Using Social Science to Reduce Violent Offending

American Psychology-Law Society Series

Using Social Science to Reduce Violent Offending

Edited by

Joel A. Dvoskin, Jennifer L. Skeem,

Raymond W. Novaco, and Kevin S. Douglas

OXFORD
UNIVERSITY PRESS

OXFORD
UNIVERSITY PRESS

Oxford University Press, Inc., publishes works that further
Oxford University's objective of excellence
in research, scholarship, and education.

Oxford New York
Auckland   Cape Town   Dar es Salaam   Hong Kong   Karachi
Kuala Lumpur   Madrid   Melbourne   Mexico City   Nairobi
New Delhi   Shanghai   Taipei   Toronto

With offices in
Argentina   Austria   Brazil   Chile   Czech Republic   France   Greece
Guatemala   Hungary   Italy   Japan   Poland   Portugal   Singapore
South Korea   Switzerland   Thailand   Turkey   Ukraine   Vietnam

Copyright © 2012 by Oxford University Press.

Published by Oxford University Press, Inc.
198 Madison Avenue, New York, New York 10016
www.oup.com

Library of Congress Cataloging-in-Publication Data

Using social science to reduce violent offending/edited by Joel A. Dvoskin ... [et al.].
p. cm.—(American Psychology-Law Society series)
Includes index.
ISBN 978-0-19-538464-2
1. Violent crimes—United States. 2. Violent offenders—Rehabilitation—United States.
3. Crime prevention—United States. 4. Crime—Sociological aspects. I. Dvoskin, Joel A. (Joel Alan)
II. Title. III. Series.
HV6789.A67 2011
364.4—dc22
2011003681

Printed in the United States of America
on acid-free paper

To our friend and colleague Don Andrews,
who devoted his life to discovering and sharing "what works"
to reduce reoffending

Series Foreword

This book series is sponsored by the American Psychology-Law Society (APLS). APLS is an interdisciplinary organization devoted to scholarship, practice, and public service in psychology and law. Its goals are to advance the contributions of psychology to the understanding of law and legal institutions through basic and applied research; promote the education of psychologists in matters of law and the education of legal personnel in matters of psychology; and inform the psychological and legal communities and the general public of current research, educational, and service activities in the field of psychology and law. APLS membership includes psychologists from the academic research and clinical practice communities as well as members of the legal community. Research and practice is represented in both the civil and criminal legal arenas. APLS has chosen Oxford University Press as a strategic partner because of its commitment to scholarship, quality, and the international dissemination of ideas. These strengths will help APLS reach its goal of educating the psychology and legal professions and the general public about important developments in psychology and law. The focus of the book series reflects the diversity of the field of psychology and law, as we continue to publish books on a broad range of topics.

This latest book in the APLS series, *Using Social Science to Reduce Violent Offending*, focuses on approaches to reducing violent crime. The editors of this volume, Joel Dvoskin, Jennifer Skeem, Raymond Novaco, and Kevin Douglas, sought to bring together researchers and policy makers to examine ways in which research on "what works" can be applied to corrections practice. They brought together key players in an invitation-only 2-day conference to address the intriguing question, "How can expert psychological knowledge about shaping prosocial behavior be applied to design a criminal justice system?" The conference afforded the opportunity for researchers, policy makers, and practitioners to discuss the current state of corrections practice and what reforms might be implemented to more effectively reduce the level of violent offending.

I am especially pleased to publish a book on prevention and treatment in this series. Research on risk assessment has identified the factors that are associated with violent offending, but our field has been slow to apply this work to interventions that can serve to reduce such offending. The "get tough on crime" policies of the past two decades have placed a disproportionate amount of resources into the construction and maintenance of jails and prisons, and appreciably less on interventions either in prison or in the community. Indeed, the direct consequence of pouring money into prison construction is that there is little left to fund community-based programs that have proven to be effective. This book appears at an opportune time, as the editors correctly note that policy makers are now acknowledging that the policies that have led to longer sentences and overcrowded prisons are neither economically sustainable nor effective in reducing recidivism or increasing public safety.

It is in this political climate that this book deserves the attention of researchers, policy makers, and practitioners. The editors have assembled an impressive list of contributors to provide a blueprint for creating change in the criminal justice system. The coverage includes both youth and adult offenders, including special populations such as sex offenders and those with mental health problems. In their concluding chapter the editors pose the question, "What if psychology redesigned the criminal justice system?" Their book shows that the application of principles based on psychological research and theory will lead to a more scientifically informed justice policy, one that will ultimately help change the lives of offenders for the better, reduce the level of violent offending, and ultimately do more to promote public safety than the current, and largely ineffective, justice system approaches.

Ronald Roesch
Simon Fraser University
Series Editor

Preface

There can be little doubt that criminal justice policy in the United States today is much harsher and more punitive than it was 40 years ago. America now has the highest rate of incarceration in the world, with over seven million people under criminal justice control as a result of incarceration, probation, or parole. The number of imprisoned people in the United States has soared from 300,000 in the early 1970's to more than 2.3 million today. We have sentenced thousands of people to death, condemned more than 2500 juveniles to life imprisonment without parole for homicide and non-homicide crimes, and sentenced hundreds of thousands of nonviolent offenders to spend decades in prison. We have declared a costly war against people with substance abuse problems; nearly a half-million people are in state or federal prisons for drug offenses today, compared to 41,000 in 1980.[1]

Writing a bad check, petty theft, or a minor property crime can result in a 20- or 30-year prison sentence. We employ aphorisms like "three strikes, you're out" and have abolished parole and behavior modification programs in many states. We prosecute 11- and 12-year-old children as adults and send them to prison for decades. We have institutionalized policies that reduce people to their worst acts and permanently label them "criminal," "murderer," "rapist," "thief," "drug dealer," "sex offender," or "felon"—identities that they cannot change regardless of the circumstances of their crimes or the improvements in their lives.

The collateral consequences of our correctional policies have been equally profound. We ban poor women and, inevitably, their children from receiving food stamps and public housing if they have prior drug convictions. And we have created a new caste system that forces thousands of people into home-lessness, residentially banned from their families and communities and rendered virtually unemployable. Some states permanently strip people with criminal convictions of the right to vote; as a result, in several Southern states disenfranchisement among African-American men has reached levels unseen since before the Voting Rights Act of 1965.

We also make terrible mistakes. More than 140 innocent people have been exonerated after being sentenced to death and nearly executed. Hundreds more have been released after being proved innocent through DNA testing. Presumptions of guilt, poverty, racial bias, and a host of other social, structural, and political dynamics have created a system that is defined by error, where potentially thousands of innocent people now suffer wrongly in prison.

However, arrested people and their families are not the only ones who pay the costs of ineffective reliance on incarceration. Corrections spending by state and federal governments has risen from $6.9 billion in 1980 to $68 billion in 2006.[2] During the ten-year period between 1985 and 1995, prisons were constructed at a pace of one new prison opening each week.[3] State governments have been forced to shift funds from public services, education, health, and welfare to pay for incarceration and now face unparalleled economic crises as a result.

The news about criminal justice policy is pretty bleak. Horrific crimes are sensationalized and magnified through extensive media reports. Terrorism and heightened anxiety about random victimization have intensified the demand for harsh punishment. The politics of fear and anger has created an environment where honest discourse about rational and effective responses to crime and criminal behavior is hard to accomplish. If there has ever been a time when new ideas and new strategies for addressing crime and behavior modification of offenders have been needed, that time is now.

The encouraging news is that there is growing hope that the economics of uninformed and ineffective correctional policy and increasing dissatisfaction with the consequences of many of our sentencing choices have created an opportunity to entertain new ways of thinking about old problems. Unquestionably, science, particularly the science of human behavior, has a lot to teach us about more rational and effective responses to crime.

In 2002, social scientists played a critical role in persuading the United States Supreme Court that a different measure of culpability should apply to people with mental retardation, leading the Court to ban the death penalty for those diagnosed with mental retardation in *Atkins v. Virginia*.[4] In 2005, psychologists, psychiatrists, neuroscientists, and others played an influential role in persuading the Court to re-evaluate the differences between children and adults when assessing the propriety of certain punishments. By explaining biological, psychological, and developmental science, mental health professionals helped the Court to articulate new protections for children and banned the death penalty for juveniles in *Roper v. Simmons*.[5] A similar effort recently resulted in a ban against life-imprisonment-without-parole sentences for children convicted of most offenses in *Graham v. Florida.*[6]

These interventions from social scientists and the resulting decisions from the United States Supreme Court are hopeful models for practitioners and policymakers working for reform in the criminal justice system, but challenging and increasingly urgent questions remain: What can social science teach us about human behavior that might promote more effective modification of improper conduct? How can we improve public safety and remediate human behavior that is violent, destructive, and dangerous? Are people no more than the worst thing they have ever done? Should we give up on the imprisoned?

Using Social Science to Reduce Violent Offending provides an invaluable resource for addressing these issues by promoting an approach to criminal justice policy based on an informed and nuanced understanding of human behavior. New research and insights into violence, brain science, adolescent development, substance abuse treatment and behavior modification are presented in this text and there is tremendous potential through social science to reduce the cost of current correctional policy while improving public safety. The policy recommendations presented here also have the added advantage of helping offenders whose lives have been plagued by violence and the misery of criminality improve the prospects for recovery. Moreover, much of what's presented in this book is innovative and well-researched but also practical. Many of the ideas and strategies are ready for practitioners, correctional officials and policymakers to implement today, which is exciting for anyone who is serious about reform.

There is no denying that violence and crime are realities that require effective strategies and responses. Anyone who has been victimized by crime appreciates the danger and disruption that inadequate attention to violence and criminality can create. But ultimately we cannot incarcerate everyone we fear, distrust, or suspect in a misguided effort to promote public safety. That approach unnecessarily victimizes not just individuals but communities, the poor, racial minorities, and anyone who is disfavored. A just society similarly cannot eliminate everyone who commits a crime or treat them unfairly or unjustly because we have the power to do so.

We have the option of learning from experts whose study of crime and human behavior offers important insights that could lead to improved public safety *and* more humane, responsible, and just punishment. The research and analysis presented here has a lot to offer in advancing that process.

Sometimes it is worth reminding ourselves that the civility of a society, the justness of a community or country, is not found in how we treat the rich, the powerful, the celebrated and esteemed. Rather, we must the judge the character of a community by how it treats the poor, the incarcerated, and the marginalized. There is a growing need for reform, reorientation and new direction when it comes to punishment in America. This wonderful collection of essays and research findings is a great place to start.

Notes

1. "A 25-Year Quagmire: The War on Drugs and Its Impact on American Society," *The Sentencing Project* (Sept. 2007), pg. 2.
2. U.S. Department of Justice, Bureau of Justice Statistics, Sourcebook of Criminal Justice Statistics 31st Edition (2008), *available at* www.albany.edu/sourcebook.
3. *See* Marc Mauer, Race to Incarcerate 1, 9 (1999) ("[m]ore than half of the prisons in use today have been constructed in the last twenty years."); *see also* Michael Tonry & Joan Petersilia, *American Prisons at the Beginning of the Twenty-First Century, in* Prisons 1, 12 (Michael Tonry & Joan Petersilia eds., 1999).
4. *Atkins v. Virginia,* 536 U.S. 304 (2002).
5. *Roper v. Simmons,* 543 U.S. 551 (2005).
6. *Graham v. Florida,* 130 S.Ct. 2011 (2010).

Bryan Stevenson
Professor of Clinical Law
New York University School of Law

Introduction

Although thousands of articles, books, chapters, and reports have been written on violent crime, the number of people under correctional supervision in the United States and elsewhere has soared. We have a wealth of knowledge about "what works" to reduce recidivistic violent crime, but this knowledge has been detached from correctional practice. This book aims to remedy that disconnect by fostering collaboration between social scientists and policy makers.

For nearly three decades, chiefly for sociopolitical reasons documented elsewhere (Cullen & Gendreau, 2000), our criminal justice system has operated under a model that is unapologetically punitive. During this period, the number of people in the United States under criminal justice supervision has mushroomed to over 7 million—3 of every 100 American adults are now under correctional supervision (Glaze & Bonczar, 2006; Pew Center on the States, 2009). The United States leads the world in its rate of incarceration, being 5–8 times higher than that of Canada and Western Europe (Walmsley, 2006). As the entrance to U.S. prisons has expanded, the exit has telescoped. Most inmates are eventually released, but most quickly return to prison, despite community monitoring (Glaze & Bonczar, 2006). The cost of building and operating prisons to house this population has skyrocketed.

These developments are troublesome, particularly given that this approach has done little to reduce crime (e.g., Levitt, 2004; Spelman, 2000). This state of affairs has led international observers to declare it "a truism that the criminal justice system of the United States is an inexplicable deformity" (Vivien Stern, Secretary General, Penal Reform International, 2002). However, mounting concerns about prison overcrowding and failed prisons policy are not unique to the United States. For example, imprisonment in the United Kingdom between 1997 and 2007 increased by one-third (Ministry of Justice, 2007), and the U.K. prison system was said to be in crisis by that country's own chief inspector of prisons (Owens, 2007). Since then, the population in custody in England and Wales has continued to grow from 80,067 at year end of 2007 to 85,600 at end of August 2010 (Ministry of Justice, 2010).

The time is ripe for a sea change in attitude, policy, and practice. Three factors are at work in encouraging this change. First, both liberal and conservative policy makers recognize that the current proliferation of prisons is not economically or practically sustainable. Second, there is growing awareness that the current approach does not provide for public safety, as the "tough on crime" movement amounts to little more than being tough on criminals. Third, attention is shifting to evidence on "what works" in corrections, which points to the reintroduction of rehabilitative efforts to better protect public safety. Indeed, former Governor Schwarzenegger renamed one of the largest correctional systems in the United States the "California Department of Corrections *and Rehabilitation*" and created a "strike team" to implement a multibillion-dollar measure to "shift our approach to rehabilitating prisoners in California" (Maile, 2007). This is symbolic of a larger movement. Across the nation, stakeholders have become interested in results-driven policies and "evidence-based" criminal justice programs (Aos, Miller, & Drake, 2006). In short, the notion that robust research evidence can be applied to increase public safety is gaining traction.

The challenge is to ensure that "evidence-based criminal justice programs" are transformed from a hollow mantra to a widespread reality. The challenge is substantial, given the chasm between science and practice in this field. As an elementary example, psychological research has long indicated that *(a)* punishment is an effective means of changing human behavior in the short run, but only with the right contingencies and proper scrutiny (Bandura, 1973; Matson & Kazdin, 1981), and *(b)* positive reinforcement can induce enduring behavior change, even after reinforcement ceases predictably to occur (Bandura, 1977). Nevertheless, visits to prisons by one of the editors (Dvoskin) in more than half of the nation's states have yet to reveal a program that appropriately and systematically applies punishment and reinforcement to improve inmate behavior or improve prosocial skills.

Other examples abound. For instance, it has been repeatedly established that aggressive behavior is acquired by social learning, which includes observing others model aggression, processing social information in a manner disposed to aggression, and the inculcation of values conducive to violence. Nevertheless, prison environments are replete with aggression-engendering elements and are all too thin on prosocial antidotes (Ireland, 2000; Magan, 1999). The rewards for anger and aggression are in the present. The rewards for their control are in the future. Without a stake in the future, there is little reason for someone to control violent behavior or to adopt prosocial values.

To bridge such gaps between scientific knowledge and practice, science must be translated to produce clear and feasible recommendations for practice.

How are we to accomplish the admittedly ambitious goal of using social science to inform correctional policy and reduce recidivistic violent crime? In our view, simply writing an academically oriented book would not suffice. To reach and truly inform the people who can implement change in correctional practice, we needed a novel approach. The approach described next recognizes that translating social science into practice will require active collaboration by scientists and correctional policy makers. This book represents a step toward facilitating this collaboration. In it, the best and brightest scholars of our time articulate how social science can be applied to reduce violent crime, based in part on their conversations with policy makers and practitioners.

Book Project Development Process

1. Collaborating With Stakeholders

Because it was essential to have stakeholders help shape this project, we organized a 2-day conference to facilitate interaction between (a) most of the authors of this book and (b) correctional administrators and front-line practitioners, judges, victims' advocates, and offenders. On the first day, chapter authors presented their intended main points to stakeholders and received structured feedback on how to maximize the relevance of the chapter's content and format to policy and practice. On the second day of the conference, the book editors met with chapter authors to discuss feedback from stakeholders about how to shape the book for maximum impact. This process was as uncommon as it was valuable; the voices of stakeholders thread through each chapter.

2. Consolidating Knowledge

Through our stakeholder conference, we finalized the desired contents and goals of this book, which is essentially a sourcebook of evidence for knowledge translation efforts. The book is written at a level that is advanced yet accessible to professionals without training in methodology or statistics. The principal target audiences for this book are (a) administrators and practitioners who design and implement programs in corrections, and (b) social science researchers and educators, particularly those in criminal justice and correctional psychology. These audiences are most relevant to our goals of distilling research into clear recommendations for practice (now) and advancement of knowledge (in the future). Although the book focuses on U.S. policy and practice, its content is of relevance to other nations such as Canada, the United Kingdom, and Australasia, given overlap in correctional theory, research, and (to a lesser extent) practice across these countries.

3. Translating Knowledge for Implementation

The essential elements of this book will be distilled to produce a small series of summaries and guides for both policy-makers and practitioners.

These will be designed for easy digestion by busy stakeholders but clearly linked to research on "what works." We will work with national policy groups to disseminate these guides.

Content and Foci

The book is divided into four sections. The first section describes the scope of violent crime. First, Alfred Blumstein (Chapter 1) describes rates of crime and incarceration in the United States and key factors that have influenced these rates over time (e.g., availability of crack cocaine; three-strikes laws). He demonstrates that longer prison sentences alone are unlikely to reduce recidivism. Next, Clive Hollin (Chapter 2) discusses the rise and fall of differing penal orientations (punitive; rehabilitative) over time, and how these have been influenced by prevailing theories on causes of crime. Hollin begins with the *Magna Carta* and ends with the *Risk-Need-Responsivity* (RNR) model, a leading empirically supported approach for reducing recidivism that forms the centerpiece of this book.

In the second section, chapter authors address key contextual factors that contribute to rates of violent crime and incarceration. In Chapter 3, David Farrington discusses family, peer, socioeconomic, neighborhood, and situational factors that predict violent crime. Then, Muniba Saleem and Craig Anderson (Chapter 4) discuss the influence of the media on violent behavior, and how "prosocial" media might be used to reduce it. Finally, Tom Tyler and Lindsay Rankin (Chapter 5) explain how public attitudes help shape penal policy. If public attitudes about crime and incarceration could be shifted, they argue, then penal policy might be revised to encompass evidence-based practices and thereby reduce recidivism.

The third and largest section of the book distills research relevant to improving interventions to reduce violent recidivism. The first chapter of this section—Chapter 6—is the book's focal point. In this chapter, Don Andrews reviews the principles of, and evidence for, the *Risk-Need-Responsivity* (RNR) model of effective correctional programming. According to the *Risk* principle, higher risk offenders should receive more intensive correctional programming than lower risk offenders. The *Need* principle holds that risk reduction efforts must focus on criminogenic needs, or changeable factors that predict crime and violence. The *Responsivity* principle holds that correctional programming should be delivered in a format that matches, or is responsive to, the learning styles of offenders. In most cases, this means that programs are structured—delivered in cognitive-behavioral or social learning formats.

The remaining chapters in this section evaluate the evidence for the RNR model within specific settings and/or with particular offender populations. More broadly, these chapters distill scientific evidence about "what works" in a readable, nontechnical fashion, outline any gaps in our present knowledge, and arrive at three to five clear recommendations for improving our approach to offenders.

The remaining two chapters in this section concern particular settings. In Chapter 7, Gendreau and Smith focus on institutional settings. In their view, prisons can be places of growth, learning, and personal improvement. In Chapter 8, Turner and Petersilia focus on the prisoner reentry and/or community supervision on parole. Besides discussing the applicability of RNR principles to the parole context, they also draw attention to the benefits of so-called ecological models of crime reduction.

The last three chapters in this section focus on particular offender groups: young offenders (Barbara Oudekerk and N. Dickon Reppucci, Chapter 9), sexual offenders (Judith Becker and Jill Stinson, Chapter 10), and offenders with mental illness (John Monahan and Henry Steadman, Chapter 11). First, Oudekerk and Reppucci demonstrate that, unlike service-based approaches, punishment-only-based approaches do not reduce violent recidivism for youth. Although there is some evidence that RNR principles apply to youth, these authors note that further research is needed, particularly with girls. Second, Becker and Stinson conclude that the principles of RNR are applicable to sexual offenders, although more research is required on their potentially unique criminogenic needs for this group. Finally, Monahan and Steadman argue that mental illness should be the focus of risk reduction efforts only when psychiatric symptoms cause violence for a given individual. In the case of offenders for whom mental illness does not drive violence potential, traditional criminogenic needs like antisocial attitudes should be the focus of intervention.

In the fourth and final section of the book, we highlight methods for overcoming system inertia to implement the recommendations made in preceding chapters. First, in Chapter 12, James McGuire points out that RNR approaches can reduce costs as well as violence. He discusses "exonovation" getting rid of policies that have been shown not to work; he also provides a rationale for shifting resources from institutional to community-based supervision and programming. In the final chapter, the editors distill key principles noted throughout the book and offer recommendations for implementing them.

This volume reflects considerable investment of effort over a lengthy period of time. The work was made possible by grants from the University of California, Irvine (The Newkirk Center for Science and Society, and The School of Social Ecology) and from the American Psychology-Law Society. We greatly appreciate the efforts of Jillian Peterson and Sarah Manchak—fantastic doctoral students at the University of California, Irvine (UC Irvine)—who helped us to finalize this draft and to carry out a spectacular working meeting between stakeholders and authors. We are also profoundly grateful to our stakeholders for providing insightful suggestions for making this work useful, and to our authors for their scholarly contributions and their patience in making any revisions necessary to fit the book's framework and produce a coherent whole.

We assembled a truly impressive cast of stakeholders and authors, consisting of highly respected leaders of their respective fields, to contribute their thoughts about how best to use social science to reduce violent crime. Both groups took their tasks seriously. As a result, our authors have produced exceptional syntheses of their respective areas of expertise, along with important pragmatic recommendations.

References

Aos, S., Miller, M., & Drake, E. (2006). *Evidence-based adult corrections programs: What works and what does not.* Olympia: Washington State Institute for Public Policy.

Bandura, A. (1973). *Aggression: A social learning analysis.* Englewood Cliffs, NJ: Prentice Hall.

Council of State Governments. (2002). *Criminal Justice/Mental Health Consensus Project.* Retrieved from http://www.ncjrs.gov/pdffiles1/nij/grants/197103.pdf.

Cullen, F., & Gendreau, P. (2000). Assessing correctional rehabilitation: Policy, practice, and prospects. *Criminal Justice, 3,* 109–175.

Glaze, L., & Bonczar, T. (2006). *Probation and parole in the United States, 2005.* Washington, DC: US Department of Justice, Office of Justice Programs, Bureau of Justice Statistics Bulletin.

Haney, C. (2006). *Reforming punishment: Psychological limits to the pains of imprisonment.* Washington, DC: American Psychological Association.

Ireland, J. L. (2000). "Bullying" among prisoners: A review of research. *Aggression and Violent Behavior, 5,* 201–215.

Levitt, S. (2004). Understanding why crime fell in the 1990s: Four factors that explain the decline and six that do not. *Journal of Economic Perspectives, 18,* 163–190.

Maghan, J. (1999). Dangerous inmates: Maximum security incarceration in the state prison systems of the United States. *Aggression and Violent Behavior, 4,* 1–2.

Maile, B. (2007). Governor Schwarzennegger creates strike teams to implement historic prison reform plan. *CDCR Press Release.* Retrieved from http://www.cya.ca.gov/Communications/press2007_0511_2.html

Matson, J. L., & Kazdin, A. E. (1981). Punishment in behavior modification: Pragmatic, ethical, and legal issues. *Clinical Psychology Review, 1,* 197–210.

Ministry of Justice. (2007). *Penal policy: A background paper.* National Offender Management Service. London: Author.

Ministry of Justice. (2010). *Population in custody month tables August 2010 England and Wales.* London: Author. Retrieved from http://www.justice.gov.uk/publications/docs/pop-in-custody-aug2010.pdf

Owens, A. (2007, June 24). Sentenced to filth, chaos and mayhem in our jails. *The Sunday Times.* Retrieved from http://www.timesonline.co.uk/tol/news/uk/crime/article1976782.ece

Pew Center on the States. (2009). *One in 31: The long reach of American corrections.* Washington, DC: Pew Charitable Trusts.

Spelman, W. (2000). The limited importance of prison expansion. In A. Blumstein & J. Wallman (Eds.), *The crime drop in America.* Cambridge, England: Cambridge University Press.

Stern, V. (2002). The international impact of U.S. policies. In M. Mauer & M. Chesney-Lind (Eds.), *Invisible punishment: The collateral consequences of mass imprisonment* (pp. 279–292). New York: The New Press.

Walmsley, R. (2006). *World prison population list (6th ed.).* London: King's College, International Centre for Prison Studies.

Contents

Contributors

Craig A. Anderson, Ph.D.
Department of Psychology
Iowa State University
Ames, IA

D. A. (Don) Andrews, Ph.D.
Department of Psychology
Carleton University

Judith V. Becker, Ph.D.
Department of Psychology
University of Arizona
Tucson, AZ

Alfred Blumstein, Ph.D.
H. John Heinz III College
Carnegie Mellon University
Pittsburgh, PA

Kevin S. Douglas, LL.B., Ph.D.
Department of Psychology
Simon Fraser University
Burnaby, BC, Canada

Joel A. Dvoskin, Ph.D., ABPP
Department of Psychiatry
University of Arizona College of Medicine
Tucson, AZ

David P. Farrington, Ph.D.
Institute of Criminology
University of Cambridge
Cambridge, UK

Paul Gendreau, O.C., Ph.D.
Department of Psychology
University of New Brunswick
Saint John, NB

Clive R. Hollin, Ph.D.
School of Psychology
University of Leicester
Leicester, UK

James McGuire, Ph.D.
Division of Clinical Psychology
University of Liverpool
Liverpool, UK

John Monahan, Ph.D.
School of Law
University of Virginia
Charlottesville, VA

Raymond W. Novaco, Ph.D.
Department of Psychology and Social Behavior
University of California, Irvine
Irvine, CA

Barbara A. Oudekerk
Department of Psychology
University of Virginia
Charlottesville, VA

Joan Petersilia, Ph.D.
Stanford Law School
Stanford University

Lindsay E. Rankin
Department of Psychology
New York University

N. Dickon Reppucci, Ph.D.
Department of Psychology
University of Virginia
Charlottesville, VA

Muniba Saleem, M.S.
Department of Psychology
Iowa State University

Jennifer L. Skeem, Ph.D.
Department of Psychology and Social Behavior
University of California, Irvine
Irvine, CA

Paula Smith, Ph.D.
Corrections Institute
University of Cincinnati

Henry J. Steadman, Ph.D.
Policy Research Associates
Delmar, New York

Jill D. Stinson, Ph.D.
Fulton State Hospital
Fulton, Missouri

Susan Turner, Ph.D.
Department of Criminology, Law and Society
University of California, Irvine
Irvine, CA

Tom R. Tyler, Ph.D.
Department of Psychology
New York University
New York

Part I

DEFINING THE PROBLEM: CRIME,
INCARCERATION, AND RECIDIVISM
IN THE UNITED STATES

1

Crime and Incarceration in the United States

Alfred Blumstein

One of the more complex policy issues the United States has grappled with for over 30 years involves the question of crime—how much there is, what we should do about it, and how much that costs in terms of dollars and intrusiveness. The question is made particularly difficult because of the degree to which public perceptions are strongly affected by media portrayals of heinous individual crimes; "If it bleeds, it leads" is a common media motto. This stimulates a public concern of vulnerability to becoming the next victim and demanding the political system to "do something." The issue is further compounded by the degree to which criminal justice policy has evolved into a major partisan divide, with conservatives typically arguing for more incarceration and liberals more typically emphasizing efforts at preventing crime.

This partisan divide is complicated by a fairly simplistic understanding on the public's part of the effect of incarceration: Locking away the offender will avoid the crime, and the more we lock away and the longer the time served, the less crime we will have to suffer. That perception may well be reasonable for some offenders, especially for those who persistently and frequently engage in violence. The issue is much more complex with illicit-market crimes such as burglars working for a fence or drug dealers, where an incarcerated offender could be replaced by someone else to carry out his or her transactions. The situation becomes even more complex when violence is associated with an illicit market as its dominant form of dispute resolution. Thus, it becomes important to recognize the differential effect of punishment on different kinds of crimes and offenders. Unfortunately, the political system has come to recognize the myopic nature of the public's response and so has exploited it by consistently taking a position of "tough on crime," which almost certainly trumps an opponent who can be labeled as "soft on crime." Thus, calling for more incarceration has certainly been shown to be effective, at least politically, but its effectiveness in controlling crime is much more complex and subtle.

In this context of a highly polarized political debate and simplistic perspectives by the public, it would be desirable to bring perspectives of social science to aid in enhancing the rationality of decisions about violent crime and how to deal with it. Enhancing that rationality is made difficult by the inherent complexity of the problem of crime: its occurrence is often difficult to measure because of the variety of incentives faced by victims and observers to avoid reporting or revealing details. Crime spans many levels of seriousness with considerable diversity in the public's concerns. And its rates can be affected by a wide variety of factors in developmental processes, in the social environment, and in the actions of public institutions and especially the components of the criminal justice system responsible for responding to reported crimes. It is also difficult to get accurate measurements of crime as experienced by victims or as recorded by police, since victims can have incentives to not report some victimization experiences to the police, and the police can have incentives to not record what gets reported to them.

There are corresponding complexities in understanding the factors contributing to changes in prison populations. If we have more crime, it would be understandable for the prison population to increase. If we have less crime while incarceration is going up, then those who favor more punishment are tempted to claim that the increase in punishment is "causing" the crime to come down, and so we should do more. That has been a dominant theme of American criminal justice policy for over 30 years, and those policies have led to the United States having the world's highest incarceration rate. With states increasingly facing severe budget pressures, there have been a variety of efforts to rethink those policies.

In this chapter, I try to address some of these complexities in measuring crime and understanding the factors contributing to changes in crime rates and in gaining a better understanding of the factors contributing to changes in incarceration rates. Then I examine the interaction between the two, especially the impacts of incarceration on various kinds of crime. Gaining a better understanding of that interaction represents a major challenge to social science research, especially an understanding of how changes in incarceration policies affect crime rates.

Crime and Crime Measurement

Crime measurement has always been a complex problem for most crimes because there is no disinterested observation of the event. Traditionally, crime measurement has depended on the victim of a crime reporting it to the police and the police maintaining counts of those reported crimes, and then reporting those counts to the FBI, which publishes an annual Uniform Crime Report (UCR), available at http://www.fbi.gov/ucr/ucr.htm.

That leaves many concerned with what became known as the "dark figure" of crime, that is, crimes known to the victim but not reported to the police. There could be many reasons for not reporting the crime to the police. If the perpetrator was someone known to the victim, perhaps the victim would not want to create difficulties for the perpetrator. If the victim saw the crime as sufficiently minor, he or she may not want to involve the police in the incident. Or the victim may have had some role in precipitating the crime and so did not see himself as a totally innocent victim. Nonreporting would be particularly high for those who would like to avoid contact with the police, such as undocumented aliens or those engaged in illicit activity themselves.

Additionally, there are many crimes that are labeled "victimless" because they regulate individual behavior such as possessing or selling prohibited drugs or pornography. Such events would not ordinarily come to police attention without some form of aggressive police action to seek it out. Information about such crimes has to be obtained through arrest or, more generally, through some form of survey. For that purpose, the National Survey on Drug Use and Health, formerly called the National Household Survey on Drug Abuse, is conducted by the Substance Abuse and Mental Health Services Administration (SAMHSA) in conjunction with The National Institute of Drug Abuse and its data are available at http://www.oas.samhsa.gov/data.cfm In this survey, SAMHSA asks people about what drugs they have used and how often. Substance abuse by young people is of special concern, and so the Monitoring the Future project at the University of Michigan conducts an annual survey of 8th, 10th, and 12th graders asking about their use of illicit drugs as well as legal drugs such as alcohol and tobacco (their data are available at http://monitoringthefuture.org/).

Victimization Survey

For the more common crimes, the Bureau of Justice Statistics (Sabol, West, & Cooper, 2009) has been conducting the National Crime Victimization Survey (NCVS) since 1973. In that survey they draw a sample of households and ask every member of the household aged 12 years or above whether he or she has been a victim of any of an array of crimes over the past 6 months, what the consequences of that victimization experience were, and whether he or she reported that crime to the police. The instrument for collecting victimization experiences is available at http://bjs.ojp.usdoj.gov/content/pub/pdf/ncvs204. pdf, and the data series are available at http://www.icpsr.umich.edu/NACJD/ NCVS/. The survey is conducted in a panel format so that a household is queried twice a year over a period of 3.5 years; if the family living in that household should move and be replaced by a different family at any time, then the new family becomes the respondent. To accommodate the vagueness of memory of whether an event occurred within or prior to 6 months ago, the initial interview of a household is taken as a "bounding interview" and not counted in the survey results. For all subsequent interviews, the events reported in the previous interviews serve that bounding purpose. If a new family replaces the initial family in a panel, their first interview remains unbounded.

The NCVS covers about 60,000 households, almost half the number they started with in 1973. As a result of the smaller sample size as well as the lower rate of victimization recently, the precision of the national estimates of victimization rates have decreased to the point where it is often difficult to find a "statistically significant difference" between one year and the next, particularly for the low-rate offenses like forcible rape, leading to estimates based on 2 years rather than a single year.

The NCVS sampling plan is designed to be representative of the population in the United States and also within a limited number of the larger metropolitan areas. But because considerations of privacy are very salient, estimates are generated only for the United States as a whole and are not available for any disaggregated unit, even as large as a state or a major metropolitan area. Thus, environmental characteristics like the socioeconomic status of a respondent can be incorporated into analyses of the survey, but not those of his or her neighborhood. It should be possible, however, to generate environmental information of a respondent's census tract, introducing some limited amount of randomized error around those estimates to avoid precise matching of the respondent's census tract, in order to generate the relationship between such environmental characteristics and victimization rates. A study by the National Research Council (Groves & Cork, 2008) provided a wide variety of suggestions for improving the value of the NCVS, including the approaches to providing subnational estimates of victimization rates, at least for the major metropolitan areas.

Uniform Crime Reports

The long-standing crime measurement data come from crimes reported to the police, tabulated by police departments, most typically reported to a state agency, and then forwarded to the Federal Bureau of Investigation (FBI) for compilation in an annual report (currently made available on the FBI Web site) known as the UCR. This is a report by individual municipality of all the crimes reported to their police department aggregated into two groups: violent crimes (including murder and nonnegligent manslaughter, forcible rape, robbery, and aggravated assault) and property crimes (including burglary or breaking and entering, larceny or theft, motor vehicle theft, and arson), collectively known as the Part I crimes. Those aggregate reports for the first 6 months of each year are published early in the following year with reports of Part I crimes (formerly known as "index" crimes) for cities with a population exceeding 100,000. In the fall of that following year, a full report of the Part I crimes is provided by the individual reporting municipality and aggregated up to the metropolitan area, state, and national levels. Since less than all police departments report their data, imputation procedures are used to estimate the aggregate numbers and rates.

The other important series in the UCR is the count of the number of arrests by crime type. The UCR provides arrests for each of the eight Part I crimes but also for an additional 20 Part II crimes, including many of the victimless crimes, simple assault (1.3 million assaults that are less serious than the 0.4 million Part I "aggravated assault" arrests), and a wide variety of property crimes and "public order" crimes. In total, police record about 14 million arrests, including 1.8 million for drug offenses, 1.5 million for driving under the influence, and about 4 million for the many "other" offenses not even tabulated specifically in the UCR.

An important virtue of the arrest information in the UCR is that it provides a demographic breakdown of the arrests by age, race, and gender, but not all combinations of these. The race information is provided only for two age groups: 18 and over and under 18, and a particularly gap is the breakout by age and race. This demographic information is key to understanding the demographic characteristics of arrestees, and by inference, of offenders if one ignores the differential vulnerability to arrest by different demographic groups.

One of the problems associated with the UCR is that reporting by individual police departments is erratic, with some departments reporting late, others reporting not at all, and some others finding ways to distort their reports to gain public approval (e.g., Rashbaum, 2010). In publishing its annual report, the FBI tries to account for nonreporting problems by generating imputed national estimates. All of their tables of demographically disaggregated arrest numbers are the numbers of arrests actually reported; their table of Estimated Total Arrests represents the result of the national imputation, which is typically about 50% larger than the actual reported arrests, with that scale factor varying by individual crime type.

There are other sources of data that could be drawn on for verification or comparison. For example, the National Center for Health Statistics publishes regular mortality data by cause of death, and one of the causes included is homicide.

Trends in Violent Crime in the United States

In our discussion of violent crime in the United States, we focus primarily on murder and robbery. Both are well-defined crimes and are reasonably well reported. Data on rape are troubled by the low and highly variable rate of reporting to the police and the relatively small number of incidents reported in the victimization survey.

Data on aggravated assault raise concern because of the varying discretion on what makes an assault "aggravated" compared to the "simple" assault. Additionally, there has been a large change in the manner in which police choose to characterize domestic assaults as "aggravated," largely to follow suggestions deriving from experimental research that arrest can be more effective than counseling in avoiding subsequent recidivism.

There is another important feature of aggravated assault that complicates its measurement. Police generally cannot make an arrest for a simple assault unless they have seen it, whereas they can make an arrest for aggravated assault even if it has only been reported to them. An experimental study of police responses to domestic violence in Minneapolis (Sherman & Berk, 1984) that was prominently reported on in the *New York Times* (Boffey, 1983) showed that arrest was more effective than counseling in reducing subsequent domestic violence. This gave rise to a widespread policy change that encouraged police to follow their preferred inclinations. It was later established that this finding applied specifically to spouses (predominantly males) who were employed at the time of the incident. Partly because of this distortion of the presumably randomized control of the experiment and partly to strengthen the conclusion, the National Institute of Justice, which had sponsored the initial Minneapolis experiment, replicated it with eight separate similar experiments in eight different cities. The interesting result from the replications was considerable ambiguity of the initial findings: Some cities confirmed the initial results, and other cities contradicted the results (Garner, Fagan, & Maxwell, 1995). Nevertheless, regardless of the complications resulting from the replications, the policy changes favoring arrest in domestic violence cases have largely persisted.

This has introduced some important complexities in the time series of aggravated assaults. In 1983 and previously, the ratio of aggravated assaults to homicides was quite flat with age at a ratio of about 18:1. Subsequent to the change to arrest for domestic assaults, which were largely classified as "aggravated assault" because they were largely not seen by the arresting officers, that ratio changed significantly with age, remaining at about 18:1 at the younger ages, then rising to a peak of about 35:1 at about age 30, and then declining subsequently (Blumstein, 1998). This suggests that the changed policy favoring arrest contributed to a rise in the number of domestic assaults that were classified as "aggravated" when they were likely to have been less than aggravated. Thus, aside from discrepancies across jurisdictions, this trend in classification of aggravated assault raises concerns about using this offense as an important indicator of trends in violence.

Thus, to get a more robust assessment of the trends in "violent crime," we focus here on the time patterns of the other two violent crimes: robbery and murder. Their trends have followed each other impressively closely over the past 35 years. Figure 1.1 depicts the national rates of murder and robbery (with robbery scaled down by a factor of 25 to put it on the same scale as murder), and it is striking how close to each other their peaks and troughs occur.

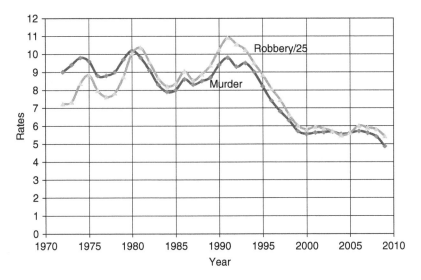

Figure 1.1. Uniform Crime Reports of murder and robbery rates (1972–2009).

The peak in 1980 was largely attributable to demographic shifts as the "baby boomers" (typically described as those born between 1946 and 1964, with a peak cohort in 1960) were moving out of the high-crime ages of 16 to 20 (Blumstein, Cohen, & Miller, 1980). By 1980, the 1960 peak cohort had already reached 20, just past the peak age of most age-crime curves (depicting the number of arrests for a particular crime type by people of age *a* divided by the population of age *a*), and subsequent cohorts contributing to the peak would be smaller.

The emergence of crack cocaine and the violence associated with crack markets were major factors in the subsequent turning points. Crack started to be marketed, predominantly by African Americans, in the early 1980s and that market was associated with considerable violence, either as a competitive instrument among competing sellers or for the settlement of buyer-seller disputes in that marketplace. That violence contributed to major public demands to crack down on drugs more generally and on crack specifically, and so Congress and many state legislatures did so aggressively. Most typically, they did so by imposing mandatory-minimum sentences for drug offending, which had previously been dealt with rather lightly. An illustration of this response is provided by the 1986 federal Drug Abuse Act with its notorious 100:1 crack to cocaine differential: Conviction would require the same 5-year mandatory-minimum sentence for 500 grams of cocaine or for just 5 grams of crack. In 2010, Congress passed the Fair Sentencing Act, which maintained a crack-powder disparity but reduced the ratio from 100:1 to 18:1. Many states started with a mandatory-minimum sentence of 2 years, were disappointed that this did not have a discernible effect on the market, raised it to 5 years, and finally raised it to 10 years, still without much effect.

As a result, this early period saw a major growth in the incarceration of crack sellers. That growth certainly satisfied the public's demand to "do something," but that did not do very much about reducing the volume of transactions. As pointed out in Blumstein's late November 1992 presidential address for the American Society of Criminology (Blumstein, 1993), in hopeful anticipation that the election of Bill Clinton as a new president would change existing policy, incarceration of drug sellers was not likely to be effective in averting transactions as long as there would be a supply of replacements to respond to the demand. Locking up drug sellers incapacitated them, and perhaps other crimes they might have engaged in, but it did not avert their drug transactions, which were taken over by replacements. Similarly, any deterrent effect resulting from the escalating sanctions causing a seller to abandon his or her post would be nullified by any replacement.

It turned out that those replacements were indeed far more troublesome on the street than their predecessors. The replacements were predominantly young and, like their predecessors, had to carry guns to protect themselves against street robbers. But these young sellers were far less restrained in their use of those guns than were the people they replaced (see Steinberg, 2007). Furthermore, because young people are tightly networked, the carrying of guns diffused to other young people in their neighborhoods not involved in the drug markets (Blumstein, 1995). That gave rise to a major arms race among young African American males and the associated consequences of a major rise in their homicides. This rise is depicted in Figure 1.2 (Blumstein, 2000), which depicts the age–crime curve for murder for 1985, which was very representative of previous years, and of 1993, which was close to the peak year

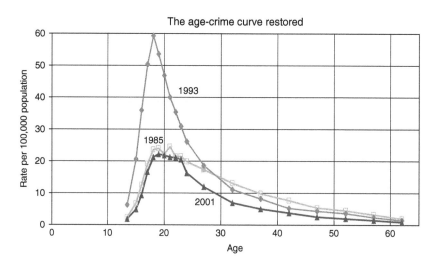

Figure 1.2. Murder arrest rate by age: 1985, 1993, and 2001.

for murder, as shown in Figure 1.1. Figure 1.2 also shows how the anomalous 1993 pattern was restored to one much closer to 1985 by 2001.

A different version of the data in Figure 1.2 is shown in Figure 1.3, which depicts in the upper figure the ratio of the homicide arrest rate by age in 1993 compared to 1985. This shows that arrests of 15-year-olds tripled between 1985 and 1993, and that the arrest rate for all ages of 20 and below more than doubled. What is less well recognized is the pattern for age 30 and above. While the rate for young people increased dramatically, the rate for all ages of 30 and above decreased by about 25% between 1985 and 1993. That decrease is presumably attributable to the major growth in prison population between 1985 and 1993 and the resulting incapacitative effect at the older ages, when people who have remained criminally active are most likely to persist in their criminal careers. The lower figure highlights the fact that by 2001 homicides by young people had declined to below their 1985 level and that homicides by those 30 and above had declined still further to a level about half that which prevailed in 1985.

These analyses provide the opportunity for explaining the other turning points in Figure 1.1. The trough in 1985 that disrupted the demographic decline was created by the recruitment of young people into the crack markets that began in 1985 and continued after that; they armed themselves and their peers did likewise, and the spike in young people's homicide was the major contributor to the 25% increase in homicide between 1985 and 1993. Crack markets were also significant factors in the even larger growth in robberies over that period, because crack users turned to robbery as a means of "one-stop shopping" for money to buy their drugs. This was in contrast to burglary, which declined steadily during that period, and which typically provided

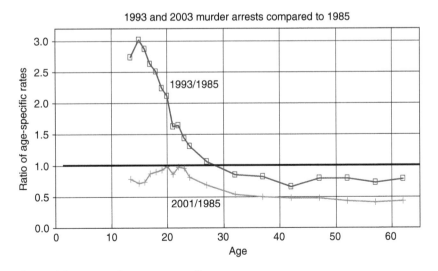

Figure 1.3. Ratios of recent age-specific rates.

products rather than money and had to be sold in the street or to a fence to get the money.

The next peak occurred in 1991 for robbery and in 1991 and 1993 for murder. That was an important peak because it was the start of the end of the crack epidemic. Those who tracked the crack phenomenon (see Johnson, Golub, & Dunlap, 2000) noted that young potential initiators saw what crack had done to parents, older siblings, and older friends and came to recognize the personal harm associated with crack. That realization, much more so than the TV commercials beamed at them, had a significant impact in reducing the demand for crack. That led to a growth in their demand for "blunts" (cigars hollowed out and filled with marijuana), a much more benign drug that saw far less violence associated with the transactions. As a result, the market had less need for the young replacements, and there was a robust economy that could absorb them. Furthermore, police had become much more aggressive about cracking down on illicit gun carrying, particularly in the inner-city neighborhoods where the crack markets had been flourishing. This shift gave rise to a decline of over 40% in both the murder and robbery rates.

This decline was particularly noted in the transition in 1993 of the armaments race of the late 1980s and earlier 1990s into a disarmament race. This pattern is reflected in Figure 1.4, which shows the use of guns in homicide by three age groups: adults (25–45), youth (18–24), and kids (under 18). The graphs are all anchored to an index value of 100 in 1985. What they show is that there was not much growth in the use of guns in homicides by adults, growth by a factor of 2.5 for youth, and by a factor of 5 for the kids. The peak in all of these occurred in 1993 and all came down rather sharply by 2000. By 2000, the homicide and robbery rates had declined to levels that had not been seen since the late 1960s.

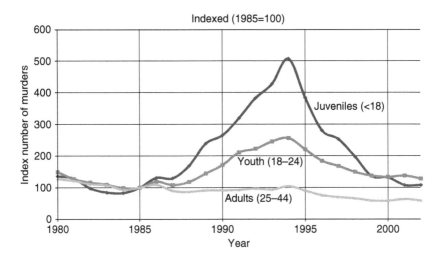

Figure 1.4. Use of handguns in murders by three age groups.

As shown in Figure 1.1, the national pattern between 2000 and 2007 was impressively flat. Year-to-year changes were typically in the order of 1%–2% up or down. But this aggregate pattern hides the presence of considerable variation within individual cities. Over that period, a number of cities like St. Louis; Birmingham, Alabama; and Oakland, California, had some year-to-year increases of more than 30%. Other cities went down, some went up, some went up and down, and others went down and up.

Previous trends had been strongly influenced by national phenomena: the demographics of the baby boomers and the recruitment of young people into crack markets. Then, in the waning of crack and police aggressiveness in capturing guns that had become widely available in inner-city areas where crack was marketed, counteracted the rise in violence associated with the crack markets. The flat national trend that followed 2000 highlighted the local characteristics of the cities, outbreaks within them, and the varying abilities of the cities and especially their police departments to respond to local growth in violence.

It is interesting to note from annual UCR data that the three largest cities, New York, Los Angeles, and Chicago, had generally declining violence rates over that 2000–2007 period. This is likely a tribute to the sophistication of their management and to the fact that they had slack patrol resources readily available to them to be sent into neighborhoods where violence was escalating. Often this growth in violence was initiated by the inner-city "street people" described by Elijah Anderson (1999) as young men who saw little future for themselves and who had very sensitive egos, and so would respond with great intensity to any insult or a sign of disrespect. In many cases, these communities were organized into gangs or mini-gangs that would generate a sequence of retaliatory strikes in response to such insults. The ready availability of guns left over from the crack era accentuated the lethality of those responses. As a result, when there was a sharp increase of violence in any particular city it was likely a reflection of young black males killing other young black males.

In contrast to the generally flat trend that prevailed from 2000–2007, there was a drop in 2008 (3.6% in homicide and 1.6% in robbery) (UCR, 2008) and then a very surprisingly large drop of 10% in homicide and 6.5% drop in robbery in the first 6 months of 2009 (UCR, 2009). This was surprising because there was widespread anticipation that the financial crisis of late 2008 and the recession in 2009 would give rise to an increase in crime, certainly in robbery because of financial needs and the large number of people unemployed, and in homicide because of tensions in domestic violence escalating to homicide.

It is too early to begin to understand the implications of this large change in 2009, especially in homicide. It is reasonable to open some speculation about possible factors that might have contributed. What changed in 2009 that could have led to a decrease in homicide? One interesting speculation is the possibility of an "Obama effect" associated with an African American president appearing in the White House (Zeleny, 2010). It is conceivable that such a radical change that was certainly unanticipated even a few years earlier could have had an effect on at least some of Anderson's "street people," and thereby have impacted the phenomenon of young black males killing other young black males, which constitutes such a large fraction of homicides in the larger cities. The drop was considerable, with New York dropping by 19%, Los Angeles by 29%, and a number of other cities with populations over 100,000 that dropped more than 20%, and these declines could have a major impact on the national rate (UCR, 2009, preliminary).

Obviously, this speculation must be assessed by comparing the race mix of offenders and victims. The "Obama effect" hypothesis anticipates that the frequency of black involvement as both victims and offenders would be reduced appreciably more than that of whites. Even then, it would not be enough to see the effect on homicides, but also one would want to see the effect displayed in other domains like a 2009 reduction in high-school drop-out rates greater for African Americans than for other racial or ethnic groups. This opens an intriguing area of research to assess the degree to which having an African American president can contribute to addressing the continuing and perplexing challenge of bringing inner-city "street people" into mainstream America.

Trends in Incarceration in the United States

Incarceration Trends

Incarceration is most commonly thought of as the most appropriate societal response to violence. Certainly, it is the natural mode of retribution or pun-ishment for an act of violence inflicting serious harm on an innocent victim. Also in terms of crime control, removing the perpetrator from the commu-nity is appropriate, especially if he or she has demonstrated a propensity for repeated acts of violence, thereby incapacitating any such crimes he or she might commit in the community. That still leaves much to be addressed in terms of what level of violence and what indicators of propensity warrant incarceration and for how long. Those are issues that could be addressed most effectively by social science research, but such guidance has been largely preempted in recent decades by the politicization of incarceration policy.

The changes in that policy are best reflected in Figure 1.5, a graph of the U.S. incarceration rate in state and federal prisons from the 1920s until 2007. The data are available from Blumstein and Cohen (1973) at http://bjs.ojp. usdoj.gov/index.cfm?ty=pbdetail&iid=2061 and http://bjs.ojp.usdoj.gov/ index.cfm?ty=pbdetail&iid=1763. The first 50 years of that period until the early 1970s show an impressive stability and trendlessness, with a mean incar-ceration rate of 110 per 100,000 population and with a coefficient of variation (standard deviation/mean) of only 8%. Struck by that observation and seeing

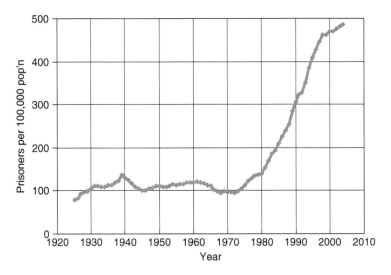

Figure 1.5. Growth of U.S. incarceration rate.

similar patterns in a number of other countries, Blumstein and Cohen (1973) proposed "A Theory of the Stability of Punishment." Under that theory, a society tries to maintain a reasonably stable incarceration rate in order to deliver a reasonable level of punishment but not go too far in order to avoid generating a political reaction from those punished and those who identify with them. That can take the form of a homeostatic process (Blumstein, Cohen, & Nagin, 1976) that was under the control of the criminal justice system. When crime rates get high and more prison capacity was needed, the longer serving prisoners can be let out earlier on parole. When crime rates are low, that provides the capacity to punish for more marginal crimes, like pornography or simple assault.

Almost simultaneously with the publication of that paper, the United States began an incarceration escalation that raised incarceration rates at an exponential rate of 6% to 8% per year. That growth was a result of the confluence of a variety of factors, particularly the increasing crime rates that began in the 1960s associated with the baby boomer population bulge. Its politicization was fueled, perhaps initially in the 1964 presidential election by Barry Goldwater, who introduced "crime in the streets" as a salient campaign issue—even though his opponent, Lyndon Johnson, had little to do with the pent-up fertility demand following the separation of the sexes induced by World War II. Other contributing factors included the increasing saliency of crime as a lead issue by the media, the emergence of the popularity of the cell door slamming as a major theme in political TV commercials, and the growing realization by political candidates that "tough on crime" was a winning campaign strategy.

The problem here is that the political system has only a limited repertoire for responding to the public's concern about crime. It wants to be able to "do something" that would be seen to be visible quickly. That would rule out investments in improved socialization of young children whose family situation or whose behavior demonstrates that they are at high risk of becoming offenders. The political figures also want to act without incurring large immediate budget costs. Research strongly suggests (American Academy of Pediatrics Council on Child and Adolescent Health, 1998) the desirability of major investments in socializing young children and their parents where the family situation indicates a high risk for crime. But that would represent a high initial cost and the payoff would occur on someone else's watch. Police forces could be increased, but that would incur immediate costs and the benefits have always been hard to measure. The easy approach was to find means of increasing sentences and to increase commitments to prison by requiring mandatory-minimum sentences.

This political transition represents a major change from an earlier view that saw the "corrections" system as targeted primarily at "correcting" the offender who committed a crime. Under that model, the major purpose of the corrections system was rehabilitation, and significant efforts were formerly directed at that goal. In the search for improved approaches to that goal, a variety of randomized experimental evaluations were conducted in the 1950s and 1960s. These experiments presumably invoked the gold standard of experimental science to generate their findings. In contrast to most attempts at carrying out randomized experiments in the criminal justice system (at least in part because of the difficulty of finding good social placebos), this was reasonably easy to do when there was a surplus of candidates available for the treatment, then one could randomly assign those candidates to a treatment or control group.

In general, most of those evaluations showed a "null effect" in which the treatment group showed no lower recidivism than the control group. Of course, these results were disappointing and led to a highly contentious paper by Robert Martinson (1976) based on work by Lipton, Martinson, and Wilkes (1973) summarizing the results of these experiments and concluding that "nothing works." This conclusion was largely endorsed by a National Research Council report (Sechrest, White, & Brown, 1979).

One possible explanation for the frequency of the null effects was that each of the experimental evaluations was for a particular, narrowly defined method or "technology" of rehabilitation. Given the diversity of needs and problems associated with an offending population, it is not surprising that any particular technology would be helpful to only a minority of offenders. Rather, what was needed was a toolkit of methodologies from which a therapist could draw for each individual offender as his or her needs were identified. Of course, running carefully controlled randomized experiments with that kind of diverse, individually targeted interventions would be extremely difficult.

The initial reaction to the null effects came from the left, which argued that since there was no good evidence of how to rehabilitate offenders or that they could be rehabilitated, then we should do less in terms of incarcerating them and interfering with their lives. Of course, the rejoinder from the right was very simple: "Lock 'em up—and throw away the key" (Wilson, *NY Times*, 1975, and *Thinking About Crime*, 1983). As usual, the right's position was much more attuned to the public's desires and so it captured the public support. It was much easier for the public and its political representatives to accept incarceration as an understandable solution to the then-growing concern about the crime problem than the unproven—or perhaps even seen as disproven—approach of rehabilitation.

That resolution represented an important contribution to policy developments over the next 30 years. Contributing to that resolution was a variety of economic analyses that related punishment policy (or the equivalent of "price") to the "demand" for crime, and not surprisingly, seemed to find the expected negative association documenting the presumed deterrent effect of incarceration, at least in those studies that got published in the economic literature. This work was initiated in theory by Gary Becker (1968), and there were a number of empirical efforts to follow, most notably by Isaac Ehrlich (1973), but there were serious methodological problems in many of those studies (Blumstein, Cohen, & Nagin, 1978) and more recently on the research on the death penalty (Donohue & Wolfers, 2005).

Prior to the transition wrought by the null-effect experiments, the predominant sentencing policy in most states was one of "indeterminate" sentences, with specification of a minimum sentence the offender had to serve before he or she became eligible for parole, and a maximum sentence after which the offender had to be released from custody, with the maximum sentence constrained by statute. The judge would hand down the sentence (say, 2 to 5 years). Then, after having served the 2-year minimum, he or she would become eligible for parole, and the parole board would decide when the offender was ready for release. That usually occurred at or shortly after the minimum sentence was served, and there was a strong incentive not to wait until the 5-year maximum sentence, which would require transferring the offender from prison to an unsupervised condition in the community with no opportunity for the help or supervision that the parole system was intended to deliver.

As the pressure for rehabilitation slackened and incarceration became the dominant goal, the desire for more rather than less became a continuing pressure (e.g., Wilson, 1975). There then followed a variety of sentencing innovations that moved sentencing discretion from judges to legislatures with legislatively prescribed determinate sentences replacing the indeterminate sentences. The discretion was removed from judges because they were seen as too lenient for the punitive environment that was developing. The statutory changes include determinate sentencing, where the statute specifies the sentence to be imposed for a particular offense type; that allows the legislature to increase the sentence at almost any provocation. The other favorites include mandatory-minimum sentences intended to prevent judges from giving a sentence of probation or even a light sentence. Most of that discretion in individual cases was transferred to prosecutors, who decide what offense is to be charged; being tougher in that regard enhances their power in the plea bargains that are the predominant mode of disposition of criminal cases, and it helps them retain their positions because they typically hold their positions through election. Congress got into the act by passing a Truth in Sentencing law that induced the states to increase incarceration. The 1994 law provided money for constructing prisons to those states that required individuals imprisoned for certain violent offenses to serve at least 85% of their maximum sentence.

The ultimate innovations were the "three strikes and you're out" laws, invoking a baseball metaphor to mandate a life sentence for those convicted a third time for a specified set of offenses. In most cases, the specified offenses involved serious violent crimes, and so the impact was generally limited. California, which adopted a "three strikes" law in 1994, the second state to do so after Washington adopted one in 1993, created a very broad window for the third "strike." This was challenged by two offenders who were convicted of relatively minor third strikes, golf clubs in one case and children's videos in the other, but the U.S. Supreme Court upheld the life sentences that followed (*Ewing v. California*, No. 01–6978; *Lockyer v. Andrade*, No. 01–1127).

The other major contributor to the growth in the prison population was the increasing criminalization of drug use and drug dealing. The roots of this increase can probably be traced to the initiatives of Henry J. Anslinger, who was appointed as the first Commissioner of the Treasury Department's Federal Bureau of Narcotics (FBN) in 1930 and held that office for 32 years until 1962. Anslinger was responsible for escalating the presumed seriousness of marijuana (the "killer weed") and for waging a very aggressive assault on a wide variety of illicit drugs. But the impact on the criminal justice system and on prisons in particular did not become serious until the 1970s as young people started experimenting with drugs, primarily marijuana and a variety of psychedelic drugs, escalating in a limited degree to heroin and cocaine. The impact increased profoundly with the introduction of crack cocaine, a smokable version of cocaine mixed with baking soda, which could be sold at a low price of $5–$10 per hit, well below the cost for a minimum quantity of powder cocaine.

The growing public concern about the effects of drugs on their teenage children generated public pressure to attack the drug problem, which had otherwise been seen as relatively minor and where sentences of probation were not unusual. The political response was to pass laws requiring a mandatory-minimum sentence, initially of 2 years, but when that did not do much good, to change it to 5 years and then to 10 years. There is still considerable question of how much good resulted from any of these changes.

Factors Contributing to the Growth in Incarceration

The dramatic growth of incarceration led to various attempts to estimate the contribution of the various stages of processing in the criminal justice system to the growth. Those could be any combination of the following: more crimes, more arrests per crime (reflecting police effectiveness), more commitments to prison per arrest (reflecting prosecutorial charging and judicial decision making regarding prison or community sentencing such as probation), longer time served (including recommitments of parolees, reflecting judges' sentences and parole release and recommitment decisions).

Blumstein and Beck (1999, 2005) explored this issue by analyzing the prison growth from 1980 to 2001. They examined six crime types (murder, robbery, assault, sex offenses, burglary, and drug offenses). Collectively, these crime types accounted for 75%–80% of prison populations. They found that over that entire period, there was no contribution attributable to more crimes and no contribution attributable to more arrests per crime, even though that had been a period of significant advance in police technology, training, and management sophistication. The entire contribution to the growth was attributable to a mixture of the decision to commit convicted offenders to prison (53% of the growth) and the time they served (47%), with an important portion of the time served attributable to changes in parole release and recommitment policies. If one ignored the incarceration for drug crimes, those percentages were reversed—45% attributable to commitments and 55% to time served.

The results could be partitioned into two periods, 1980–1992 and 1992–2001, and the results were somewhat different in each period. For the first period from 1980 until 1992, a time of increasing crime, the growth in crime rates accounted for 22% of the growth. For the second period, a time of largely declining crime rates, there was no contribution of crime to the growth. In both periods, there was no contribution of growth in arrests.

The two dominant aspects of the policy choices, commitment and time served, contributed quite differently in the two periods—in the first period, the growth was predominantly commitment (63%) and changes in time served were relatively minor (15%). After 1992, time served became much more salient (60%) and commitment less so (40%). The passage of mandatory sentencing laws was a major factor in the early period, and the lengthening of the time served became much more salient in the later period, especially with the growth in resentencing because of parole violation. A major factor contributing to that parole violation was the larger number of drug offenders in prison and the high risk that a drug offender, especially if that offender was an addict, would fail a urinalysis test, and that would lead to a recommitment.

California was particularly high in this regard. Of people released to parole, about 75% would be recommitted to prison for about 9 months, they would then be released for about 9 months, and again would suffer a 75%

chance of recommitment. Thus, there would have several cycles of release and recommitment before their sentence expired.

It is clear that both of these policy choices—commitments and time served—are highly discretionary, affected by the legislature through statutes setting determinate sentences, raising statutory maximums, or imposing sentencing constraints on judges through requiring mandatory minimums. For any particular offense, prosecutors have a choice of which version of that offense to charge, the version invoking a mandatory minimum or not, all of which enters the plea negotiation with defense counsel and is affected inevitably by the strength of the evidence available. Judges choose a sentencing range, in some states affected by sentencing guidelines established by sentencing commissions. And parole authorities, which previously released prisoners most often at or shortly after they served their minimum sentence, tended to become more conservative in that release decision and became more aggressive in deciding to recommit to prison people who committed technical violations or were accused of relatively minor offenses.

Figure 1.6 depicts the results of the growth in incarceration rate for the six crime types addressed in Blumstein and Beck (2005). As is evident from the figure, the largest factor contributing to the growth in incarceration has been the intense reliance on incarceration for dealing with the nation's drug problems. While the incarceration rate for all other offenses increased appreciably, the incarceration rate for drug offenses increased by a factor of 10, making it the single largest crime type represented in prison. Drug offenders comprise over 20% of the prisoners in state prisons and over 50% of those in federal prisons, and so account for the largest single crime type in incarceration.

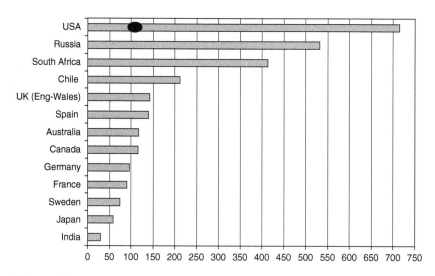

Figure 1.6. National incarceration rates per 100,000 population.

Despite this enormous increase in incarceration of drug offenders, it has become clear that incarceration has made only a limited contribution to dealing with the nation's drug problems. In contrast to incarceration of a pathological rapist or of an otherwise violent individual, where the incarceration has a certain incapacitation effect during the time of incarceration and perhaps a deterrent effect on those who can weigh the costs and benefits of their individual criminal acts, the crime-control effects of incarceration of drug offenders or of any other such market crimes are limited by the resilience of the market to respond to the extraction of any limited number of individuals from that market. As long as the demand persists, replacements can be recruited or can simply move in to cover the turf of those removed from the market. These replacements would nullify any potential incapacitation effect intended by the incarceration. Similarly, any deterrent effect of incarceration would also be nullified as long as a replacement could cover the territory of anyone scared off the street by the threat of incarceration. As long as drug sellers are willing to risk lethal exposure in the street to competitors or to robbers, it seems unlikely that the threat imposed by the criminal justice system would be sufficient to dry up the supply of replacements.

Recognition of the futility of incarceration for drug offenders was undoubtedly an impelling force in inducing California to pass Proposition 36 mandating treatment rather than incarceration for drug sellers. After almost 30 years of the "drug war" with only limited evidence of success in reducing drug transactions and with expenditures in the order of $100 billion in enforcement with still no clear indication of a meaningful impact on drug abuse, there are increasing moves to reconsider the policies. That rethinking has focused initially on marijuana, which is seen as the most benign of the various illicit drugs. The following are indications of those moves:

- In 2008, Massachusetts voted to decriminalize marijuana.
- Other states have voted to put marijuana as a low priority for enforcement.
- The Obama administration has announced that it does not intend to interfere with the distribution of medical marijuana in states that have legalized marijuana for medical purposes.

Recent Declines in Prison Population

With the recession of 2007–2010 and the sizable budget deficits being carried by many states, there has been some significant rethinking of the wisdom and effectiveness of the growing incarceration rates. The growth in corrections expenditures has been a major component of the growth in state budgets over the past 30 years. A number of states for the first time are actually seeing a reduction in their prison populations. New York in particular has finally revised in a major way the infamous Rockefeller drug laws that represented a major factor in the growth of their prison populations. California, with about

150,000 prisoners in a system with a capacity of about 100,000, is considering releasing as many as 50,000 prisoners.

Nationally, 2008 saw a major reduction from the previous growth in prison populations that had averaged about 6% to 8% per year since 1980. The 2008 rate dropped to only 0.8%, with almost as many states reducing their prison populations as increasing them. New York and Texas were particularly impressive notable for having posted reductions of over 30% compared to 2003 (Sabol et al., 2009). It has been particularly notable that the jurisdictions that reduced their prison population have not seen any notable increase in crime.

Intense political response emerges when a released prisoner commits a particularly heinous offense. Parole boards, recognizing the inevitable response to a risky decision, try to be judicious in deciding whom to release. It is always possible, however, for an unanticipated explosive crime to occur and to force a defensive political response. This is exemplified by the murder of a police officer in Philadelphia by a paroled offender, and the immediate response by the governor to call a halt to all further parole releases until the decision on that particular release was reviewed. That review took about 3 months, but it contributed to a steady growth in Pennsylvania's prison population. As a result, Pennsylvania led the nation with a prison population growth of 30% in 2008 (BJS, 2009).

The reduction of incarceration has been politically feasible because the budget crisis comes at a time when crime rates are at their lowest levels since the 1960s. Thus, while any single heinous crime can stir up political activism, there does seem to be a growing recognition of the need for rethinking the relentless drive for more incarceration. There was considerable astonishment in response to a Pew report (2008) that pointed out that 1% of the U.S. adult population was currently behind bars in prison or local jails. This observation was not surprising because the incarceration rate in prison is about 500 per 100,000 total population, and an additional 250 in jails, and about three quarters of the U.S. population are adults, but seeing the rate as 1 per 100 certainly captured attention. As shown in Figure 1.5, the fact that the United States was able to operate for over 50 years with an incarceration rate of 110 (or 0.11%) is testimony to the dramatic growth of incarceration in the United States. As can be seen in Figure 1.7, most of the other industrialized countries we identify with have rates similar to our earlier rates, in the neighborhood of 50–150. It was only recently that the United States passed Russia, whose incarceration rate is about 500, to take the world's leadership position. The formerly stable rate of 110 is shown as a circle on the U.S. bar.

The fiscal crisis has also brought with it a desire for prison-impact estimates to be appended to bills intended to raise sentences. In contrast to many other legislative actions, which are usually accompanied by a fiscal-impact statement, it is rare to find judiciary committees requiring such statements. Most typically, they change their policies in response to a particularly visible crime or to some public outcry that stimulates change, almost always upward. Most often those changes are simply introduced as legislation, and once they leave the judiciary committee it is virtually impossible for them not to garner

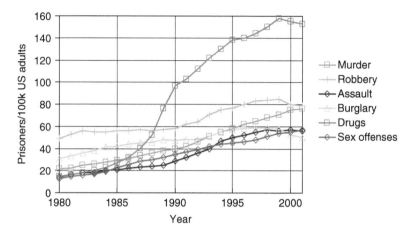

Figure 1.7. Incarceration rate by crime type.

a strong majority on the floor of any legislative body. It is only later that the costs in terms of prison impact are seen. And that assessment can occur quite a bit later as the effect of the legislative change accumulates over time. Increasingly, legislatures in states with sentencing commissions, whose major role is developing sentencing guidelines, are asking the commissions to develop prison-impact estimates for new legislation being introduced.

One of the more striking efforts at rethinking sentencing policy was initiated by the Pennsylvania General Assembly in a sequence of four bills (Acts 81–84 of 2008) that called on the Pennsylvania Commission on Sentencing to develop new guidelines for release decisions by parole authorities or by judges who sentenced offenders to the local jail, for resentencing decisions for offenders on parole release who violate the conditions of parole, either as a new offense or as a technical violation. The legislation also introduced the concept of risk assessment as a consideration to account for an actuarial assessment of the likelihood of recidivism by a released offender. Indeed, the legislation opened the door to permit early release of individuals serving a mandatory minimum sentence. This was a first step by the Pennsylvania legislature to start rethinking its large array of mandatory minimum sentences. Other states, including Michigan, will have moved forward more aggressively to repeal their mandatory minimum sentences. The Pennsylvania action stopped short of repeal, but it effectively put them into a sunset mode so that analyses by the Sentencing Commission could lead to recommendations to repeal those that could not be shown to have been effective.

Effects of Incarceration on Crime

The trends we have seen in crime and incarceration raise the question of the effect of incarceration on crime. Certainly the rhetoric favoring incarceration tends to view that as the dominant influence on crime. That rhetoric was reinforced during the crime drop of the 1990s, a time when incarceration was increasing, and it was easy to claim that the growth in incarceration was the cause of the drop. Of course, incarceration was also increasing during the crime rise from 1985 to 1993. This highlights the complexity of the interaction between incarceration and crime and argues against any simplistic explanation.

The two principal modes of effect are incapacitation and deterrence. Incapacitation occurs by removing the offender from the community and thereby preventing him or her from inflicting crimes on the community. If we know something about the nature of an offender's criminal career, particularly the frequency of offending (often denoted as λ) and the anticipated residual duration, that would allow us to estimate the crime reduction associated with a particular sentence.

A key associated question is whether the incarceration has any effect on an individual's future offending patterns. It could be rehabilitative (a reduction in the offending rate λ or a shortening of the criminal career) through either the pain of the experience or through skills learned that would be helpful after release. Or it could lead to criminalization (an increase in the offending rate or a lengthening of the criminal career) as a result of the difficulty in gaining employment, atrophy of existing pro-social life skills, or from the crime skills learned from fellow inmates. This has been a difficult issue on which much research has been attempted, but with only limited success because of the difficulty in controlling for the selection effect associated with the judges' decisions to incarcerate and to set a sentence. Nieuwbeerta, Nagin, and Blokland (2009) used sophisticated methods of trajectory analysis (Nagin 2005), propensity scores (Rosenblatt & Rubin, 1984), and individual matching to reduce that selection bias and find some positive criminogenic effects of incarceration in a Dutch sample.

The deterrence effect is more complex than incapacitation, and it is supposed to occur by imposing punishment on convicted offenders and thereby sending the message to others that they could suffer similarly. There has been considerable research, primarily by economists, since one of their basic principles is that increase in price (i.e., punishment) should reduce the demand (i.e., the willingness to do crime). The issues here are complex in that they require econometric models that account for the various factors other than punishment that could also affect crime rates in any particular jurisdiction. It is also possible that the relationship between crime and incarceration is endogenous, since a jurisdiction with high crime rates might be more impelled to ration its limited incarceration capacity. Since the estimates of the deterrent effect depends very strongly on the specific econometric model used to make such estimates, and those models differ considerably in the variables included and in the degree to which they account for the reverse influence of crime rates on incarceration, the estimates of those effects can vary considerably. Many models and associated estimates have been proposed and critiqued, and no strongly consistent estimates are available. The most consistent findings about deterrence are the strongest influence of *certainty* of punishment (i.e., the probability that a crime would lead to incarceration) and the relative weakness of *severity* (the duration of the sentence). The state of that research has been summarized by Nagin (1998) and more recently by Durlauf and Nagin (2011).

Recent policy innovations have focused on a third aspect of deterrence, *celerity* (the speed with which the punishment is imposed). That has given rise to efforts exemplified by Project HOPE in Hawaii, where drug offenders are subjected to frequent urinalysis, and those who fail are quickly sent to a local jail, but for only a few days. The substitution of celerity for severity has been shown to generate a significant reduction in recidivism (Kleiman, 2009).

There is little question that incarceration can have a meaningful impact on offending through incapacitation. An individual who commits crime at an annual rate λ sentenced to S years of incarceration can be expected to avert $\lambda*S$ crimes during that period through incapacitation. But that estimate is valid only if the following are true:

1) The individual's criminal career does not terminate before the S years have passed.
2) The incarceration has no effect on that individual's criminal career through either rehabilitation (a reduction in the offending rate λ or a shortening of the criminal career) or through criminalization (an increase in the offending rate or a lengthening of the criminal career).
3) The crimes that individual would have committed are not replaced by recruitment of a replacement, as is likely to occur with vice crimes or even with burglary managed by a fence (Blumstein, Cohen, Roth, & Visher, 1986).

These conditions certainly suggest the following:

1) Avoiding excessively long sentences that keep an individual in prison long after he would have stopped offending
2) Developing approaches in incarceration that facilitate rehabilitation rather than criminalization, and especially discerning which prisoners are more likely to be rehabilitated and which are more likely to be criminalized
3) Using incarceration selectively for market crimes and developing approaches like individual treatment and strategic disruption of the markets

Two separate and independent analyses of the effect of incarceration on the significant crime drop of over 40% from 1993 to 2000 estimated that incarceration contributed to 25% of that drop. Spelman (2000) based his estimate on an econometric model that took account of both deterrence and incapacitation generally. Rosenfeld (2000) based his estimate on an incapacitation effect by assuming that the offending frequency λ of people in prison was about the same as those in a highly disadvantaged neighborhood.

A detailed exposition of the limits of our ability to assess the usefulness of incarceration in reducing crime, is beyond the scope of this chapter, but it is clear that our policies in this regard are driven much more strongly by ideology than by informed research. Whatever the limits of our knowledge, it is clear that even with our limited research, we can pursue much more rational policies. But given the importance of the issue, the resources involved, and the disruption to many people's lives, further research to illuminate these issues is very much needed. That research should address at least the following issues:

- Improved econometric models of the relationship between punishment and crime
- New research into the parameters of criminal careers and their determinants, most important of all, the offending frequency (λ) and the rate of desistance to update the latest work that dates back to the 1970s
- Assessment of the effects of incarceration, both in terms of the decision to commit to prison and the time spent there, on those who leave in order to assess the degree of rehabilitation compared to criminalization, and specifically to assess those who might be amenable to various forms of treatment
- Assessment of the trade-offs among the various components of deterrence and specifically celerity compared to severity

Each of these issues could comprise a significant research program. There is little question that addressing these could make a significant improvement in the efficiency and the effectiveness of the criminal justice system, for which incarceration is a primary policy choice. At a time when U.S. crime rates are the lowest they have been in over 40 years and the public's concern about crime is reasonably calm, this represents an important opportunity for bringing rationality into the operation of the nation's criminal justice system.

Conclusion

The growth of the U.S. incarceration rate certainly suggests a level of punitiveness that one would not have anticipated in a nation that prides itself on being a liberal democracy. But a liberal democracy is also likely to be responsive to the wishes of its people, and those wishes can become quite intense when faced with a serious crime problem. Thus, when we compare the incarceration rate of the United States to the other countries with which we typically identify ourselves, mostly Western Europe, shown in Figure 1.7, we can readily see how far deviant the United States has become. As incarceration has moved from a small governmental function to a major "prison–industrial complex," the interests of those involved in that industry becomes a major political force. The California corrections officers' union is reputed to be the largest financial contributor in gubernatorial elections. When the New York governor wanted to create a commission somewhat like the military base closing commission charged with deciding which prisons to close down as the prison population decreased, he encountered stiff opposition from the rural legislators whose districts saw prisons as a major part of their economy. The initiation of private prisons by profit oriented corporations represents another political influence to keep the prison population from shrinking too much. Thus, as violent crime rates have stayed reasonably steady since 2000, and as incarceration rates have grown, but at a much slower rate than previously, and as a number of states have found the means to reduce their prison populations, it appears extremely unlikely that the United States will ever revert to its previously stable rate of 110 per 100,000. In light of the political appeal of punitiveness, perhaps the best we might hope for is stabilization at a rate of 500 in state and federal prisons with another 250 in local jails, keeping 1% of the U.S. adult population behind bars. Even that would be preferable to reverting to the 1980–2000 growth rate of 6 to 8% per year.

And that restoration of a stable rate appears likely to continue as long as major crime rates stay within control. In addition to the costs, the profound racial disproportionality in prisons could be an unsettling effect on forcing a rethinking of the intensity of involvement of the criminal justice system in people's daily lives. Furthermore, the growing ubiquity of background checking as a condition of employment will undoubtedly force some attention to the redemption of individuals hampered by a stale criminal history that happened over 20 years ago that prevents them from getting a job. It is likely, however, that incarceration will continue to be seen as the proper mode of response to those who commit violent crimes at a high rate because prison is demonstrably effective at incapacitating their offenses.

Bringing social science research to address these issues is certainly an important need. We started with a discussion of crime trends, and we are reasonably good—but far from perfect—at explaining past trends, although there is still considerable debate over each of the turning points discussed in the crime trends section here. But we are extremely weak at making forecasts for the future, and such forecasts are necessary in order to allocate resources intelligently. The previous section discussed some research needs in order to become more rational in our use of incarceration for controlling crime. It is clear that there are major unmet needs for social science research to address these issues and to restore the public's confidence in the rationality and responsibility of the criminal justice system. The resources committed to the National Institute of Justice, the agency responsible for carrying out that research, are much below what is needed to make significant progress in that direction. Some few tens of millions of dollars are far too limited to make a major dent in the $200 billion operation of the criminal justice system.

References

American Academy of Pediatrics Council on Child and Adolescent Health. (1998). The role of home-visitation programs in improving health outcomes for children and families. *Pediatrics, 101*(3), 486–489.

Anderson, E. (1999). *Code of the street.* New York, NY: W.W. Norton and Co.

Becker, G. S. (1968). Crime and punishment: An economic analysis. *Journal of Political Economy, 78,* 169–217.

Blumstein, A. (1993). Making rationality relevant. The American Society of Criminology Presidential Address. *Criminology, 31,* 1–16.

Blumstein, A. (1995). Youth violence, guns, and the illicit-drug industry. *Journal of Criminal Law and Criminology, 86*(4), 10–36.

Blumstein, A. (1998). Violence certainly is the problem. *University of Colorado Law Review, 69,* 945–967.

Blumstein, A. (2000). Disaggregating the violence trends. In A. Blumstein & J. Wallman (Eds.), *The crime drop in America* (pp. 13–44). Cambridge, England: Cambridge University Press.

Blumstein, A., & Beck, A. J. (1999). Population growth in U.S. prisons, 1980–1996. In M. Tonry & J. Petersilia (Eds.), *Crime and justice: A review of research* (pp. 17–61). Chicago, IL: University of Chicago Press.

Blumstein, A., & Beck, A. J. (2005). Reentry as a transient state between liberty and recommitment. In J. Travis & C. Visher (Eds.), *Prisoner reentry and crime in America* (pp. 50–79). Cambridge, England: Cambridge University Press.

Blumstein, A., & Cohen, J. (1973). A theory of the stability of punishment. *Journal of Criminal Law, Criminology and Police Science, 63,* 198–207.

Blumstein, A., Cohen, J., & Miller, H. (1980). Demographically disaggregated projections of prison populations. *Journal of Criminal Justice, 8,* 1–25.

Blumstein, A., Cohen, J., & Nagin, D. (1976). The dynamics of a homeostatic punishment process. *Journal of Criminal Law and Criminology, 67,* 317–334.

Blumstein, A., Cohen, J., & Nagin, D. (Eds.). (1978). *Deterrence and incapacitation: Estimating the effects of criminal sanctions on crime rates.* Washington, DC: National Academy of Sciences.

Blumstein, A., Cohen, J., Roth, J. A., & Visher, C. A. (Eds.). (1986). *Criminal careers and career criminals.* Report of the National Research Council Panel on Research on Criminal Careers, National Academy Press.

Boffey, P. M. (1983, April 5). Domestic violence: Study favors arrest. *New York Times,* Section C, Page 1, Column 1.

Donohue, J., & Wolfers, J. (2005). Uses and abuses of empirical evidence in the death penalty debate. *Stanford Law Review, 58,* 791–846.

Durlauf, S. N., & Nagin, D. S. (2011). The deterrent effect of imprisonment.

Ehrlich, I. (1973). Participation in illegitimate activities: A theoretical and empirical investigation. *Journal of Political Economy, 81,* 521–565.

Garner, J., Fagan, J., & Maxwell, C. (1995). Published findings from the Spouse Assault Replication Program: A critical review. *Journal of Quantitative Criminology, 11,* 3–28.

Groves, R. M., & Cork, D. L. (Eds.). (2008). *Surveying victims: Options for conducting the National Crime Victimization Survey.* Report of the Panel to Review the Programs of the Bureau of Justice Statistics, National Research Council of the National Academies. Washington, DC: National Academies Press.

Johnson, B. D., Golub, A., & Dunlap, E. (2000). The rise and decline of hard drugs, drug markets, and violence in inner-city New York. In A. Blumstein & J. Wallman (Eds.), *The crime drop in America* (pp. 164–206). Cambridge, England: Cambridge University Press.

Kleiman, M. (2009). When Brute Force Fails: How to Have Less Crime and Less Punishment. Princeton University Press.

Lipton, D., Martinson, R., & Wilkes, J. (1973). *The effectiveness of correctional treatment: A survey of treatment evaluation studies.* New York, NY: Praeger Publishers.

Martinson, R. (1976). What works?–Questions and answers about prison reform. *Public Interest, 35,* 22–54.

Nagin, D. S. (1998). Criminal deterrence research: A review of the evidence and a research agenda for the outset of the 21st century. In M. Tony (Ed.), *Crime and justice: An annual review of research* (Vol. 23, pp. 1–42). Chicago, IL: University of Chicago Press.

Nagin, D. (2005). *Group-based modeling of development.* Cambridge, MA: Harvard University Press.

Nieuwbeerta, P., Nagin, D. S., & Blokland, A. (2009). The relationship between first imprisonment and criminal career development: A matched samples comparison. *Journal of Quantitative Criminology, 25,* 227–257.

Rashbaum, W. K. (2010, February 6). Retired officers raise questions on crime data. *New York Times,* p. 1.

Rosenblatt, P. R., & Rubin, D. B. (1984). Reducing bias in observational studies using subclassification on the propensity scores. *Journal of the American Statistical Association, 79,* 516–524.

Rosenfeld, R. (2000). Patterns in adult homicide: 1980–1995. In A. Blumstein & J. Wallman (Eds.), *The crime drop in America* (pp. 130–163). Cambridge, England: Cambridge University Press.

Sabol, W. J., West, H. C., & Cooper, M. (2009). *Prisoners in 2008.* Report No. NCJ 228417. Washington, DC: Bureau of Justice Statistics, U.S. Department of Justice.

Sechrest, L., White, S. O., & Brown, E. (Eds.). (1979). *The rehabilitation of criminal offenders: Problems and prospects.* Report of the Panel on Research on Rehabilitative Techniques., Washington, D.C: National Academy of Sciences Press.

Sherman, L., & Berk, R. (1984). The specific deterrent effects of arrest for domestic assault. *American Sociological Review, 49,* 261–272.

Spelman, W. (2000). The limited importance of prison expansion. In A. Blumstein & J. Wallman (Eds.), *The crime drop in America* (pp. 97–129). Cambridge, England: Cambridge University Press.

Steinberg, L. (2007). Risk-taking in adolescence: New perspectives from brain and behavioral science. *Current Directions in Psychological Science, 16*(2), 55–59.

Wilson, J. Q. (1975, March 9). Lock em up and other thoughts on crime. *New York Times Magazine,* p. SM3.

Wilson, J.Q, *Thinking About Crime* (1983). Basic Books.

Zeleny, J. (2010, January 12). The Obama effect on an Indiana contest. *New York Times.* http://thecaucus.blogs.nytimes.com/2010/01/12/the-obama-effect-on-an-indiana-contest/

2

A Short History of Corrections: The Rise, Fall, and Resurrection of Rehabilitation Through Treatment

Clive R. Hollin

The broad concern of this chapter is with the changes over time in enthusiasm for a correctional or rehabilitative approach to managing crime. Crime is not a new phenomenon, and throughout history all societies have experienced the consequences of criminal behavior. Given that crime is not going to go away completely, the issue becomes one of damage limitation: How can the incidence of crime be prevented and reduced? The question of how to reduce crime, particularly violent crime, and the associated harm it brings to people's lives is a puzzle that many societies have struggled to answer for centuries. To trace correctional history from its beginnings to the present day and to speculate on what the future may hold, it is necessary to move through a range of topics. These topics include the relationships between criminology, philosophy, and psychology; the tensions between different models of criminal behavior and associated methods to reduce crime; and the emergence of evidence-based practice in correctional systems.

Solutions of the Past

The solution to a problem may well depend on how we explain its causes. One of the earliest explanations for why people committed crimes was a belief in possession by spirits. The basis of this explanation of crime, evident in many countries and cultures, lies in the perception of the lawbreaker as someone who is possessed by evil spirits and demons. A belief in spirits and the power of the deity underpinned practices such as *trial by ordeal*, a procedure in which the guilt or innocence of the accused was determined by an extremely painful test. As God would miraculously intercede on behalf of the blameless—the principle of *judicium Dei*, a judgment by God in favor of the innocent—it was believed that the accused would emerge unscathed from the trial while the guilty would suffer or die.

The tradition in 10th-century Saxon Europe, until it was banned by the Church in 1215 (in England the year of Magna Carta), was for trial by fire or water. Ordeal by fire entailed grasping a red-hot iron or walking across red-hot metal; ordeal by water involved picking a stone from boiling liquid by hand, drinking poisoned water, or submersion in water. Another form of trial, *trial by combat*, was common in 16th-century Europe. In trial by combat, also calling on *judicium Dei*, the protagonists fought until one was dead or disabled, with the victor declared the winner of the dispute.

As time passed, so trial by ordeal and trial by combat were discarded and widely replaced with *trial by jury*. The notion of a jury drawn from the community was not new; a similar system had existed in ancient Greece, and in England there was precedent in Anglo-Saxon law with the jury of accusation. If the outcome of a trial was that the accused was found guilty, then the person was sentenced in accordance with the law of the land. A sentence sought to serve several purposes, the most common of which was to inflict punishment on the guilty.

Our ancestors' imaginations knew no bounds when it came to devising forms of punishment. Those convicted of crimes were, at different times, punished in many ways: There was public humiliation as with the pillory; mutilation by cutting off limbs, ears, noses, or the upper lip, and the plucking out of eyes; and whipping, flogging, and branding. There were many forms of execution such as burning to death, hanging, and *peine forte et dure* ("the strong and hard pain"), which involved pressing the person to death (usually by placing him or her under a wooden board and putting weights on the board until the person was crushed). In addition, there was the option in England of deportation to the colonies.

We should not think of extreme forms of punishment as just belonging to ancient history: In mid-18th-century England, there were over 100 offenses that were punishable by death. Pettifer (1939/1992) notes of this period that:

> Death had become the cure for all but the most trivial crimes, the remedy for nearly all felonies. Offences which, to-day, would be dealt with by admonition and a small fine, or helpful periods of probation, such as damaging shrubs in public gardens; larceny of property over the value of a shilling; breaking down the head of a fishpond so that the fish might escape; cutting a hop-bind in a hop plantation; and a hundred others, were all punishable by death by hanging. (p. 17)

Those 18th-century criminals who were sent to jail were subjected to harsh regimes, including being held in body irons, extensive periods in solitary confinement (including the wearing of masks to prevent prisoners from look-ing at each other), hard labor, and peculiarities such as the treadmill and the crack (a machine that the prisoner turns by rotating a handle to make cups revolve to scoop up sand; when the cups are full, they have considerable weight), which demanded extreme physical effort to the point of exhaustion.

The seeds of change that saw a shift away from the widespread use of extreme punishment, and which proved to be the precursor to many contem-porary criminal justice systems, were sown in the mid-1700s. As explanations for criminal behavior based on possession by demons faded, a new level of understanding emerged, this time with its basis in philosophy. The *classical school* of philosophy has a lineage that can be traced to Immanuel Kant (1724–1804) and the Enlightenment philosophers.

Classical Theory

The basis of Enlightenment philosophy was that human action is the product of our reason and free will. The credit for applying the principles of Enlightenment philosophy to crime is generally given to the Italian mathema-tician and economist Cesare Bonesana Marchese de Beccaria (1738–1794) and to the English philosopher and jurist Jeremy Bentham (1748–1832).

Beccaria's contribution to the history of criminal justice is to be found in a single book, published in 1764, *Dei Delitti e Delle Pene* (*On Crimes and Punishments*). Beccaria's principal concern is with the greater good—"la mas-sima felicita divisa nel maggior numero" (the greatest happiness for the great-est number)—acknowledging that some individual freedoms may have to be surrendered for the benefit of the majority. Beccaria (1764/1963) developed this view in arguing that criminal law, defining all crimes and punishments, applies to *all* members of society and so should be written and accessible to all. Furthermore, the restrictions imposed by criminal law on individual freedom should be limited and the individual should be protected by being presumed innocent until proved guilty. It is implicit in Beccaria's work that criminals act in a rational manner in committing their crimes. The purpose of punishment is to deliver retribution and so to deter the criminal from further criminal acts. It follows that the severity of punishment, which should be certain and immediate, should fit the crime and not the criminal. The amount and degree of punishment should be proportionate to that required to prevent and deter crime. Thus, the overarching goal of a criminal justice system should be crime prevention.

Jeremy Bentham, contemporaneous with Beccaria, also advocated that a rational calculation of the balance between profit and pain guided the indi-vidual's free choice of whether to commit a criminal act. In keeping with this position, Bentham (1996) advocated a *utilitarian* approach as the foundation for criminal law. Utilitarianism holds that we judge the moral value of an action by the contribution it makes to the greater good. Thus, like Beccaria, Bentham came to the view that the administration of punishment should be regulated so that it can prevent crime. Bentham held that punishment should seek to achieve four outcomes: *(1)* to prevent crime; *(2)* if prevention is not achieved, to convince a criminal to commit a less serious crime; *(3)* to reduce the harm inflicted during a crime; and *(4)* to prevent crime as cheaply as possible.

In essence, classical theory maintains that, given an opportunity to commit a crime, each individual can make a free, rational choice between criminal and noncriminal behavior. What factors might a person given the opportunity to commit a crime consider when making a rational choice? According to Roshier (1989), "The goal of our rationality is personal satisfaction; rational self-interest is the key motivational characteristic that governs our relationship with crime and conformity" (pp. 14–15). Thus, in anticipation of Freud's pleasure principle, we have a picture of the criminal as a hedonist, estimating the gains and losses of his or her actions in a personal equation of avoiding pain and gaining gratification. Lilley et al. (2002) have dubbed this approach to understanding crime the "criminal as calculator."

There are two key assumptions within classical theory: first, that we exercise free will in making choices about our actions; second, that we act in a rational manner in making those choices. If crimes are rational acts of free will, it follows that the purpose of punishment must be to change the individual's decision making so that in the future he or she will decide not to commit a crime. As with any theory, the assumptions underpinning classical theory are open to question. Where does free will come from and does everyone have the same capacity to exercise free will (Honderich, 1993)? Why do some people and not others decide to commit criminal acts? Do we really obey the law simply because we fear punishment?

The practical implications of a utilitarian philosophy were to affect profoundly legal systems across 18th-century Europe. Contrary to the belief of the day, utilitarianism argued that excessive punishment is both unnecessary and, indeed, counterproductive in terms of preventing crime. The level of punishment, classical theorists argued, should be in proportion to the severity of the crime (see von Hirsch, 1993). The reasoning behind proportionality of punishment is plain. If all crimes carry an equally harsh penalty, then there can be no selective, differential effect of punishment. For example, if the crimes of child abuse and murder were both punishable by the death penalty, then logically the child abuser would have little reason not to kill the child in order to prevent disclosure of the abuse. In other words, matching the crime to the punishment creates the possibility that punishment can act as a deterrent and so prevent crime.

The legacy of classical theory is clearly seen in the modern-day legal systems of Europe and the United States. Classical theory was the dominant force in Europe and America in the late 18th and the 19th centuries, guiding both judicial philosophers and the functioning of the criminal justice system of the time.

Some of the basic tenets of classical theory are highly familiar today. The principle of *mens rea*, guilty intent, lies close to the concept of free will.

We accept that, with due allowance for age and in some cases mental disorder, criminals are responsible for their crimes. We take it as a given that the severity of punishment should be proportional to the crime and that extreme punitive measures are not acceptable. The dispensation of punishments that fit the crime with the purpose of deterring further offending owes much to utilitarian thinking. It is taken as axiomatic that the punishment of the individual can be of benefit to the majority: The experience of punishment deters the individual from committing further crimes, now termed *special or specific deterrence*; and the threat of punishment also deters others from engaging in crime, now called *general deterrence.*

In many contemporary criminal justice systems, the aim of deterrence through punishment is unchanged, but the methods are different, relying on two basic approaches (that can occur simultaneously): *(1)* remove something that the individual values; and *(2)* forcibly impose conditions that the individual dislikes. To achieve the former, the law allows removal of an individual's assets, mainly property and money but arguably children, as well as more subtle possessions such as self-esteem and social standing. The criminal's liberty may be curtailed by means such as curfew and electronic tagging, or by loss of freedom through a period of imprisonment. The ultimate personal loss is present in those jurisdictions where the death penalty is administered. The latter approach, imposition of aversive conditions, may be realized through the use of punitive institutional regimes such as "short, sharp, shocks" and boot camps, or with cruel and unusual forms of punishment as with long periods of solitary confinement, corporal punishment, and hard labor (Thornton, Curran, Grayson, & Holloway , 1984).

The evolution from the spiritual to the philosophical was, in the late 18th century, followed by the emergence of the psychological.

Psychological Theory and Criminal Behavior

The psychoanalytic theory of Sigmund Freud (1856–1939) is the traditional starting place in the history of theoretical developments within mainstream psychology. After Freud, plotting the historical lineage according to the major theoretical milestones, the next important influence was Ivan Pavlov (1849–1936) and B. F. Skinner (1904–1990) and the development of learning theory, then Gordon W. Allport (1897–1967), Raymond B. Cattell (1905–1998), and Hans J. Eysenck (1916–1997) in the articulation of personality theory. The line of descent from traditional learning theories continues to social learning and cognitive-behavioral theory, as typified by the work of Julian Rotter and Albert Bandura. This theoretical line finally takes us to the door of cognitive psychology as seen, for example, in contemporary theories of information processing and speculation on the nature of human consciousness (Hardcastle, 1995). Peering through the door, we glimpse an ever more biological future, particularly with the advent of neuroscience and its impact on behavioral and social science (Gazzaniga, Ivry, & Mangun, 2002).

As they were developed, so psychological theories have been used to formulate explanations of criminal behavior. If we follow the same historical route by which the theories were developed, we encounter first psychodynamic accounts of criminal behavior. Thus, the early psychological theorists drew on psychoanalytic concepts, as seen with the application of the reality principle (e.g., Alexander & Healy, 1935) and sublimation (e.g., Healy & Bronner, 1936), to explain criminal behavior. The influential writings of John Bowlby (1907–1990) on attachment, maternal deprivation, and delinquency apply psychodynamic theory to account for the developmental process associated with delinquency (Bowlby, 1944).

The influence of operant learning theory in explaining criminal behavior is seen in the work of the criminologist Edwin Sutherland (1883–1950) who developed differential association theory (Sutherland, 1947) and in differential reinforcement theory (Jeffery, 1965). Social learning theory (Bandura, 1977) has been used to develop a theory of crime (Akers, 1977). Finally, Hans Eysenck has applied personality theory to provide an explanation of criminal behavior (Eysenck, 1964).

The impact of cognitive psychology in formulating an understanding of criminal behavior is evident in two distinct bodies of research. The first set of studies is concerned with social cognition and social information processing in offenders. This literature includes studies of the association between criminal behavior and aspects of cognition such as empathy, social problem solving, moral reasoning, and social perception (Ross & Fabiano, 1985). The concept of social information processing has been used to formulate a model of the development of aggressive and violent delinquent behavior (e.g., Crick & Dodge, 1996; Huesmann, 1988). The second literature draws upon a particular aspect of cognitive theory, decision making, to understand the criminal as a rational decision maker (e.g., Cornish & Clarke, 1986). The view of the criminal as a calculating *rational* decision maker stands comparison with classical theory, although less so with social information processing where the vagaries of emotionality, particularly anger (Novaco, 1994), and irrationality are allowed their eccentric influences on human behavior (see Finkel & Parrott, 2006).

Multifactor Models

There have been several attempts to draw together the large body of evidence on psychology and crime generally (Bartol & Bartol, 2005; Blackburn, 1993; Feldman, 1977; Hollin, 1989; Nietzel, 1979); or specifically around themes such as biologically based explanations for crime (Rafter, 2008; Raine, 1993). There are also large-scale research projects, typically employing longitudinal research designs, which chart the individual and social factors that may discriminate delinquent life course trajectories (e.g., Thornberry & Krohn, 2002). In looking at the key predictors of delinquency drawn from longitudinal research,

Farrington (2002) concludes that for males "Impulsivity, low intelligence, poor parenting, a criminal family and socio-economic deprivation, despite their interrelations, all contribute independently to the development of delinquency" (p. 680).

Risk-Needs Model

The development of a psychology of criminal conduct (Andrews & Bonta, 1994, 2003) has informed the risk-needs model of criminal behavior. This model suggests that offenders have a range of needs, not all of which are related to their offending. As Andrews and Bonta (1994) explain:

> Many offenders, especially high-risk offenders, have a variety of needs. They need places to live and work and/or they need to stop taking drugs. Some have poor self-esteem, chronic headaches or cavities in their teeth. These are all "needs." The need principle draws our attention to the distinction between *criminogenic* and *noncriminogenic* needs. Criminogenic needs are a subset of an offender's risk level. They are dynamic attributes of an offender that, when changed, are associated with changes in the probability of recidivism. Noncriminogenic needs are also dynamic and changeable, but these changes are not necessarily associated with the probability of recidivism. (p. 176)

As described in Chapter 9, Andrews and Bonta developed a measure of need and risk, the Level of Service Inventory (Andrews & Bonta, 1995), which assesses a range of empirically derived criminogenic needs and produces an estimate of the individual offender's risk of reoffending. The Level of Service Inventory functions appropriately for both male and female offenders (Gendreau, Little, & Goggin, 1996; Palmer & Hollin, 2007).

The growth in complex models of criminal behavior underscores the interplay between a range of individual, social, and economic factors. As the research base grew so the theoretical focus sharpened to highlight specific types of crime. In particular, attention turned to the various crimes that involve violent behavior.

Psychology and *Violent* Criminal Behavior

The immediate issue in focussing on violence becomes one of terminology and definition. The terms *aggression* and *violence*, often used synonymously, may lose precision so that, as Berkowitz (1993) notes, there are "all too many meanings" (p. 3). A report from the World Health Organization (WHO; Krug et al., 2002), which refers to violence as a global public health problem, tackles the etymological complexity hidden within the word *violent*. The WHO report makes a distinction between four classes of violence: these four are "physical," "sexual," "psychological," and "deprivation and neglect." Furthermore, the violence may be "self-directed," "interpersonal," or "collective" in nature: self-directed violence includes self-harm and suicide, interpersonal violence includes physical and sexual assault, and collective violence includes genocide and acts of war.

In WHO terms, the present concern is with acts of physical violence against the person that are forbidden in criminal law, specifically where physical injury is the outcome (here excluding acts of sexual and domestic violence). The focus on *criminal* law also specifically excludes violent acts by people with a mental disorder (Hodgins & Müller-Isberner, 2000). The present focus therefore captures criminal acts such as murder and attempted murder, manslaughter, wounding, assault, and robbery.

Set against this background, and drawing parallels with theories of criminal behavior in general, there have been several psychologically informed accounts of violence. Thus, there have been explanations for violent behavior couched within the conceptual strictures of biology (Loeber & Pardini, 2008), psychodynamic theory (Lerner, 1999), learning theory (Bandura, 1973), personality theory (McMurran & Howard, 2009), and cognition (Gannon, Ward, Beech, & Fisher, 2007). However, it is evident that relationships between many factors must be understood to have a full understanding of violent crime. Hollin and Palmer (2003) reported that criminal history, companions, education and employment, and alcohol and drugs were risk factors that distinguished violent from nonviolent imprisoned offenders. The development of multifactor models of violence represents a significant conceptual advance in this regard.

Multifactor Models of Violence

Nietzel, Hasemann, and Lynam (1999) presented a four-stage model of the development of violent offending. With illustrative examples given in Table 2.1, this model progresses through the life span highlighting key risk factors at each stage. As Nietzel et al. (1999) note, some relationships between factors are more certain than others and there will be more than one pathway through the model.

The model in Table 2.1 hints at the difficulties involved in fully understanding violent behavior. The developmental changes associated with violent behavior that take place from childhood to adolescence are themselves intricate and complex (Reid, Patterson, & Snyder, 2002) as, indeed, is the case over the life span (Farrington, 2007). The process of building theoretical models can become increasingly wide ranging: for example, multisystemic therapy, developed for adolescent offenders, has its theoretical origins in theories of social ecology and family systems (Henggeler, Schoenwald, Borduin, Rowland, & Cunningham, 1998).

Table 2.1 Developmental Model of Violence

Distal Antecedents	Early Indicators	Developmental Processes	Maintenance Variables
Biological			
Genes			
Hormones	Conduct disorder	School failure	Peer group
Psychological	Ineffective parenting	Substance use	Rewards of violence
IQ			
Temperament			
Environmental			
Family processes			
Neighborhood			

Source: After Nietzel et al., 1999.

Applying Theory: The Rehabilitative Ideal

As psychological theories became more sophisticated and gathered empirical support, so they were applied to real-life problems, including criminal behavior, with the aim of bring about some beneficial change.

The Rise of Treatment

The history of rehabilitation for criminals can be traced back to the great social reformers of the 18th century. In Britain, John Howard (1726–1790) and Elizabeth Fry (1780–1845) sought to change prisons from institutions of deep despair and cruel punishment to places that were humane and held the potential to reform prisoners' lives. In the United States, similar social changes were underway: Samuel June Barrows (1845–1909) was appointed by President Cleveland to represent the United States on the International Prison Commission and, when he was elected to Congress, Barrows worked for prison reform.

As efforts to rehabilitate criminals became more widespread in the early 19th century, precipitating changes in social and welfare policy for prisons and prisoners, so psychologists were at pains to offer treatment as a means to rehabilitation. To follow the theories outlined earlier, we can chart the use of treatment within corrections according to the broad traditions of psychodynamic psychotherapy, behavior modification and behavior therapy, and cognitive-behavioral and cognitive therapies. In practice there are many variations on themes and the divisions between types of therapy may become blurred, but most psychologists would recognize these broad churches of therapy.

The earliest therapeutic work with delinquents was from a psychoanalytic tradition (e.g., Aichhorn, 1955) and saw delinquent behavior as the product of a failure in psychological development. It was the task of the therapist to amend this developmental failure and so bring about an end to the delinquency. The use of psychodynamic treatment methods with offenders continued to develop up to the 1960s, with significant contributions by such notable figures as Melanie Klein (Klein, 1934/1975). The use of group and milieu therapies, including group counseling, psychodrama, reality therapy, transactional analysis, and therapeutic communities, proved popular in both Britain and America in the 1940s, 1950s, and 1960s (Lester & Van Voorhis, 2004a; Lipton, 2001). Although the popularity of psychotherapeutic methods in the criminal justice system has waned, the practice of forensic/correctional psychotherapy remains, although perhaps as a specialty requiring high levels of professional training (Cordess, 2001; Lester & Van Voorhis, 2004b).

As psychotherapeutic methods faded from correctional practice, the 1970s saw their replacement with such behavioral methods as token economies, response cost procedures, and time out (Lester, Braswell, & Van Voorhis, 2004; Milan, 2001). These behavioral methods were applied in a range of settings, from prisons and residential homes to the community, often with young offenders (Hollin, 1990). Indeed, several innovative projects for young offenders, based on behavioral models, were developed during this period, including Achievement Place in Kansas (Kirigin, Braukmann, Atwater, & Wolf, 1982) and the work of the Oregon Social Learning Center (Reid et al., 2002).

The Fall of Treatment

In the 1950s and 1960s efforts to rehabilitate offenders through treatment were evident throughout the criminal justice system. However, there were criticisms of psychological treatment on two grounds. The first set of criticisms was based on the appropriateness of treatment as a strategy for changing the behavior of those who have committed crimes. As Jeffery (1960) notes, a treatment philosophy contains three assumptions, *determinism, differentiation,* and *pathology.* Determinism implies that the individual's behavior is caused by factors—biological, psychological, social, or some combination of all three—that are outside the individual's control. Differentiation holds that criminals are in some way, be it biologically, psychologically, or socially, different from noncriminals. The notion of pathology, the next logical step after differentiation, holds that the difference between criminals and noncriminals is one of abnormality.

There are exceptions, as with some mentally disordered offenders, but a system of rehabilitation through treatment that is based on determinism, differentiation, and pathology is a direct contradiction to a criminal justice system based on the rational exercise of free will, punishment, and deterrence. This contradiction is seen most clearly in Skinner's radical behaviorism (Skinner, 1974) and associated methods of changing behavior, which understand human behavior in terms of a genotype–environment interaction, with no time for the ghost in the machine of free will.

Yet further, there were academic criticisms, most notably from criminology, which reached a peak with the publication of *The New Criminology* (1973) by the British criminologists Taylor, Walton, and Young (1973). With its roots in deviancy theory, labeling theory, and European philosophy, the new criminology presented a Marxist analysis of crime and was outright in its rejection of psychological theory and practice (see Hollin, 2007).

The second set of criticisms was based on empirical grounds. The publication in 1974 of Robert Martinson's paper "What Works? Questions and Answers About Prison Reform"—preempting a substantial report by Lipton, Martinson, and Wilks (1975)—was a tipping point in the shift away from treatment and toward punishment. As with the American reviews, a Home Office publication by Brody (1976) also found little support for the thesis that treatment could rehabilitate offenders and reduce crime.

There is an inescapable association between crime, criminal justice, and politics (O'Malley, 2004), which touches many levels from the financial to the philosophical, which for myriad reasons varies in nature at different times in different countries. The effects of this political influence on the criminal justice system were evident in the early 1980s. It was during the first years of the 1980s that the pessimistic reviews of the 1970s, notwithstanding Martinson's (1979) later recantation of his earlier paper, suited the punitive political philosophies of the day. Thus, the position was taken that treatment had been shown not to work and should be abandoned. It might have been possible to take the alternative view that this null finding provided the opportunity to try new methods of changing behavior: however, the opportunity was lost as the criminal justice system returned to the business of punishing offenders. The era dawned when prisons had no greater aspiration than "humane containment" and the delivery of the offender's "just desserts," while juvenile offenders were consigned to boot camps and to custodial regimes designed to administer a "short, sharp, shock." There were continued arguments in support of treatment (e.g., Gendreau & Ross, 1979) and accusations of "knowledge destruction" with respect to the effectiveness of treatment (Andrews & Wormith, 1989), but the world was not listening.

The Return to Treatment

The resurrection of treatment in the 1990s is directly attributable to the impact of the meta-analyses of the offender treatment literature. Garrett's (1985) meta-analysis was the forerunner of a large number of similar analyses over the next decade: In an overview of the literature McGuire (2002) refers to "30 meta-analytic reviews published between 1985 and 2001" (p. 13). There are several highly cited meta-analyses from this period (Andrews et al., 1990; Lipsey, 1992; Lösel & Koferl, 1989) that gave rise to several syntheses of their findings (Gendreau, 1996; Hollin, 1999; Lipsey, 1995; Lösel, 1995). In adopting a phrase from the title of Martinson's (1974) paper, the collective interest in applying the lessons from the meta-analyses to inform rehabilitative practice with offenders became known as "What Works?" (McGuire, 1995).

What Works?

The meta-analyses indicated that the interventions that were most effective in reducing offending were cognitive-behavioral in orientation, had an explicit focus on offense behavior, and were structured in format. Andrews (1995) describes the formulation of principles for the delivery of effective correctional treatment to reduce reoffending. These principles concerned individual differences across offenders in terms of risk, need, and responsivity. The *risk principle* maintains that the intensity of service delivery should correspond with the risk of reoffending. Intensive services are necessary for offenders with a high risk of reoffending; a lighter touch is needed for offenders with a low risk of reoffending. The misallocation by risk of offenders to treatment, both too high risk and too low risk, can mask the treatment effects for correctly allocated offenders (Palmer et al., 2008, 2009).

The *need principle* demands clarity in treatment focus: If an intervention's intended outcome is a reduction in reoffending, then it must target criminogenic needs. This is not to say that noncriminogenic needs should be ignored, rather services that target only these factors will "fail" when offending is not reduced. The *responsivity principle* highlights the need for a close match between mode of delivery and offender characteristics such as age, gender, and intellectual ability. Andrews (1995) expanded these three basic principles to include *treatment integrity*: the need to ensure a close match between treatment design and actual service delivery (see Hollin, 1995).

As large practice agencies, such as the English and Welsh Prison Service, began to translate these principles into practice, there were two significant developments. First, following the lead of Correctional Services in Canada, there was an increased use of offending behavior programs (Robinson & Porporino, 2001). Second, there was a recognition of the need for clear, explicit criteria by which to judge whether a program is fit for purpose (Hollin & Palmer, 2006; Lipton, Thornton, McGuire, Porporino, & Hollin, 2000). In addition, the organizational coherence and standards of management necessary to implement programs—including levels of practitioner training to deliver programs, the importance of managing treatment integrity, and collecting monitoring and evaluation data—became more clearly articulated (Gendreau, Goggin, & Smith, 2002).

The advent of offending behavior programs led to the development of programs to develop the cognitive skills of all offenders (Hollin & Palmer, 2009) as well as a range of offense-specific programs, including programs for violent offenders such as Aggression Replacement Training (ART; Goldstein, Glick, & Gibbs, 1998; Goldstein, Nensén, Daleflod, & Kalt, 2004). The ART program, which incorporates skills training, anger control, and moral reasoning training, was used successfully by the English and Welsh Probation Service with adult male violent offenders in the community (Hatcher et al., 2008).

There have been several reviews of programs for violent offenders (Lipsey & Wilson, 1998; McGuire, 2008a; Polaschek, 2006). McGuire drew three conclusions: first, there is ample evidence that treatment can reduce violent behavior; second, there is room for more high-quality outcome research; third, to be successful, the amount and intensity (i.e., "dosage") of interventions for violent offenders needs to be greater than for nonviolent offenders.

History has taught us a great deal about the efforts demanded by effective crime reduction and prevention and we continue to learn empirically, practically, and politically. Indeed, with respect to the interaction between researchers and politicians (with practitioners caught in the cross fire), there are echoes today of the early 1980s in the grave misgivings expressed by UK researchers about the way in which evidence is (mis)used within the criminal justice system. These misgivings center on the charges of manipulation by central government of the evidence that emerged from the government's Crime Reduction programme in order to support changes in policy (Hollin, 2008; Hope, 2004; Raynor, 2004; Walters, 2008).

What Next?

If we peer into the near future, where might we boldly go? It is my view that there are two pressing issues, one parochial to researchers, the other much wider in scope. First, to sustain evidence-based practice there is a need for research to adapt yet further to the realities of working within the criminal justice system. It is held that randomized studies are the gold standard in research design. Although this view is debatable (Hollin, 2008), there are legal and ethical issues associated with the use of randomized designs in criminal justice settings. However, rather than dismissing nonrandomized studies as "suboptimal" (Chitty, 2005), researchers can with confidence adopt alternative designs such as propensity analysis (McGuire et al., 2008) to widen the evidence base. Any insistence on a particular research methodology is counterproductive. For example, it is evident that dropping out of a program is contraindicated (Hollin et al., 2008) and to improve practice we need to understand why this is the case. However, to dismiss the empirical evidence and sit back saying we must have randomized studies (Chitty, 2005) simply will not do when it is perfectly possible to compensate for an absence of random assignment to treatment and control conditions by statistically equating groups on, say, risk factors for violence.

Second, there are wider issues with which to become involved. At a time when questions are being asked about the effectiveness of punishment in reducing crime and the effectiveness of sentencing (Hollin, 2002; McGuire, 2008b), there is the opportunity to introduce constructive practice into the criminal justice system on a substantial scale. To take this opportunity means formulating not only an empirical base to the argument but also being prepared to counter arguments of the "treatment equals pathology" type.

In conclusion, if we can seize the moment at this point in history, then, looking into the distant future, perhaps the punitive emphasis of the criminal justice system may be replaced with a commitment to more constructive and skill-building practices as one means by which to prevent violent crime.

References

Aichhorn, A. (1955). *Wayward youth.* New York: Meridian Books.

Akers, R. L. (1977). *Deviant behavior: A social learning* approach (2nd ed.). Belmont, CA: Wadsworth.

Alexander, F., & Healy, W. (1935). *Roots of crime.* New York: Knopf.

Andrews, D. A. (1995). The psychology of criminal conduct and effective treatment. In J. McGuire (Ed.), *What works: Reducing reoffending* (pp. 35–62). Chichester, England: John Wiley & Sons.

Andrews, D. A., & Bonta, J. (1994). *The psychology of criminal conduct.* Cincinnati, OH: Anderson Publishing Company.

Andrews, D. A., & Bonta, J. (1995). *LSI-R: The Level of Service Inventory-Revised.* Toronto: Multi-Health Systems.

Andrews, D. A., & Bonta, J. (2003). *The psychology of criminal conduct* (3rd ed.). Cincinnati, OH: Anderson Publishing Company.

Andrews, D. A., & Wormith, J. S. (1989). Personality and crime: Knowledge destruction and construction in criminology. *Justice Quarterly, 6,* 289–309.

Andrews, D. A., Zinger, I., Hoge, R. D., Bonta, J., Gendreau, P., & Cullen, F. T. (1990). Does correctional treatment work? A clinically relevant and informed meta-analysis. *Criminology, 28,* 369–404.

Bandura, A. (1973). *Aggression: A social learning analysis.* Englewood Cliffs, NJ: Prentice-Hall.

Bandura, A. (1977). *Social learning theory.* New York: Prentice-Hall.

Bartol, C. R., & Bartol, A. M. (2005). *Criminal behavior: A psychosocial approach* (7th ed.). Upper Saddle River, NJ: Pearson Educational.

Beccaria, C. (1963). *On crimes and punishments* (H. Paolucci, Trans.). Indianapolis, IN: Bobbs-Merrill. (Original work published in 1764).

Bentham, J. (1996). An introduction to the principles of morals and legislation. In J. H. Burns & H. L. A. Hart (Eds.), *The collected works of Jeremy Bentham.* Oxford, England: Oxford University Press.

Berkowitz, L. (1993). *Aggression: Its causes, consequences, and control.* New York: McGraw-Hill.

Blackburn, R. (1993). *The psychology of criminal conduct: Theory, research and practice.* Chichester, England: John Wiley & Sons.

Bowlby, J. (1944). Forty-four juvenile thieves. *International Journal of Psychoanalysis, 25,* 1–57.

Brody, S. (1976). *The effectiveness of sentencing.* Home Office Research Study 35. London: HMSO.

Chitty, C. (2005). The impact of corrections on re-offending: Conclusions and the way forward. In G. Harper & C. Chitty (Eds.), *The impact of corrections on re-offending: A review of "what works"* (2nd ed., pp. 73–82). Home Office Research Study 291. London: Home Office.

Cordess, C. (2001). Forensic psychotherapy. In C. R. Hollin (Ed.), *Handbook of offender assessment and treatment* (pp. 297–329). Chichester, England: John Wiley & Sons.

Cornish, D. B., & Clarke, R. V. G. (Eds.). (1986). *The reasoning criminal: Rational choice perspectives on crime.* New York: Springer-Verlag.

Crick, N. R., & Dodge, K. A. (1996). Social information-processing mechanisms in reactive and proactive aggression. *Child Development, 67,* 993–1002.

Eysenck, H. J. (1964). *Crime and personality.* London: Routledge and Kegan Paul.

Farrington, D. P. 2002. Developmental criminology and risk-focused prevention. In M. Maguire, R. Morgan, & R. Reiner (Eds.), *The Oxford handbook of criminology* (3rd ed., pp. 657–701). Oxford, England: Oxford University Press.

Farrington, D. P. (2007). Origins of violent behavior over the lifespan. In D. J. Flannery, A. T. Vaszonyi, & I. D. Waldman (Eds.), *The Cambridge handbook of violent behavior and aggression* (pp. 19–48). Cambridge, England: Cambridge University Press.

Feldman, M. P. (1977). *Criminal behaviour: A psychological analysis.* Chichester, England: John Wiley & Sons.

Finkel, N. J., & Parrott, W. G. (2006). *Emotions and culpability: How the law is at odds with psychology, jurors, and itself.* Washington, DC: American Psychological Association.

Gannon, T. A., Ward, T., Beech, A., & Fisher, D. (Eds.). (2007). *Aggressive offenders' cognition: Theory, research and practice.* Chichester, England: John Wiley & Sons.

Garrett, C. G. (1985). Effects of residential treatment on adjudicated delinquents: A meta-analysis. *Journal of Research in Crime and Delinquency, 22,* 287–308.

Gazzaniga, M. S., Ivry, R. B., & Mangun, G. R. (2002). *Cognitive neuroscience: The biology of the mind* (2nd ed.). London: W. W. Norton.

Gendreau, P. (1996). Offender rehabilitation: What we know and what needs to be done. *Criminal Justice and Behavior, 23,* 144–161.

Gendreau, P., Goggin, C., & Smith, P. (2002). Implementation guidelines for correctional programs in the "real world." In G. A. Bernfeld, D. P. Farrington, & A. W. Leschied (Eds.), *Offender rehabilitation in practice: Implementing and evaluating effective programs* (pp. 228–268). Chichester, England: John Wiley & Sons.

Gendreau, P., Little, T., & Goggin, C. (1996). A meta-analysis of predictors of adult offender recidivism: What works! *Criminology, 34,* 401–433.

Gendreau, P., & Ross, B. (1979). Effective correctional treatment: Bibliotherapy for cynics. *Crime and Delinquency, 25,* 463–489.

Goldstein, A. P., Glick, B., & Gibbs, J. C. (1998). *Aggression Replacement Training: A comprehensive intervention for aggressive youth* (rev. ed.). Champaign, IL: Research Press.

Goldstein, A. P., Nensén, R., Daleflod, B., & Kalt, M. (Eds.). (2004). *New perspectives on Aggression Replacement Training: Practice, research, application.* Chichester, England: John Wiley & Sons.

Hardcastle, V. G. (1995). A critique of information processing theories of consciousness. *Minds and Machines, 5,* 89–107.

Hatcher, R. M., Palmer, E. J., McGuire, J., Hounsome, J. C., Bilby, C. A., & Hollin, C. R. (2008). Aggression Replacement Training with adult male offenders within community settings: A reconviction analysis. *Journal of Forensic Psychiatry and Psychology, 19,* 517–532.

Healy, W., & Bronner, A. F. (1936). *New light on delinquency and its treatment.* New Haven, CT: Yale University Press.

Henggeler, S. W., Schoenwald, S. K., Borduin, C. M., Rowland, M. D., & Cunningham, P. B. (1998). *Multisystemic treatment for antisocial behavior in youth*. New York: Guildford.

Hodgins, S., & Müller-Isberner, R. (Eds.). (2000). *Violence, crime and mentally disordered offenders*. Chichester, England: John Wiley & Sons.

Hollin, C. R. (1989). *Psychology and crime: An introduction to criminological psychology*. London: Routledge.

Hollin, C. R. (1990). *Cognitive-behavioral interventions with young offenders*. Elmsford, NY: Pergamon Press.

Hollin, C. R. (1995). The meaning and implications of "programme integrity." In J. McGuire (Ed.), *What works: Reducing reoffending* (pp. 195–208). Chichester, England: John Wiley & Sons.

Hollin, C. R. (1999). Treatment programmes for offenders: Meta-analysis, "what works," and beyond. *International Journal of Psychiatry and Law, 22*, 361–372.

Hollin, C. R. (2002). Does punishment motivate offenders to change? In M. McMurran (Ed.), *Motivating offenders to change: A guide to enhancing engagement in therapy* (pp. 235–249). Chichester, England: John Wiley & Sons.

Hollin, C. R. (2007). Criminological psychology. In M. R. Maguire, R. Morgan, & R. Reiner (Eds.), *The Oxford handbook of criminology* (4th ed., pp. 43–77). Oxford, England: Oxford University Press.

Hollin, C. R. (2008). Evaluating offending behaviour programmes: Does only randomisation glister? *Criminology and Criminal Justice, 8*, 89–106.

Hollin, C. R., McGuire, J., Hounsome, J. C., Hatcher, R. M., Bilby, C. A. L., & Palmer, E. J. (2008). Cognitive skills offending behavior programs in the community: A reconviction analysis. *Criminal Justice and Behavior, 35*, 269–283.

Hollin, C. R., & Palmer, E. J. (2003). Level of Service Inventory-Revised profiles of violent and non-violent prisoners. *Journal of Interpersonal Violence, 18*, 1075–1086.

Hollin, C. R., & Palmer, E. J. (Eds). 2006. *Offending behaviour programmes: Development, application, and controversies*. Chichester, England: John Wiley & Sons.

Hollin, C. R., & Palmer, E. J. (2009). Cognitive skills programmes for offenders. *Psychology, Crime, and Law, 15*, 147–164.

Honderich, T. (1993). *How free are you? The determinism problem*. Oxford, England: Oxford University Press.

Hope, T. (2004). Pretend it works: Evidence and governance in the evaluation of the Reducing Burglary initiative. *Criminal Justice, 4*, 287–308.

Huesmann, L. R. (1988). The role of social information processing and cognitive schema in the acquisition and maintenance of habitual aggressive behavior. In R. G. Green & E. D. Donnerstein (Eds.), *Human aggression: Theories, research, and implications for social policy* (pp. 73–109). San Diego, CA: Academic Press.

Jeffery, C. R. (1960). The historical development of criminology. In H. Mannheim (Ed.), *Pioneers in criminology* (pp. 364–394). London: Stevens.

Jeffery, C. R. (1965). Criminal behavior and learning theory. *Journal of Criminal Law, Criminology and Police Science, 56*, 294–300.

Kirigin, K. A., Braukmann, C. J., Atwater, J., & Wolf, M. M. (1982). An evaluation of Achievement Place (Teaching-Family) group homes for juvenile offenders. *Journal of Applied Behavior Analysis, 15*, 1–16.

Klein, M. (1975). Criminal tendencies normal children. In M. Klien (Ed.), *The collected writings of Melanie Klein. Volume 1 Love, Guilt and Reparation: And Other Works 1921–1945* (pp. 170–185). London: Hogarth Press. (Original work published in 1934).

Krug, E. G., Dahlberg, L. L., Mercy, J. A., Zwi, A. B., & Lozano, R. (Eds.). 2002. *World report on violence and health*. Geneva, Switzerland: World Health Organization.

Lerner, H. D. (1999). Psychodynamic theories. In V. B. Van Hasselt & M. Hersen (Eds.), *Handbook of psychological approaches with violent offenders: Contemporary strategies and issues* (pp. 67–82). New York: Kluwer Academic/ Plenum.

Lester, D., Braswell, M., & Van Voorhis, P. (2004). Radical behavioral interventions. In P. Van Voorhis, M. Braswell, & D. Lester (Eds.), *Correctional counseling & rehabilitation* (5th ed., pp. 61–83). Cincinnati, OH: Anderson Publishing Co.

Lester, D., & Van Voorhis, P. (2004a). Early approaches to group and milieu therapy. In P. Van Voorhis, M. Braswell, & D. Lester (Eds.), *Correctional counseling & rehabilitation* (5th ed., pp. 85–110). Cincinnati, OH: Anderson Publishing Co.

Lester, D., & Van Voorhis, P. (2004b). Psychoanalytic therapy. In P. Van Voorhis, M. Braswell, & D. Lester (Eds.), *Correctional counseling & rehabilitation* (5th ed., pp. 41–60). Cincinnati, OH: Anderson Publishing Co.

Lilly, J. R., Cullen, F. T., & Ball, R. A. (2002). *Criminological theory: Context and consequences* (3rd ed.). Thousand Oaks, CA: Sage Publications.

Lipsey, M. W. (1992). Juvenile delinquency treatment: A meta-analytic inquiry into the variability of effects. In T. D. Cook, H. Cooper, D. S. Cordray, H. Hartmann, L. V. Hedges, R. J. Light, T. A. Louis, & F. Mosteller (Eds.), *Meta-analysis for explanation: A casebook* (pp. 83–127). New York: Russell Sage Foundation.

Lipsey, M. W. (1995). What do we learn from 400 studies on the effectiveness of treatment with juvenile delinquents? In J. McGuire (Ed.), *What works: Reducing reoffending* (pp. 63–111). Chichester, England: John Wiley & Sons.

Lipsey, M. W., & Wilson, D. B. (1998). Effective intervention for serious juvenile offenders: A synthesis of research. In R. Loeber & D. P. Farrington (Eds.), *Serious and violent juvenile offenders: Risk factors and successful interventions* (pp. 313–345). Thousand Oaks, CA: Sage Publications.

Lipton, D. S. (2001). Therapeutic community treatment programming in corrections. In C. R. Hollin (Ed.), *Handbook of offender assessment and treatment* (pp. 155–177). Chichester, England: John Wiley & Sons.

Lipton, D. S., Martinson, R., & Wilks, J. (1975). *The effectiveness of correctional treatment: A survey of treatment evaluation studies*. New York: Praeger.

Lipton, D. S., Thornton, D. M., McGuire, J., Porporino, F. J., & Hollin, C. R. (2000). Program accreditation and correctional treatment. *Substance Use and Misuse, 35*, 1705–1734.

Loeber, R., & Pardini, D. (2008). Neurobiology and the development of violence: Common assumptions and controversies. *Philosophical Transactions of the Royal Society B, 363*, 2491–2503.

Lösel, F. (1995). Increasing consensus in the evaluation of offender rehabilitation: Lessons from recent research syntheses. *Psychology, Crime, and Law, 2*, 19–39.

Lösel, F., & Koferl, P. (1989). Evaluation research on correctional treatment in West Germany: A meta-analysis. In H. Wenger, F. Lösel, & J. Haisch (Eds.), *Criminal behavior and the justice system: Psychological perspectives* (pp. 67–92). Chichester, England: John Wiley & Sons.

Martinson, R. (1974). What works? Questions and answers about prison reform. *The Public Interest, 35*, 22–54.

Martinson, R. (1979). New findings, new views: A note of caution regarding sentencing reform. *Hofstra Law Review, 7*, 243–258.

McGuire, J. (Ed.). (1995). *What works: Reducing reoffending.* Chichester, England: John Wiley & Sons.

McGuire, J. (2002). Integrating findings from research reviews. In J. McGuire (Ed.), *Offender rehabilitation and treatment: Effective programmes and policies to reduce reoffending* (pp. 3–38). Chichester, England: John Wiley & Sons.

McGuire, J. (2008a). A review of effective interventions for reducing aggression and violence. *Philosophical Transactions of the Royal Society B, 363*, 2577–2597.

McGuire, J. (2008b). What's the point of sentencing? In G. Davies, C. R. Hollin, & R. Bull (Eds.), *Forensic psychology* (pp. 265–291). Chicester, England: John Wiley & Sons.

McGuire, J., Bilby, C. A. L., Hatcher, R. M., Hollin, C. R., Hounsome, J., & Palmer, E. J. (2008). Evaluation of structured cognitive-behavioural treatment programmes in reducing criminal recidivism. *Journal of Experimental Criminology, 4*, 21–40.

McMurran, M., & Howard, R. (Eds.). (2009). *Personality, personality disorder and violence.* Chichester, England: John Wiley & Sons.

Milan, M. A. (2001). Behavioral approaches to correctional management and rehabilitation. In C. R. Hollin (Ed.), *Handbook of offender assessment and treatment* (pp. 139–1154). Chichester, England: John Wiley & Sons.

Nietzel, M. T. (1979). *Crime and its modification: A social learning approach.* Oxford, England: Pergamon Press.

Nietzel, M. T., Hasemann, D. M., & Lynam, D. (1999). Behavioral perspective on violent behavior. In V. B. Van Hasselt & M, Hersen (Eds.), *Handbook of psychological approaches with violent offenders: Contemporary strategies and issues* (pp. 39–66). New York: Kluwer Academic/Plenum.

Novaco, R. W. (1994). Anger as a risk factor for violence among the mentally disordered. In J. Monahan & H. J. Steadman (Eds.), *Violence and mental disorder: Developments in risk assessment* (pp. 21–59). Chicago, IL: University of Chicago Press.

O'Malley, P. (2004). Penal policies and contemporary politics. In C. Summer (Ed.), *The Blackwell companion to criminology* (pp. 183–195). Oxford, England: Blackwell.

Palmer, E. J., & Hollin, C. R. (2007). The Level of Service Inventory-Revised with English women prisoners: A needs and reconviction analysis. *Criminal Justice and Behavior, 34*, 971–984.

Palmer, E. J., McGuire, J., Hatcher, R. M., Hounsome, J. C., Bilby, C. A. L., & Hollin, C. R. (2008). *International Journal of Offender Therapy and Comparative Criminology, 52*, 206–221.

Palmer, E. J., McGuire, J., Hatcher, R. M., Hounsome, J. C., Bilby, C. A. L., & Hollin, C. R. (2009). Allocation to offending behaviour programmes in the

English and Welsh Probation Service. *Criminal Justice and Behavior, 36,* 909–922.

Pettifer, E. W. (1992). *Punishments of former days.* Winchester, England: Waterside Press. (Original edition published by the author in 1939).

Polaschek, D. L. L. (2006). Violent offender programmes: Concept, theory, and practice. In C. R. Hollin & E. J. Palmer (Eds.), *Offending behaviour programmes: Development, application, and controversies* (pp. 113–154). Chichester, England: John Wiley & Sons.

Rafter, N. (2008). *The criminal brain: Understanding biological theories of crime.* New York: New York University Press.

Raine, A. (1993). *The psychopathology of crime: Criminal behavior as a clinical disorder.* San Diego, CA: Academic Press.

Raynor, P. (2004). The Probation Service "Pathfinders": Finding the path and losing the way? *Criminal Justice, 4,* 309–325.

Reid, J. B., Patterson, G. R., & Snyder, J. J. (2002). *Antisocial behavior in children and adolescents: A developmental analysis and model for intervention.* Washington, DC: American Psychological Association.

Robinson, D., & Porporino, F. J. (2001). Programming in cognitive skills: The Reasoning and Rehabilitation programme. In C. R. Hollin (Ed.), *Handbook of offender assessment and treatment.* Chichester, England: John Wiley & Sons.

Roshier, B. (1989). *Controlling crime: The classical perspective in criminology.* Milton Keynes, England: Open University Press.

Ross, R. R., & Fabiano, E. A. (1985). *Time to think: A cognitive model of delinquency prevention and offender rehabilitation.* Johnson City, TN: Institute of Social Sciences and Arts.

Skinner, B. F. (1974). *About behaviourism.* London: Jonathan Cape.

Sutherland, E. H. (1947). *Principles of criminology* (4th ed.). Philadelphia, PA: Lippincott.

Taylor, I., Walton, P., & Young, J. (1973). *The new criminology: For a social theory of deviancy.* London: Routledge & Kegan Paul.

Thornberry, T. P., & Krohn, M. D. (Eds.). 2002. *Taking stock of delinquency: An overview of findings from contemporary longitudinal studies.* New York: Kluwer/ Plenum Press.

Thornton, D. M., Curran, L., Grayson, D., & Holloway, V. (1984). Tougher regimes in detention centres: Report of an evaluation by the Young Offender Psychology Unit. London: HMSO.

von Hirsch, A. (1993). *Censure and sanctions.* Oxford, England: Clarendon Press.

Walters, R. (2008). Government crime policy and moral contamination. *Criminal Justice Matters, 72,* 39–41.

Part II

TARGETING CONTEXTUAL
CONTRIBUTORS TO THE PROBLEM

3

Contextual Influences on Violence

David P. Farrington

The main aim of this chapter is to review contextual influences on violence. The most basic definition of violence is behavior that is intended to cause, and that actually causes, physical or psychological injury. The main focus is on the most important violent crimes that are defined by the criminal law, namely homicide, assault, robbery, and forcible rape. However, because of space limitations, sex offenses will not be reviewed here (see, e.g., van Wijk et al., 2005). The main contextual influences that are reviewed are family, peer, socioeconomic, neighborhood, and situational factors. School influences are not reviewed, since most of the relevant research focuses on bullying or peer aggression in schools (see, e.g., Ttofi & Farrington, 2010).

This chapter focuses on knowledge gained in studies of individual offenders. Research on victims of violence is not reviewed, although they often overlap with violent offenders (see, e.g., Rivara, Shepherd, Farrington, Richmond, & Cannon., 1995). Similarly, research on aggregate rates of violence in areas or countries is not reviewed (see, e.g., MacDonald & Gover, 2005). The main emphasis here is on results obtained in the United States and Great Britain and similar Western countries, and on stranger or street violence, not domestic or within-family violence (see, e.g., Desmarais, Gibas, & Nicholls, 2010). Most research focuses on male offenders and on the offenses of assault and homicide.

Risk Factors and Prospective Longitudinal Studies

Within a short chapter, it is impossible to review everything that is known about contextual influences on violence. This chapter will focus especially on knowledge gained in major prospective longitudinal studies of offending, in which community samples of at least several hundred people are followed up from childhood into adulthood, with repeated personal interviews as well as the collection of record data. More extensive information about violence can be found in Delisi and Conis (2008), Ferguson (2010), Flannery, Vaszonyi, and Waldman (2007), and Riedel and Welsh (2008).

During the 1990s, there was a revolution in criminology as the risk factor prevention paradigm became influential (see Farrington, 2000). The basic idea of this paradigm is very simple: Identify the key risk factors for offending and implement prevention methods designed to counteract them. This paradigm was imported into criminology from public health, where it had been used successfully for many years to tackle illnesses such as cancer and heart disease, by pioneers such as Hawkins and Catalano (1992). The risk factor prevention paradigm links explanation and prevention; links fundamental and applied research; and links scholars, policy makers, and practitioners. Loeber and Farrington (1998) presented a detailed exposition of this paradigm as applied to serious and violent juvenile offenders.

A risk factor for violence is defined as a variable that predicts a high probability of violence. To determine whether a risk factor is a predictor or possible cause of violence, the risk factor needs to be measured before the violence. Therefore, prospective longitudinal surveys are needed to investigate risk factors for violence.

The paradigm typically also emphasizes protective factors, suggesting that intervention methods to enhance them should also be implemented. However, in the past the term "protective factor" has been used ambiguously. Some researchers have suggested that a protective factor is the opposite end of the scale to a risk factor. For example, if poor parental supervision is a risk factor, good parental supervision might be a protective factor. However, unless a protective factor has no corresponding, symmetrically opposite risk factor, this seems to be using two terms for the same variable. Other researchers have suggested that a protective factor interacts with a risk factor to minimize or buffer its effects. Typically, the impact of a protective factor is then studied in the presence of a risk factor.

Loeber, Farrington, Stouthamer-Loeber, and White (2008) suggested a new terminology. They defined promotive factors as variables that predict a low probability of violence, and protective factors as variables that predict a low probability of violence among persons exposed to risk factors. They also extended these definitions to the prediction of desistance. Remedial promotive factors were variables that predicted a high probability of desistance among those who had previously offended, while hindering risk factors were variables that predicted a low probability of desistance. There is not space to review the predictors of desistance in this chapter (see, e.g., Kazemian & Farrington, 2010; Lodewijks, De Ruiter, & Doreleijers, 2010).

This chapter will focus especially on results obtained in two prospective longitudinal surveys: the Cambridge Study in Delinquent Development (United Kingdom) and the Pittsburgh Youth Study (United States). The Cambridge Study is a prospective longitudinal survey of over 400 London males from age 8 to age 48 (see Farrington et al., 2006; Piquero, Farrington, & Blumstein, 2007). These males were originally assessed in 1961–1962, when they were attending six state primary schools in London and were aged 8–9. Therefore, the most common year of birth of the males is 1953. The study males have been interviewed and assessed nine times between ages 8 and 48. Attrition has been very low; for example, 95% of those still alive were interviewed at age 18, 94% at age 32, and 93% at age 48.

The assessments in schools measured such factors as intelligence, personality, and impulsiveness, while information was collected in the interviews about such topics as living circumstances; employment histories; relationships with females; leisure activities such as drinking, drug use, and fighting; and of course violence and offending behavior. The boys' parents were also interviewed about once a year from when the boys were aged 8 until when they were aged 15. The parents provided details about such matters as family income, family composition, their employment histories, their child-rearing practices (including discipline and supervision), and the boy's temporary or permanent separations from them. Also, the boys' teachers completed questionnaires when the boys were aged about 8, 10, 12, and 14. These furnished information about such topics as their restlessness or poor concentration, truancy, school attainment, and disruptive behavior in class. Searches of the criminal records of the males, of their biological relatives (fathers, mothers, brothers, and sisters), of their wives and female partners, and of any person who ever offended with any of our males, were also carried out. Up to age 40, 40% of the males were convicted (or adjudicated) of a criminal or juvenile offense, including 16% who were convicted of violence (assault, robbery, carrying or using weapons; see Farrington, 2007b).

In the Pittsburgh Youth Study, over 1,500 Pittsburgh boys were followed up (see Loeber, Farrington, Stouthamer-Loeber, & Van Kammen, 1998; Loeber et al., 2008). Initially, 500 were in first grade (aged about 7), 500 were in fourth grade (aged about 10), and 500 were in seventh grade (aged about 13), of public schools in the City of Pittsburgh. These boys were mostly born between 1974 and 1980. The youngest and oldest cohorts were assessed at least once a year for 12 years, from age 7 to age 19 (youngest) and from age 13 to age 25 (oldest). The middle cohort was assessed every 6 months until age 13, and then finally at age 22. Information was collected from the boys, their mothers, and their teachers.

By age 19, 26% of the boys in the youngest cohort had been arrested for serious violence (homicide, attacking to injure, robbery, or forcible rape). By age 25, 35% of the boys in the oldest cohort had been arrested for serious violence. Special analyses were carried out to investigate the boys who were convicted homicide offenders (see Farrington, Loeber, Stallings, & Homish, 2008; Loeber et al., 2005).

Public Health Versus Criminal Justice

Apart from the focus on risk and protective factors, there are advantages in adopting a public health perspective rather than a criminal justice perspective in studying violence (see, e.g., Dahlberg, 2007; Hoffman, 2004). Public health emphasizes preventing the occurrence or recurrence of illnesses, whereas criminal justice emphasizes retribution, deterrence, incapacitation, and rehabilitation. Public health focuses on victims and consequences, whereas criminal justice targets offenders and is concerned with blame. Public health aims to establish the prevalence and incidence of illnesses (epidemiology) and focuses not only on risk and protective factors and early identification but also on situational factors and "criminogenic commodities" such as guns, alcohol, and drugs (Moore, 1995). Particularly, public health aims to use knowledge about risk and protective factors to design and implement intervention programs, whereas criminal justice measures (except perhaps rehabilitation) are rarely based on demonstrated risk and protective factors. Public health focuses especially on primary prevention: preventing the first act of violence. It is assumed that prevention is better than cure.

Public health approaches have provided alternative methods of measuring violence, for example, using injury data from accident and emergency departments of hospitals (Shepherd, 2007). However, for the purposes of this chapter, their greatest contribution has been to emphasize risk and protective factors and their linkages with interventions. Risk factors that cannot be changed (e.g., gender and race) will not be reviewed here, and neither will individual factors such as impulsiveness and low empathy.

Violence Over the Life Course

Measurement and Prevalence

The most common ways of identifying violent offenders are by using police or court records or self-reports of offending. For example, in the Seattle Social Development Project, which is a follow-up of over 800 youths from age 10 to age 30, 8.6% self-reported a robbery and 3.3% had a court referral for robbery as juveniles (Farrington, Jolliffe et al., 2003). The discrepancy was greater for assault, where 61.3% self-reported but only 12.7% were referred to court. The comparison between self-reports and official records gives some indication of the probability of a violent offender being caught and officially processed. Self-reported violence had predictive validity in the Seattle study: 14% of those who admitted assault had a later court referral for assault, compared with 4% of the remainder (Jolliffe et al., 2003).

Violent offending tends to peak in the teenage years in many different countries. In the United States in 2008, the peak age of arrest for robbery and forcible rape was 18, and for murder and aggravated assault it was 19 (Sourcebook of Criminal Justice Statistics, 2009, Table 4.7). Similar results have been obtained in self-report surveys. For example, in the 2003 English national self-report survey, the percentage admitting violence in the previous year peaked at 23% of males at age 16–17 and 12% of females at age 14–15 (Budd, Sharp, & Mayhew, 2005).

Many theories have been proposed to explain why offending (especially by males) peaks in the teenage years. There may be changes with age in physical capabilities and opportunities for crime, linked to changes in "routine activities" (Cohen & Felson, 1979), such as going to bars in the evenings with other males. The most popular explanation emphasizes the importance of contextual influences (Farrington, 1986), which are the main focus of this chapter. From birth, children are under the influence of their parents, who generally discourage offending. However, during their teenage years, juveniles gradually break away from the control of their parents and become influenced by their peers, who may encourage offending in many cases. After age 20, offending declines again as peer influences give way to a new set of family influences hostile to offending, originating in spouses and female partners.

Continuity

In general, there is continuity from juvenile to adult violence. In the Cambridge Study, 34% of the boys convicted for youthful violence were reconvicted for adult violence, compared with only 8% of those not convicted for youthful violence (Farrington, 2007b). For self-reported violence, 29% of youthful violent offenders were also adult violent offenders, compared with 12% of nonviolent youth. While it is possible that part of the continuity in officially recorded violence may be attributable to continuity in police targeting, the continuity in self-reported violence indicates that there is real continuity in violent behavior.

Generally, an early age of onset of violence predicts a relatively long career of violence, as found in the Pittsburgh Youth Study (Loeber et al., 2008). Moffitt (1993) suggested that the "life-course persistent" offenders who started early (around age 10) and had long criminal careers were fundamentally different from the "adolescence-limited" offenders who started later (around age 14) and had short criminal careers. Trajectory analyses for violence in the Pittsburgh Youth Study identified an early onset-chronic trajectory and an early desistance trajectory, in agreement to some extent with Moffitt's typology (Loeber, Lacourse, & Homish, 2005).

One likely explanation of the continuity in violence over time is that there are persisting individual differences in an underlying potential to commit antisocial, aggressive, or violent behavior. In any cohort, the people who are relatively more aggressive at one age also tend to be relatively more aggressive at later ages, even though absolute levels of aggressive behavior and behavioral manifestations of violence are different at different ages.

Specialization or Versatility

In most research, violent offenders tend to be versatile rather than specialized. They tend to commit many different types of crimes and also show other problems such as heavy drinking, drug use, an unstable job record, and sexual promiscuity (West & Farrington, 1977, p. 149). There is also versatility in types of violence. For example, males who assault their female partners are significantly likely to have convictions for other types of violent offenses (Farrington, 1994), and soccer hooligans are very similar to other types of violent offenders (Farrington, 2006a).

As an indication of their versatility, violent people typically commit more nonviolent offenses than violent offenses. In the Oregon Youth Study, which is a follow-up study of over 200 boys between ages 10 and 30, the boys arrested for violence had an average of 6.6 arrests of all kinds (Capaldi & Patterson, 1996). In the Cambridge Study, the likelihood of committing a violent offense increased steadily with the total number of offenses committed, and violent offenders were very similar to nonviolent frequent offenders (Farrington, 1991). Piquero (2000) and Piquero and Buka (2002) also found that violent offenders were versatile rather than specialized, in the Philadelphia and Providence perinatal cohorts, respectively.

Unfortunately, there is a great deal of controversy about whether violent offenders are specialized or versatile, and conclusions depend on the statistical techniques and samples used (e.g., the Forward Specialization Coefficient versus Latent Class Analysis, community versus offender samples). For example, Osgood and Schreck (2007) hypothesized that specialization was a latent variable, used item response theory, and concluded that there was substantial specialization in violence. McGloin, Sullivan, Piquero, and Pratt (2007) suggested that the degree of specialization depended partly on an enduring criminal propensity and partly on changes in local life circumstances. In a later analysis, McGloin, Sullivan, and Piquero (2009) concluded that there was specialization in the short term but versatility in the long term. Felson (2009, p. 33) suggested that the "versatility cup is half empty and half full." It seems likely that there is some specialization in violence superimposed on some versatility, but the relative importance of specialization versus versatility has yet to be firmly established.

Contextual Influences

Violent offenses, like other crimes, arise from interactions between offenders and victims in contexts. Some violent acts are probably committed by people with relatively stable and enduring violent tendencies, while others are committed by more "normal" people who find themselves in contexts that are conducive to violence. This chapter summarizes knowledge about contextual influences on the development of violent persons (i.e., persons with a relatively high probability of committing violent acts in any situations) and the occurrence of violent acts.

Antisocial Parents

Numerous family factors predict violence. In the Cambridge Study, the strongest childhood predictor of adult convictions for violence was having a convicted parent by the tenth birthday; 20% of boys with convicted parents were themselves convicted, compared with 7% of the remainder (Farrington, 2007b). In the Seattle Social Development Project, parental criminality and parental violence predicted a child's violence (Herrenkohl et al., 2000). The meta-analysis by Derzon (2010) also confirms that parental antisocial behavior is a significant predictor of a child's violence. However, it is not clear that there is any specialized intergenerational transmission from violent parents to violent children, as opposed to general transmission from criminal parents to delinquent children (McCord, 1977).

Substance use by parents also predicts violence by children, and smoking by the mother during pregnancy is a particularly important risk factor. A large-scale criminal record follow-up of a general population cohort of over 5,600 males in Finland showed that maternal smoking during pregnancy doubled the risk of violent offending by male offspring, after controlling for other biopsychosocial risk factors (Rasanen et al., 1999). Similar results were obtained in a Copenhagen birth cohort study of over 4,100 males (Brennan, Grekin, & Mednick, 1999), and in the Philadelphia perinatal project of McGloin, Pratt, and Piquero (2006).

Farrington, Jolliffe, Loeber, Stouthamer-Loeber, and Kalb (2001) reviewed six possible explanations of why antisocial behavior was concentrated in families and transmitted from one generation to the next. First, there may be intergenerational continuities in exposure to multiple risk factors such as poverty, disrupted families, and living in deprived neighborhoods. Second, assortative mating (the tendency of antisocial females to choose antisocial males as partners) facilitates the intergenerational transmission of antisocial behavior. Third, family members may influence each other (e.g., older siblings may encourage younger ones to be antisocial). Fourth, the effect of an antisocial parent on a child's antisocial behavior may be mediated by environmental mechanisms such as poor parental supervision and inconsistent discipline. Fifth, intergenerational transmission may be mediated by genetic mechanisms. Sixth, there may be labeling and police bias against known criminal families.

Child-Rearing Factors

In her classic follow-up of 250 Boston boys in the Cambridge-Somerville Youth Study, McCord (1979) found that the strongest predictors at age 10 of later convictions for violence (up to age 45) were poor parental supervision, parental aggression (including harsh, punitive discipline), and parental conflict. In her later analyses, McCord (1996) showed that violent offenders were less likely than nonviolent offenders to have experienced parental affection and good discipline and supervision.

Similar results have been obtained in other surveys. In the Pittsburgh Youth Study, poor parental supervision, poor parent–boy communication, and physical punishment predicted the boy's violence (Loeber et al., 2005). In the Cambridge Study, harsh parental discipline and poor parental supervision predicted the boy's official and self-reported violence (Farrington, 2007b). In the Seattle Social Development Project, poor family management (poor supervision, inconsistent rules, and harsh discipline) predicted self-reported violence (Herrenkohl et al., 2000). The meta-analysis by Derzon (2010) confirmed that parental supervision, involvement, and discipline were significantly related to a child's violent behavior.

In the Pittsburgh Youth Study, harsh physical punishment predicted violence for Caucasians but not for African Americans (Farrington, Loeber, & Stouthamer-Loeber, 2003). It has been suggested (e.g., by Deater-Deckard, Dodge, Bates, & Pettit, 1996; Kelley, Power, & Wimbush, 1992) that this is because physical discipline is associated with neglect and coldness in Caucasian families but with concern and warmth in African American families. In the Cambridge-Somerville Youth Study, McCord (1997) found that physical punishment predicted convictions for violence especially when it was combined with low parental warmth and affection. According to Straus (2001), physical punishment predicts violence because children learn from their parents that violence is an acceptable method of solving problems.

Child Abuse

In a longitudinal study of over 900 abused children and nearly 700 controls, Widom (1989) discovered that recorded child physical abuse and neglect predicted later arrests for violence, independently of other predictors such as gender, ethnicity, and age. Predictability was greater for females than for males (Widom & White, 1997). Child sexual abuse also predicted adult arrests for sex crimes (Widom & Ames, 1994). Similarly, child abuse predicted later violence in the Pittsburgh Youth Study (Loeber et al., 2005) and in a Swedish longitudinal survey of nearly 300 delinquents and controls followed up in criminal records to their 40s (Lang, af Klinteberg, & Alm, 2002). Interestingly, there is evidence that a genetic factor connected with MAOA can protect against the undesirable effects of child maltreatment (Kim-Cohen et al., 2006; Widom & Brzustowicz, 2006).

Possible environmental causal mechanisms linking childhood victimization and later violence were reviewed by Widom (1994). First, childhood victimization may have immediate but long-lasting consequences (e.g., shaking may cause brain injury; see also Heide & Solomon, 2006). Second, childhood victimization may cause bodily changes (e.g., desensitization to pain) that encourage later violence. Third, child abuse may lead to impulsive or dissociative coping styles that, in turn, lead to poor problem-solving skills or poor school performance. Fourth, victimization may cause changes in self-esteem or in social information-processing patterns that encourage later violence. Fifth, child abuse may lead to changed family environments (e.g., being placed in foster care) that have deleterious effects. Sixth, juvenile justice practices may label victims, isolate them from prosocial peers, and encourage them to associate with delinquent peers.

Broken Families and Exposure to Violence

Parental conflict and coming from a broken family predicted violence in both the Cambridge and Pittsburgh studies, and living in a single-parent female-headed household predicted violence in Pittsburgh (Farrington, 1998). A broken family was the strongest explanatory predictor of homicide offending in the Pittsburgh Youth Study (Farrington et al., 2008). Parental conflict also predicted youth violence in the Seattle Social Development Project (Herrenkohl et al., 2000). The meta-analysis by Derzon (2010) found that family discord and parental separation were significantly related to violent behavior, but that coming from a broken home was not.

If a child is exposed to violence between his parents, this predicts the child's later antisocial behavior (Chan & Yeung, 2009). In the Christchurch (New Zealand) longitudinal study of over 1,300 children from birth to age 25, Fergusson and Horwood (1998) found that children who witnessed violence between their parents were more likely to commit both violent and property offenses according to their self-reports. The importance of witnessing violence held up after controlling for other risk factors such as parental criminality, parental substance use, parental physical punishment, a young mother, and low family income. Nofziger and Kurtz (2005) discussed various explanations of the link between witnessing and committing violence, and they concluded that both were aspects of a continuing violent family lifestyle.

Large Family Size

Large family size (number of children) predicted youth violence in both the Cambridge and Pittsburgh studies (Farrington, 1998). In the Oregon Youth Study, large family size at age 10 predicted self-reported violence at age 13–17 (Capaldi & Patterson, 1996). There are many possible reasons why a large number of siblings might increase the risk of a child's delinquency (Brownfield & Sorenson, 1994). Generally, as the number of children in a family increases, the amount of parental attention that can be given to each child decreases. Also, as the number of children increases, the household tends to become more overcrowded, possibly leading to increases in frustration, irritation, and conflict. In the Cambridge Study, large family size did not predict delinquency for boys living in the least crowded conditions, with two or more rooms than there were children (West & Farrington, 1973, p. 33). This suggests that household overcrowding might be an important factor mediating the association between large family size and offending.

Young Mothers

Young mothers (mothers who had their first child at an early age, typically as a teenager) tended to have violent sons in the Pittsburgh Youth Study (Loeber et al., 2005). A young mother also predicted homicide offending (Farrington et al., 2008). Later analyses in which risk and promotive factors were carefully distinguished demonstrated that the most important effect was that the sons of older mothers had low rates of violence, rather than the sons of younger mothers having high rates (Loeber et al., 2008, p. 200). A teenage mother predicted self-reported violence in the Cambridge Study (Farrington, 2007b). Interestingly, the relationship between a young mother and a convicted son in this study disappeared after controlling for other variables, notably large family size, a convicted parent, and a broken family (Nagin, Pogarsky, & Farrington, 1997). A young mother also predicted self-reported violence in the Rochester Youth Development Study of 1,000 children between ages 13 and 32 (Pogarsky, Lizotte, & Thornberry, 2003). In the Dunedin (New Zealand) study of over 1,000 children from birth to age 32, Jaffee, Caspi, Moffitt, Belsky, and Silva (2001) concluded that the link between teenage mothers and violent children was mediated by maternal characteristics (e.g., intelligence, criminality) and family factors (e.g., harsh discipline, family size, disrupted families).

Peer Influences

Having delinquent friends is an important predictor of youth violence (see Vitaro, Boivin, & Tremblay, 2007), but it is not clear whether there is a specialized effect of peer violence. Peer delinquency and gang membership predicted self-reported violence in the Seattle Social Development Project (Hawkins et al., 1998). What is less clear is the extent to which the link between delinquent friends and violence is a consequence of co-offending, which is particularly common under age 21 (Reiss & Farrington, 1991). However, in the National Longitudinal Study of Adolescent Health, which is a follow-up of over 14,000 youth originally aged 11–19, Haynie and Osgood (2005) concluded that the major intervening mechanisms were socialization by peers and opportunity to offend. In the same study, Haynie, Steffensmeier, and Bell (2007) found that having opposite-sex friends increased female violence but decreased male violence. In the Pittsburgh Youth Study, peer delinquency predicted both violence (Loeber et al., 2005) and homicide offending (Farrington et al., 2008). However, Farrington, Loeber, Yin, and Anderson (2002) found that peer delinquency did not predict a boy's delinquency within individuals (unlike poor parental supervision), suggesting that it was a correlate of offending rather than a cause. Interestingly, the impact of peer delinquency on youth violence was much reduced by a concurrent good relationship with peers (Loeber et al., 2008, p. 201).

It is clear that young people increase their offending after joining a gang. In the Seattle Social Development Project, Battin et al. (1998) found this and also showed that gang membership predicted delinquency above and beyond having delinquent friends. In the Pittsburgh Youth Study, Gordon et al. (2004) reported not only a substantial increase in drug selling, drug use, violence, and property crime after a boy joined a gang but also that the frequency of offending decreased to pre-gang levels after a boy left a gang. Thornberry, Krohn, Lizotte, Smith, and Tobin (2003) in the Rochester Youth Development Study and Gatti, Tremblay, Vitaro, and McDuff (2005) in the Montreal longitudinal-experimental study of over 1,000 youth followed up between ages 10 and 26 also found that young people offended more after joining a gang. Several of these studies contrasted the "selection" and "facilitation" hypotheses and concluded that future gang members were more delinquent to start with but became even more delinquent after joining a gang. In the Chicago Youth Development Study of over 300 boys followed up between ages 11 and 25, Tolan, Gorman-Smith, and Henry (2003) found that gang membership led to peer violence and then to individual violence.

Socioeconomic Status

In general, coming from a low socioeconomic status (SES) family predicts violence. For example, in the U.S. National Youth Survey of over 1,700 children followed up between ages 14 and 40, the prevalences of self-reported felony assault and robbery were about twice as high for lower class youth as for middle class ones (Elliott, Huizinga, & Menard, 1989). The strongest predictor of official violence in the Pittsburgh Youth Study was family dependence on welfare benefits (Farrington, 1998), and this also predicted homicide offenders (Farrington et al., 2008). In the Cambridge Study, coming from a low SES family (having a father with an unskilled manual job) did not significantly predict the boy's youthful violence but did predict his adult violence (Farrington, 2007b). Low family income predicted youthful and adult convictions and youthful self-reported violence, while poor housing predicted youthful violence.

The meta-analysis by Derzon (2010) concluded that low SES was a significant, although weak, predictor of violence. Several researchers have suggested that the link between a low SES family and antisocial behavior is mediated by family socialization practices. For example, Larzelere and Patterson (1990) in the Oregon Youth Study concluded that the effect of SES on delinquency was entirely mediated by parental management skills. Fergusson, Swain-Campbell, and Horwood (2004) in the Christchurch Health and Development Study in New Zealand found that the effect of SES on delinquency disappeared after controlling for family factors, conduct problems, truancy, and deviant peers, suggesting that these may have been mediating factors.

Neighborhood Influences

Generally, people living in urban areas are more violent than those living in rural areas. In the U.S. National Youth Survey, the prevalence of self-reported felony assault and robbery was considerably higher among urban youth (Elliott et al., 1989), and Derzon (2010) found that urban housing predicted criminal behavior. Within urban areas, people living in high-crime neighborhoods are more violent than those living in low-crime neighborhoods. In the Rochester Youth Development Study, living in a high-crime neighborhood significantly predicted self-reported violence (Thornberry, Huizinga, & Loeber, 1995). Similarly, in the Pittsburgh Youth Study, living in a bad neighborhood (either as rated by the mother or based on census measures of poverty, unemployment, and female-headed households) significantly predicted official and reported violence (Farrington, 1998) and homicide offending (Farrington et al., 2008). Interestingly, violence in advantaged neighborhoods seemed to be predicted mainly by individual factors, whereas violence in disadvantaged neighborhoods seemed to be predicted mainly by social and contextual factors (Beyers, Loeber, Wikström, & Stouthamer-Loeber, 2001). In this survey, living in a bad neighborhood, low SES, and the family on welfare were among the factors that best predicted homicide offenders out of other violent offenders (Loeber et al., 2005). However, good neighborhoods had promotive effects (Loeber et al., 2008, pp. 178–179).

Several researchers have attempted to identify the characteristics of neighborhoods that have an influence on violent crime (see Wikström, 2007). In the National Longitudinal Study of Adolescent Health, Bellair, Roscigno, and McNulty (2003) concluded that the preponderance of low-wage service sector employment opportunities in an area directly increased the likelihood of violence. In the Seattle Social Development Project, Herrenkohl et al. (2000) found that community disorganization, residential mobility, the availability of drugs, and the number of neighborhood adults who were involved in crime predicted youth violence.

Sampson, Raudenbush, and Earls (1997) studied community influences on violence in the Project on Human Development in Chicago Neighborhoods, which is a three-wave multiple-cohort study of over 6,300 persons originally aged from birth to age 18. The most important community predictors were concentrated economic disadvantage (as indexed by poverty, the proportion of female-headed families, and the proportion of African Americans), immigrant concentration (the proportions of Latinos or foreign-born persons), residential instability, and low levels of informal social control and social cohesion. They suggested that the "collective efficacy" of a neighborhood, or the willingness of residents to intervene to prevent antisocial behavior, might act as a protective factor against crime (see Odgers et al., 2009). In the same project, Sampson, Morenoff, and Raudenbush (2005) concluded that most of the difference between African Americans and Caucasians in violence could be explained by racial differences in exposure to risk factors, especially living in a bad neighborhood. Similar conclusions were drawn in the Pittsburgh Youth Study (Farrington, Loeber, & Stouthamer-Loeber, 2003) and in the National Longitudinal Study of Adolescent Health (Kaufman, 2005).

Situational Factors

It might be argued that all the contextual factors reviewed so far in this section—family, peer, socioeconomic, and neighborhood—essentially influence the development of a long-term individual potential for violence. In other words, they contribute to between-individual differences: why some people are more likely than others, given the same situational opportunity, to commit violence. Another set of influences—situational factors—explain how the potential for violence becomes the actuality in any given situation. Essentially, they explain short-term within-individual differences: why a person is more likely to commit violence in some situations than in others. Situational factors may be specific to particular types of crimes: robberies as opposed to rapes, or even street robberies as opposed to bank robberies. One of the most influential situational theories of offending is routine activities theory (Cohen & Felson, 1979). This suggests that, for a predatory crime to occur, the minimum requirement is the convergence in time and place of a motivated offender and a suitable target, in the absence of a capable guardian. Felson and Boba (2010, pp. 27–34) have provided a more recent description of how predatory and violent crimes occur, and Tita and Griffiths (2005) investigated how routine activities theory could explain homicide incidents in Pittsburgh.

In their Montreal longitudinal study of over 400 delinquents between ages 15 and 40, LeBlanc and Frechette (1989) provided detailed information about motives and methods used in different offenses at different ages. For example, for violence at age 17, the main motivation was utilitarian or rational. For all crimes, however, the primary motivation changed from hedonistic (searching for excitement, with co-offenders) in the teenage years to utilitarian (with planning, psychological intimidation, and use of instruments such as weapons) in the 20s (Le Blanc, 1996). In the Cambridge Study, motives for physical fights depended on whether the boy fought alone or with others (Farrington, 1993). In individual fights, the boy was usually provoked, became angry, and hit his opponent to discharge his own internal feelings of tension. In group fights, the boy often said that he became involved to help a friend or because he was attacked, and rarely said that he was angry. The group fights were more serious, occurring in bars or streets, and they were more likely to involve weapons, produce injuries, and lead to police intervention. Fights often occurred when minor incidents escalated, because both sides wanted to demonstrate their toughness and masculinity and were unwilling to react in a conciliatory way.

Many of the boys in the Cambridge Study fought after drinking alcohol, and it is clear that alcohol intoxication is an immediate situational factor that precipitates violence. In England, most violence occurs on weekend nights around pubs and clubs and involves young males who have been drinking (Allen, Nicholas, Salisbury, & Wood, 2003). In the National Longitudinal Study of Adolescent Health, Felson, Teasdale, and Burchfield (2008) showed that, even though drinkers were more likely to commit violence while sober, there was a causal effect of intoxication on violence. Further reviews of violence in and around drinking establishments, and methods of reducing it, can be found in Scott and Dedel (2006) and Graham and Homel (2008).

In the United States, guns and drugs are situational factors that are associated with violence. In the Pittsburgh Youth Survey, gang membership, drug selling, and gun carrying predicted homicide offenders (Farrington et al., 2008). Gangs were discussed earlier. In a longitudinal survey of over 4,500 high school seniors in California and Oregon, drug selling was one of the strongest risk factors for violence, especially among girls (Saner & Ellickson, 1996). Brennan and Moore (2009) have provided a useful review of knowledge about weapons and violence. Wells and Horney (2002) analyzed more than 2,000 violent and potentially violent events described by offenders, and they found that, after controlling for individual differences and self-reported intent to harm, weapons were associated with an increased probability of attack and serious injury. More research on situational influences on violent acts needs to be incorporated in prospective longitudinal studies, in order to link up the developmental and situational perspectives.

A Theory of Violence

To develop theories of violence, it is important to establish how risk factors have independent, additive, interactive, or sequential effects. Generally, the probability of violence increases with the number of risk factors (Farrington, 2001a). For example, in the Cambridge Study, the percentage of boys convicted for violence between ages 10 and 20 increased from 2% of those with none of the five vulnerability risk factors at age 8–10 to 28% of those with four or five (out of low family income, large family size, convicted parent, poor child-rearing, and low intelligence). This type of research gives some indication of how accurately violence might be predicted. The most extensive review of theories of violence can be found in Zahn, Brownstein, and Jackson (2004).

Numerous investigations of independent predictors of violence have been carried out in the Cambridge Study. For example, Farrington (2001a) reported that the most important independent childhood predictors of adult violence convictions were a convicted parent, low family income, dishonesty, and harsh discipline; the most important independent childhood predictors of adult self-reported violence were a broken family, low SES, nervousness, and a young mother. As an example of a study of sequential effects, Johnson, Smailes, Cohen, Kasen, and Brook (2004), in a longitudinal survey of nearly 1,000 New York State children, concluded that poor parenting mediated the relationship between antisocial parents and violence by the children as adults.

Developmental and life-course theories aim to explain development, risk factors, and the effect of life events (Farrington, 2005). Such theories can help to explain how and why biological factors such as a low heart rate, individual factors such as impulsiveness or low intelligence, family factors such as poor parental supervision, peer factors, socioeconomic factors, and neighborhood factors influence the development of an individual potential for violence. For example, living in a bad neighborhood and suffering socioeconomic deprivation may in some way cause poor parenting, which in some way causes impulsivity and school failure, which in some way causes a high potential for violence. Theories can also help in specifying more general concepts that underlie violence potential, such as low self-control or weak bonding to society. Theories can also help in specifying how a potentially violent person interacts with situational factors to produce violent acts.

Figure 3.1 shows the key elements of my theory (Farrington, 2003). It was designed to explain offending by lower class males and can easily be modified to explain violence. I have called it the integrated cognitive antisocial potential (ICAP) theory. It integrates ideas from many other theories, including strain, control, learning, labeling, and rational choice approaches; its key construct is antisocial potential (AP); and it assumes that the translation from antisocial potential to antisocial and violent behavior depends on cognitive (thinking and decision-making) processes that take account of opportunities and victims. Figure 3.1 is deliberately simplified in order to show the key elements of the ICAP theory on one sheet of paper; for example, it does not show how the processes operate differently for onset compared with desistance or at different ages.

The key construct underlying offending is antisocial potential (AP), which refers to the potential to commit antisocial acts, including violence. Long-term persisting between-individual differences in AP are distinguished from short-term within-individual variations in AP. Long-term AP depends on impulsiveness, on strain, modeling and socialization processes, and on life events, while short-term variations in AP depend on motivating and situational factors. The ICAP theory suggests that long-term individual, family, peer, school, and neighborhood influences lead to the development of long-term, fairly stable, slowly changing differences between individuals in the potential for violence.

Regarding long-term AP, people can be ordered on a continuum from low to high. The distribution of AP in the population at any age is highly skewed; relatively few people have high levels of AP. People with high AP are

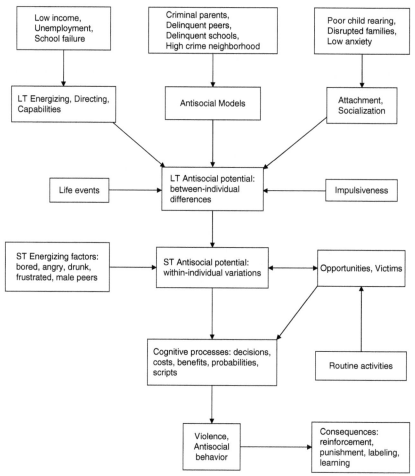

Figure 3.1. The integrated cognitive antisocial potential (ICAP) theory.

more likely to commit many different types of antisocial acts including violence. Hence, offending and antisocial behavior are versatile and not specialized. The relative ordering of people on AP (long-term between-individual
variation) tends to be consistent over time, but absolute levels of AP vary with
age, peaking in the teenage years, because of changes within individuals in the
contextual factors that influence long-term AP (e.g., from childhood to adolescence, the increasing importance of peers and decreasing importance of
parents).

Following strain theory, the main energizing factors that potentially lead
to high long-term AP are desires for material goods, status among intimates,
excitement, and sexual satisfaction. However, these motivations only lead to

high AP if antisocial methods of satisfying them are habitually chosen. Antisocial methods tend to be chosen by people who find it difficult to satisfy their needs legitimately, such as people with low income, unemployed people, and those who fail at school. However, the methods chosen also depend on physical capabilities and behavioral skills; for example, a 5-year-old would have difficulty stealing a car. For simplicity, energizing and directing processes and capabilities are shown in one box in Figure 3.1.

Long-term AP also depends on attachment and socialization processes. AP will be low if parents consistently and contingently reward good behavior and punish bad behavior. (Withdrawal of love may be a more effective method of socialization than hitting children.) Children with low anxiety will be less well socialized, because they care less about parental punishment. AP will be high if children are not attached to (prosocial) parents, for example, if parents are cold and rejecting. Disrupted families (broken homes) may impair both attachment and socialization processes.

Long-term AP will also be high if people are exposed to and influenced by antisocial models, such as criminal parents, delinquent siblings, and delinquent peers, for example, in high-crime schools and neighborhoods. Long-term AP will also be high for impulsive people, because they tend to act without thinking about the consequences. Also, life events affect AP; it decreases after people get married or move out of high-crime areas, and it increases after separation from a partner (see Farrington & West, 1995; Theobald & Farrington, 2009). There may also be interaction effects between the influences on long-term AP. For example, people who experience strain or poor socialization may be disproportionally antisocial if they are also exposed to antisocial models. In the interests of simplicity, Figure 3.1 does not attempt to show such interactions.

Figure 3.1 attempts to show some of the processes by which risk factors have effects on AP. It does not show biological factors, but these could be incorporated in the theory at various points. For example, the children of criminal parents could have high AP partly because of genetic transmission, excitement-seeking could be driven by low cortical arousal, school failure could depend partly on low intelligence, and high impulsiveness and low anxiety could both reflect biological factors.

According to the ICAP theory, the commission of offenses and other types of antisocial acts depends on the interaction between the individual (with his immediate level of AP) and the social environment (especially criminal opportunities and victims). Superimposed on long-term between-individual differences in violence potential are short-term within-individual variations. Short-term AP varies within individuals according to short-term energizing factors such as being bored, angry, drunk, or frustrated, or being encouraged by male peers. Criminal opportunities and the availability of victims depend on routine activities. Encountering a tempting opportunity or victim may cause a short-term increase in AP, just as a short-term increase in AP may motivate a person to seek out criminal opportunities and victims.

Faced with an opportunity for violence, whether a person with a certain level of AP actually is violent depends on cognitive processes, including considering the subjective benefits, costs, and probabilities of the different outcomes and stored behavioral repertoires or scripts (based on previous experiences). The subjective benefits and costs include immediate situational factors such as the perceived utility of hurting someone and the likelihood and consequences of being caught by the police. They also include social factors such as likely disapproval by parents or female partners, and encouragement or reinforcement from peers. In general, people tend to make decisions that seem rational to them, but those with low levels of AP will not commit offenses even when (on the basis of subjective expected utilities) it appears rational to do so. Equally, high short-term levels of AP (e.g., caused by anger or drunkenness) may induce people to commit offenses when it is not rational for them to do so.

The consequences of violence may, as a result of a learning process, lead to changes in long-term AP and in future cognitive decision-making processes. This is especially likely if the consequences are reinforcing (e.g., gaining pleasure or peer approval) or punishing (e.g., receiving legal sanctions or parental disapproval). Also, if the consequences involve labeling or stigmatizing the offender, this may make it more difficult for him to achieve his aims legally, and hence may lead to an increase in AP. (It is difficult to show these feedback effects in Figure 3.1 without making it very complex.)

This approach is an explicit attempt to integrate developmental and situational theories. The interaction between the individual and the environment is seen in decision making in criminal opportunities, which depends both on the underlying potential for antisocial behavior and on situational factors (costs, benefits, probabilities). Also, the double-headed arrow shows the possibility that encountering a tempting opportunity may cause a short-term increase in antisocial potential, just as a short-term increase in potential may motivate a person to seek out an opportunity for violence. The theory includes cognitive elements (perception, memory, decision making) as well as the social learning and causal risk factor approaches. An independent test of the ICAP theory in the Netherlands by Van Der Laan, Blom, and Kleemans (2009) concluded that serious delinquency was related to an accumulation of long-term risk factors and also to situational factors such as using alcohol or drugs.

As in most criminological theories, there is insufficient attention to typologies of offenders. Perhaps some people are violent primarily because of their high violence potential (e.g., "life-course-persistent" offenders), while others are violent primarily because they happen to be in violent situations. Or perhaps some people are violent primarily because of short-term influences (e.g., getting drunk frequently) and others primarily because of the way they think and make decisions in potentially violent situations. From the point of view of both explanation and prevention, it would be useful to classify people according to their most influential risk factors and most important reasons why they commit violent acts.

Conclusions

Research Implications

The most important contextual influences on violence are family factors (e.g., poor supervision, harsh discipline, child physical abuse, a violent parent, large family size, a young mother, a broken family), peer delinquency, low socio-economic status, urban residence, and living in a high-crime neighborhood. These results may be useful in developing risk assessment instruments, which should take account of contextual as well as individual factors. Important short-term situational factors include the motives of potential offenders (e.g., anger, a desire to hurt), alcohol consumption, drugs, guns, and actions leading to violent events (e.g., the escalation of a trivial altercation).

More research is needed specifically searching for protective factors against violence, for example, by investigating why aggressive children do not become violent adults. More research is also needed on protective factors that encourage desistance. Some protective factors may have similar effects on onset and persistence, but others (e.g., life events such as getting married and getting a satisfying job) may have more specific effects on desistance. The discovery of protective factors could have important implications for the prevention and treatment of violence.

More research is needed to investigate the topic of specialization in violence and also whether there are specific effects of violent parents or violent peers (over and above the general effects of antisocial parents and delinquent peers). This research could have important policy implications. For example, if offending was totally versatile, violence could be reduced just as effectively by targeting frequent nonviolent offenders as by targeting specifically violent offenders. Explaining the intergenerational transmission of violence is an especially important topic.

More research is needed on types of offenders and on the neglected topic of adult onset (see, e.g., Zara & Farrington, 2009). More research is needed to explain gender and racial/ethnic differences in violence. Previous research suggests that males and females, and African Americans and Caucasians, differ more in their number of risk factors than in their relationships between risk factors and violence (Farrington, Loeber, & Stouthamer-Loeber, 2003; Moffitt, Caspi, Rutter, & Silva, 2001), but this needs to be investigated further. More research is needed on the costs and benefits of prevention and treatment programs for violence, in comparison with the costs and benefits of prison, policing, and other criminal justice measures.

To investigate development and risk factors for violence and the effects of life events, longitudinal studies are needed. Such studies should include multiple cohorts, in order to draw conclusions about different age groups from birth at least to the mid-20s. They should include both males and females and the major racial/ethnic groups, so that results can be compared for different subgroups. Longitudinal studies should measure a wide range of risk and especially protective factors, and seek to discover interaction effects.

They should be based on large, high-risk samples, especially in inner-city areas, incorporating screening methods to maximize the yield of violent offenders while simultaneously making it possible to draw conclusions about the total population. They should include frequent assessments and a variety of data from different sources (e.g., interviews with participants and parents, official record data). They should include long-term follow-ups to permit conclusions about developmental pathways. They should make a special effort to study careers of violence and to link developmental and situational data.

The most pressing problem is to advance knowledge about causes of violence. More tests of alternative causal mechanisms that may intervene between risk factors and violence are needed, and especially more within-individual analyses should be carried out (Murray, Farrington, & Eisner, 2009). Virtually all knowledge about risk factors is based on between-individual analyses, but variables that are related to violence between individuals may not be related within individuals. Longitudinal studies with frequent data collection are needed for within-individual analyses. Such analyses may radically alter our conclusions about the causes of violent behavior over the life span. This is the new frontier.

Policy Implications

While public health and criminal justice approaches to violence reduction are not mutually exclusive, more public health approaches are needed. In particular, violence reduction programs should be based on knowledge about risk and protective factors (Farrington, 2001b, 2007a). More systematic reviews and meta-analyses of these factors are needed, and more randomized experiments should be mounted to evaluate the effectiveness of risk-focused prevention. High-quality evaluation research shows that many types of programs are effective, and that in many cases their financial benefits outweigh their financial costs (Farrington & Welsh, 2007). However, there have been relatively few attempts to study effects on violence specifically or to follow up experimental and control individuals in repeated interviews (see Farrington, 2006b).

The major policy implications are as follows: Smoking, drinking, and drug use in pregnancy, and also early child abuse, should be targeted by home visiting programs in which nurses give advice to mothers about prenatal and postnatal care of the child, about infant development, and about the importance of proper nutrition and avoiding substance use in pregnancy (Olds, Sadler, & Kitzman, 2007). Poor parental supervision and inconsistent discipline should be targeted by behavioral parent management training (Webster-Stratton, 1998). Negative peer influence should be targeted by community-based mentoring programs (Jolliffe & Farrington, 2008) and by treatment foster care (Chamberlain & Reid, 1998).

It is also desirable to implement programs in schools to encourage prosocial development. For example, anti-bullying programs are effective

(Farrington & Ttofi, 2009), and programs to encourage stable relationships and discourage early pregnancy should be mounted (Theobald & Farrington, 2010). Community programs that encourage cohesiveness, collective efficacy, and intervention to prevent crimes can also be recommended. For example, a quasi-experimental evaluation of an improved street lighting program concluded that the environmental investment led to improved community pride and informal social control, which in turn was followed by decreased crime (Painter & Farrington, 1997).

Communities That Care (CTC) is one of the most promising community-based prevention programs (Hawkins & Catalano, 1992). It is modeled on large-scale community-wide public health programs, and it is a multiple-component program including interventions that have been proved to be effective in high-quality research. The choice of intervention strategies depends on empirical evidence about what are the most important risk and protective factors in a particular community. The interventions aim to reduce the identified risk factors and enhance the identified protective factors. CTC has been shown to be effective in reducing substance use and delinquency in a large randomized experiment involving 24 communities (Hawkins et al., 2009).

It is also important to target immediate situational influences on violence such as alcohol, guns, gangs, and drugs. For example, the gang prevention program GREAT (Gang Resistance Education and Training) reduced victimization, instilled more negative views about gangs among youth, improved attitudes toward police, and increased the number of prosocial peers (Howell, 2009, p. 161). However, it did not prevent youth from joining gangs. As another example, Macintyre and Homel (1997) in Australia found that violence in nightclubs was caused by crowding as well as drunkenness. They made recommendations about how nightclubs could be redesigned to reduce crowding, by changing pedestrian flow patterns (e.g., to and from restrooms). Following the ICAP theory, it would also be desirable to try to change decision making by potential offenders in criminal opportunities, by decreasing subjectively perceived benefits and increasing subjectively perceived costs of violence.

Risk-focused prevention should also target individual factors not reviewed in this chapter. For example, impulsiveness should be targeted by skills training (Lösel & Beelmann, 2006), and low school achievement should be targeted by preschool intellectual enrichment programs (Schweinhart et al., 2005). The time is ripe to adopt a public health approach and embark on risk-focused prevention on a large scale, perhaps based on Communities That Care, in order to reduce crime and violence. This approach would have many additional benefits, including improving mental and physical health and life success in areas such as education, employment, relationships, housing, and child-rearing. It is crucial to interrupt the intergenerational transmission of crime and violence, and the financial benefits of risk-focused prevention seem very likely to exceed the financial costs. Let's do it!

References

Allen, J., Nicholas, S., Salisbury, H., & Wood, M. (2003). Nature of burglary, vehicle and violent crime. In C. Flood-Page & J. Taylor (Eds.), *Crime in England and Wales 2001/2002: Supplementary volume* (pp. 41–68). London: Home Office.

Battin, S. R., Hill, K. G., Abbott, R. D., Catalano, R. F., & Hawkins, J. D. (1998). The contribution of gang membership to delinquency beyond delinquent friends. *Criminology, 36*, 93–115.

Bellair, P. E., Roscigno, V. J., & McNulty, T. L. (2003). Linking local labor market opportunity to violent adolescent delinquency. *Journal of Research in Crime and Delinquency, 40*, 6–33.

Beyers, J. M., Loeber, R., Wikström, P-O. H., & Stouthamer-Loeber, M. (2001). Predictors of adolescent violence by neighborhood. *Journal of Abnormal Child Psychology, 29*, 369–381.

Brennan, I. R., & Moore, S. C. (2009). Weapons and violence: A review of theory and research. *Aggression and Violent Behavior, 14*, 215–225.

Brennan, P. A., Grekin, E. R., & Mednick, S. A. (1999). Maternal smoking during pregnancy and adult male criminal outcomes. *Archives of General Psychiatry, 56*, 215–219.

Brownfield, D., & Sorenson, A. M. (1994). Sibship size and sibling delinquency. *Deviant Behavior, 15*, 45–61.

Budd, T., Sharp, C., & Mayhew, P. (2005). *Offending in England and Wales: First results from the 2003 Crime and Justice Survey*, Research Study No. 275. London: Home Office.

Capaldi, D. M., & Patterson, G. R. (1996). Can violent offenders be distinguished from frequent offenders? Prediction from childhood to adolescence. *Journal of Research in Crime and Delinquency, 33*, 206–231.

Chamberlain, P., & Reid, J. B. (1998). Comparison of two community alternatives to incarceration for chronic juvenile offenders. *Journal of Consulting and Clinical Psychology, 66*, 624–633.

Chan, Y-C., & Yeung, J. W-K. (2009). Children living with violence within the family and its sequel: A meta-analysis from 1995–2006. *Aggression and Violent Behavior, 14*, 313–322.

Cohen, L. E., & Felson, M. (1979). Social change and crime rate trends: A routine activity approach. *American Sociological Review, 44*, 588–608.

Dahlberg, L. L. (2007). Public health and violence: Moving forward in a global context. In D. J. Flannery, A. T. Vaszonyi, & I. D. Waldman (Eds.), *The Cambridge handbook of violent behavior and aggression* (pp. 465–485). Cambridge, England: Cambridge University Press.

Deater-Deckard, K., Dodge, K. A., Bates, J. E., & Pettit, G. S. (1996). Physical discipline among African American and European American mothers: Links to children's externalizing behaviors. *Developmental Psychology, 32*, 1065–1072.

Delisi, M., & Conis, P. J. (Eds.). (2008). *Violent offenders: Theory, research, public policy, and practice*. Sudbury, MA: Jones and Bartlett.

Derzon, J. H. (2010). The correspondence of family features with problem, aggressive, criminal, and violent behavior: A meta-analysis. *Journal of Experimental Criminology, 6*(3), 263–292.

Desmarais, S. L., Gibas, A., & Nicholls, T. L. (2010). Beyond violence against women: Gender inclusiveness in domestic violence research, policy, and practice. In C. J. Ferguson (Ed.), *Violent crime: Clinical and social implications* (pp. 184–206). Thousand Oaks, CA: Sage.

Elliott, D. S., Huizinga, D., & Menard, S. (1989). *Multiple problem youth: Delinquency, substance use, and mental health problems.* New York: Springer-Verlag.

Farrington, D. P. (1986). Age and crime. In M. Tonry & N. Morris (Eds.), *Crime and justice* (Vol. 7, pp. 189–250). Chicago: University of Chicago Press.

Farrington, D. P. (1991). Childhood aggression and adult violence: Early precursors and later life outcomes. In D. J. Pepler & K. H. Rubin (Eds.), *The development and treatment of childhood aggression* (pp. 5–29). Hillsdale, NJ: Lawrence Erlbaum.

Farrington, D. P. (1993). Motivations for conduct disorder and delinquency. *Development and Psychopathology, 5,* 225–241.

Farrington, D. P. (1994). Childhood, adolescent and adult features of violent males. In L. R. Huesmann (Ed.), *Aggressive behavior: Current perspectives* (pp. 215–240). New York: Plenum.

Farrington, D. P. (1998). Predictors, causes, and correlates of youth violence. In M. Tonry & M. H. Moore (Eds.), *Youth violence* (pp. 421–475). Chicago: University of Chicago Press.

Farrington, D. P. (2000). Explaining and preventing crime: The globalization of knowledge—The American Society of Criminology 1999 Presidential Address. *Criminology, 38,* 1–24.

Farrington, D. P. (2001a). Predicting adult official and self-reported violence. In G-F. Pinard & L. Pagani (Eds.), *Clinical assessment of dangerousness: Empirical contributions* (pp. 66–88). Cambridge, England: Cambridge University Press.

Farrington, D. P. (2001b). The causes and prevention of violence. In J. Shepherd (Ed.), *Violence in health care* (2nd ed., pp. 1–27). Oxford, England: Oxford University Press.

Farrington, D. P. (2003). Developmental and life-course criminology: Key theoretical and empirical issues. *Criminology, 41,* 221–255.

Farrington, D. P. (Ed.). (2005). *Integrated developmental and life-course theories of offending. Advances in criminological theory, Vol. 14.* New Brunswick, NJ: Transaction.

Farrington, D. P. (2006a). Comparing football hooligans and violent offenders: Childhood, adolescent, teenage and adult features. *Monatsschrift fur Kriminologie und Strafrechtsreform* [Journal of Criminology and Penal Reform], *89,* 193–205.

Farrington, D. P. (2006b). Key longitudinal-experimental studies in criminology. *Journal of Experimental Criminology, 2,* 121–141.

Farrington, D. P. (2007a). Childhood risk factors and risk-focussed prevention. In M. Maguire, R. Morgan, & R. Reiner (Eds.), *The Oxford handbook of criminology* (4th ed., pp. 602–640). Oxford, England: Oxford University Press.

Farrington, D. P. (2007b). Origins of violent behavior over the life span. In D. J. Flannery, A. J. Vaszonyi, & I. D. Waldman (Eds.), *The Cambridge handbook of violent behavior and aggression* (pp. 19–48). Cambridge, England: Cambridge University Press.

Farrington, D. P., Coid, J. W., Harnett, L., Jolliffe, D., Soteriou, N., Turner, R., & West, D. J. (2006). *Criminal careers up to age 50 and life success up to age 48: New findings from the Cambridge Study in Delinquent Development.* Research Study No. 299. London: Home Office.

Farrington, D. P., Jolliffe, D., Hawkins, J. D., Catalano, R. F., Hill, K. G., & Kosterman, R. (2003). Comparing delinquency careers in court records and self-reports. *Criminology, 41,* 933–958.

Farrington, D. P., Jolliffe, D., Loeber, R., Stouthamer-Loeber, M., & Kalb, L. M. (2001). The concentration of offenders in families, and family criminality in the prediction of boys' delinquency. *Journal of Adolescence, 24,* 579–596.

Farrington, D. P., Loeber, R., Stallings, R., & Homish, D. L. (2008). Early risk factors for homicide offenders and victims. In M. J. Delisi & P. J. Conis (Eds.), *Violent offenders: Theory, research, public policy, and practice* (pp. 79–96). Sudbury, MA: Jones and Bartlett.

Farrington, D. P., Loeber, R., & Stouthamer-Loeber, M. (2003). How can the relationship between race and violence be explained? In D. F. Hawkins (Ed.), *Violent crime: Assessing race and ethnic differences* (pp. 213–237). Cambridge, England: Cambridge University Press.

Farrington, D. P., Loeber, R., Yin, Y., & Anderson, S. J. (2002). Are within-individual causes of delinquency the same as between-individual causes? *Criminal Behaviour and Mental Health, 12,* 53–68.

Farrington, D. P., & Ttofi, M. M. (2009). Reducing school bullying: Evidence-based implications for policy. In M. Tonry (Ed.), *Crime and justice* (Vol. 38, pp. 281–345). Chicago: University of Chicago Press.

Farrington, D. P., & Welsh, B. C. (2007). *Saving children from a life of crime: Early risk factors and effective interventions.* Oxford, England: Oxford University Press.

Farrington, D. P., & West, D. J. (1995). Effects of marriage, separation and children on offending by adult males. In J. Hagan (Ed.), *Current perspectives on aging and the life cycle. Vol. 4: Delinquency and disrepute in the life course* (pp. 249–281). Greenwich, CT: JAI Press.

Felson, R. B. (2009). Violence, crime, and violent crime. *International Journal of Conflict and Violence, 3,* 23–29.

Felson, M., & Boba, R. (2010). *Crime and everyday life* (4th ed.). Thousand Oaks, CA: Sage.

Felson, R. B., Teasdale, B., & Burchfield, K. B. (2008). The influence of being under the influence: Alcohol effects on adolescent violence. *Journal of Research in Crime and Delinquency, 45,* 119–141.

Ferguson, C. J. (Ed.). (2010). *Violent crime: Clinical and social implications.* Thousand Oaks, CA: Sage.

Fergusson, D. M., & Horwood, L. J. (1998). Exposure to interparental violence in childhood and psychosocial adjustment in young adulthood. *Child Abuse and Neglect, 22,* 339–357.

Fergusson, D., Swain-Campbell, N., & Horwood, J. (2004). How does childhood economic disadvantage lead to crime? *Journal of Child Psychology and Psychiatry, 45,* 956–966.

Flannery, D. J., Vaszonyi, A. T., & Waldman, I. D. (Eds.). (2007). *The Cambridge handbook of violent behavior and aggression.* Cambridge, England: Cambridge University Press.

Gatti, U., Tremblay, R. E., Vitaro, F., & McDuff, P. (2005). Youth gangs, delinquency and drug use: A test of the selection, facilitation, and enhancement hypotheses. *Journal of Child Psychology and Psychiatry, 46,* 1178–1190.

Gordon, R. A., Lahey, B. B., Kawai, E., Loeber, R., Stouthamer-Loeber, M., & Farrington, D. P. (2004). Antisocial behavior and young gang membership: Selection and socialization. *Criminology, 42,* 55–87.

Graham, K., & Homel, R. (2008). *Raising the bar: Preventing aggression in and around bars, pubs, and clubs.* Cullompton, England: Willan.

Hawkins, J. D., & Catalano, R. F. (1992). *Communities that care.* San Francisco: Jossey-Bass.

Hawkins, J. D., Herrenkohl, T., Farrington, D. P., Brewer, D., Catalano, R. F., & Harachi, T. W. (1998). A review of predictors of youth violence. In R. Loeber & D. P. Farrington (Eds.), *Serious and violent juvenile offenders: Risk factors and successful interventions* (pp. 106–146). Thousand Oaks, CA: Sage.

Hawkins, J. D. Oesterle, S., Brown, E. C., Arthur, M. W., Abbott, R. D., Fagan, A. A., & Catalano, R. F. (2009). Results of a type 2 translational research trial to prevent adolescent drug use and delinquency: A test of Communities that Care. *Archives of Pediatrics and Adolescent Medicine, 163,* 789–798.

Haynie, D., & Osgood, D. W. (2005). Reconsidering peers and delinquency: How do peers matter? *Social Forces, 84,* 1107–1128.

Haynie, D. L., Steffensmeier, D., & Bell, K. E. (2007). Gender and serious violence: Untangling the role of friendship sex composition and peer violence. *Youth Violence and Juvenile Justice, 5,* 235–253.

Heide, K. M., & Solomon, E. P. (2006). Biology, childhood trauma, and murder: Rethinking justice. *International Journal of Law and Psychiatry, 29,* 220–233.

Herrenkohl, T. I., Maguin, E., Hill, K. G., Hawkins, J. D., Abbott, R. D., & Catalano, R. F. (2000). Developmental risk factors for youth violence. *Journal of Adolescent Health, 26,* 176–186.

Hoffman, J. S. (2004). *Youth violence, resilience, and rehabilitation.* New York: LFB Scholarly Publishing.

Howell, J. C. (2009). *Preventing and reducing juvenile delinquency.* Thousand Oaks, CA: Sage.

Jaffee, S., Caspi, A., Moffitt, T. E., Belsky, J., & Silva, P. A. (2001). Why are children born to teen mothers at risk for adverse outcomes in young adulthood? Results from a 20-year longitudinal study. *Development and Psychopathology, 13,* 377–397.

Johnson, J. G., Smailes, E., Cohen, P., Kasen, S., & Brook, J. S. (2004). Antisocial parental behavior, problematic parenting, and aggressive offspring behavior during adulthood. *British Journal of Criminology, 44,* 915–930.

Jolliffe, D., & Farrington, D. P. (2008). *The influence of mentoring on reoffending.* Stockholm, Sweden: National Council for Crime Prevention.

Jolliffe, D., Farrington, D. P., Hawkins, J. D., Catalano, R. F., Hill, K. G., & Kosterman, R. (2003). Predictive, concurrent, prospective and retrospective validity of self-reported delinquency. *Criminal Behaviour and Mental Health, 13,* 179–197.

Kaufman, J. M. (2005). Explaining the race/ethnicity violence relationship: Neighborhood context and social psychological processes. *Justice Quarterly, 22,* 224–251.

Kazemian, L., & Farrington, D. P. (2010). The developmental evidence base: Desistance. In G. J. Towl & D. A. Crighton (Eds.), *Forensic psychology* (pp. 133–147). Oxford, England: Blackwell.

Kelley, M. L., Power, T. G., & Wimbush, D. D. (1992). Determinants of disciplinary practices in low-income black mothers. *Child Development, 63,* 573–582.

Kim-Cohen, J., Caspi, A., Taylor, A., Williams, B., Newcombe, R., Craig, I. W., & Moffitt, T. E. (2006). MAOA, maltreatment, and gene-environment interaction predicting children's mental health: New evidence and a meta-analysis. *Molecular Psychiatry, 11,* 903–913.

Lang, S., af Klinteberg, B., & Alm, P-O. (2002). Adult psychopathy and violent behavior in males with early neglect and abuse. *Acta Psychiatrica Scandinavica, 106,* 93–100.

Larzelere, R. E., & Patterson, G. R. (1990). Parental management: Mediator of the effect of socioeconomic status on early delinquency. *Criminology, 28,* 301–324.

LeBlanc, M. (1996). Changing patterns in the perpetration of offenses over time: Trajectories from early adolescence to the early 30's. *Studies on Crime and Crime Prevention, 5,* 151–165.

LeBlanc, M., & Frechette, M. (1989). *Male criminal activity from childhood through youth.* New York: Springer-Verlag.

Lodewijks, H. P. B., De Reuter, C., & Doreleijers. T. (2010). The impact of protective factors in desistance from violent offending: A study in three samples of adolescent offenders. *Journal of Interpersonal Violence, 25,* 568–587.

Loeber, R., & Farrington, D. P. (Eds.). (1998). *Serious and violent juvenile offenders: Risk factors and successful interventions.* Thousand Oaks, CA: Sage.

Loeber, R., Farrington, D. P., Stouthamer-Loeber, M., & Van Kammen, W. B. (1998). *Antisocial behavior and mental health problems: Explanatory factors in childhood and adolescence.* Mahwah, NJ: Lawrence Erlbaum.

Loeber, R., Farrington, D. P., Stouthamer-Loeber, M., & White, H. R. (2008). *Violence and serious theft: Development and prediction from childhood to adulthood.* New York: Routledge.

Loeber, R., Pardini, D., Homish, D. L., Wei, E. H., Crawford, A. M., Farrington, D. P., Stouthamer-Loeber, M., Creemers, J., Koehler, S. A., & Rosenfeld, R. (2005). The prediction of violence and homicide in young men. *Journal of Consulting and Clinical Psychology, 73,* 1074–1088.

Lösel, F., & Beelmann, A. (2006). Child social skills training. In B. C. Welsh & D. P. Farrington (Eds.), *Preventing crime: What works for children, offenders, victims, and places* (pp. 33–54). Dordrecht, Netherlands: Springer.

MacDonald, J. M., & Gover, A. R. (2005). Concentrated disadvantage and youth-on-youth homicide: Assessing the structural covariates over time. *Homicide Studies, 9,* 30–54.

Macintyre, S., & Homel, R. (1997). Danger on the dance floor: A study of interior design, crowding and aggression in nightclubs. In R. Homel (Ed.), *Policing for prevention: Reducing crime, public intoxication, and injury* (pp. 91–113). Monsey, NY: Criminal Justice Press.

McCord, J. (1977). A comparative study of two generations of Native Americans. In R. F. Meier (Ed.), *Theory in criminology* (pp. 83–92). Beverly Hills, CA: Sage.

McCord, J. (1979). Some child-rearing antecedents of criminal behavior in adult men. *Journal of Personality and Social Psychology, 37*, 1477–1486.

McCord, J. (1996). Family as crucible for violence: Comment on Gorman-Smith et al. (1996). *Journal of Family Psychology, 10*, 147–152.

McCord, J. (1997). On discipline. *Psychological Inquiry, 8*, 215–217.

McGloin, J. M., Pratt, T. C., & Piquero, A. R. (2006). A life-course analysis of the criminogenic effects of maternal cigarette smoking during pregnancy: A research note on the mediating impact of neuropsychological deficit. *Journal of Research in Crime and Delinquency, 43*, 412–426.

McGloin, J. M., Sullivan, C. J., & Piquero, A. R. (2009). Aggregating to versatility? Transitions among offender types in the short term. *British Journal of Criminology, 49*, 243–264.

McGloin, J. M., Sullivan, C. J., Piquero, A. R., & Pratt, T. C. (2007). Local life circumstances and offending specialization/versatility: Comparing opportunity and propensity models. *Journal of Research in Crime and Delinquency, 44*, 321–346.

Moffitt, T. E. (1993). Adolescence-limited and life-course-persistent antisocial behavior: A developmental taxonomy. *Psychological Review, 100*, 674–701.

Moffitt, T. E., Caspi, A., Rutter, M., & Silva, P. A. (2001). *Sex differences in antisocial behavior.* Cambridge, England: Cambridge University Press.

Moore, M. H. (1995). Public health and criminal justice approaches to prevention. In M. Tonry & D. P. Farrington (Eds.), *Building a safer society: Strategic approaches to crime prevention* (pp. 237–262). Chicago: University of Chicago Press.

Murray, J., Farrington, D. P., & Eisner, M. P. (2009). Drawing conclusions about causes from systematic reviews of risk factors: The Cambridge Quality Checklists. *Journal of Experimental Criminology, 5*, 1–23.

Nagin, D. S., Pogarsky, G., & Farrington, D. P. (1997). Adolescent mothers and the criminal behavior of their children. *Law and Society Review, 31*, 137–162.

Nofziger, S., & Kurtz, D. (2005). Violent lives: A lifestyle model linking exposure to violence to juvenile violent offending. *Journal of Research in Crime and Delinquency, 42*, 3–26.

Odgers, C. L., Moffitt, T. E., Tach, L. M., Sampson, R. J., Taylor, A., Matthews, C. L., & Caspi, A. (2009). The protective effects of neighborhood collective efficacy on British children growing up in deprivation: A developmental analysis. *Developmental Psychology, 45*, 942–957.

Olds, D. L., Sadler, L., & Kitzman, H. (2007). Programs for parents of infants and toddlers: Recent evidence from randomized trials. *Journal of Child Psychology and Psychiatry, 48*, 355–391.

Osgood, D. W., & Schreck, C. J. (2007). A new method for studying the extent, stability, and predictors of individual specialization in violence. *Criminology, 45*, 273–311.

Painter, K. A., & Farrington, D. P. (1997). The crime reducing effect of improved street lighting: The Dudley project. In R. V. Clarke (Ed.), *Situational crime prevention: Successful case studies* (2nd ed., pp. 209–226). Guilderland, NY: Harrow and Heston.

Piquero, A. (2000). Frequency, specialization, and violence in offending careers. *Journal of Research in Crime and Delinquency, 37*, 392–418.

Piquero, A. R., & Buka, S. L. (2002). Linking juvenile and adult patterns of criminal activity in the Providence cohort of the National Collaborative Perinatal Project. *Journal of Criminal Justice, 30,* 259–272.

Piquero, A. R., Farrington, D. P., & Blumstein, A. (2007). *Key issues in criminal career research: New analyses of the Cambridge Study in Delinquent Development.* Cambridge, England: Cambridge University Press.

Pogarsky, G., Lizotte, A. J., & Thornberry, T. P. (2003). The delinquency of children born to young mothers: Results from the Rochester Youth Development Study. *Criminology, 41,* 1249–1286.

Rasanen, P., Hakko, H., Isohanni, M., Hodgins, S., Jarvelin, M., & Tiihonen, J. (1999). Maternal smoking during pregnancy and risk of criminal behavior among adult male offspring in the Northern Finland 1966 birth cohort. *American Journal of Psychiatry, 156,* 857–862.

Reiss, A. J., & Farrington, D. P. (1991). Advancing knowledge about co-offending: Results from a prospective longitudinal survey of London males. *Journal of Criminal Law and Criminology, 82,* 360–395.

Riedel, M., & Welsh, W. (2008). *Criminal violence: Patterns, causes, and prevention* (2nd ed.). Oxford, England: Oxford University Press.

Rivara, F. P., Shepherd, J. P., Farrington, D. P., Richmond, P. W., & Cannon, P. (1995). Victim as offender in youth violence. *Annals of Emergency Medicine, 26,* 609–614.

Sampson, R. J., Morenoff, J. D., & Raudenbush, S. (2005). Social anatomy of racial and ethnic disparities in violence. *American Journal of Public Health, 95,* 224–232.

Sampson, R. J., Raudenbush, S. W., & Earls, F. (1997). Neighborhoods and violent crime: A multilevel study of collective efficacy. *Science, 277,* 918–924.

Saner, H., & Ellickson, P. (1996). Concurrent risk factors for adolescent violence. *Journal of Adolescent Health, 19,* 94–103.

Schweinhart, L. J., Montie, J., Zongping, X., Barnett, W. S., Belfield, C. R., & Nores, M. (2005). *Lifetime effects: The High/Scope Perry Preschool Study through age 40.* Ypsilanti, MI: High/Scope Press.

Scott, M. S., & Dedel, K. (2006). *Assaults in and around bars* (2nd ed.). Washington, DC: Office of Community Oriented Policing Services.

Shepherd, J. (2007). Preventing violence-caring for victims (the King James IV Lecture). *The Surgeon, 5,* 114–121.

Sourcebook of Criminal Justice Statistics. (2009). Retrieved from http://www.albany.edu/sourcebook/

Straus, M. A. (2001). *Beating the devil out of them: Corporal punishment in American families and its effects on children.* New Brunswick, NJ: Transaction.

Theobald, D., & Farrington, D. P. (2009). Effects of getting married on offending: Results from a prospective longitudinal survey of males. *European Journal of Criminology, 6,* 496–516.

Theobald, D., & Farrington, D. P. (2010). Should policy implications be drawn from research on the effects of getting married on offending? *European Journal of Criminology, 7,* 239–247.

Thornberry, T. P., Huizinga, D., & Loeber, R. (1995). The prevention of serious delinquency and violence: Implications from the program of research on the causes and correlates of delinquency. In J. C. Howell, B. Krisberg,

J. D. Hawkins, & J. J. Wilson (Eds.), *Sourcebook on serious, violent and chronic juvenile offenders* (pp. 213–237). Thousand Oaks, CA: Sage.

Thornberry, T. P., Krohn, M. D., Lizotte, A. J., Smith, C. A., & Tobin, K. (2003). *Gangs and delinquency in developmental perspective.* New York: Cambridge University Press.

Tita, G., & Griffiths, E. (2005). Traveling to violence: The case for a mobility-based spatial typology of homicide. *Journal of Research in Crime and Delinquency, 42*, 275–308.

Tolan, P. H., Gorman-Smith, D., & Henry, D. B. (2003). The developmental ecology of urban males' youth violence. *Developmental Psychology, 39*, 274–291.

Ttofi, M. M., & Farrington, D. P. (2010). School bullying: Risk factors, theories and interventions. In F. Brookman, M. Maguire, H. Pierpoint, & T. Bennett (Eds.), *Handbook of crime* (pp. 427–457). Cullompton, England: Willan.

Van Der Laan, A., Blom, M., & Kleemans, E. R. (2009). Exploring long-term and short-term risk factors for serious delinquency. *European Journal of Criminology, 6*, 419–438.

Van Wijk, A., Loeber, R., Vermeiren, R., Pardini, D., Bullens, R., & Doreleijers, T. (2005). Violent juvenile sex offenders compared with violent juvenile nonsex offenders: Explorative findings from the Pittsburgh Youth Study. *Sexual Abuse, 17*, 333–352.

Vitaro, F., Boivin, M., & Tremblay, R. E. (2007). Peers and violence: A two-sided developmental perspective. In D. J. Flannery, A. T. Vaszonyi, & I. D. Waldman (Eds.), *The Cambridge handbook of violent behavior and aggression* (pp. 361–387). Cambridge, England: Cambridge University Press.

Webster-Stratton, C. (1998). Preventing conduct problems in Head Start children: Strengthening parenting competencies. *Journal of Consulting and Clinical Psychology, 66*, 715–730.

Wells, W., & Horney, J. (2002). Weapon effects and individual intent to do harm: Influences on the escalation of violence. *Criminology, 40*, 265–295.

West, D. J., & Farrington, D. P. (1973). *Who becomes delinquent?* London: Heinemann.

West, D. J., & Farrington, D. P. (1977). *The delinquent way of life.* London: Heinemann.

Widom, C. S. (1989). The cycle of violence. *Science, 244*, 160–166.

Widom, C. S. (1994). Childhood victimization and adolescent problem behaviors. In R. D. Ketterlinus & M. E. Lamb (Eds.), *Adolescent problem behaviors* (pp. 127–164). Hillsdale, NJ: Lawrence Erlbaum.

Widom, C. S., & Ames, M. A. (1994). Criminal consequences of childhood sexual victimization. *Child Abuse and Neglect, 18*, 303–318.

Widom, C. S., & Brzustowicz, L. M. (2006). MAOA and the "cycle of violence": Childhood abuse and neglect, MAOA genotype, and risk for violent and antisocial behavior. *Biological Psychiatry, 60*, 684–689.

Widom, C. S., & White, H. R. (1997). Problem behaviors in abused and neglected children grown up: Prevalence and co-occurrence of substance use, crime and violence. *Criminal Behavior and Mental Health, 7*, 287–310.

Wikström, P-O. H. (2007). The social ecology of crime: The role of the environment in crime causation. In H. J. Schneider (Ed.), *International handbook of criminology* (Vol. 1., pp. 333–357). Berlin: De Gruyter.

Zahn, M. A., Brownstein, H. H., & Jackson, S. L. (2004). *Violence: From theory to research.* Lexis Nexis-Anderson.

Zara, G., & Farrington, D. P. (2009). Childhood and adolescent predictors of late onset criminal careers. *Journal of Youth and Adolescence, 38,* 287–300.

4

The Good, the Bad, and the Ugly of Electronic Media

Muniba Saleem and Craig A. Anderson

A person's knowledge about how the world works comes from many sources. In modern societies the primary sources of culture-defining stories are entertainment media corporations. The ideas, beliefs, and scripts that people acquire from stories are put to use in the real world, where they have consequences. For example, people exposed mostly to stories involving deceit, crime, and violence will tend to learn that the world is a hostile, mean, and violent place; that others are not to be trusted; that one must be on the lookout for possible threats; and that one must be ready to respond to threats aggressively. Such a hostile outlook can, in fact, create the hostile world that is expected in a type of self-fulfilling prophecy (Anderson, Buckley, & Carnagey, 2008). People with such an outlook tend to elicit hostile behavior from others and are unaware that their hostile expectations actually created others' hostile behavior. Instead, they feel validated in their belief about hostile others.

Our basic thesis is that changing maladaptive behavior patterns requires changing the underlying maladaptive knowledge structures and their reinforcing dynamics. In this chapter we *(a)* discuss the importance of studying aggression and violence through a risk and protective factor approach, *(b)* clarify some common misunderstandings regarding media violence studies, *(c)* describe a psychological perspective on how humans can learn through direct and indirect observations, and *(d)* summarize evidence on the effects of media violence, especially within field experiments. We conclude by presenting hypotheses on how prosocial media may be used to reduce antisocial cognition and behavior and offer policy relevant suggestions.

Framework: Media Violence—A Risk Factor of Aggression

Aggression is defined as behavior intended and expected to harm another person, who is believed by the perpetrator to be motivated to avoid the harm (e.g., Anderson & Bushman, 2002a). *Violence* is aggression that is severe enough to inflict serious physical injury. Risk and protective factors precede and either increase or decrease (respectively) the likelihood of aggression and violence. Such factors vary across developmental stages and involve individual, biological, and social factors (see Chapters 3 and 6).

Exposure to media violence is a risk factor at both the individual and societal levels. At the individual level, high exposure to media violence detrimentally affects normative beliefs about the acceptability of aggressive behavior and cognitive scripts that can drive aggressive behavior automatically (Carnagey & Anderson, 2003). At the societal level, high use of violent entertainment media increases the proportion of the population that endorses proviolence attitudes, beliefs, and expectations, and thereby increases the frequency of aggression-inducing provocations (Anderson et al., 2003). Because aggression and violence are multidetermined (see Chapter 3; Anderson, Gentile, & Buckley, 2007), media violence is best viewed as *one* of the many causal risk factors that increase the likelihood of aggression.

Still, the effects of media violence on aggression are larger than the effects of calcium intake on bone mass or of lead exposure on IQ in children (Anderson & Bushman, 2001). Media violence effects on aggression are larger than many other aggression risk factors such as low IQ and child abuse (see Figure 4.1). Media violence predicts real violence even when other risk factors

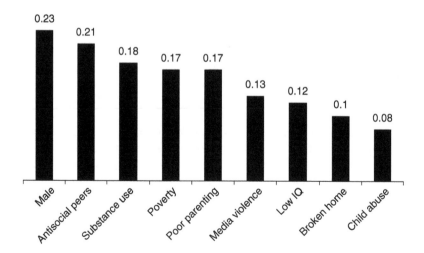

Figure 4.1. Effect sizes of risk factors for violence at age 15 to 18. (Adapted from Surgeon General Report of Youth Violence, 2001.)

are statistically controlled (Boxer, Huesmann, Bushman, O'Brien, & Moceri, 2009). But, unlike most risk factors, media violence is unique in that most people are exposed to it and it costs little to reduce exposure.

Mechanism: Observational Learning

Observing (and subsequently imitating) other people's behavior is one of the most important sources of learned behavior (Bandura, 1973, 2002). In fact, observational learning is a key component of every theoretical account of media violence effects (Anderson et al., 2003). Once an observer attends to and remembers a new behavior, this new knowledge can guide future behavior. Use of such knowledge depends on motivation, which among other things is influenced by whether the observed behavior was rewarded or punished.

Observations of real behavior as well as symbolic observations, such as TV, video games, and other media, yield observational learning. Early childhood observations influence the construction and modification of knowledge structures, rules, attitudes, and behaviors that persist even in adulthood (Huesmann & Miller, 1994). Concerning antisocial cognitions and behaviors, media influences learning by *(a)* modeling specific behaviors (prosocial, neutral, antisocial); and *(b)* showing which types of behaviors are rewarded, punished, or ignored.

What Is Observed Through Television, Movies, and Video Games

Television, in the average U.S. household, is watched almost 5 hours a day (Nielson Company, 2009). In the United States, 68% of 8–18-year-olds and 33% of children from birth to age 6 have a TV in their bedroom (Kaiser Family Foundation, 2005). Nearly two-thirds of TV programs contain some physical violence (Smith et al., 1998). A typical hour of television features an average of six different violent exchanges (Wilson, Colvin, & Smith, 2002). In programs targeted to young children, violence is even more prevalent. Roughly 70% of children's programs (compared to 60% of adult programs) contain violence (Wilson et al., 2002), whereas only 10% of the most popular children's shows contain prosocial lessons (Woodard, 1999). Fewer than 4% of violent programs shown on U.S. television contain any antiviolence theme (National Television Violence study [NTVS], 1998). Although far less is known about movie content, a content analysis of G-rated movies revealed that almost all contain violence, which often is portrayed as a response to a conflict. This content analysis also revealed that the duration of screen violence has increased significantly in the last 40 years (Yokota & Thompson, 2000).

Video games are very popular, and time spent playing them is on the rise (Escobar-Chavez & Anderson, 2008). Content analyses have shown that most video games contain some violent content, even children's games. For example,

Gentile (2009) found that 91% of video games rated as appropriate for 10 year olds are violent, as are 31% of games for younger children. Furthermore, violent games are preferred by children. More than half of 4th–8th-grade children report a preference for games in which the main action is violent (Buchman & Funk, 1996). The vast majority of 4th–12th-grade children play industry rated "mature" video games, which include graphic violence (Walsh et al., 2005).

The next section reveals that people (including children) extract the general meaning of what they see and apply these ideas, beliefs, and scripts to real-life situations. For example, playing violent video games involving war with fictitious aliens increases real aggression against real people in nonwar contexts (Anderson et al., 2004; Anderson, Gentile, & Buckley, 2007; Sheese & Graziano, 2005).

Effects of Violent TV and Movies on Aggressive Behavior, Attitudes, and Desensitization

Effects on Aggressive Behavior

Research robustly indicates that television and film violence is associated with aggression (see Anderson et al., 2003 for a detailed review). For example, meta-analysis of over 200 studies involving over 43,000 participants demonstrated that the evidence for negative effects of media violence is strong and its strength is increasing (Anderson & Bushman, 2002b; Bushman & Anderson, 2001). Furthermore, no group—distinguished by age (children, adolescents, young adults), sex, or personality type—is immune to these effects.

Studies With Children

Decades of experiments reveal that violent media increases children's aggression (e.g., Bandura, Ross, & Ross, 1961; Bjorkqvist, 1985; Liebert & Baron, 1972). For example, children who watched a single violent *Power Rangers* episode committed significantly more intentional acts of aggression inside the classroom (e.g., hitting, kicking, shoving, and insulting) than those in a control condition (Boyatzis, Matillo, & Nesbitt, 1995). Indeed, for every aggressive act perpetrated by children in the control group, there were seven aggressive acts committed by children in the *Power Rangers* group.

Longitudinal studies reveal that early childhood exposure to media violence uniquely predicts later aggression and violence, even after controlling for other causal risk factors (Huesmann, Moise, Podolski, & Eron, 2003). Indeed, these researchers found that TV violence exposure in childhood significantly predicted adulthood violent and criminal behavior.

Studies With Adolescents and Adults

Leyens and colleagues (1975) studied delinquent boys in a residential facility who were randomly assigned to cottages and to viewing either a violent or nonviolent film every evening for a week. Boys exposed to the violent films engaged in significantly more physical assaults on their cottage mates compared to boys exposed to nonviolent films. Correlational studies of violence yield similar effects (see Paik & Comstock, 1994 for a review). For example, McLeod, Atkin, and Chaffee (1972) studied the link between "aggressive behavioral delinquency" (fighting, hitting, etc.) and TV viewing habits of junior high and high school students. Exposure to TV violence was positively linked to aggressive behavioral delinquency for both boys and girls. In a longitudinal study, Johnson and colleagues (2002) found that TV exposure at age 14 predicted assault and fighting behavior at age 16 and 22, even after controlling for other risk factors. More recent results from experiments using undergraduate students are consistent with these findings (see Anderson et al., 2003).

Effects on Aggressive Attitudes and Beliefs

The media often glamorizes criminal acts (Garofalo, 1981; Marsh, 1991), and it may be an important source of inaccurate beliefs about the consequences of crime (e.g., Kappeler, Blumberg, & Potter, 1993). Studies indicate that media violence changes beliefs and attitudes toward violence among children, adolescents, and adults (see Anderson et al., 2003). Exposure to media violence leads viewers to see the world as more hostile than it really is, and it increases the acceptability of violence. Longitudinal studies reveal that exposure to TV violence in childhood increases the acceptance of violence 15 years later (e.g., Huesmann & Moise, 1999).

Effects on Desensitization

Another way media violence can influence aggression is by reducing the normal inhibitions that most people have against such behavior. Desensitization occurs when there is an extinction of fear and anxious reactions toward violence, which can be manifested through decreased attention to violent events, decreased sympathy for violence victims, and decreased negative attitudes toward violence. A consequence is moral disengagement, in which someone not only fails to refrain from behaving inhumanely but also fails to invest in social obligations (Bandura, 1999). Those who are morally disengaged are more likely to aggress, because they rationalize or justify the use of violence and do not adopt countervailing social values.

Exposure to violent media is associated with tolerance for violence, willingness to engage in aggression, lower empathy for violence victims, and lower willingness to intervene on behalf of a victim (Anderson et al., 2003; Bushman & Anderson, 2009). These effects have been found for children, adolescents, and adults (Linz, Donnerstein, & Penrod, 1984; Mullin & Linz, 1995; Thomas & Drabman, 1975). The increased frequency, realism, and graphic portrayal of violence in media may indicate that modern societies (such as the

United States) have become desensitized and have a higher tolerance for violence than ever before (Hayes, 2007).

Effects of Violent Video Games

Video game violence may have greater effects on behavior than other forms of media violence (Gentile & Anderson, 2003). Meta-analytic reviews demonstrate that video game violence exposure increases aggressive cognitions, aggressive behaviors, hostile affect, desensitization, and physiological arousal, and decreases prosocial behavior and empathy (Anderson et al., 2010). Longitudinal studies indicate that children and adolescents who frequently play violent video games become more aggressive and delinquent over time, even after controlling for earlier aggressiveness and other variables (e.g., Anderson et al., 2007, 2008; Hoph, Huber, & Weis, 2008; Moller & Krahe, 2009). Video game violence also increases aggression-related beliefs and attitudes, including beliefs that other people intend to harm one (e.g., Anderson et al., 2007; Moller & Krahe, 2009). Similarly, such exposure leads to violence desensitization and reduced empathy for victims of violence (e.g., Bushman & Anderson, 2009).

Factors That Influence the Effects of Media Violence

Effect-Boosting Factors

Media violence is more likely to elicit aggressive behavior if it is portrayed as unpunished or rewarded (Bandura, 1986), effective (Tan, 1986), justified (Bandura, 1973), lacking consequences (Potter, 1997); if the viewer identifies with the perpetrator of violence (Bandura, 1986) and perceives it as realistic (Huesmann & Eron, 1986); and if it is arousing (Mustonen & Pulkkinen, 1993). The portrayal of consequences (or lack thereof) is especially central to what is learned (Bandura et al., 1961). An extensive study of 2,500 hours of U.S. television programs found that only 19% of aggressive actors were punished for their aggressive actions and 8% were both punished and rewarded (NTVS, 1997). Similarly, most violent video games reward their characters (and players) with points, money, or status for aggression, and such rewards increase later aggression (Carnagey & Anderson, 2005). Thus, violent actions in these forms of media are more likely to be learned and to lead to future aggression.

Effect-Attenuating Factors

In contrast, some factors *reduce* the effects of media violence on aggression, including parental involvement (Anderson et al., 2007; Nathanson, 1999) and focusing on the consequences to the victim (Wilson et al., 1999). Focusing on the victim prompts aversive reactions that decrease the likelihood of imitation. Such a focus also prompts perspective taking, which in turn might increase prosocial behavior (Hoffman, 2008).

Media Exposure Effects on Other Risk Factors for Aggression

Media exposure may also have indirect effects on aggression by causing attentional problems, poor educational and reading performance, and substance abuse (see Chapter 3). Recent research indicates that high exposure to television (entertainment rather than educational) programs and video games is associated with attentional problems (e.g., Bailey, West, & Anderson, 2010, in press; Bioulac, Arfi, & Bouvard, 2008; Johnson, Cohen, Kasen, & Brook, 2007; Swing, Gentile, & Anderson, 2010). Some studies suggest that TV viewing (Koolstra & Van der Voort, 1996), particularly entertainment viewing (Ennemoser & Schneider, 2007), is negatively associated with reading achievement. Longitudinal studies indicate that there is strong association between exposure to alcohol advertisements and early alcohol use (e.g., Collins, Ellickson, McCaffrey, & Hambarsoomians, 2007). Alcohol use is depicted in more than 70% of popular television shows among 12-to-17-year-olds (Christensen, Henriksen, & Roberts, 2000) and in most (92%) popular movies (Sargent, Wills, Stoolmiller, Gibson, & Gibbons, 2006). Furthermore, nearly 20% of PG-13 movies portray illegal drug use (Roberts, Henriksen, & Christenson, 1999). These exposures are associated with more favorable attitudes toward alcohol, early initiation of alcohol use, and increases in alcohol consumption (e.g., Pechmann & Shih, 1999; Sargent et al., 2006).

Effects of Prosocial Media Content

Effects of Prosocial Media

Prosocial behavior is action that benefits another being. Although pure, non-violent prosocial behavior is relatively rare in the media, documented effects of such media include increases in friendliness, positive social interactions, altruism, cooperation, self-control, and delay of gratification; and reduction of stereotypes (see Mares & Woodard, 2005, for a detailed review). A meta-analysis of 34 studies involving more than 5,000 children found that viewing prosocial media enhances children's prosocial behavior (Mares & Woodard, 2005). Several studies on prosocial content have focused on *Sesame Street.* Beyond educational benefits, *Sesame Street* viewing increased social skills and prosocial attitudes, including nonracist attitudes and behaviors (Ball & Bogatz, 1970; Huston & Wright, 1998; Rice, Huston, Truglio, & Wright, 1990). Similar effects have been observed for other prosocial shows like *Mr. Rogers' Neighborhood* (Hearold, 1986).

Some shows presented as "prosocial" are not. "Prosocial" media in which the "good guys" achieve social justice by beating up the "bad guys" actually decreases prosocial behavior (Mares & Woodard, 2005). Similarly, frequent viewers of superhero shows in which the heroes defeat villains with physical violence (e.g., *Power Rangers*) are relatively likely to judge aggression in hypothetical situations as morally correct (Krcmar & Curtis, 2003) and to behave more aggressively and less prosocially (Liss, Reinhardt, & Fredriksen, 1983).

Prosocial video game exposure also relates positively to prosocial behavior (Gentile et al., 2009). In correlational and longitudinal studies, adolescents who frequently played prosocial video games were significantly more likely to display prosocial behavior (e.g., cooperation, empathy, helping someone in need). In an experimental study, participants who were randomly assigned to play a prosocial video game were more likely to help others on a subsequent task than those who played neutral or violent games.

Effects of Educational Media Content

Educational media can teach or improve personal skills. In a longitudinal study of low–socioeconomic status preschoolers, Wright et al. (2001a) found that viewing educational TV programs (such as *Sesame Street*) positively predicted time spent reading, letter-word knowledge, math skills, vocabulary size, and school readiness 3 years later, even after controlling for demographic variables and preschool attendance (see also Wright et al., 2001b). In a study that exposed children ages 5–8 to a safety videotape that portrayed children engaging in both injurious recreational behavior and alternative safe behavior, Potts and Swisher (1998) found that children's willingness to take physical risks was decreased and their identification of injury hazards was increased. Moreover, educational video games have been shown to increase performance in a range of areas from algebra to computer programming (e.g., Fery & Ponserre, 2001; Murphy, Penuel, Means, Korbak, & Whaley, 2002; Subrahmanyam & Greenfield, 1994). Video games also have been used to teach life skills to students with severe learning disabilities (Standen & Cromby, 1996) and health self-care behaviors to children with asthma and diabetes (Lieberman, 2001).

Using Media for Good

Media are being used to target global problems such as overpopulation, illiteracy, women's inequality, environmental destruction, and AIDS (see Singhal, Cody, Rogers, & Sabido, 2004). Bandura (2001) and his colleagues have designed dramatic serials on television and radio to inform and motivate people to change their behavior to alter detrimental societal norms and practices.

For example, a serial drama was aired to address family planning issues in a region in Kenya. Compared to the control region (with additional statistical controls), contraception use in the broadcast region increased by 58% and family size declined 24% (Westoff & Rodriguez, 1995). Thus, media models can activate, channel, and support prosocial behavior (Bandura, 1986).

Although these results are promising, caution is warranted. First, media campaigns have shown limited effectiveness with children as isolated strategies for prevention (Schilling & McAlister, 1990), although they seem to enhance the effects of other school- and community-based prevention programs (Perry, Kelder, Murray, & Klepp, 1992) in addressing issues as substance abuse (e.g., Pentz et al., 1989; Perry et al., 1992). Second, among late adolescents and adults, media campaigns sometimes seem to exacerbate negative target attitudes (i.e., boomerang effects) and behaviors instead of inducing positive change (see Cantor & Wilson, 2003, for a review).

Implications for Correctional Practice

One implication of media effects research for correctional practice is that violent media are likely to reinforce offenders' antisocial ideas, beliefs, and scripts, and to increase the likelihood of violent behavior. Relevant research in correctional settings is limited, but Waite, Hillbrand, and Foster (1992; see also Parke, Berkowitz, Leyens, West, & Sebastian, 1977) longitudinally examined the effects of disallowing MTV in a forensic hospital on aggressive behavior. At the time, MTV showed mostly music videos, which tend to focus on sexual and violent themes. Disallowing MTV reduced verbal (32%) and physical (47%) aggression. Although there are methodological limitations to this study, results suggest that reducing exposure to media violence exposure may reduce aggression in correctional settings. Of course, more research with better methodological controls is needed to support this idea.

A second implication is that positive media could promote prosocial behavior. Antisocial cognition, including beliefs supportive of crime, anger, and criminal identity (Andrews, Bonta, & Wormith, 2006), is one of the main risk factors for aggression and other crime (see Chapter 6). Research shows that these cognitions are easily learned and conditioned but are resistant to change (Huesmann, Eron, & Dubow, 2002). Thus, it could be the case that prosocial media makes little difference if provided late (i.e., adulthood intervention) rather than early (i.e., childhood prevention). Still, whether positive media promotes prosocial behavior among juvenile and adult offenders is a question open to empirical testing. Social-cognitive theories suggest that this may be a fruitful avenue of research. Exposure to prosocial media could (*a*) increase the accessibility of prosocial thoughts and scripts, providing adaptive alternatives to aggression, (*b*) reduce risky thinking (e.g., believing the world is hostile) that can foster aggression, (*c*) reduce the likelihood of imitating aggression by avoiding its glamorization and showing realistic consequences, *(d)* increase the likelihood of prosocial behavior by showing that it is rewarded, *(e)* increase empathy and perspective taking toward victims of aggression (Shechtman, 2008), perhaps "re-sensitizing" individuals by increasing their normal negative emotional response to violence (see Nathanson & Cantor, 2000). More research is needed to investigate whether media (which is low cost) can enhance the effectiveness of cognitive behavioral interventions in reducing antisocial cognition and violent recidivism.

Media and Public Policy

Given parents' and others' concerns about the amount of violence in today's media (Gentile & Walsh, 1999) and the overwhelming evidence of its detrimental effects, it is surprising that little has been done to minimize children's exposure to media violence. In this section, we summarize past attempts to do so before making recommendations for progress.

Past Attempts

Although attempts have been made to reduce children's media exposure in the United States, most have failed (see Anderson et al., 2003; Kunkel et al., 2001). For example, children's access to violent video games has not been effectively restricted because the courts do not perceive a sufficiently strong causal connection between such media and aggression to warrant First Amendment intrusion (Gentile, Saleem, & Anderson, 2007). Still, the industry has adopted "voluntary" regulatory policies, including attaching age-based ratings to their products. However, these ratings have been criticized as inconsistent, inaccurate, and confusing to parents (e.g., Gentile, 2009; Greenberg, 2001). For example, independent analyses suggest that the Entertainment Software Review Board (ESRB) underreports violence in video games by almost half (Thompson & Haninger, 2001). Furthermore, age-based ratings encourage children to seek older fare (e.g., Cantor, 1998), perhaps because they desire what is forbidden (Bushman & Stack, 1996). Fundamentally, there is the option for parents to discourage or regulate children's TV viewing and video game playing. Two small-scale intervention studies suggest that such actions can improve children's outcomes, including the reduction of aggression (e.g., Huesmann et al., 1983; Robinson et al., 2001).

Suggestions for Policy and Practice

Based on past research, we make the following policy suggestions to mitigate children's exposure to media violence:

1. Implement (or emphasize) content code ratings rather than age-based ratings. Content code ratings would specify questionable material

(e.g., sex and violence). There is evidence that content ratings are more informative and less likely to attract young viewers (Cantor, 1998) than age-based ratings.

2. Use a single rating system rather than the multitude that currently exist. A science-based organization that is independent of the media industry (such as the American Psychological Association, the Association for Psychological Science, or the American Academy of Pediatrics) should develop a reliable and valid system that is informed by research on what content is harmful, and that is informative to parents. An independent organization should implement the rating system; and media might be encouraged, such as by market forces, to label their products with this organization's ratings. Organizations that have a vested interest in producing and selling media products (such as media companies) should not be allowed to interfere with the creation, composition, or deliberations of the independent organization(s) charged with creating and implementing the systems.

3. Conduct a media campaign to correct misconceptions and increase awareness about media effects, with three target audiences: parents, schools, and pediatricians. First, the campaign should target getting parents actively involved in reducing their child's exposure to violent media (see Nathanson, 1999). For example, the American Academy of Pediatrics (2007) recommends that children under 2 not be exposed to any screen media, and those over age 2 not spend more than 2 hours per day exposed to electronic screens (e.g., TV, movies, video games, Internet). Second, the campaign should target schools and school boards, which can implement media literacy programs to educate children about unrealistic portrayals observed in media, including the unrealistic consequences of aggressive and violent acts (for an example of an effective program, see Robinson et al., 2001). Third, the campaign should target pediatricians, who could provide information to parents about unhealthy media habits and their outcomes (e.g., increase in aggression, favorable attitudes toward alcohol and drugs, and attention problems).

Policy-Relevant Gaps to Address in Future Research

First, although there is preliminary evidence that prosocial media can affect positive societal changes, there are only a handful of media interventions that have achieved successful short-term and long-term outcomes. Thus, there is a need for controlled experimental research to identify what kinds of factors in a media intervention can successfully influence attitudes and behaviors in the long term, and how unanticipated boomerang effects can be avoided. Second, the effect of prosocial media on offenders' aggression is essentially unknown. It would be useful to test the effects of prosocial media (e.g., TV, movies, video games) embedded in cognitive-behavioral interventions on offenders' recidivism. The work of Bandura and others on the use of serial dramas to affect positive attitudinal and behavioral changes in several domains of risky behavior could serve as a model for the creation of engaging, entertaining electronic media for use in correctional settings. Third, truly large-scale longitudinal research is needed to examine the unique, additive, and interactive effects of media violence and other known risk factors on violence from childhood to adulthood.

Conclusion

Electronic media have immense effects on socialization. Given the prevalence and glamorization of violent media in our society, it is not surprising that antisocial cognition and behaviors are common. If we want a society that is less prone to aggression and violence, we need to promote media that teach prosocial problem solving. Also, rather than eliminate war movies, police drama, or first-person shooter video games, we must change the context of the stories being told and the audiences that are exposed to potentially harmful content. Because of the dearth of positive media, a potential untapped market is opened up to media conglomerates that would also, in turn, benefit society. Improvements in each of these factors should reduce societal acceptance and prominence of antisocial cognitions, norms, and behaviors.

References

American Academy of Pediatrics. (2007). *Television and the family.* Retrieved from: http://www.aap.org/publiced/BR_TV.htm

Anderson, C. A., Berkowitz, L. Donnerstein, E., Huesmann, L. R., Johnson, J. D., Linz, D., Malamuth, N. M., & Wartella, E. (2003). The influence of media violence on youth. *Psychological Science in the Public Interest, 4,* 81–110.

Anderson, C. A., Buckley, K. E., & Carnagey, N. L. (2008). Creating your own hostile environment: A laboratory examination of trait aggression and the violence escalation cycle. *Personality and Social Psychology Bulletin, 34,* 462–473.

Anderson, C. A., & Bushman, B. J. (2001). Effects of violent video games on aggressive behavior, aggressive cognition, aggressive affect, physiological arousal, and prosocial behavior: A meta-analytic review of the scientific literature. *Psychological Science, 12,* 353–359.

Anderson, C. A., & Bushman, B. J. (2002a). Human aggression. *Annual Review of Psychology, 53,* 27–51.

Anderson, C. A., & Bushman, B. J. (2002b). The effects of media violence on society. *Science, 295,* 2377–2378.

Anderson, C. A., Carnagey, N. L., Flanagan, M., Benjamin, A. J., Eubanks, J., & Valentine, J. C. (2004). Violent video games: Specific effects of violent content on aggressive thoughts and behavior. *Advances in Experimental Social Psychology, 36,* 199–249.

Anderson, C. A., Gentile, D. A., & Buckley, K. E. (2007). *Violent video game effects on children and adolescents.* New York: Oxford University Press.

Anderson, C. A., Sakamoto, A., Gentile, D. A., Ihori, N., Shibuya, A., Yukawa, S., Naito, M., & Kobayashi, K. (2008). Longitudinal effects of violent video games aggression in Japan and the United States. *Pediatrics, 122,* e1067–e1072.

Anderson, C. A., Shibuya, A., Ihori, N., Swing, E. L., Bushman, B. J., Sakamoto, A., Rothstein, H. R., & Saleem, M. (2010). Violent video game effects on aggression, empathy, and prosocial behavior in Eastern and Western countries. *Psychological Bulletin, 136,* 151–173.

Andrews, D. A., Bonta, J., & Wormith, S. J. (2006). The recent past and near future of risk and/or need assessment. *Crime and Delinquency, 52,* 7–27.

Bailey, K., West, R., & Anderson, C. A. (2010). A negative association between video game experience and proactive cognitive control. *Psychophysiology, 47,* 34–42.

Bailey, K., West, R., & Anderson, C. A. in press. The influence of video games on social, cognitive, and affective information processing. In J. Decety & J. Cacioppo (Eds.), *Handbook of social neuroscience.* New York: Oxford University Press.

Ball, S., & Bogatz, G. A. (1970). *The first year of Sesame Street: An evaluation.* Princeton, NJ: Educational Testing Service.

Bandura, A. (1973). *Aggression: A social learning analysis.* Englewood Cliffs, NJ: Prentice Hall.

Bandura, A. (1986). *Social foundations of thought and action: A social cognitive theory.* Englewood Cliffs, NJ: Prentice-Hall.

Bandura, A. (1999). Moral disengagement in the perpetration of inhumanities. *Personality and Social Psychology Review, 3,* 193–209.

Bandura, A. (2001). Social cognitive theory of mass communication. *Media Psychology, 3,* 265–298.

Bandura, A. (2002). Social cognitive theory of mass communication. In J. Bryant & D. Zillmann (Eds.), *Media effects* (pp. 121–153). Mahwah, NJ: Lawrence Erlbaum Associates.

Bandura, A., Ross, D., & Ross, S. A. (1961). Transmission of aggression through imitation of aggressive models. *Journal of Abnormal and Social Psychology, 63,* 575–582.

Bioulac, S., Arfi, L., & Bouvard, M. P. (2008). Attention deficit/hyperactivity disorder and video games: A comparative study of hyperactive and control children. *European Psychiatry, 23,* 134–141.

Bjorkqvist, K. (1985). *Violent films, anxiety, and aggression.* Helsinki, Finland: Finnish Society of Sciences and Letters.

Boxer, P., Huesmann, L. R., Bushman, B. J., O'Brien, M., & Moceri, D. (2009). The role of violent media preference in cumulative developmental risk for violence and general aggression. *Journal of Youth and Adolescence, 38,* 417–428.

Boyatzis, C. J., Matillo, G. M., & Nesbitt, K. M. (1995). Effects of "The Mighty Morphin Power Rangers" on children's aggression with peers. *Child Study Journal, 25,* 45–55.

Buchman, D. D., & Funk, J. B. (1996). Video and computer games in the "90s: Children's time commitment and game preference. *Children Today, 24,* 12–16.

Bushman, B. J., & Anderson, C. A. (2001). Media violence and the American public: Scientific facts versus media misinformation. *American Psychologist, 56,* 477–489.

Bushman, B. J., & Anderson, C. A. (2009). Comfortably numb: Desensitizing effects of violent media on helping others. *Psychological Science, 20,* 273–277.

Bushman, B. J., & Stack, A. D. (1996). Forbidden fruit versus tainted fruit: Effects of warning labels on attraction to television violence. *Journal of Experimental Psychology: Applied, 2,* 207–226.

Cantor, J. (1998). Ratings for program content: The role of research findings. *Annals of the American Academy of Political and Social Science, 557,* 54–69.

Cantor, J., & Wilson, B. J. (2003). Media and violence: Intervention strategies for reducing aggression. *Media Psychology, 5,* 363–406.

Carnagey, N. L., & Anderson, C. A. (2003). The role of theory in the study of media violence: The General Aggression Model. In D. A. Gentile (Ed.), *Media violence and children* (pp. 87–106). Westport, CT: Praeger.

Carnagey, N. L., & Anderson, C. A. (2005). The effects of reward and punishment in violent video games on aggressive affect, cognition, and behavior. *Psychological Science, 16,* 882–889.

Christensen, P. G., Henriksen, L., and Roberts, D. F. (2000). *Substance use in popular prime-time television.* Washington, DC: Office of National Drug Control Policy.

Collins, R. L., Ellickson, P. L., McCaffrey, D. F., & Hambarsoomians, K. (2007). Early adolescent exposure to alcohol advertising and its relationship to underage drinking. *Journal of Adolescent Health, 40,* 527.

Ennemoser, M., & Schneider, W. (2007). Relations of television viewing and readings: Findings from a 4-year longitudinal study. *Journal of Educational Psychology, 99,* 349–368.

Escobar-Chaves, S. L., & Anderson, C. A. (2008). Media and risky behaviors. *Future of Children, 18,* 147–180.

Fery, Y-A., & Ponserre, S. (2001). Enhancing the control of force in putting by video game training. *Ergonomics, 44,* 1025–1037.

Garofalo, J. (1981). Crime and the mass media: A selective review of research. *Journal of Research in Crime and Delinquency, 18,* 319–350.

Gentile, D. A. (2009). The rating systems for media products. In S. Calvert & B. J. Wilson (Eds.), *Handbook of children, media, and development.* Blackwell Publishing Ltd., Oxford, UK. doi: 10.1002/9781444302752.ch23.

Gentile, D. A., & Anderson, C. A. (2003). Violent video games: The newest media violence hazard. In D. A. Gentile (Ed.), *Media violence and children* (pp. 131–152). Westport, CT: Praeger.

Gentile, D. A., Anderson, C. A., Yukawa, S., Ihori, N., Saleem, M., Ming, L. K., Shibuya, A., Liau, A. K., Khoo, A., & Sakamoto, A. (2009). The effects of prosocial video games on prosocial behaviors: International evidence from correlational, experimental, and longitudinal studies. *Personality and Social Psychology Bulletin, 35,* 752–763.

Gentile, D. A., Saleem, M., & Anderson, C. A. (2007). Public policy and the effects of media violence on children. *Social Issues and Policy Review, 1,* 15–61.

Gentile, D. A., & Walsh, D. A. (1999). *National survey of family media habits, knowledge, and attitudes.* Minneapolis, MN: National Institute on Media and the Family.

Greenberg, B. S. (2001). *The alphabet soup of television program ratings.* Creskhill, NJ: Hampton Press.

Hayes, J. (2007). Films and TV up the ante on graphic torture scenes. *Pittsburgh Post Gazette.* Retrieved from http://www.post-gazette.com/pg/07019/755004-237.stm

Hearold, S. (1986). A synthesis of 1043 effects of television on social behavior. In G. Comstock (Ed.), *Public communication and behavior* (Vol. 1, pp. 65–130). Orlando, FL: Academic Press.

Hoffman, M. L. (2008). Empathy and prosocial behavior. In M. Lewis, J. M. Haviland-Jones, & L. F. Barrett (Eds.), *Handbook of emotions* (Vol. 3, pp. 440–455). New York: Guilford Press.

Hopf, W., Huber, G. L., & Weis, R. H. (2008). Media violence and youth violence: A 2-year longitudinal study. *Journal of Media Psychology, 20,* 79–96.

Huesmann, L. R., & Eron, L. D. (1986). *Television and the aggressive child: A cross-national comparison.* New York: Lawrence Erlbaum.

Huesmann, L. R., Eron, L. D., & Dubow, E. F. (2002). Childhood predictors of adult criminality: Are all risk factors reflected in childhood aggressiveness? *Criminal Behavior and Mental Health, 12,* 185–208.

Huesmann, L. R., Eron, L. D., Klein, R., Brice, P., & Fischer, P. (1983). Mitigating the imitation of aggressive behaviors by changing children's attitudes about media violence. *Journal of Personality and Social Psychology, 44,* 899–910.

Huesmann, L. R., & Miller, L. S. (1994). Long term effects of repeated exposure to media violence in childhood. In L. R. Huesmann (Ed.), *Aggressive behavior: Current perspective* (pp. 153–186). New York: Plenum Press.

Huesmann, L. R, & Moise, J. (1999). *The role of cognitions in mediating the effect of childhood exposure to violence on adult aggression: A 15-year comparison of youth in four countries.* Paper presented at the IXth European Conference on Developmental Psychology, Spetses, Greece.

Huesmann, L. R., Moise, J., Podolski, C. L., & Eron, L. D. (2003). Longitudinal relations between childhood exposure to media violence and adult aggression and violence: 1977–1992. *Developmental Psychology, 39,* 201–221.

Huston, A. C., & Wright, J. C. (1998). Mass media and children's development. In I. E. Sigel & K. A. Renninger (Eds.), *Handbook of child psychology* (Vol. 4, pp. 999–1058). New York: John Wiley & Sons.

Johnson, J. G., Cohen, P., Smailes, E. M., Kasen, S., & Brook, J. S. (2002). Television viewing and aggressive behavior during adolescence and adulthood. *Science, 295,* 2468–2471.

Johnson, J. G., Cohen, P., Kasen, S., & Brook, J. S. (2007). Extensive television viewing and the development of attention and learning difficulties during adolescence. *Archives of Pediatric Adolescent Medicine, 161,* 480–486.

Kaiser Family Foundation. (2005). *Generation M: Media in the lives of 8–18 year-olds.* Retrieved from: http://www.kff.org/entmedia/entmedia030905pkg.cfm

Kappeler, V., Blumberg, M., & Potter, G. (1993). *The mythology of crime and criminal justice.* Washington, DC: U.S. Department of Justice.

Koolstra, C. M., & van der Voort, T. H. A, (1996). Longitudinal effects of television on children's leisure-time reading: A test of three explanatory models. *Human Communication Research, 23,* 4–35.

Krcmar, M., & Curtis, S. (2003). Mental models: Understanding the impact of fantasy violence on children's moral reasoning. *Journal of Communication, 53,* 460–499.

Kunkel, D., Maynard Farinola, W. J., Cope, K. M., Donnerstein, E., Biely, E., Zwarun, L., & Rollin, E. (2001). Assessing the validity of V-chip rating judgments: The labeling of high-risk programs. In B. S. Greenberg (Ed.), *The alphabet soup of television program ratings* (pp. 51–68). Cresskill, NJ: Hampton Press.

Leyens, J-P., Camino, L., Parke, R. D., & Berkowitz, L. (1975). Effects of movie violence on aggression in a field setting as a function of group. *Journal of Personality and Social Psychology, 32,* 346–360.

Lieberman, D. A. 2001. Management of chronic pediatric diseases with interactive health games: Theory and research findings. *Journal of Ambulatory Care Management, 24,* 26–38.

Liebert, R. M., & Baron, R. A. (1972). Some immediate effects of televised violence on children's behavior. *Developmental Psychology, 6,* 469–475.

Linz, D., Donnerstein, E., & Penrod, S. (1984). The effects of long-term exposure to filmed violence against women. *Journal of Communication, 34,* 130–147.

Liss, M. B., Reinhardt, L. C., & Fredriksen, S. (1983). TV heroes: The impact of rhetoric and deeds. *Journal of Applied Developmental Psychology, 4,* 175–187.

Mares, M. L., & Woodard, E. (2005). Positive effects of television on children's social interactions: A meta-analysis. *Media Psychology, 7,* 301–322.

Marsh, H. L. (1991). A comparative analysis of crime coverage in newspapers in the United States and other countries from 1960 to 1989: A review of the literature. *Journal of Criminal Justice, 19,* 67–80.

McLeod, J. M., Atkin, C. K., & Chaffee, S. H. (1972). Adolescents, parents, and television use: Adolescent self-report measures from Maryland and Wisconsin samples. In G. A. Comstock & E. A. Rubinstein (Eds.), *Television and social behavior: A technical report to the Surgeon General's Scientific Advisory Committee on Television and Social Behavior* (Vol. 3, pp. 173–238). Washington, DC: U.S. Government Printing Office.

Moller, I., & Krahe, B. (2009). Exposure to violent video games and aggression in German adolescents: A Longitudinal analysis. *Aggressive Behavior, 35,* 75–89.

Mullin, C. R., & Linz, D. G. (1995). Desensitization and resensitization to sexualized violence: Effects of exposure to sexually violent films on judgments of domestic violence victims. *Journal of Personality and Social Psychology, 69,* 449–459.

Murphy, R., Penuel, B., Means, B., Korbak, C., & Whaley, A. (2002). E-DESK: A *review of recent evidence on the effectiveness of discrete educational software.* Menlo Park, CA: SRI International. Retrieved from http://ctl.sri.com/publications/downloads/Task3_FinalReport3.pdf

Mustonen, A., & Pulkkinen, L. (1993). Aggression in television programs in Finland. *Aggressive Behavior, 19,* 175–183.

Nathanson, A. I. (1999). Identifying and explaining the relationship between parental mediation and children's aggression. *Communication Research, 26,* 124–143.

Nathanson, A. I., & Cantor, J. (2000). Reducing the aggression-promoting effect of violent cartoons by increasing children's fictional involvement with the victim. *Journal of Broadcasting and Electronic Media, 44,* 125–142.

National Television Violence Study. (1997). *Technical Report, 2.* Thousand Oaks, CA: Sage.

National Television Violence Study. (1998). *Technical Report, 3.* Thousand Oaks, CA: Sage.

Nielson Company. (2009). Average TV viewing for 2008-09 TV season at all-time high. Retrieved from http://blog.nielsen.com/nielsenwire/media_entertainment/average-tv-viewing-for-2008-09-tv-season-at-all-time-high/

Paik, H., & Comstock, G. (1994). The effects of television violence on antisocial behavior: A meta-analysis. *Communication Research, 21,* 516–546.

Parke, R. D., Berkowitz, L., Leyens, J. P., West, S. G., & Sebastian, R. J. (1977). Some effects of violent and nonviolent movies on the behavior of juvenile delinquents. In L. Berkowitz (Ed.), *Advances in experimental social psychology* (pp. 135–172). New York: Academic Press.

Pechmann, C., & Shih, C. F. (1999). Smoking scenes in movies and antismoking advertisements before movies: Effects on youth. *Journal of Marketing, 63,* 1–13.

Pentz, M. A., Dwyer, J. H., MacKinnon, D. P., Flay, B. R., Hansen, W. B., Wang, E. U. I., & Johnson, C. A. (1989). A multi-community trial for primary prevention of adolescent drug abuse: Effects on drug use prevalence. *Journal of American Medical Association, 261,* 3259–3266.

Perry, C. L., Kelder, S. H., Murray, D. M., & Klepp, K. I. (1992). Community wide smoking prevention: Long term outcomes of the Minnesota Heart Health Program and Class of 1989 study. *American Journal of Public Health, 82,* 1210–1216.

Potter, W. J. (1997). The problem of indexing risk of viewing television aggression. *Critical Studies in Mass Communication, 14,* 228–248.

Potts, R., & Swisher, L. (1998). Effects of televised safety models on children's risk taking and hazard identification. *Journal of Pediatric Psychology, 23,* 157–163.

Rice, M. L., Huston, A. C., Truglio, R., & Wright, J. C. (1990). Words from "Sesame Street": Learning vocabulary while viewing. *Developmental Psychology, 26,* 421–428.

Roberts, D. F., Henriksen, L., & Christenson, P. G. (1999). *Substance use in popular movies and music.* Washington, DC: Office of National Drug Control Policy.

Robinson, T. N., Wilde, M. L., Navracruz, L. C., Haydel, K. F., & Varady, A. (2001). Effects of reducing children's television and video game use on aggressive behavior: A randomized controlled trial. *Archives of Pediatric Adolescent Medicine, 155,* 17–23.

Sargent, J. D., Wills, T. A., Stoolmiller, M., Gibson, J., & Gibbons, F. X. (2006). Alcohol use in motion pictures and its relation with early-onset teen drinking. *Journal of Studies on Alcohol, 67,* 617–637.

Schilling, R. F., McAlister, A. L. (1990). Preventing drug use in adolescents through media interventions. *Journal of Consulting and Clinical Psychology, 58,* 416–424.

Shechtman, Z. (2008). *Treating child and adolescent aggression through bibliotherapy.* New York: Springer-Verlag.

Sheese, B. E., & Graziano, W. G. (2005). Deciding to defect: The effects of video-game violence on cooperative behavior. *Psychological Science, 16,* 354–357.

Singhal, A., Cody, M. J., Rogers, E. M., & Sabido, M. (Eds.). (2004). *Entertainment-education and social change: History, research, and practice.* Mahwah, NJ: Erlbaum Associates.

Smith, S. L., Wilson, B. J., Kunkel, D., Linz, D., Potter, J., Colvin, C. M., & Donnerstein, E. (1998). Violence in television programming overall: University of California, Santa Barbara Study. *National Television Violence Study: Volume 3.* Thousand Oaks, CA: Sage.

Standen, P. J., & Cromby, J. J. (1996). Can students with developmental disability use virtual reality to learn skills which will transfer to the real world? In H. J. Murphy (Ed.), *Proceedings of the Third International Conference on Virtual Reality and Persons with Disabilities.* Northridge: California State University Center on Disabilities.

Subrahmanyam, K., & Greenfield, P. M. (1994). Effect of video game practice on spatial skills in girls and boys. *Journal of Applied Developmental Psychology, 15,* 13–32.

Swing, E. L., Gentile, D. A., & Anderson, C. A. (2010). Television and video game exposure and the development of attention problems. *Pediatrics, 126,* 214–221.

Tan, A. S. (1986). Social learning of aggression from television. In J. Bryant & D. Zillmann (Eds.), *Perspectives on media effects* (pp. 41–55). Hillsdale, NJ: Erlbaum.

Thomas, M. H., & Drabman, R. S. (1975). Toleration of real life aggression as a function of exposure to televised violence and age of subject. *Merrill-Palmer Quarterly, 21,* 227–232.

Thompson, K. M., & Haninger, K. (2001). Violence in E-rated video games. *Journal of the American Medical Association, 286,* 591–598.

Waite, B. M., Hillbrand, M., & Foster, H. G. (1992). Reduction of aggressive behavior after removal of music television (MTV). *Hospital and Community Psychiatry, 43,* 173–175.

Walsh, D., Gentile, D. A., Walsh, E., Bennett, N., Robideau, B., Walsh, M., Strikland, S., & McFadden, D. (2005). *Tenth annual MediaWise® video game report card.* Minneapolis, MN: National Institute on Media and the Family.

Westoff, C. F., & Rodriguez, G. (1995). The mass media and family planning in Kenya. *International Family Planning Perspectives, 21*(1), 26–31.

Wilson, B. J., Colvin, C. M., & Smith, S. L. (2002). Engaging in violence on American television: A comparison of child, teen, and adult perpetrators. *Journal of Communication, 52,* 36–60.

Wilson, B. J., Linz, D., Federman, J., Smith, S. L., Paul, B., Nathanson, A., Donnerstein, E., & Lingsweiler, R. W. (1999). *The choices and consequences evaluation: A study of court TV's anti-violence curriculum.* Santa Barbara: Center for Communication and Social Policy, University of California.

Wilson, B. J., Smith, S. L., Potter, W. J., Kunkel, D., Linz, D., Colvin, C. M., & Donnerstein, E. (2002). Violence in television programming: Assessing the risks. *Journal of Communication, 52,* 5–35.

Woodard, E. H. (1999). *The 1999 state of children's television report: Programming for children over broadcast and cable television.* (Report No. 28). Philadelphia: University of Pennsylvania, Annenberg Public Policy Center.

Wright, J. C., Huston, A. C., Murphy, K. C., St. Peters, M., Piñon, M., Scantlin, R., & Kotler, J. (2001a). The relations of early television viewing to school readiness and vocabulary of children from low income families: The Early Window project. *Child Development, 72,* 1347–1366.

Wright, J. C., Huston, A. C., Scantlin, R., & Kotler, J. (2001b). The Early Window project: Sesame Street prepares children for school. In S. M. Fisch & R. T. Tuglio (Eds.), *G. is for growing: Thirty years of research on children and Sesame Street* (pp. 97–114). Mahwah, NJ: Lawrence Erlbaum Associates.

Yokota, F., & Thompson, K. M. (2000). Violence in G-rated animated films. *Journal of the American Medical Association, 283,* 2716–2720.

5

Public Attitudes and Punitive Policies

Tom R. Tyler and Lindsay E. Rankin

There is probably no more dramatic example of the problems in the U.S. criminal justice system than the size of the American prison population (Haney & Zimbardo, 1998). As noted in Part I of this book, the incarceration rates and the costs of the current penal model are staggering. The United States is among the world leaders in the proportion of citizens it holds in prison. In 2000, there were over 2 million Americans in jail or prison (Pew Center for the States, 2008; United States Department of Justice, 2001), far surpassing incarceration rates in Europe and elsewhere (Garland, 2001).

These high rates of punishment reflect a trend in recent decades in the United States in which the exercise of legal authority has become primarily associated with the use of threat and punishment aimed at deterring people from engaging in criminal behavior (Nagin, 1998). In this instrumental approach, the focus is (and should be) on the power of legal authorities and institutions to shape behavior by threatening to deliver negative sanctions for rule breaking. For this model to be credible those who break rules have to receive punishment for their crimes, leading to a need for widespread incarceration. Of course, the model is not only about punishment: it also involves the need for a substantial police force to detect wrongdoing when it occurs. Within legal circles, this way of viewing the instrumental relationship of legal authorities with citizens is referred to as the "deterrence" or "social control" model, and it is this model of human behavior that—for better or worse—currently dominates law and public policy.

We will argue that the current focus is too strongly and too exclusively on such an instrumental approach given its cost and benefit tradeoffs and how it compares to the alternative models that exist. And, we will argue, this overly instrumental orientation is true both in the practices of the legal system and in the opinions of the public. But first, we point out that the attitudes of the public regarding how to prevent and deal with crime is not *solely* instrumental and not *solely* focused on punishment.

We want to first consider how society ended up with such an instrumental system. We will argue that public views can be generally characterized in several ways. First, when the issue is how to prevent crime, members of the public are primarily interested in building people's character or instilling appropriate morals and values. Values are internalized feelings about obligation or right and wrong. They see such values as lacking in those who commit criminal behavior. Second, when considering how to deal with those who have already committed crimes, members of the public have a very pessimistic view of the possibility of rehabilitating these wrongdoers. We characterize this public view as reflecting the belief that there are people beyond the capability of having or being open to influence by morals and values. Such people will commit crimes unless there is a severe threat of punishment to deter them. For this group a value-based approach is not possible and members of the public support an instrumental approach in the form of using punishment to respond to past crime and to deter future crime. The public does not view this punishment approach as effective, but instead sees it as the only possibility for those they regard as beyond the influence of morals and values. This view of criminals as "outsiders" who are not subject to the same motivations and values as the average citizen has dominated the criminal justice system.

In this chapter we will discuss such public attitudes and will consider how these views have led American society to an ambivalent embrace of an instrumental approach to motivating lawful behavior. We note that this strategy is costly and results in negative side effects, and we explore what alternatives are possible. We also discuss the nature of the public opinion that policy makers must confront when seeking to make policy changes.

Public Views on Preventing Crime

How does the public think individuals can be encouraged to behave in accordance with the law? To examine public perceptions about how to motivate such behavior, we can look at research by Tyler and Boeckmann (1997), who interviewed California residents in the wake of the passage of the three-strikes initiative. They asked people about the effectiveness of several different approaches to controlling crime, and the results indicate that people generally believe that shaming and moral education are the most effective ways to control the problem. For example, 70% of those interviewed indicated that shaming people by printing their names in the paper would lower crime, while 85% said that using schools to encourage the development of values such as respect and responsibility to follow rules in children would be effective. These approaches are based on values, specifically social and moral values, and indicate public support for a long-term view of preventing crime by effective socialization in childhood and by the activation of values via responses to wrongdoing like shaming that call upon the values that properly socialized people would hold.

Public support for these approaches that encourage following the law is consistent with research findings that similarly suggest that childhood value creation is a viable approach to encouraging rule following among adults. Specifically, psychologists have studied how to encourage the internalization of social values, that is, the taking values on as one's own and feeling responsible for behaving in accord with them (e.g., Hoffman, 1977). For example, researchers study the factors that shape children's willingness to break rules under conditions in which they believe they are not being observed. Their findings indicate that how children are raised by their parents shapes the degree to which they do or do not break rules under these circumstances. These findings speak to considerations of developing moral values in an effort to prevent later undesirable behavior.

Classic developmental psychological research points to the effectiveness of two types of child-rearing strategies for building values. One approach involves building social ties with caring others, leading to "identification," that is, the adoption of parental values (Hoffman, 2000; Tangney & Dearing, 2002). The other approach involves the development of reasoning skills through dialogue and discussion with children, so that their moral values become advanced and engaged in guiding their behavior (Blasi, 1980). Both of these strategies are based on the idea of values, rather than an instrumental approach based upon punishment or reward, in an effort to encourage desired behavior. They speak to efforts to prevent or correct misbehavior because research on developmental strategies has also been linked to law-abiding behavior among adults. Specifically, research suggests that strategies of socialization that encourage the development of social ties and cognitive reasoning skills are linked to law-abiding behavior among both adolescents and adults (Jurkovic, 1980; Turiel, 1987).

However, parents do not solely pursue values approaches and in dealing with misbehavior physical discipline is also common. In a recent national sample of American parents of 1–2 year olds, 63% reported using physical discipline, while by fifth grade 80% of children had been physically punished (Gershoff & Bitansky, 2007, p. 232). This supports our argument, expanded upon later, that there is a general culture of punitiveness in the United States. While debate continues about the usefulness of physical discipline, many if not most, researchers argue that it is of very little benefit and carries a substantial risk of harm. For example, Gershoff and Bitansky (2007) conclude that "if parents' goals are to increase children's moral internalization and to decrease their aggressive and antisocial behavior, there is little evidence that corporal punishment is effective in achieving these goals" (p. 235). And physical discipline is linked directly to aggression and violence toward others both in childhood and adolescence (Fine, Trentacosta, Izard, Matow, & Campbell, 2004). So physical punishment is likely ineffective in leading to long-term compliance; does not promote internalization of values; and can lead to aggression. Later, we will argue that similar findings apply to the excessive use of punitive policies in our criminal justice system, but first we turn to public attitudes regarding offenders and prospects of preventing them from engaging in future criminal behavior.

Public Views on Offenders

People do not just want to punish criminals for punitive or retributive reasons. They are also concerned with moral issues. There is a long-standing finding in psychological research on responses to wrongdoing that people punish to restore a moral balance (Vidmar & Miller, 1980). It has recently been affirmed in a compelling series of studies in which appropriate sentencing decisions in criminal cases are driven by moral judgments about deservingness rather than by instrumental judgments concerning how to deter future criminal conduct (Carlsmith, 2006). In making decisions within experimental contexts about whom to punish and/or how severely to punish, people focus primarily upon the issue of moral wrong.

If it were up to the members of the public, in other words, they accept punishment when it accords with their moral sense of what is appropriate given the level and type of wrong committed, but just as important they would prefer to have sincere apologies and other signs that wrongdoers recognized and acknowledge their moral wrongs and were likely to follow their moral values in the future and be law abiding.

But if people view crime as a moral issue, how can they be described as instrumental in their approach to criminals? How does this moral view of punishment contrast with the high rates of incarceration and punitive nature of the criminal justice system? To understand this seeming paradox, we again turn to the study of Californians conducted in the wake of the passage of the three-strikes initiative (Tyler & Boeckmann, 1997). The results on the perceived viability of several different approaches to punishment in response to rule breaking indicated that people had generally pessimistic views about the effectiveness of punishment as a response to wrongdoing. Only 55% said that putting criminals in prison for life would lower the crime rate and only 44% felt that using the death penalty more often would lower the crime rate. Hence, the public generally felt that deterrence in the form of severe punishment was not an especially effective response to crime. But this sample of Californians expressed even higher levels of skepticism regarding rehabilitation, with only 24% indicating that it was possible to rehabilitate burglars and only 5% saying it was possible to rehabilitate violent offenders.

Tyler and Boeckmann (1997) argue that people hold a pessimistic view of rehabilitation both because they believe that there are no common core values that wrongdoers share with others in the community and because they doubt the ability of government to effectively manage the rehabilitation process (Zimring & Johnson, 2006). For whatever reason people see the reconnection of offenders with common moral values as unlikely to occur. Similarly, in that survey of California residents the public supported severe punishment when they felt that children did not learn moral values (Tyler & Boeckmann, 1997). Those respondents who endorsed these views supported the three-strikes initiative and generally punitive policies for law breakers. Again, it seems that people see wrongdoers as lacking the communities' moral values, and therefore appeals to these values will not prevent unlawful behavior. Hence, effective deterrence will necessitate the threat and use of punishment.

In other words, of the alternatives, people expressed reluctant support for deterrence. And, of course, since punishment is not viewed as leading to rehabilitation, it is necessary to impose longer sentences on offenders, who upon their release from jail or prison will pose a danger similar to that which led them to break rules in the first place. As noted, believing that offenders lack moral values is linked to supporting longer sentences (and in the case of the three-strikes law lifetime sentences). The result is the public support for America's currently highly and "unapologetically" punitive policies for dealing with crime and criminals (Roberts & Stalans, 2004).

While the public's ambivalent views of human motivation are supportive of the current instrumental approaches, we will argue that both the public and many policies fail to fully recognize the shortcoming and the problems associated with trying to deter wrongdoing by the threat and use of punishment. Those problems include the material and social costs of deterrence and punishment, as well as the unintended consequence that instrumental approaches contribute to the problem of preventing rule breaking by undermining other human motivations, such as people's values, that could also play a role in keeping people from engaging in criminal behavior. Hence, we will suggest that people ought to be more skeptical of deterrence as a way of preventing crime and punishment as a way of preventing repeat offending, and that greater use of values approaches should be incorporated into public policy. And, as noted, we suggest that such a values-based approach finds resonance within the public, at least if it focuses upon value creation in society, especially among the young, rather than efforts to rehabilitate adult offenders.

Instrumental Approaches in the Legal System

A person looking at American society in the 1960s might have projected a future of declining punishment and increasing efforts at rehabilitation and reintegration for offenders (Garland, 2001). That is, in fact, the direction taken by much of Europe. However, the United States has not moved in that direction. Instead, it has remained a punitive society in which harsh punishment is central to reactions to rule breaking (Garland, 2001). Central to this punitive society are beliefs under which the primary way of motivating compliance with the law is via the application of sanctions.

This instrumental approach of a punishment-based deterrence policy that has come to dominate the legal system has two aspects. First is the suggestion that people's law-related behavior is shaped by their expectations about the punishment that will result from rule breaking. People could potentially be influenced by their estimates of the likelihood of being caught and punished, by their expectation of the severity of punishment, or both. Second, if they are caught and punished for wrongdoing, deterrence models suggest that the severity of the punishment that people receive shapes the likelihood of postpunishment wrongdoing. It is the role of severe punishment in preventing recidivism that is particularly relevant to issues of punitiveness.

The influence of the threat of punishment is ubiquitous in the law. Judges, for example, attempt to influence people's acceptance of their decisions by threatening fines or jail time for failure to comply. Similarly, police officers carry guns and clubs, and they are empowered to threaten citizens with physical injury and incapacitation, among other penalties. The goal is to establish legal authority and, as Reiss (1971) points out, "The uniform, badge, truncheon, and arms all may play a role in asserting authority" in the effort to "gain control of the situation" (p. 46). The police thereby seek to gain control over the individual's behavior "by manipulating an individual's calculus regarding whether 'crime pays' in any particular instance" (Meares 2000, p. 396). All of these authorities seek to bring behavior into line with the law by threatening people with punishment.

More generally, the legal system is charged with producing compliant behavior and based on an instrumental approach it attempts to shape environmental contingencies in such a way that citizens will be faced with the prospect of heavy losses (e.g., incarceration) that are intended to outweigh the anticipated gains of engaging in criminal behavior. This deterrence model dictates that the responsibility of lawmakers is to decide which acts should be prevented, and then to specify sufficiently strict penalties—generally fines or prison terms—so that the prohibited behavior is rarely enacted. The notion that people's behavior with respect to the law is shaped by calculations of expected gains and losses is a core premise of rational choice theory, which is derived from neoclassical economics (Nagin, 1998).

According to the assumptions of rational choice theory, most people will calculate expected utilities by multiplying the probability of an outcome (e.g., getting caught for armed robbery or drunk driving) by its valence (very good to very bad). If the laws are well calibrated, people will arrive at the desired conclusion that they should follow the law. Thus, rational self-interest is the motivational engine of the deterrence/social control model. To regulate behavior, this model suggests that decision makers should adjust criminal sanctions to the needed level so that the expected losses associated with law breaking will minimize the likelihood that people will break the law.

Instrumental Views in General Public Attitudes

The general tenor of recent times in the United States is captured by the case of support for the death penalty. During the 1960s, a majority of adult Americans favored ending the death penalty, while public opinion polls during the 1980s and 1990s typically found that 80% or more of those interviewed favored the death penalty (Ellsworth & Gross, 1994). The focus of public discussion has been, both on the issue of the death penalty and punishment more generally, on the view that the legal system is too lenient and that there need to be harsher ways to punish those who commit crimes.

The punitive nature of public views is a theme in most recent writing about the American public. But given some of the support for value building that we discussed earlier, why does the public support ever harsher punishments? We see punitiveness as an expression of frustration in a public who perceives moral values to be in decline and the set of shared values that define a common community transforming into a set of subcommunities of "outsiders" and "strangers" who either lack values or have different values. In this changing social landscape, people view punishment as a mechanism that still works to maintain social order. However, as we are about to argue, its actual effectiveness in preventing law breaking is limited, and over time the appeal of ever more severe sanctions is, in our view, irresistible, since the deterrence model is not preventing crimes and the use of strategies based upon this model has undermined the role of other values in securing compliance. Once rules are broken the general deterrence model can be enhanced by the costly route of building more prisons, as has occurred to a considerable extent in America. Severe punishments hold the promise of keeping dangerous people off the street and, to the degree they can be afforded, seem the only effective route to take. In other words, incapacitation becomes the most seemingly viable option in the wake of failed deterrence strategies. If people cannot be deterred ever more severe punishments can be used to keep criminals under control because they can at least keep them off the streets for lengthy periods of time. In the case of the death penalty the threat posed by someone is completely eliminated by their execution.

Shortcomings of Instrumental Views

Despite such institutional and public support, we argue that the deterrence model is both too costly and at best a minimally effective system of social control. The high costs come in the form of material costs of implementing such a system, the social costs of the negative effects that these methods of surveillance and punishment have on communities and their relationship with the law and law enforcement, and the self-defeating effect that this approach has in undermining individuals' internal motivations for law abiding behavior.

Material Cost of Instrumental Approach

The high material cost of the system stems from the need to create and maintain a credible threat of punishment. According to an instrumental view, people will only change their behavior when they feel that there is a reasonable risk of being caught and punished for wrongdoing. Of course people will try to hide their illegal behavior, so a system of surveillance will be needed to identify wrongdoing.

The problems of surveillance are central to deterrence models, because research suggests that it is the probability of punishment, more than punishment severity, that shapes rule-related behavior (Tyler, 2006a, 2006b). In other words, if a person is considering rule breaking, he or she is more influenced by the likelihood that he or she will be caught and punished at all than by considerations of how severe that punishment will be. As a consequence, a system for detecting wrongdoing must be created and maintained. For this reason, as Meares (2000) notes, the effectiveness of "instrumental means of producing compliance always depend[s] on resource limits" (p. 401). It is not realistic to substitute draconian punishments for a more costly system that creates credible risks of being detected while engaging in wrongdoing because it will not be effective in motivating behavior. The relevant questions are how much in terms of financial and other benefits and burdens authorities are willing to expend in order to control crime, and how much power to intrude into citizens' lives people are willing to allow the authorities to have?

Deterrence works reasonably well in at least some cases, such as murder, because society has devoted considerable resources to making the risk of being caught high and to enforcing penalties for it by punishing those who commit murder with lengthy incarceration. The objective risk of being caught and punished for murder is relatively high: approximately 45% (Robinson & Darley, 1997). The likelihood of being caught for committing a murder is high enough for deterrence to be effective in lowering the murder rate. Even in this case, however, criminals are not as sensitive to the magnitude of the penalty as they are to the estimated probability of being apprehended. As a result, capital punishment does not serve to deter murder more effectively than does life imprisonment (Ellsworth & Mauro, 1998).

For offences less severe than murder, using surveillance to shape law-related behavior becomes even more problematic. For example, in examining the problem of drunk driving, Ross (1982) suggests that raising risk estimates to a level that is high enough to lower the rate of law-breaking behavior, while not necessarily impossible, involves prohibitively high costs in terms of police manpower and people's willingness to accept state intrusions into their personal lives. Ross further points out that even the intensive efforts of Scandinavian authorities to create high estimates of risk using random road blocks and other similarly expensive and intrusive law enforcement measures are insufficient to create and maintain subjective risk estimates that are high enough to deter drunk driving over the long term.

In addition to deterring a potential offender, the instrumental approach would argue that punishing an individual after he or she does something wrong discourages the individual from future law breaking, which provides an additional reason for incarceration. This is referred to as specific deterrence, the belief that punishing a person for wrongdoing leads that person to be less likely to commit rule-breaking behavior in the future. The high material costs of this extension of the instrumental strategy are incurred through the administration of the actual punishment such as incarceration time, as discussed in Part I of this book.

However, just as we have argued that the threats of severe punishment fail to motivate behavior, the delivery of punishments is also a strategy of uncertain effectiveness. This is true of the practice of widespread punishment for minor crimes. One example is the use of what is called the broken windows approach to policing. That approach argues that the police should punish minor crimes to discourage more serious crimes. However, evaluations suggest that the use of this approach does not lower the rate of serious crime (Harcourt & Ludwig, 2006). More broadly, variations in the severity of punishment are not found to be related to the rate of reoffending among offenders (Lipsey & Cullen, 2007; Lynch & Sabol, 1997), while among juveniles incarceration increases the risk of recidivism (McCord, Widom, & Crowell, 2001; Mendel, 2002).

As already noted, it would be wrong to argue that estimates of risk and punishment have *no* effect on behavior. Research does support the argument that variations in the perceived certainty of punishment do affect people's compliance with the law, at least to some degree in some cases. People's behavior is often, though not always, shaped by their estimate of the likelihood that, if they disobey the law, they will be caught and punished (Nagin, 1998). But perceptions of the likelihood of being caught and punished generally have a relatively *minor* influence on people's behavior. Consequently, social control strategies based exclusively on a deterrence model of human behavior have at best limited success (Tyler, 2009).

Further demonstrating the minor effect of deterrence by examining both the certainty and severity of punishment, MacCoun (1993) found that these considerations account for approximately 5% of the variance in drug use behavior, a finding consistent with the suggestion of Paternoster (1987) that "perceived certainty [of punishment] plays virtually no role in explaining deviant/criminal conduct" (p. 191). A recent review similarly concluded that the relationship between crime/deviance and variables specified by deterrence theory is "modest to negligible" (Pratt, Cullen, Blevins, Daigle, & Madensen, 2008, p. 383). And after decades of research the voluminous literature on the deterrence effects of the death penalty suggests that "the relationship between executions and murders still lacks clear proof" (Weisberg, 2005, p. 163). Hence, deterrence is a very high cost strategy that yields, at best, identifiable but weak results.

Social Costs of Instrumental Approaches

Deterrence involves material investments of resources and would require high costs to be effective. Further, the implementation of deterrence strategies also results in social costs. Many material costs are concrete and visible on state and federal budgets. In contrast, social costs, by which we mean the negative effects on the relationships of people within a community and between communities and law enforcement, may be more invisible but no less important to consider. The heavy costs of the large-scale imprisonment to individuals and communities have had a strong impact, especially on urban communities and especially among members of racial and ethnic minority groups, which are overrepresented in the prison system (Patillo, Weiman, & Western, 2004).

For example, surveillance systems have deleterious effects on the social climate of groups because their use implies distrust, which decreases people's ability to feel positively about themselves, their groups, and the system itself (Kramer & Tyler, 1996). Furthermore, people may experience intrusions into their lives as procedurally unfair, leading to anger and other negative emotions often associated with perceptions of injustice (e.g., Gurr, 1970). Whether surveillance works or not, then, it is often demotivating and introduces new costs in terms of distrust and perhaps even paranoia in subsequent social interaction. Such costs are borne by groups, organizations, and societies to which people belong, as they lose the gains that occur when people are willing to cooperate with each other.

Research suggests that the increasing use of deterrence strategies and social control has exerted precisely this type of negative influence on the American social climate. It has created an adversarial relationship between legal authorities and members of the communities they serve, especially with respect to racial and ethnic minority group members (Tyler & Huo, 2002), leading the public to grow less compliant with the law and less willing to help the police to fight crime (Sunshine & Tyler, 2003).

Undermining of Motivation Through Instrumental Approach

Furthermore, general principles of human motivation suggest that if people comply with the law only in response to coercive power, they will be less likely to obey the law in the future because acting in response to external pressures diminishes internal motivations to engage in a behavior. This follows from the well-known distinction in social psychology between intrinsic and extrinsic motivation. Research shows that when people are motivated solely by the prospect of obtaining external rewards and punishments they become less likely to perform the desired behavior in the absence of such environmental reinforcements (e.g., Deci, 1975). On the other hand, if people are motivated by intrinsic reasons for behaving in a certain way, then their compliance becomes much more reliable and less context dependent. And external contingencies that are too strong can even dampen the motivation for behaviors that were previously intrinsically motivated, even for formerly enjoyable activities.

The undermining effects of deterrence do not only occur among the people being regulated. When authorities manage people by surveillance, they do not build up any basis for trusting them. For example, employees who have been given the opportunity to follow rules for internal reasons demonstrate to workplace authorities when they do so that they can be trusted. Subsequently, authorities are more comfortable allowing those individuals to work without supervision. However, when authorities are constantly present, they have no basis for trust and can suspect that the moment they leave people will stop following the rules (Strickland, 1958). Hence, the very behavior of surveillance creates the conditions requiring future surveillance. And, as noted earlier, their suspicions are at least partially justified, since their surveillance has probably had the effect of undermining people's value-based motivations for obeying the law.

Thus, overall the deterrence or instrumental model has, at best, only minor influence on people's behavior. In the social sciences even small effects can be meaningful, but as we have outlined, these small effects come at high costs in terms of resources for enforcement and punishment and in terms of negative social impact. Therefore, these small effects, we argue, are not worth these high costs, and furthermore the side effects over time can be cumulative because it can create a self-fulfilling prophecy, a perpetuating cycle of lessening intrinsic motivation and trust in authorities which lead to less voluntary cooperation and rule following and greater reliance and enforcement of deterrence models by both law enforcement and in the minds of the public. Despite these disadvantages, our society is currently committed to a deterrence approach to bringing behavior into line with rules. This commitment is strong in spite of empirical evidence that suggests that this approach is not very effective and that value-based regulation is more effective. As we have noted, the public is focused upon moral issues when dealing with the law, so the deterrence approach is a poor fit to "true" public concerns. However, the public has a generally skeptical view about both the possibility of who can be motivated to adhere to rules based upon values and of preventing recurrences of wrongdoing based upon rehabilitation. As a consequence, the public focuses reluctantly upon deterrence and incapacitation (Tonry, 1999). Our argument is that in reality empirical findings support the value of the approach that the public actually favors, a focus upon preventing rule-breaking behavior through the development and maintenance of the values that support rule following.

Alternative Value-Based Approaches Rather Than Instrumental

We noted that the public generally falls back on instrumental approaches for motivating rule following, despite recognizing the limits of punishment.

They see punishment as more effective or at least the only option for dealing with individuals who have committed crimes because they view rehabilitation as not viable. However, while the public has a generally negative view about the possibility of rehabilitation, the public is more positive toward efforts to prevent criminal behavior, not by deterrence, but by the development of values. This strong public support for values is important because, we will suggest, there is considerable evidence that values are a viable and effective approach to motivating rule adherence. Hence, it may be more politically reasonable to focus upon changing approaches to preventing wrongdoing, and it may require more convincing of the public that similar efforts can be directed at rehabilitating those who have committed crimes.

Our argument is that there is an alternative model to deterrence that can inform criminal justice policies, a self-regulatory model in which individuals' behavior is internally motivated by their values. In this chapter, we use the term *values* to refer to internalized feelings that people have about their obligations to obey authorities and follow moral principles; that is, we focus on the values of legitimacy and moral beliefs (see Tyler, 2009). Because these values are held by people as their own, they are motivated to follow them irrespective of whether there are punishments or rewards associated with such actions. Hence, their behavior in following rules is voluntary and occurs without surveillance. We argue that people are more likely to obey a law if they think it is legitimate and/or consistent with their moral values. We will argue that these values are actually better at preventing criminal behavior than instrumental approaches, that such values can be developed and encouraged, and that people who have committed crimes are still sensitive to these values despite public skepticism about such motivations within people who have committed crimes in the past.

Legitimacy

Legitimacy is the feeling of responsibility and obligation to follow the law; to accept the decisions of legal authorities; and to cooperate with and help legal authorities to do their jobs. Legitimacy is defined as "a property that a rule or an authority has when others feel obligated to voluntarily defer to that rule or authority. In other words, a legitimate authority is one that is regarded by people as entitled to have its decisions and rules accepted and followed by others" (Skogan & Frydl, 2004 , p. 297). Legitimacy, therefore, is a quality that people perceive an authority, a law, or an institution to possess that leads others to feel obligated to obey its decisions and directives. Successful leaders and institutions use more than brute force to execute their will. They strive to gain the consent of the governed so that their commands will be voluntarily accepted.

One way to think about legitimacy is people's belief that it is a property of an institution. Studies of the legitimacy of legal authorities typically ask people to evaluate their general feelings of responsibility and obligation to obey the law and legal authorities (see Tyler, 2006a). This focus on the importance of legitimacy reflects concern with the circumstances under which people follow the directives of social rules and social authorities. Legitimacy is important to the success of such authorities because they are enabled to gain public deference to a range of decisions by virtue of their social role (Tyler, 2006a, 2006b). Widespread voluntary cooperation with the law and legal authorities allows those authorities to concentrate their resources most effectively on pursuing the long-term goals of society. The authorities do not need to provide incentives or sanctions to all citizens to get them to support every rule or policy they enact, and the resources needed for order maintenance can be deployed in other ways.

Legitimacy can also be perceived as the property of a person. In early policing, for example, the beat officer patrolled a particular area, an area in which he or she often lived. They developed personal relationships with the public—that is, people knew them. So they had legitimacy as individuals, and they built or undermined that legitimacy by the manner in which they exercised their authority. In modern police forces, which are rooted in police cars, the officer who steps out of a car to respond to a particular situation is generally someone that the people involved do not know. That officer has institutional legitimacy, marked by a uniform, a cap, a badge. Their authority comes from the authority of their office, not from anything about them as particular people.

Legitimacy can be created by the actions of the institution or individuals. One of the primary ways examined in research that legitimacy is created in the minds of people is through authorities' use of pair procedures. This means by making decisions via neutral procedures and by treating people fairly and with respect, ideas referred to in the psychological literature as procedural justice (Tyler, 2009). The centrality of procedural justice to legitimacy suggests that policy makers can effectively create and maintain legitimacy and can, therefore, enact strategies based upon legitimacy (Tyler, 2009).

Moral Values

The second social value we are discussing is personal morality—the motivation to behave in accord with one's sense of what is appropriate and right to do in a given situation. The influence of moral values is based on the internalization of feelings of responsibility to follow principles of personal morality (see Robinson & Darley, 1995). A core element of moral values is that people feel a personal responsibility to follow those values and feel guilty when they fail to do so. Hence, moral values, once they exist, are self-regulatory in character, and those who have such values are personally motivated to bring their conduct into line with their moral standards. And, like the social value of legitimacy, morality is internal and shapes actions distinct from consideration of being caught and punished for wrongdoing. What unites the study of legitimacy and morality? In both cases, the key is that people accept as their own feelings of responsibility and obligation for their actions in society.

These feelings about the morality of particular behaviors also shape people's rule-following behavior. People are less likely to obey laws not consistent with their moral values (Tyler, 2006b). Further, discrepancies can generalize beyond a particular law and shape adherence to a broader range of laws. This can pose problems for the legal system, but looked at from the other direction people are more willing to comply with the law to the extent that they view it as consistent with their moral values; their internalized sense of morality acts as a force for law abidingness (e.g., Robinson & Darley, 1995; Tyler, 2006a).

Robinson and Darley (1995) and Finkel (1995) show gaps between law and public morality. To the extent that such gaps are widely known, they would undermine public compliance with the law. The law can enlist people's moral values as a motivational force supporting deference to the law by pursuing ends that people view as moral. They argue that the law is less likely to be able to call upon people's moral motivations to support the legal system when its values are viewed as discrepant from those of the public. Hence, the law can engage moral values when and if the law is consistent with the moral values held by the public.

Building upon moral values requires first that people have moral values and that they are widely shared within the community. It is precisely this issue that forms the focus of public concern, with the lack of common moral values seen as a problem, and the building of moral values seen as the best long-term solution to issues of crime. Here, we suggest, public views and our arguments converge. We join the public in arguing that creating moral values is the best approach to exercising social control. How do you build such values? One focus should be upon childhood socialization because, as we have indicated, psychological research supports the importance of socializing values in children. And that developmental literature is directed at moral values. Second, studies of adults suggest that procedural justice, which as we have noted increases legitimacy, also increases moral value congruence. If legal authorities enforce the law using fair procedures, people also infer that they share their moral values (Tyler & Blader, 2005).

Values Advantages Over Instrumental Approaches

In empirical studies of the general population, legitimacy and morality are found to be as or more important in shaping compliance than instrumental approaches. Tyler (2006a, 2006b, 2009), for example, compared the risk of deterrence to that of legitimacy and moral value congruence and found that both values were stronger predictors of compliance than was estimated risk. In other words, when these alternative value-based models are compared to deterrence, the alternative models are found to be stronger. Further, studies find that results "consistent with a large body of research that shows than when other inhibitions are strong (such as those provided by one's moral beliefs), the deterrent effect of sanction threats are irrelevant [to whether adolescents and young adults engage in criminal behavior]" (Wright, Caspi, Moffit, & Paternoster, 2004, p. 206).

In other words, when people have values, such as their morality or belief in an institution's legitimacy, risk calculations may become less relevant or even irrelevant to their behavioral calculations. Tyler (2005) similarly found that values and risk perceptions interacted in shaping peoples' everyday law-related behavior, with risk calculations assuming a smaller role in behavioral choices when values were important. Further, values are more important than sanctions in shaping both the voluntary acceptance of rules and willing cooperation with legal authorities. Because voluntary acceptance and cooperation are gains to the legal system, self-regulation is a superior strategy.

Given the positive effects of values on influencing behavior, we think policy should include promotion of legitimacy and moral values as approaches to preventing and dealing with crime. There have been institutions that have beneficially moved from instrumental approaches toward self-regulation based upon values, as demonstrated in the research on business (Tyler & Blader, 2005). Employee behavior was traditionally thought of as being shaped by command and control models in which authorities shaped actions by providing rewards and/or threatening punishments, but it has been recognized within the regulatory community that more self-regulatory models are important and that businesses need to tap into the values that exist within their workplaces, drawing upon employees own motivations to follow rules and policies in their workplace. Such self-regulatory approaches have the advantage we have noted—they minimize surveillance costs and maximize behavior based upon employee values (see Tyler, Dienhart, & Thomas, 2007). Hence, efforts to deal with recent corporate crises should focus on building value-based cultures in work organizations.

The average employee might, understandably, be seen by the public as quite different from the average person in contact with the criminal justice system. We would not argue that a self-regulation model will prevent all crime, just as the deterrence model cannot prevent murders even when its detection and punishment rates are high. And we would not argue that punishment and instrumental methods should never be used; for one thing, people have reactions to extreme injustice, and deterrence is not the only reason for the use of punishment. But once a crime has been committed, if just putting people in jail or prison does not lower the rate of reoffending, what can be done? Many strategies of rehabilitation focus on reconnecting people with their values and their ties to society and its rules and authorities (Braithwaite, 2002; Tyler, 2006c) and by building social ties and encouraging the development and engagement of values (Gendreau, 1996).

Developing Values

A large psychological literature speaks to the idea of value socialization in childhood (see Chapter 3). That literature makes clear that it is possible to socialize values and that doing so shapes both adolescent and adult law-related behavior. Further, specific approaches to value development have been identified and proven to be effective. Hence, it is possible enact the public's agenda with considerable confidence of success.

The more challenging issue—in the public's mind, at least—is to get adults who have committed crimes to develop and act on their values. Is this possible to do once a person is beyond childhood? Public opinion seems to be skeptical, but research suggests that many approaches to rehabilitation are successful. While Part III of this book will address in greater detail specific strategies to reduce recidivism, for the purposes of arguing that values can be engaged in such a population we will point out a few methods and findings in this area of research relevant to our arguments about the contexts that succeed and fail at steering people away from crime.

One specific approach of a successful program is restorative justice. Restorative justice involves conferences that include the offender, the offender's family, the victim, and members of the community. At the conference all of those involved discuss the offender's behavior, the offender acknowledges responsibility for wrongdoing, and the group crafts an approach to restoring justice. The focus is on a "bad behavior, good person" approach in which those present seek to reconnect the offender to his or her values, with the goal of motivating the offender to want to follow the rules in the future. The restorative justice approach seeks ways to heighten the offender's future motivations to engage psychologically and behaviorally in society. This engagement includes developing or becoming more committed to social values that promote self-regulation, and consequently adhering more closely to laws and social regulations in the future, that is, to lower levels of rearrest. In other words, one important goal is being able to create better community members. Research results support the facilitative role of restorative justice conferences (Roberts & Stalans, 2004; Sherman, 1999). Studies suggest that, at least with regard to some types of crime such as those committed by juveniles who have social ties, participating in a restorative justice conference leads to greater cooperation with the law in the future (Bradshaw, Roseborough, & Umbriet, 2006; Latimer, Dowden, & Muise, 2005; Nugent, Williams, & Umbreit, 2003; Poulson, 2003). Such conferences, it seems, do increase the motivation to accept the law and the decisions of legal authorities and to be a law-abiding citizen.

Latimer, Dowden, and Muise (2005) directly examined evidence concerning the impact of restorative justice on recidivism in adults. They concluded that in approximately two-thirds of the programs studied, restorative justice programs "yielded reductions in recidivism compared to nonrestorative approaches to criminal behavior" (p. 137), a difference which they found statistically significant. While these authors do not examine the psychological mechanisms by which these effects occur, we argue that they are using approaches consistent with our argument for an increased focus on values and a less singular focus on instrumental approaches.

Of course, we do not want to overstate our case. Studies suggest that rehabilitation is most successful among adolescents. It can be effective among adults, but results are weaker. We know it is most difficult to change "hardened" criminals such as violent or career offenders. Is it possible to do so at all? Research reviewed elsewhere in this volume suggests that the answer is yes.

We noted at the beginning that it is almost as if the public sees criminals as different and not subject to motivations related to values. Evidence addressing some aspects of this view contradicts these beliefs and shows that this group is sensitive to issues of values. For example, Casper, Tyler, and Fisher (1988) analyzed the results of a panel study of defendants arrested for felonies, defendants who were generally young, minority, and male, demographic characteristics that are common among much of the population in contact with criminal justice in the United States. They found that the evaluations of the procedural justice of the case disposition process made by these defendants had a strong influence upon both their satisfaction with their experiences and was the primary factor shaping their generalization from their personal experience to their overall views about the legitimacy of the law and the legal system. And elsewhere we have argued that legitimacy corresponds with rule-following behavior. Other studies similarly suggest that procedural justice plays an important role in shaping the attitudes and behaviors of "criminals" (see Tyler, 2009).

Summary

The general message of this chapter is that law enforcement and the public have ambivalently embraced an instrumental approach, that is, the threat of or actual punishment as a mechanism through which to shape the behavior of both wrongdoers and people in general. This is not to say that others approaches do not exist, or that people do not disagree; however, the dominant model clearly follows instrumental approaches. We have argued that not only does empirical research show that this approach is not particularly effective in determining behavior, but it also is very costly in terms of both resources and negative side effects. Hence, there is a widespread disconnect between policy and empiricism. It has led to a dramatic growth in the American prison population and has soured the relationship between the law, legal authorities, and the members of society. It has had a particularly negative impact on the minority community.

Given these problems it is important to emphasize that there are alternatives to a solely instrumental approach. In particular, we point to a series of findings that suggest the importance of focusing on values, an approach which has the goal of enhancing self-regulation. But the main purpose of considering these issues is to ask whether alternatives to instrumental approaches that do receive empirical support can actually be implemented with public support or at least without widespread resistance. That is, one problem lies in public punitiveness—the support of the public for harsh punishment. These public views are linked to public conceptions of human nature. In particular, the issue is whether people believe that people can develop and act on values.

The public seems to generally favor and see the potential of approaches that build values and mutual respect among members of the public. The findings of Tyler and Boeckmann (1997) suggest that people support efforts to build values and rely on self-regulation methods to prevent crime. Thus, policy makers would do well to focus on building on these existing beliefs of people in order to shift from dependency on a purely surveillance deterrence model to a model that encourages the development and activation of moral values and beliefs in the legitimacy of the legal system (Tyler, 2009).

The core to the effectiveness of a value-based strategy is value socialization. Studies show it works, but they clearly suggest that it works most effectively among children and adolescents. The socialization of adults is harder and the socialization of rule breakers may be especially difficult. While rehabilitation can work, it is not an optimum place to start.

Further, policy changes related to rehabilitation face more resistance from the public. Of course, additional research is clearly needed to establish the nature of punitive attitudes, but the findings of Tyler and Boeckmann (1997) suggest that the public does not see rehabilitation as feasible, especially for violent adult offenders. Thus, in the case of the rehabilitation of adults who are already criminals, policy makers would not be able to rely solely on emphasizing certain aspects of the existing attitudes of the public and instead would have to focus more on communicating to people that there are methods that *are* effective or that the preventative measures the public abstractly support *can* also be applied to reducing recidivism. And, of course, that would be more difficult because the research evidence is less strikingly positive for programs aimed at adult offenders.

Is value creation a panacea that can increase law abidingness among everyone? No, it is not. Public skepticism is justified to a degree. But we suggest that it is clearly a superior strategy in general, particularly when societies begin with a focus on value creation during childhood and adolescence and do not wait until people have already offended to attempt to create or reactivate values. While restoration can occur, it is not as effective as is a strategy focused on value creation prior to offending. And the public reveals considerable awareness of these distinctions. As a result, the public supports the superior strategy of childhood value creation when it feels that effectively implementing such a strategy is feasible.

References

Blasi, A. (1980). Bridging moral cognition and moral action. *Psychological Bulletin, 88,* 1–45.

Bradshaw, W., Roseborough, D., & Umbriet, M. S. (2006). The effects of victim offender mediation on juvenile offender recidivism. *Journal of Conflict Resolution, 24,* 87–98.

Braithwaite, J. (2002). *Restorative justice and responsive regulation.* Oxford, England: Oxford University Press.

Carlsmith, K. M. (2006). The roles of retribution and utility in determining punishment. *Journal of Experimental Social Psychology, 42*, 437–451.

Casper, J. D., Tyler, T., & Fisher, B. (1988). Procedural justice in felony cases. *Law and Society Review, 22*(3), 483–507.

Deci, E. L. (1975). *Intrinsic motivation.* New York: Plenum Press.

Ellsworth, P. C., & Gross, S. R. (1994). Hardening of the attitudes: Americans' views on the death penalty. *Journal of Social Issues, 50*, 19–52.

Ellsworth, P. C., & Mauro, R. (1998). Psychology and law. In D. T. Gilbert, S. T. Fiske, & G. Lindzey (Eds.), *Handbook of social psychology* (pp. 684–732). New York: McGraw Hill.

Fine, S. E., Trentacosta, C. J., Izard, C. E., Mastow, A. J., & Campbell, J. L. (2004). Anger perception, caregivers' use of physical discipline, and aggression in children at risk. *Social Development, 13*, 213–228.

Finkel, N. J. (1995). *Commonsense justice: Juror's notions of the law.* Cambridge, MA: Harvard University Press.

Garland, D. (2001). *The culture of control.* Chicago: University of Chicago Press.

Gendreau, P. (1996). The principles of effective intervention with offenders. In A. T. Harland (Ed.), *Choosing correctional interventions that work: Defining the demand and evaluating the supply* (pp. 117–130). Newbury Park, CA: Sage.

Gershoff, E. T., & Bitensky, S. H. (2007). The case against corporal punishment of children. *Psychology, Public Policy, and Law, 13*, 231–272.

Gurr, T. R. (1970). *Why men rebel.* Princeton, NJ: Princeton University Press.

Haney, C., & Zimbardo, P. (1998). The past and future of U.S. prison policy: Twenty-five years after the Stanford prison experiment. *American Psychologist, 53*, 709–727.

Harcourt, B. E., & Ludwig, J. (2006). Broken windows: New evidence for NYC and a five-city social experiment. *University of Chicago Law Review, 73*, 271–320.

Hoffman, L. W. (1977). Changes in family roles, socialization and sex differences. *American Psychologist, 32*, 644–657.

Hoffman, M. L. (2000). *Empathy and moral development: Implications for caring and justice.* Cambridge, England: Cambridge University Press.

Jurkovic, G. J. (1980). The juvenile delinquent as a moral philosopher: A structural-developmental perspective. *Psychological Bulletin, 88*, 709–727.

Kramer, R. M., & Tyler, T. R. (Eds.). (1996). *Trust in organizations.* Thousand Oaks, CA: Sage.

Latimer, J., Dowden, C., & Muise, D. (2005). The effectiveness of restorative justice practices. *The Prison Journal, 85*, 127–144.

Lipsey, M. W., & Cullen, F. T. (2007). The effectiveness of correctional rehabilitation: A review of systematic reviews. *Annual Review of Law and Social Science, 3*, 297–320.

Lynch, J. P., & Sabol, W. J. (1997). *Did getting tough on crime pay?* Crime Policy Report. Washington, DC: American University, The Urban Institute.

MacCoun, R. J. (1993). Drugs and the law: A psychological analysis of drug prohibition. *Psychological Bulletin, 113*, 497–512.

McCord, J., Widom, C. S., & Crowell, N. A. (2001). *Juvenile justice.* Committee on Law and Justice, National Research Council, Juvenile Justice. Washington, D.C.

Meares, T. L. (2000). Norms, legitimacy, and law enforcement. *Oregon Law Review, 79*, 391–415.

Mendel, R. A. (2002). *Less hype, more help: Reducing juvenile crime: What works and what doesn't.* Washington, DC: National Urban League, American Youth Policy Forum.

Nagin, D. S. (1998). Criminal deterrence at the onset of the 21st century. *Crime and Justice, 23,* 1–42.

Nugent, W., Williams, M., & Umbreit, M. S. (2003). Participation in victim-offender mediation and the prevalence and severity of subsequent delinquent behavior. *Utah Law Review, 2003,* 137–166.

Paternoster, R. (1987). The deterrent effect of the perceived certainty and severity of punishment: A review of the evidence and issues. *Justice Quarterly, 4*(2), 173–217.

Patillo, M., Weiman, D., & Western, B. (Eds.). (2004). Imprisoning America: The social effects of mass incarceration. New York: Russell-Sage.

Pew Center for the States. (2008). One in 100: Behind bars in America. *Pew's Public Safety Performance Project.* Washington, D.C. www.pewcenteronthestate.org.

Poulson, B. (2003). A third voice: A review of empirical research on the psychological outcomes of restorative justice. *Utah Law Review, 2003,* 167–203.

Pratt, T. C., Cullen, F. T., Blevins, K. R., Daigle, L. E., & Madensen, T. D. (2008). The empirical status of deterrence theory: A meta-analysis. In F. T. Cullen, J. P. Wright, & K. R. Blevins (Eds.), *Taking stock: The status of criminological theory* (pp. 367–396). New Brunswick, NJ: Transaction.

Reiss, A. J. (1971). *The police and the public.* New Haven, CT: Yale University Press.

Roberts, J. V., & Stalans, L. J. (2004). Restorative sentencing: Exploring the views of the public. *Social Justice Research, 17,* 315–334.

Robinson, P. H., & Darley, J. (1995). *Justice, liability, and blame.* Boulder, CO: Westview.

Robinson, P. H., & Darley, J. (1997). The utility of desert. *Northwestern University Law Review, 91,* 453–499.

Ross, H. L. (1982). *Deterring the drinking driver: Legal policy and social control.* Lexington, MA: Lexington Books.

Sherman, L. (1999, January). *Consent of the governed*: Police, democracy and diversity Presentation at the Law School of Hebrew University. Jerusalem.

Skogan, W. G., & Frydl, K. (Eds.). (2004). *Fairness and effectiveness in policing: The evidence.* Washington, DC: The National Academies Press.

Strickland, L. H. (1958). Surveillance and trust. *Journal of Personality, 26,* 200–215.

Sunshine, J., & Tyler, T. R. (2003). The role of procedural justice and legitimacy in shaping public support for policing. *Law and Society Review, 37*(3), 555–589.

Tangney, J. P., & Dearing, R. L. (2002). *Shame and guilt.* Oxford, England: Oxford University Press.

Tonry, M. (1999). Why are US incarceration rates so high? *Crime and Delinquency, 45,* 419–437.

Turiel, E. (1987). Potential relations between the development of social reasoning and childhood aggression. In D. H. Crowell, I. M. Evans, & C. R. O'Connell (Eds.), *Childhood aggression and violence* (pp. 95–114). New York: Plenum.

Tyler, T. R. (2005). Managing conflicts of interest within organizations: Does activating social values change the impact of self-interest on behavior.

In D. Moore, D. Cain, G. Loewenstein, & M. Bazerman (Eds.), *Conflicts of interest* (pp. 13–35). Cambridge, England: Cambridge University Press.

Tyler, T. R. (2006a). Legitimacy and legitimation. *Annual Review of Psychology, 57,* 375–400.

Tyler, T. R. (2006b). *Why people obey the law.* Princeton, NJ: Princeton University Press.

Tyler, T. R. (2006c). Restorative justice and procedural justice: Dealing with rule breaking. *Journal of Social Issues, 62,* 307–326.

Tyler, T. R. (2009). *Legitimacy and criminal justice: The benefits of self-regulation.* Reckless/Dinize Memorial Lecture. Retrieved from http://moritzlaw.osu.edu/osjcl/Articles/Volume7_1/Tyler-FinalPDf.pdf

Tyler, T. R., & Blader, S. L. (2005). Can businesses effectively regulate employee conduct?: The antecedents of rule following in work settings. *Academy of Management Journal, 48,* 1143–1158.

Tyler, T. R., & Boeckmann, R. J. (1997). Three strikes and you are out, but why? The psychology of public support for punishing rule breakers. *Law and Society Review, 31,* 237–265.

Tyler, T. R., Dienhart, J., & Thomas, T. (2007). The ethical commitment to compliance. *California Management Review, 50,* 31–51.

Tyler, T. R., & Huo, Y. (2002). *Trust in the law.* New York: Russell-Sage.

United States Department of Justice, Bureau of Justice Statistics. (2001). *Prisoners in 2000.* Washington, DC: US Department of Justice

Vidmar, N., & Miller, D. T. (1980). The social psychology of punishment. *Law and Society Review, 14,* 565–602.

Weisberg, R. (2005). The death penalty meets social science. *Annual Review of Law and Social Science, 1,* 151–170.

Wright, B. R. E., Caspi, A., Moffitt, T. E., & Paternoster, R. (2004). Does the perceived risk of punishment deter criminally prone individuals? *Journal of Research in Crime and Delinquency, 41,* 180–213.

Zimring, F. E., & Johnson, D. T. (2006). Public opinion and the governance of punishment in democratic political systems. *The Annals of the American Academy of Political and Social Science, 605,* 265–280.

Part III

IMPROVING OUR APPROACH TO
INDIVIDUAL OFFENDERS

6

The Risk-Need-Responsivity (RNR) Model of Correctional Assessment and Treatment

D. A. (Don) Andrews

There has been an extraordinary expansion of correctional supervision and incarceration in many Western countries, including the United States. The growth in correctional populations may be traced at least in part to the collapse of support in the 1970s for "rehabilitation," that is, reducing crime by intervening to change something about offenders or their circumstances. As support for a punishment model grew, "nothing works" became the dominant perspective. This perspective began to change in the late 1980s, partially because influential reviews of research increased understanding of (*a*) the characteristics of people and their circumstances that are robust risk factors for involvement in criminal activity, and (*b*) the major factors of correctional intervention programs that "work" in deliberate efforts to reduce crime.

This chapter presents the "Risk-Need-Responsivity" (RNR) model of correctional assessment and treatment in three major sections. The first section outlines principles of effective crime reduction, referencing research on major risk factors for crime and "what works" to reduce it. The second section highlights gaps in the knowledge base for policy and practice. The third section enumerates implications for (*a*) the supervision and treatment of individual offenders and (*b*) the system-level structuring of correctional systems or programs. Because specialization in particular types of crime is very unusual and the predictors of violent and nonviolent crime are very similar, this chapter considers general offending rather than violent offending in particular. To facilitate understanding, a glossary is provided (see Appendix A) to define key terms (e.g., dynamic risk factors or criminogenic needs) and statistics (e.g., the Pearson product moment correlation coefficient as a measure of effect size).

Distilling Evidence About "What Works" in Corrections

The dominant model of "what works" is the RNR model of correctional assessment and correctional interventions (Ogloff & Davis, 2004). The RNR model is based on a summary of what psychology knows about changing human behavior, with specific attention to criminal behavior. That is, RNR is closely connected to General Personality and Cognitive Social Learning (GPCSL) models of human behavior. GPCSL models are holistic, interdisciplinary, and open to the full range of potential factors, including biological, personal, interpersonal, familial, structural, and cultural. Although a review of the model is beyond the scope of this chapter, which focuses more narrowly on RNR, Andrews and Bonta (2010) show that no perspective more strongly explains the acquisition, maintenance, and modification of human behavior in the context of both moment-to-moment functioning and deliberate intervention programs.

Introduction to the Principles of Risk-Need-Responsivity

An initial reading of Appendix B, which provides an overview of the RNR principles of effective assessment and intervention, will greatly enhance understanding of this chapter. In this section, I introduce the core and overarching principles of RNR.

The core RNR principles are based on research findings, which are summarized in the next section of this chapter. First of these core principles, "Introduce Human Service" (Principle 4, Appendix B), is an explicit recognition that sole reliance on principles of justice will not enhance crime reduction efforts. The remaining three principles are the crux of RNR itself. According to the *risk principle* (Principle 5, Appendix B), nothing positive in terms of crime prevention can be derived from delivering services to persons who are at low risk of reoffending in the absence of service. The effect will be nil at best and an increase in offending at worst. It is the recidivism of higher risk cases that will be reduced through the delivery of appropriate services. According to the *need principle*, for purposes of crime prevention, it is important for services to target changeable risk factors for crime or "criminogenic needs" predominately (Principle 6, Appendix B) and with consideration of breadth (Principle 9). The *responsivity principle* (Principle 7) holds that services will best prevent crime, if they are delivered in a manner that fits the learning styles of offenders generally (e.g., cognitive-behavioral and other structured skill-building approaches), as well as specific characteristics of individuals (e.g., gender-, age-, cognitive-skill level, or motivation-specific approaches).

Unlike the core RNR principles, the overarching principles of RNR are fundamentally value based, in the sense that they refer to the normative context of assessment and intervention. Adherence with normative principles is expected regardless of whether that adherence reduces crime. Principle 1 is "Respect for the Person and the Normative Context" (Appendix B). Correctional programming, like medical and social services, is expected to be offered with respect for the person and to be delivered in ethical, decent, legal, and otherwise normative ways. Respect for personal autonomy is particularly important in service delivery within corrections because so much in justice is about control, coercion, surveillance, deterrence, and discipline. Because norms may vary with settings, mental health agents may want to combine crime reduction efforts with a commitment to the reduction of emotional distress. Likewise, feminist-based programs may attend to trauma along with pursuit of reduced crime through attention to factors that are more strongly linked with criminal activity.

Principle 2, "Psychological Theory" (see Appendix B), suggests that crime prevention activities are best based on an understanding of the criminal conduct of individuals rather than theories of community-wide crime rates or theories of justice. In terms of justice, the values of due process, just desert, restoration, general deterrence, and incapacitation may all be respected on normative grounds but, empirically, none of them are very helpful when it comes to reducing the postsanction criminal futures of offenders. Likewise, the correlates of aggregated crime rates are often misleading with reference to understanding risk/need factors in the prediction of the criminal recidivism of individual offenders.

Principle 3, "General Enhancement of Crime Prevention Services" (see Appendix B), recognizes that crime prevention should not be viewed as the responsibility only of justice and correctional agencies. The reduction of crime may come to be viewed as a legitimate pursuit of agencies and agents in the health, youth, family, marital, substance abuse, and social domains of human and clinical services. In conjunction with Principle 1, there is every reason to believe that effective crime prevention programs—programs in adherence with the RNR principles—may be delivered in ethical and humane ways outside of justice and corrections. Of course, this will occur only if crime prevention activities are seen as normatively appropriate. Before discussing the clinical principles of RNR, a brief look at the research literature will be helpful.

Supporting Research: Major Risk Factors for Crime

The research base for RNR includes many systematic quantitative reviews (or "meta-analyses") of relevant literatures on *(1)* predictors of criminal behavior and *(2)* the dimensions of effective correctional treatment. The number of primary studies involved is in the thousands for studies of risk/need factors and in the hundreds for controlled studies of effective correctional interventions. To complete a meta-analysis, researchers compute an effect size for each primary study and then compute the average effect size found for particular risk/need factors or for particular approaches to intervention. Appendix A describes how to interpret the Pearson correlation coefficient as a measure of effect size. Meta-analytic reviews of research allow consideration of the absolute and relative predictive power of different risk/need factors and the absolute and relative crime prevention effects of different intervention approaches. Methodological and other study characteristics may be explored as potential moderators of the effect sizes. In this section, I summarize the results of meta-analytic research on major risk factors for crime. The dimensions of effective correctional treatment will be presented in the section that follows.

Some readers may be surprised to learn that even in the early 1990s, a survey identified over 1,000 studies of the correlates and predictors of crime and meta-analyses of 372 of those studies yielded more than 1,770 estimates of the magnitude of association between the potential predictors of crime and a measure of criminal activity (Gendreau, Little, and Goggin, 1996). Based on the existing literature, it is now possible to summarize the findings of hundreds of primary studies and multiple meta-analyses of the predictors of crime (see Andrews & Bonta, 2010; McGuire, 2004).

Table 6.1 provides a narrative summary of the best-established risk/need factors, which Andrews and Bonta (2010) call "the Central Eight." The first four of these factors (the Big Four) are strongly associated with various measures of recidivism, and the second four are moderately associated with this outcome. Two points are noteworthy. First, although each of the eight risk factors is described separately, measures within the Central Eight are intercorrelated in theory and in fact. Antisocial personality pattern, in particular, shares many links with the other factors. This pattern represents emotional and behavioral tendencies that are evident in a variety of situations and contexts. As suggested in Table 6.1, two fundamental dimensions of this pattern are "low conscientiousness—low constraint" and "low agreeableness—negative emotionality." These two major trait constellations are associated with: an antisocial behavioral history; antisocial attitudes, values, and beliefs; and differential interpersonal association patterns, rewards, and satisfactions in the domains of family, school, work, and leisure. Second, each of the eight risk factors is addressable through intervention, as the last column of Table 6.1 suggests. For example, Cognitive Self Change (Bush, 1995) may enable the person to build low-risk cognitions in high-risk circumstances. Similarly, developments in understanding self-regulation (Vohs, Baumeister, & Ciaroco, 2005) open up opportunities for interventions that build expectations, plans, and strategies that are favorable to prosocial activity (Mischel & Ayduk, 2004; Mischel & Shoda, 1995). Reform-oriented narratives and personal identities (see Maruna, LeBel, Mitchell, & Naples, 2004) are additional potential foci.

Panel A of Table 6.2 provides average effect size estimates from primary research studies for each member of the Central Eight, for the pooled estimates

Table 6.1 Major Risk Factors for Recidivism: The Central Eight

	Definition	Strength	Intervention Target
The Big Four			
History of antisocial behavior	Early involvement in a number and variety of antisocial activities in a variety of settings. Major indicators include being arrested at a young age, large number of prior offenses, and rule violations while on conditional release. In assessing this risk factor, place little weight on the seriousness or amount of injury imposed by the current offense.	Antisocial behavior is absent or so rare that procriminal contributions to antisocial attitudes will be minimal.	Building new noncriminal behaviors in high-risk situations. Building self-efficacy beliefs supporting reform ("I know what to do to avoid criminal activity and know I can do what is required").
Antisocial personality pattern	Impulsive, adventurous, pleasure seeking, generalized trouble (with multiple persons across many settings), restlessly aggressive, callous disregard for others. Specific definitions emphasize, for example, (a) weak constraint, negative emotionality, and angry stress reaction (Patrick, Curtin, & Tellegen, 2002); or (b) low agreeableness and low conscientiousness (Digman, 1990; Miller & Lynam, 2001).	High restraint, thinks before acting, highly agreeable.	Build skills in self-control, anger management, and problem solving.
Antisocial cognition	Attitudes, values, beliefs, rationalizations, and a personal identity that is favorable to crime. Cognitive-emotional states associated with crime are anger, irritation, resentment, and defiance. Specific indicators include identification with criminals, negative attitudes toward the law and justice system, a belief that crime will yield rewards, and rationalizations that specify a broad range of conditions under which crime is justified (e.g., the victim deserved it, the victim is worthless).	Rejects antisocial sentiments; personal identity is explicitly anticriminal and prosocial.	Reduce antisocial thinking and feeling. Build and practice less risky thoughts and feelings.

(*Continued*)

Table 6.1 (Cont'd)

	Definition	Strength	Intervention Target
Antisocial associates	Includes both association with procriminal others and relative isolation from anticriminal others. Sometimes called "social support for crime."	Close and frequent association with anticriminal others; no association with criminal others.	Reduce association with procriminal others. Enhance association with anticriminal others.
The Moderate Four			
Family/ marital circumstances	In the family of origin (for youth) or marital relationship (for adults), there is (a) poor relationship quality and (b) few expectations that the person will avoid criminal behavior. For youth, parents may provide poor nurturance/caring and poor monitoring/supervision. Also, the young person may care little about the parent or the parent's opinions. For adults, the marital relationship or its equivalent may have little mutual caring, respect, and interest, or neutral or even procriminal behavioral expectations.	Strong nurturance caring in combination with strong monitoring and supervision.	Reduce conflict, build positive relationships, enhance monitoring and supervision.
School/work	Poor quality of interpersonal relationships within the settings of school and/or work. Low levels of performance and involvement in these settings, as well as low levels of rewards and satisfactions.	Strong attachments to fellow students or colleagues and authority figures. High performance and satisfaction at school/work.	Enhance performance, involvement, and rewards and satisfactions.
Leisure/ recreation	Low levels of involvement and satisfactions in anticriminal leisure pursuits.	High levels of involvement in and satisfaction in anticriminal leisure pursuits.	Enhance involvement and rewards and satisfactions.

Table 6.1 (Cont'd)

	Definition	Strength	Intervention Target
Substance abuse	Problems with alcohol and/or other drugs (tobacco excluded). Current problems with substances indicate higher risk than a prior history of abuse.	No evidence of risky substance abuse and sentiments tend to be negative toward substance abuse.	Reduce substance abuse. Reduce personal and interpersonal supports for substance-oriented behavior. Enhance alternatives to substance abuse.

Source: From Andrews and Bonta (2006, 2010).

Table 6.2 Utility of the Central Eight Versus Other Factors in Predicting Recidivism

Factor	Mean r	98% Confidence Interval	k
A. The Big Four			
History of antisocial behavior	.25	.18–.32	8
Antisocial personality pattern	.24	.15–.34	6
Antisocial attitudes	.27	.13–.40	6
Antisocial associates	.28	.18–.39	4
Total	.26	.22–.30	24
B. The Moderate Four			
Family/marital	.17	.11–.24	8
Education/employment	.18	.11–.25	8
Leisure/recreation	.21	—	1
Substance abuse	.13	.04–.21	6
Total	.17	.13–.20	23
C. Composites of the Central Eight			
LSI-R (women)	.35	.34–.36	27
LSI-R (men)	.36	—	4 meta-an.
LS/CMI (mixed sex)	.41	.34–.47	19

Factor	Mean r	Partial r, controlling for LSI-R[a]
D. Minor Risk Factors Emphasized in Criminological Models (Critical, Feminist, Humanistic, Sociological)[b]		
Gender (being male)	.12	.09
Age (being younger)	.10	.06
Ethnicity (being non-white)	.06	.00
Lower class origins	.06	—
Poverty/financial problems	.17	.06
Accommodation problems	.16	.03
Victimization/abuse history	.09	–.03
Emotional distress	.11	–.01

[a]The correlation with Level of Service Risk/Need controlled statistically.
[b]Mean estimates from up to eight meta-analyses (Andrews & Bonta, 2010).

of the Big Four, and/or the pooled estimates of the Moderate Four. These estimates are grand means, in that the means were derived from summary statistics reported in up to eight separate meta-analyses. Panel A also includes estimates for the Level of Services Inventory (LSI), a risk assessment tool that is a composite of the major and moderate risk/need factors. The instrument is in wide scale use in corrections. As shown in Table 6.2, the overall estimate for the Big Four is in the mid .20s and that for the Moderate Four is in the high .10s. The estimate for the LSI composites of these variables was in the mid .30s to low .40s.

For comparison purposes, Panel D of Table 6.2 presents average effect size estimates for a set of variables that are often emphasized by a small sub-group of scholars often described as critical criminologists (i.e., Marxist, Socialist, and some feminist perspectives on crime). These scholars object to social location variables such as age, gender, ethnicity, and social class of origin not being on the list of major risk factors. Similarly, some scholars from sociological, humanistic, or forensic psychological perspectives suggest that poverty, accommodation problems, victimization, and/or mental illness should be on the list. As shown in Panel D of Table 6.2, although many of these variables are risk factors, their effects seem to operate through the Central Eight, and particularly through the Big Four. The results for Panel B, like those for Panel A, were computed from up to eight meta-analytic investigations. The grand means varied from the minimal (.06) for lower class origins to the mid .10s for the socioeconomic indicators of financial and housing problems. However, after controlling for the LSI composite measure of the Central Eight, most of these variables added no incremental utility in predicting recidivism (save for being male and, for males, being of young age or white). Poverty, housing problems, abuse history, and emotional distress carried little or no predictive information not already carried by the Central Eight factors. According to the *need principle* of the RNR model, these Central Eight risk factors are prime targets for correctional intervention programs that seek to reduce recidivism (see Table 6.1, column 3). I now turn to research on "what works" in correctional intervention.

Supporting Research: Major Dimensions of Effective Correctional Interventions

The number of meta-analyses of the effects of correctional treatment was approximately 40 between 1989 and the publication of McGuire's (2004) textbook. The number is likely now over 60. The vast majority of these quantitative reviews have focused on the effectiveness of particular types of programming (e.g., family therapy, cognitive-behavioral therapy, boot camps). Although these reviews are helpful to clinicians and managers when they are considering various program possibilities, they are limited in that they fail to convey that the success of any program is dependent upon how well the implementation adheres with the principles of RNR.

According to Lipsey (2009), only two groups of researchers have concentrated on exploring the characteristics of effective programming that may apply across a range of particular types of programs—Mark Lipsey and his colleagues and D.A. Andrews and his colleagues. The two approaches are quite different. Mark Lipsey is atheoretical in his approach, focusing more on methodological considerations in meta-analysis (e.g., adjusting effect size estimates for sample size) than on any particular theory of criminal conduct or correctional treatment. In contrast, Andrews and colleagues are closely associated with GPCSL perspectives and prefer to work with simple unadjusted effect size estimates, then exploring whether factors like sample size affect the magnitude of effect size estimates.

Despite differences between the approaches of the two groups, it is clear that they agree on several important conclusions. First, there is agreement that programming that is human service-oriented (i.e., remedial, curative, clinical, or therapeutic) reduces recidivism, whereas punishment-oriented approaches yield nil through crime-inducing effects (in keeping with RNR Principle 4, see Appendix B). Second, the crime reduction effects of human service (i.e., those that attend to criminogenic needs) are strongest when the services *(a)* are delivered to higher risk cases (in support of the RNR Principle 5, Appendix B) and *(b)* employ behavioral and social learning strategies (in support RNR Principle 7, Appendix B). Third, both groups agree that these findings are true across different genders, ethnicities, and age groups and across different correctional settings (although human service programming is particularly effective in community-based corrections, in support of RNR Principle 13, Appendix B). Fourth, there is agreement that evaluations conducted by persons involved in the design or delivery of service yield higher levels of crime reduction effects. Although this is probably partly explained by experimenter bias, it is probably also because an involved evaluator promotes higher levels of fidelity to the model while implementing it. Indeed, several scholars agree that an involved evaluator functions as a proxy measure of program integrity (Andrews & Bonta, 2010; Lipsey, 2009; Petrosino & Soydan, 2005). As this summary suggests, the two groups overlap in their agreement that there is support for some of the principles that underpin the RNR model. Support for each of these principles will now be reviewed directly.

Support for Core RNR Principles

The first core RNR principle, "Introduce Human Service" (Principle 4, Appendix B), is an explicit recognition that sole reliance on principles of justice will not enhance crime reduction efforts. Studies that rely on specific deterrence have failed to establish significant and replicable reductions in criminal reoffending (see Andrews & Bonta, 2006, 2009; McGuire, 2004). Most recently, Lipsey (2009) convincingly demonstrated that "therapeutic" interventions were more effective in reducing the recidivism of young offenders than were interventions based on control, surveillance, deterrence, and discipline. As shown in Figure 6.1, the average effect of more punishment is an *increase* of 3% in recidivism relative to less punishment (i.e., a mean *r* of –.03 across 101 tests). In contrast, the average effect of some human service in a justice context is a decrease of 12% in recidivism relative to no or less human service (averaged across 273 tests). Clearly, on average, the introduction of human service is associated with reduced recidivism.

Of course, some forms of service have greater crime prevention potential than others. According to the three core RNR principles of risk, need, and general responsivity (Principles 5–7, Appendix B), services will have greater effects when they focus on higher risk cases; target dynamic risk factors or criminogenic needs (see Tables 6.1 and 6.2); and use behavioral, cognitive-behavioral, and cognitive social learning strategies. As shown in Panel A of Table 6.3, the effect of cumulative adherence with the human service principles of risk, need, and general responsivity has been demonstrated in meta-analytic reviews of effects on general recidivism, violent recidivism, sexual recidivism, and prison misconducts. Although there are few primary studies on violent offending and sexual offending per se, the pattern of findings is supportive of RNR adherence. For general recidivism, where the most data are available, the effect of providing any human service is .12 (Fig. 6.1) but reaches .26 with high adherence to RNR (Table 6.3, first row).

Panel B of Table 6.3 shows that the degree of adherence to the RNR principles corresponds to the degree of reduction in general recidivism across a variety of correctional settings (e.g., probation, prison) and across restorative and nonrestorative models of justice. Restorative justice approaches focus on repairing the harm done the victim, restoring the community that may have been disrupted by an offence, and/or holding offenders accountable. Andrews and Bonta (2010) found that the effects of restorative justice programs on recidivism are relatively small (mean *r* = .07, *k* = 80, N = 94,492), though

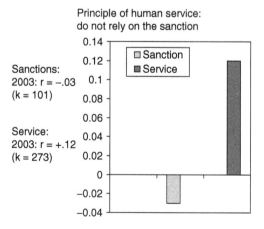

Figure 6.1. Increasing human service (vs. sanctions) increases program effect size.

Table 6.3 Effect Size (r) for Re-Offending by Level of Risk-Need-Responsivity (RNR) Adherence Across Various Contexts

	Level of RNR Adherence				Correlation With Effect Size
A. Type of Outcome	None (k)	Low (k)	Moderate (k)	High (k)	
General recidivism[a]	−.02 (124)	.02 (106)	.18 (84)	.26 (60)	.56
Violent recidivism[b]	−.01 (21)	.07 (11)	.15 (2)	.20 (8)	.56
Sexual recidivism[c]	−.02 (4)	.04 (6)	.07 (12)	.10 (1)	—
Prison misconducts[d]	—	.16 (32)	.20 (24)	.38 (10)	—
B. Correctional Setting/ Justice Model					
Community corrections	.00 (95)	.03 (74)	.22 (50)	.35 (30)	.61
Residential corrections	−.10 (29)	.01 (32)	.12 (34)	.17 (30)	.58
Restorative: No	−.03 (106)	.02 (102)	.18 (81)	.26 (55)	.57
Restorative: Yes	.02 (14)	.14 (4)	.16 (3)	.35 (1)	.59
C. Type of Offender					
Female offenders	.02 (14)	.03 (10)	.17 (9)	.36 (12)	.57
Male offenders	−.03 (110)	.02 (96)	.18 (75)	.24 (48)	.57
White offenders	−.04 (80)	−.03 (84)	.19 (62)	.26 (42)	.60
Non-white offenders	.01 (44)	.00 (22)	.13 (22)	.28 (18)	.48
Young offenders	−.02 (62)	.01 (63)	.20 (39)	.28 (42)	.58
(under 20 years)	−.02 (62)	.05 (43)	.16 (45)	.22 (18)	.53
Adult offenders (20+ years)					
D. Type of Program					
Family therapy	−.02 (6)	.06 (18)	.22 (17)	.40 (17)	.63
Academic	.03 (6)	.07 (20)	.20 (31)	.32 (15)	.47
Vocational	−.05 (5)	.05 (13)	.20 (16)	.38 (10)	.68
Substance abuse	−.06 (5)	.07 (10)	.14 (17)	.30 (4)	.61
Cognitive-behavioral	—	−.10 (01)	.14 (15)	.26 (60)	.36
E. Intermediate Targets					
Noncriminogenic needs Targeted predominately	−.03 (55)	−.00 (59)	.16 (02)	—(0)	.16
Some noncriminogenic Needs targeted	−.03 (62)	.01 (81)	.23 (26)	.24 (11)	.51

[a]Dowden and Andrews (1999).
[b]Dowden and Andrews (2000).
[c]Hanson et al. (2006).
[d]French and Gendreau (2006). RNR coded according to CPAI scores.
Source: Based on Andrews and Dowden (2007) and Andrews and Bonta (2010). k = number of tests of treatment; k = 374.

better than the effects of punishment alone (which tends to *increase* recidivism, as shown in Figure 6.1). However, the data in Table 6.3 indicate that greater effects are obtained through the introduction of services in full adherence with RNR.

The effect of RNR adherence also generalizes across gender, ethnic, and age groups. As shown in Panel C of Table 6.3, reduced reoffending is strongly associated with RNR adherence in programming with female offenders (see also Lipsey, 2009). Such evidence may be leading to a rapprochement between critical feminist and RNR approaches (see Blanchette & Brown, 2006). Consistent with the findings of gender similarities, this table reveals that the core clinical principles of RNR apply equally well with whites and non-whites and with younger and older offenders. The principles of RNR transcend conventional sociodemographic differentiations.

RNR principles also apply effectively across a variety of particular types of programs, as shown in Panel D of Table 6.3. The strong suggestion is that RNR adherence supersedes particular program typologies. Does family counseling work? Do academic and vocational programs work? Does substance abuse treatment work? Does cognitive-behavioral therapy work? They all "work" when moderate and higher risk cases are served, when criminogenic needs are targeted predominately, and when structured behavioral and cognitive social learning influence strategies are employed. Cognitive-behavioral programs tend to yield particularly impressive outcomes. This is not a surprise. As shown in Table 6.3, most of these programs manifest high levels of RNR adherence ($k = 60$ of 76, or 80% programs; Table 6.3). It appears that programmers who chose to employ cognitive social learning strategies (that is, who were in adherence with the principle of general responsivity) also chose to work with the criminogenic needs of higher risk cases.

The only programs whose crime prevention potential was not enhanced significantly by adherence with RNR were those that *predominately* targeted noncriminogenic needs, or factors that do not relate strongly to recidivism (e.g., emotional distress; see Table 6.3, Panel E). Still, RNR clearly enhanced the effectiveness of programs that set *some* noncriminogenic needs as intermediate targets of change. According to the specific responsivity principle (Principle 8, Appendix B), noncriminogenic needs may be targeted for purposes of enhancing motivation or for humanitarian or entitlement reasons. As long as noncriminogenic needs are not targeted predominately, the evidence is highly favorable to programming that is in adherence with RNR core principles. These points are revisited later. In plain words, the data presented in this section indicate that reliance on punishment without introducing human service, delivering services to lower risk cases, concentrating on noncriminogenic factors, or eschewing cognitive-behavioral strategies of change is simply not very "smart," if one aims to reduce criminal recidivism.

(Limited) Support for Specific Responsivity

As suggested earlier, sometimes the specifics of cases and their circumstances demand (or suggest) that certain accommodations be made in the delivery of service (Kazdin & Whitley, 2003). For example, child care services may be provided during treatment sessions, if a female client has child care responsibilities; or crime prevention programming may be preceded by an opportunity to reduce abusive drinking, if a client is frequently intoxicated. The RNR principle of specific responsivity (Principle 8) is straight-forward. When designing supervision and service programs, it is important to build on the strengths of the case and remove or reduce barriers to full participation.

Sometimes, however, specific responsivity concerns are misused as a way to keep doing what has always been done. For example, a focus on relieving mental illness or addressing gender-informed factors (e.g., trauma/victimization, poverty, and emotional problems) may be treated as even more important than adherence with the core RNR principles. Non-criminogenic needs that clinicians enjoy addressing may be declared mistakenly to be specific responsivity factors that demand special attention.

This is problematic for two reasons. First, the evidence in support of specific responsivity is very scattered and has not been summarized through meta-analysis (see Appendix B). Second, once the targeting of noncriminogenic needs becomes dominant, a huge problem arises. Under that condition, programs are virtually never adherent to other RNR principles (i.e., 114 of 116 programs were none-low in adherence; see Table 6.3, Panel E). Those who chose to target noncriminogenic needs also chose to work primarily with low-risk cases and/or employ less than powerful influence strategies. That constitutes crime prevention programming that is decidedly less than "smart" (Petrosino & Soydan, 2005). These "not so smart" programs are predominately found in routine or "real-world" corrections rather than short-term and highly controlled "demonstration projects." Attention to specific responsivity considerations can be rewarding and appropriate at times, but they must not lead to the suspension of adherence to the core clinical RNR considerations.

Support for Breadth in Applying the Need Principle

According to the RNR principle of breadth (Principle 9, Appendix B), the number of criminogenic needs targeted should be great, relative to the number of noncriminogenic needs targeted. In other words, the number of criminogenic needs targeted minus the number of noncriminogenic needs targeted should have a positive value (indicating that criminogenic needs are targeted predominantly). Craig Dowden (1998) coded programs for their targeting of criminogenic and noncriminogenic needs. When reports on correctional programming were silent on the matter of intermediate targets (Lipsey, 2009), the need area (criminogenic or noncriminogenic) was coded absent. The results are shown in Figure 6.4, which reveals that the crime reduction effect is strongly associated with the number of criminogenic needs targeted, relative to noncriminogenic needs. This provides support for the breadth principle.

Table 6.4 presents the mean effect sizes associated with the targeting of particular criminogenic needs and the comparable evidence for particular

Table 6.4 Needs Targeted in a Program Rank Ordered by Program Effect Size

Need Area Targeted	Percent (%)	Mean Phi (k)		Correlation With Phi	Interrater % Agreement
A. Criminogenic Needs		Not a Target	Targeted		
Personal targets	26	.04 (277)	.21 (97)	.39***	90
Antisocial cognition	21	.04 (296)	.21 (78)	.36***	80
Self-control deficits	16	.05 (315)	.22 (59)	.33***	90
Interpersonal targets	19	.05 (302)	.22 (72)	.37***	100
Family process	08	.06 (344)	.29 (30)	.33***	100
Antisocial associates	14	.06 (323)	.21 (51)	.28**	100
School/work	24	.06 (286)	.15 (88)	.21**	90
Substance abuse	10	.08 (338)	.11 (36)	.06	98
B. Noncriminogenic Needs					
Personal targets	46	.11 (203)	.04 (171)	−.18**	93
Fear of official	11	.10 (331)	−.05 (43)	−.25**	100
punishment	27	.09 (273)	.08 (101)	−.08ns	93
Personal distress	12	.08 (331)	.08 (43)	.00ns	100
Physical activity	12	.08 (331)	.08 (43)	.00ns	100
Conventional ambition	12	.09 (329)	.01 (45)	−.13*	100
Interpersonal targets Family	07	.09 (348)	.02 (26)	−.10ns	100

Notes. % = percentage of tests with need targeted; Mean Phi = mean effect size when targeted and not targeted; Correlation with Phi = correlation with effect size; Interrater % Agreement = rates of agreement among 29 raters.

* p < .05; ** p < .01; *** p < .001; ns, not significant.

noncriminogenic needs. Note that the interrater agreement rates are quite respectable, despite the fact that many reports were not explicit in describing the intermediate targets of change. In keeping with Figure 6.2, these results indicate that the targeting of criminogenic needs is associated with enhanced crime reduction, whereas the targeting of noncriminogenic needs is associated with nonsignificant effects or with increased reoffending.

(Limited) Support for the Strength and Professional Discretion Principles

Strengths or protective factors are defined in Appendix A, and the relevant principles are articulated in Appendix B. There is no compelling evidence that strengths predict recidivism, above and beyond risk factors. Likewise, there is no meta-analytic evidence that focusing on the strengths of a case acts as a specific responsivity factor to reduce recidivism. The anecdotal evidence is impressive, but systematic empirical investigations are scarce.

Similarly, I am unaware of systematic empirical support for the exercise of professional discretion or deviation from recommendations (e.g., known

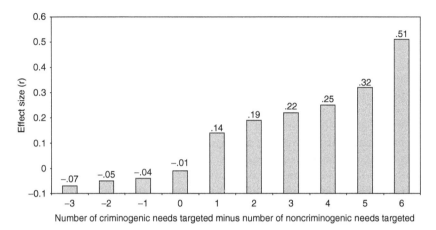

Figure 6.2. Increasing the breadth of targeting criminogenic needs (vs. noncriminogenic) needs increases program effect size.

risk factors or RNR principles) for very specific reasons. In the context of risk assessment, it is difficult to ignore the warning suggested by the well-established poor performance of unstructured professional judgment relative to the predictive validity of structured and validated assessment instruments. The exercise of professional discretion in the context of RNR-based assessment is presumably structured, but evidence in support of its value is still required.

Structured Assessment Principle

According to this principle, validated assessment instruments should be used and should inform every intervention and contact. There are a number of well-established and well-validated risk/need assessment instruments (see Andrews, Bonta, & Wormith, 2004, 2006). Be aware, however, that some non-validated instruments are being aggressively marketed. If an instrument's proponent cannot provide cross-validated and replicated evidence of its predictive validity, reject that instrument. Indeed, avoid the instrument, if a proponent cannot provide access to at least two prospective validity studies composed of at least two independent samples of offenders. Insist that the evidence be based on exactly the same instrument being used with the two samples. This may sound obvious, but proponents of some instruments, in fact, present findings that are site specific and sample specific. By "specific" I mean that the only items used in a report are the items that were significantly predictive in that particular site with that particular sample of offenders. In applied science, as in science in general, replication of the validity of *standardized* assessment instruments is essential.

Be certain that the sites employed in the validation studies correspond to the sites of intended use, such as being a community-based or institution-based site. Evaluate whether the outcome measures employed in the validation study are of direct interest to the intended sites of application. For example, are general recidivism, violent recidivism, sexual recidivism, and/or in-program misconduct reports of most interest?

The field of risk/need assessment has recently advanced significantly. Now, evidence is emerging that agencies that conduct systematic assessments and act in accordance with the findings of the assessment have greater crime *reduction* potential than other agencies. The Correctional Program Assessment Inventory–2000 (Gendreau & Andrews, 2001) is a systematic survey of the extent to which programming adheres to the principles of RNR. Lowenkamp (2004) and Lowenkamp, Latessa, and Smith (2006) found that the element of risk assessment that was most strongly associated with crime reduction was the making of differential risk designations. Eighty-seven percent of the half-way houses surveyed attended to risk factors in at least some minimal way, but only 13% differentiated cases according to level of risk. It is astounding to discover that such basic principles are often not followed even within agencies that do conduct systematic risk/need assessments.

To help correct such issues, my colleagues and I now routinely advise agencies to consider "fourth-generation" risk assessment instruments that can integrate risk assessment and case management processes (see Andrews, Bonta, & Wormith, 2006). One example of such an instrument is the Level of Service/Case Management Inventory (LS/CMI; Andrews, Bonta, & Wormith, 2004) and its youth version (Hoge & Andrews, 2002). These tools are explicit attempts to enhance adherence with the principles of RNR by structuring assessment, service planning, and service delivery from intake through case closure. The LS/CMIs also are gender informed and include surveys of specific responsivity factors and strengths. Our consultations with users revealed a clear wish for a more positive and complete assessment of offenders. There is already evidence that the structuring of increased RNR adherence is rewarded by enhanced crime reduction (Luong & Wormith, in press).

This book is concerned in particular with the prediction and reduction of violent offending. We have already seen evidence (albeit limited by a relatively small number of studies) that RNR adherence is associated with reduced violence. How does the Level of Services Inventory (LSI), an instrument designed with explicit attention to the prediction of general recidivism, do in the prediction of violent recidivism? Campbell, French, and Gendreau (2007) compared the predictive validity of the LSI with that of forensic assessment instruments that have been validated and applied as violence risk assessment tools (i.e., the VRAG, HCR20, and the PCL-R). Predictive validity was explored in relation to violent criminal offending and violent misconduct in prisons or hospitals. The LSI was not the single best predictor of either criterion measure, but its utility was statistically indistinguishable from that of the best of the specialized assessment instruments.

In a slightly different domain, there is evidence that structured assessment that is linked with differential treatment approaches (DT; for a review, see Van Voorhis, 1997) can reduce rates of revocation of probation or parole. Reducing revocation of community supervision is thought to have value because the alternative of incarceration is considerably more costly. This is particularly true when revocation is based not on reoffending, but instead on technical violations or a "bad attitude." DT assessment systems often are based on developmental considerations such as interpersonal maturity; these are included in the *specific responsivity* principle of RNR.

The Wisconsin Case Management Classification system (Harris, Gingerich, & Whittaker, 2004) is a DT system that was adopted widely across the United States and for a period in Canadian federal corrections on the basis of multiple evaluations that focused primarily upon reduced revocation rates (or reduced recommendations that community supervision be revoked). Table 6.5 provides a summary of impressive quasi-experimental evaluations of this system (as summarized in Harris et al., 2004). In five of six evaluations, there were small but statistically significant reductions in revocation rates.

Table 6.5 Effects of the Wisconsin Case Management Classification System on Recidivism

Study Site	Cases	Conditions	Outcome	Comparison	Treatment	Effect
Milwaukee	High risk	Intensive service vs. regular supervision	Revocation	30%	20%	10%*
Milwaukee	High risk	Intensive service vs. intensive supervision	Revocation	24%	20%	4%
Texas	High risk	—	Revocation	23%	15%	8%*
South Carolina	—	—	Revocation	Higher	Lower	*
Florida	—	—	Revocation	Higher	Lower	*
A south central U.S. county	—	—	Revocation	25%	16%	9%*
			arrests	31%	31%	0%
			technical violation	9%	19%	−10%*
Washington State	—	—	Prison misconducts	Higher	Lower	*ns*

*, significant difference; *ns* = not significant.

Source: Based on Harris et al. (2004). I cannot provide recidivism rates for some studies because I have not yet gained access to the papers.

A closer look at other outcomes, though, reveals that there were no significant effects on arrests or misconduct reports, and there was a significant increase in technical violations. Moreover, few measures of differential case management processes (two of nine) on the part of officers were associated with the reduced revocation rates observed in these studies (Harris et al., 2004). This pattern of results raises the very real possibility that training in the Wisconsin system changed the posttraining revocation behavior of supervision officers but did not reduce the criminal behavior of offenders. It is fascinating that training in an integrated approach to assessment and supervision may have had little impact on the antisocial conduct of offenders but radically changed officer approaches to revocation. I hasten to note that the vast majority of the outcome studies referred to in this chapter did not involve training the persons responsible for the arrest, conviction, or incarceration of offenders.

These findings support the general value of GPCSL and RNR-based assessments that were constructed to maximize the prediction of general recidivism. In large agencies with diverse populations and settings, it is also important that the assessment be based on widely applicable predictors of criminal futures. It is important to know that composite assessments of the central eight risk/need factors are widely applicable in terms of offender types (age, gender, and ethnicity), in terms of settings (probation, parole, prisons), and now in terms of various measures of violent recidivism and general recidivism.

Organizational Principles

There is relatively strong evidence for RNR organizational principles about the settings, staffing, and management of human service. The evidence base for the community-based principle (Principle 13, Appendix B) appears in Table 6.3 (Panel B). Although the effects of adherence with the core clinical RNR principles were stronger in community settings than in prison, human service was also critical in prison settings. If human service was not delivered in a prison setting, the mean effect size for incarceration was a 10 percentage point *increase* in reoffending.

Principle 14 (Core Correctional Staff Practices) expands upon the principle of general responsivity by specifying particular styles of interaction and skills that constitute effective practices. The specification forms a basis for the selection of effective service providers, for their training (pre-service and in-service), and for their clinical supervision. Generally, the desirable service provider can establish high-quality relationships with clients (i.e., respectful, caring, collaborative) and possesses the structuring skills that enhance the level and direction of interpersonal influence. Structuring skills are the concrete means of moving risk factors in the direction of becoming strengths. If one wants to increase real alternatives to procriminal ways of thinking, feeling, and acting, then the alternatives are best demonstrated and reinforced by service providers. The fundamentals of skill building are well known but infrequently practiced. They involve describing the desired behavior, modeling (demonstrating) the behavior, creating role-playing opportunities, reinforcing, correcting when necessary, reinforcing, and repeating the process.

These concrete indicators of core practices have been associated with reduced crime in corrections (Andrews, 1980), forensic mental health (Skeem, Eno Louden, Polaschek, & Camp, 2007), and family therapy (see the elements of nurturance and supervision in the family entry in Table 6.1). The elements of core correctional practice that have been explored meta-analytically are listed in Table 6.6. All elements were significantly associated with reduced reoffending.

Notably, the elements were infrequently represented in practice. For example, effective modeling and systematic skill training were found in only 10% of the evaluated programs. When will service providers actually engage in effective core correctional practices? Following GPCSL, they will when they

Table 6.6 Program Effect Size by Elements of Core Correctional Practice and Integrity

Element	% of Programs Where Present	r, Presence, and Effect Size
A. Core Correctional Practice		
Relationship skills	3	.26***
Structuring skills	12	.37***
Effective reinforcement	4	.25***
Effective modeling	10	.36***
Effective disapproval	2	.18***
Structured skill learning	10	.39***
Problem solving	12	.33***
Advocacy/brokerage	14	.10*
Effective authority	4	.19***
B. Integrity		
Staff selected for relationship skills	3	.26***
Staff trained	45	.26**
Clinical supervision of staff	18	.21**
Number hours of service	—	.20**
Rated appropriate dosage	41	.05
Printed/taped manuals	19	.30**
Monitor process or intermediate change on targets	39	.007
Specific model	54	.23***
New/fresh program	33	.20**
Small sample (less than 100)	36	.28***
Involved evaluator	21	.41***

$* p < .05; ** p < .01; *** p < .001.$

Source: Based on Andrews and Bonta (2006, 2010).

have the skills (have been trained); have a history of being rewarded for engaging in those practices; have attitudes, values, and beliefs supportive of those practices; and have associates who endorse the use of effective practices.

According to Principle 15 (Management), the task of management is to create the organizational conditions supportive of adherence with RNR. Crime prevention is viewed as an important objective of the agency when both managers and staff agree on the matter, and staff and management are rewarded for supporting crime prevention. Some elements of integrity that have been tested meta-analytically are listed in Table 6.6, section B.

As noted earlier, when people involved in the design and/or delivery of the service are also involved in the evaluation of service, both integrity and outcomes are greatly enhanced. Andrews and Dowden (2007) and Andrews and Bonta (2010) pooled the integrity elements of small sample studies and involved evaluators to create three levels of programming from "routine," through "mixed" to "demonstration project." Inspection of Table 6.7 reveals that the largest crime reduction effects are found when adherence to the core clinical principles of RNR is combined with the integrity of programming found in demonstration projects.

Figures 6.3 and 6.4 tell the story in a dramatic fashion. Integrity adds nothing to crime reduction unless the supervision or services are in adherence with the core clinical principles of RNR (Fig. 6.3). Figure 6.4 illustrates the increase in crime prevention provided by the addition of integrity of implementation to the contributions of core RNR adherence. Simply put, the quality of management and implementation matters.

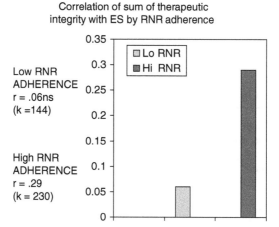

Figure 6.3. Organizational staffing/management principles increase program effect size if there is adherence to core clinical Risk-Need-Responsivity (RNR) principles. ES, effect size.

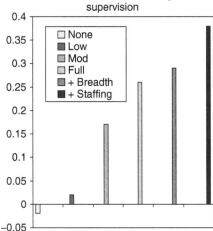

Figure 6.4. Adding breadth and organizational principles to Risk-Need-Responsivity (RNR) increases program effect size (ES).

Gaps in the Knowledge Base

Several difficulties with the research literature were noted in the review of assessment and intervention studies: (a) few meta-analysts have attended to the intermediate targets of change, (b) controlled evaluations of violence prevention programs remain relatively few in number, and (c) some areas remain

Table 6.7 Program Effect Size by Level of Risk-Need-Responsivity (RNR) Adherence and Type of Program

Program Type	Level of RNR Adherence				r, RNR Adherence, and Effect Size
	None (k)	Low (k)	Moderate (k)	High (k)	
Demonstration project	.01 (1)	.07 (7)	.35 (16)	.38 (23)	.44
Mixed program	−.04 (30)	−.02 (28)	.21 (34)	.26 (26)	.53
Real-world program	−.02 (93)	.04 (71)	.09 (34)	.15 (11)	.41

Note. Effect size = r. Number of tests of treatment = k.

Source: Based on data from Dowden and Andrews (2004).

woefully unexplored (e.g., marital counseling, a focus on leisure/recreation). There is also a lack of experimental evidence on whether deliberately induced change on dynamic risk factors is responsible for reduced criminal activity. Serious work is also required on the many issues involved in the communication of risk/need information.

Another gap in the knowledge base is that of how to make "real-world" correctional practice more like that found in demonstration projects. Why did several attempts to introduce "what works" fail to reduce crime? A plausible answer is that the principles of RNR were not followed (Andrews, 2006; Andrews & Bonta, 2010; Goggin & Gendreau, 2006). Use of RNR jargon is a lot easier than achieving adherence with the RNR principles.

Implications for Individual Offenders and Correctional Systems

Individual Offenders

The RNR model of correctional assessment, supervision, and treatment rather naturally breaks down into the implications of work with individual offenders and work with systems. The normative principles apply to both, whereas the clinical principles are explicitly about work with individual offenders. The organizational set of principles speaks to work at the system level. Of course, proponents of RNR value comprehensive implications, but my colleagues and I would never suggest anything but that the model is incomplete, nonexhaustive, and a work in progress.

In the process of admitting that the principles of RNR have proven to be far less obvious than he once thought, Andrews (2006) provided the following summary points (with a few additions to the list):

1) Employ structured and validated fourth-generation assessment instruments and actually use the information derived thereby in program design, program delivery, program modification, and case closure.
2) Introduce a human service orientation to supervision and programming. Never rely solely upon negative sanctions or official punishment to reduce postsanction criminal activity.
3) Supervision and services must be structured and employ the best-validated influence strategies (that is, always employ cognitive-behavioral and cognitive social learning strategies).
4) Never assign low-risk cases to intensive supervision and services. With reference to crime reduction, there is no replicated evidence in support of violation of this rule. From the point of view of crime prevention, violation of this rule is inexcusable. If low-risk cases present with noncriminogenic needs, seek programming that is offered outside of corrections where contact with higher risk cases is unlikely and the disruption of strengths is less likely.

5) Assign moderate and higher risk cases to intensive supervision and service. There is no documented evidence that not doing so will reduce criminal activity.

6) Target criminogenic needs predominately. The targeting of noncriminogenic needs predominately is associated with either nil effects on crime reduction or increased criminal activity. Resist the nonvalidated appeals to focus predominately on enhanced and generalized well-being. Effective programs are ones that build up rewards for noncriminal alternatives to crime and reduce the costs of noncriminal alternatives.

7) Low levels of motivation to participate in crime reduction activities are positively associated with level of risk. To increase participation and reduce premature dropout, pay attention to specific responsivity considerations such as building on strengths, reducing barriers, and applying the principles and practices of Motivational Interviewing. It is important to target the criminogenic and noncriminogenic needs that are of particular concern to higher risk cases. On balance, more criminogenic needs should be targeted than noncriminogenic ones.

Structuring Correctional Systems

1) If crime prevention is not an officially stated objective of the agency, the RNR model may be ignored. Recognize, however, that the public will learn eventually that such agencies are not enhancing public safety (except perhaps through incapacitation) and may well be enhancing criminal activity.

2) If crime prevention is an objective, then that objective must have a prominent place in agency mission statements, and success in practice should contribute meaningfully to the evaluations of managers and practitioners. The evidence is now clear that it does matter what agencies and agents "do" with the offenders with whom they are in contact. Their actions can be shown to increase crime, have no impact on crime, or reduce crime. Agencies and agents have a choice.

3) The roles of policy, managers, and practitioners should be defined such that they support adherence with the principles of RNR in order to maximize crime prevention.

4) The RNR model places a great emphasis on the cognitive social learning principles of relationship skills and structuring skills as a means of guiding the key management functions of the selection, training, and clinical supervision of direct service workers.

5) The concepts of core correctional practice and the elements of integrity in the implementation and maintenance are key to enhancing the effects of adherence with the core clinical principles of RNR.

6) Systems should make monitoring, feedback, and corrective action routine. Make it a matter of policy.

7) Existing evidence is limited. In response, involve competent and informed researchers in program design, program delivery, program review, and process and outcome evaluations.

8) Statements of policy and the actions of management must demonstrate hope with reference to crime prevention and avoid modeling despair and disrespect for the objective of crime prevention.

Applications of the RNR principles have proven to be complex, and the principles have been frequently ignored. It appears that nonadherence is much more attractive in practice than many of us realized. If applications of RNR and GPCSL can reduce criminal behavior, such applications should also be able to influence the policy of agencies and the behavior of agents.

Acknowledgments

See the fourth and fifth editions of *The Psychology of Criminal Conduct* by Andrews and Bonta (2006, 2010) for thorough references to original supporting research by multiple professionals over a period of more than 40 years. It is foolish to list contributors because it is almost certain that some will inadvertently be left off the list. However, keeping the list short, I must thank Paul Gendreau, along with Jim Bonta, Catherine Carvell, Craig Dowden, Bob Hoge, Steve Wormith, Annie Yessine, and Ivan Zinger.

Appendix A: Glossary of Key Terms

Criminogenic Need. *See* Dynamic risk factor.

Dynamic Risk Factor (or Criminogenic Need). A risk factor that may be changed and, when changed, alters the chance of future criminal behavior. Changes in the risk factor may occur naturally or may be induced through intervention. However, the causal status of dynamic risk factors is best determined through experimental research in which change is deliberately induced and is shown to reduce recidivism. Dynamic risk factors suggest appropriate targets of change to reduce offending, invoking the "need" principle of RNR (see Table 6.2).

Protective Factor and Strength Factor. Although the two terms are often used interchangeably, three separate definitions are required for strengths and protective factors.

- *Strength Factor 1.* An absence of a risk factor that has no incremental value in predicting recidivism. Here, a strength simply reflects the inverse of an association between a risk factor and recidivism.
- *Strength Factor 2.* A characteristic of people and/or their circumstances whose presence is associated with a reduced chance of crime. This effect is incremental to any effect on recidivism that it has as a risk factor.

For example, individuals may be assessed as being at one of three levels on a given characteristic: *(1)* problematic (e.g., low verbal intelligence), *(2)* intermediate (e.g., *average* intelligence), or *(3)* positive (e.g., high verbal intelligence). Low verbal intelligence is a risk marker if the "problematic" group has a higher likelihood of recidivism compared to the "intermediate" group with average intelligence. High verbal intelligence is a strength marker if the "positive" group has a lower recidivism rate than the "intermediate" group with average intelligence. Thus, four findings are possible: *(a)* intelligence is neither a risk nor a strength, *(b)* low intelligence is a risk but high intelligence is not a strength, *(c)* low intelligence is not a risk but high intelligence is a strength, or *(d)* low intelligence is a risk and high intelligence is a strength. To my knowledge there is no compelling evidence that any instrument's assessments of strengths has incremental predictive utility over its assessment of risks. Similarly, although service programs may be designed to build on the strengths of a case (e.g., using more verbal, less directive approaches for highly intelligent cases), there is to my knowledge no compelling research base for this practice.

- *Protective Factor.* A characteristic whose presence reduces the predictive validity of risk factors. For example, certain risk scores may be less strongly correlated with the recidivism of highly intelligent persons than with the recidivism of less intelligent persons. To my knowledge, there are no replicated examples of a protective effect in the applied literature.

Pearson Correlation Coefficient (r). The most frequently employed measure of effect size in the prediction and the intervention literatures. May be interpreted as a percentage point difference in recidivism rates for lower and higher risk groups or for the treatment and control groups. The greater the r value, the greater the level of predictive validity or crime reduction effect of treatment. For example, if $r = .20$, then the recidivism rate of the lower risk group is 50 minus 20/2 (or $50 - 10 = 40$). The recidivism rate of the higher risk group is 50 plus 20/2 or, $50 + 10 = 60$. The difference between 60 and 40 is 20 points. As an example for an intervention program, an r of .20 indicates that the recidivism rate of the control group is 60% ($50 + 10 = 60$) and the recidivism rate of the experimental group is 40% ($50 - 10$). The effect of treatment is a reduction in recidivism of 20 percentage points ($60 - 40 = 20$).

Recidivism. The reoccurrence of criminal activity during a follow-up of identified offenders over a specified follow-up period. It is typically measured as a discrete event (no/yes) or as the number of new occurrences. Distinctions may also be made according to seriousness of the new offence(s) or their type (e.g., violent). The occurrences may be defined by self-report, the reports of other observers (e.g., acquaintance), or by official records (e.g., police reports).

- Obviously, reports of the effects of intervention on any measure of recidivism can only refer to recidivistic events that are detected. Validity studies too only deal with detected reoffending.

- Some measures of recidivism (e.g., revocation of parole) are very indirect measures of the occurrence of new offences (and may in fact reflect violations of parole conditions that do not involve reoffending).

Risk Factor. A characteristic of people and/or their circumstances whose presence is associated with an increased chance of future criminal activity. Risk factors may be *(a)* relatively static or fixed factors such as a criminal history or *(b)* relatively dynamic and subject to change.

Appendix B. Principles of the Risk-Need-Responsivity (RNR) Model

Overarching Principles

1. **Respect for the Person and the Normative Context:** Services are delivered with respect for the person, including respect for personal autonomy, being humane, ethical, just, legal, decent, and being otherwise normative. Some norms may vary with the agencies or the particular settings within which services are delivered. For example, agencies working with young offenders may be expected to show exceptional attention to education issues and to child protection. Mental health agencies may attend to issues of personal well-being. Some agencies working with female offenders may place a premium on attending to trauma and/or to parenting concerns.
2. **Psychological Theory:** Base programs on an empirically solid psychological theory (a general personality and cognitive social learning approach is recommended).
3. **General Enhancement of Crime Prevention Services:** The reduction of criminal victimization may be viewed as a legitimate objective of service agencies, including agencies within and outside of justice and corrections.

Core RNR Principles and Key Clinical Issues

4. **Introduce Human Service:** Introduce human service into the justice context. Do not rely on the sanction to bring about reduced offending. Do not rely on deterrence, restoration, or other principles of justice.
5. **Risk:** Match intensity of service with risk level of cases. Work with moderate and higher risk cases. Generally, avoid creating interactions of low-risk cases with higher risk cases.
6. **Need:** Target criminogenic needs predominately. Move criminogenic needs in the direction of becoming strengths.
7. **General Responsivity:** Employ behavioral, social learning, and cognitive-behavioral influence and skill-building strategies.
8. **Specific Responsivity:** Adapt the style and mode of service according to the setting of service and to relevant characteristics of individual

offenders such as their strengths, motivations, preferences, personality, age, gender, ethnicity, cultural identifications, and other factors. The evidence in regard to specific responsivity is generally favorable but very scattered, and it has yet to be subjected to a comprehensive meta-analysis. Some examples of specific responsivity considerations follow:

- When working with the weakly motivated, build on strengths, reduce personal and situational barriers to full participation in treatment, establish high-quality relationships, deliver early and often on matters of personal interest, and start where the person "is at."
- Attend to the evidence on age-, gender-, and culturally responsive services.
- Attend to the evidence about differential treatment according to psychosocial maturity, interpersonal anxiety, cognitive skill levels, and the responsivity aspects of psychopathy.
- Consider targeting noncriminogenic needs to enhance motivation, reduce distracting factors, or address humanitarian and entitlement issues.

9. **Breadth (or Multimodal):** Target a great number of criminogenic needs, relative to noncriminogenic needs.
10. **Strength:** Assess strengths to enhance specific responsivity effects and, perhaps, to enhance predictive accuracy.
11. **Structured Assessment:**

    a. **Assessments of Strengths and Risk-Need-Specific Responsivity Factors:** Employ structured and validated assessment instruments.
    b. **Integrated Assessment and Intervention:** Every intervention and contact should be informed by the assessments.

12. **Professional Discretion:** Deviate from recommendations only for very specific reasons. For example, functional analysis suggests that emotional distress is a risk/need factor for this person.

Organizational Principles

13. **Community-based settings:** Community-based services are preferred, but the principles of RNR also apply within residential and institutional settings.
14. **Core Correctional Staff Practices:** Effectiveness of interventions is enhanced when delivered by therapists and staff with *high-quality relationship skills* in combination with *high-quality structuring skills.* Quality relationships are characterized as respectful, caring, enthusiastic, collaborative, and valuing of personal autonomy. Structuring practices include prosocial modeling, effective reinforcement and disapproval, skill building, problem solving, effective use of authority, advocacy/brokerage, cognitive

restructuring, and motivational interviewing. Motivational interviewing skills include both relationship and structuring aspects of effective practice.

15. **Management:** Promote the selection, training, and clinical supervision of staff according to RNR and introduce monitoring, feedback, and adjustment systems. Build systems and cultures supportive of effective practice and continuity of care. Some additional specific indicators of integrity include having program manuals available, monitoring of service process and intermediate changes, adequate dosage, and involving researchers in the design and delivery of service.

Sources: Andrews, Bonta, & Hoge, 1990; Andrews & Bonta, 1994, 2006, 2010; Andrews, Zinger, et al., 1990; Bonta & Andrews, 2007.

References

Andrews, D. A. (1980). Experimental investigations of the principles of differential association through deliberate manipulation of the structure of service systems. *American Sociological Review, 45,* 448–462.

Andrews, D. A. (2006). Enhancing adherence to risk-need-responsivity: Making quality a matter of policy. *Criminology and Public Policy, 5,* 595–602.

Andrews, D. A., & Bonta, J. (1994). *The psychology of criminal conduct.* Cincinnati, OH: Andersen Publishing.

Andrews, D. A., & Bonta, J. (2006). *The psychology of criminal conduct* (4th ed.). Newark, NJ: LexisNexis/Matthew Bender.

Andrews, D. A., & Bonta, J. (2009). *The Level of Service Inventory–Revised.* North Tonawanda, NY: Multi-Health Systems.

Andrews, D. A., & Bonta, J. (2010). *The psychology of criminal conduct* (5th ed.). Newark, NJ: LexisNexis/Matthew Bender.

Andrews, D. A., Bonta, J., & Hoge, R. D. (1990). Classification for effective rehabilitation: Rediscovering psychology. *Criminal Justice and Behavior, 17,* 19-52.

Andrews, D. A., Bonta, J., & Wormith, S. J. (2004). *The Level of Service/Case Management Inventory (LS/CMI).* Toronto, ON: Multi-Health Systems.

Andrews, D. A., Bonta, J., & Wormith, S. J. (2006). The recent past and near future of risk/need *assessment. Crime and Delinquency, 52,* 7–27.

Andrews, D. A., & Dowden, C. (2007). The risk-need-responsivity model of assessment and human service in prevention and corrections: Crime prevention jurisprudence. *Canadian Journal of Criminology and Criminal Justice, 48*(4), 439–464.

Andrews, D. A., Zinger, I., Hoge, R. D., Bonta, J., Gendreau, P., & Cullen, F. T. (1990). Does correctional treatment work? A clinically relevant and psychologically informed meta-analysis. *Criminology, 28,* 369-404.

Blanchette, K., & Brown, S. L. (2006). *The assessment and treatment of women offenders.* Chichester, England: John Wiley & Sons.

Bonta, J., & Andrews, D. A. (2007). *Risk-need-responsivity model for offender assessment and rehabilitation.* Corrections Research User Report No. 2007–06. Ottawa, ON: Public Safety Canada.

Bush, J. (1995). Teaching self-risk management to violent offenders. In J. McGuire (Ed.), *What works: Reducing reoffending* (pp. 139–154). New York: John Wiley & Sons.

Campbell, M. A., French, S., & Gendreau, P. (2007). *Assessing the utility of risk assessment tools and personality measures in the prediction of violent recidivism for adult offenders.* User Report 2007–04. Ottawa, ON: Public Safety Canada.

Digman, J. M. (1990). Personality structure: Emergence of the five factor model. *Annual Review of Psychology, 41,* 417–440.

Dowden, C. (1998). *A meta-analytic exploration of the risk-need-responsivity model of rehabilitation.* Unpublished Master's dissertation, Department of Psychology, Carleton University, Ottawa, ON.

Dowden, C., & Andrews, D. A. (1999). What works for female offenders: A meta-analytic review. *Crime and Delinquency, 45,* 438–452.

Dowden, C. & D. A. Andrews. (2000). Effective correctional treatment and violent reoffending. *Canadian Journal of Criminology, 42,* 449–467.

Dowden, C., & Andrews, D. A. (2004). The importance of staff practices in delivering effective correctional treatment: A meta-analysis of core correctional practices. *International Journal of Offender Therapy and Comparative Criminology, 48,* 203–214.

French, S., & Gendreau, P. (2006). Reducing prison misconducts: What works! *Criminal Justice and Behavior, 33,* 185–218.

Gendreau, P., & Andrews, D. A. (2001). *The Correctional Program Assessment Inventory–2000 (CPAI 2000).* Saint John: University of New Brunswick.

Gendreau, P., Little, T., & Goggin, C. (1996). A meta-analysis of the predictors of adult offender recidivism: What works! *Criminology, 31,* 401–433.

Goggin, C., & Gendreau, P. (2006). The implementation and maintenance of quality services in offender rehabilitation programmes. In C. R. Hollin & E. J. Palmer (Eds.), *Offending behaviour programmes: Development, application, and controversies* (pp. 209–246). Chichester, England: John Wiley & Sons.

Harris, P. M., Gingerich, R., & Whittaker, T. A. (2004). The "effectiveness" of differential supervision. *Crime and Delinquency, 50,* 235–271.

Hoge, R., & Andrews, D. (2002). *The Youth Level of Service/Case Management Inventory.* Toronto, ON: Multi-Health Systems.

Kazdin, A. E., & Whitley, M. K. (2003). Treatment for parental stress to enhance therapeutic change among children referred for aggressive and antisocial behavior. *Journal of Consulting and Clinical Psychology, 71,* 504–515.

Lipsey, M. W. (2009). The primary factors that characterize effective interventions with juvenile offenders: A meta-analytic overview. *Victims and Offenders, 4,* 124–147.

Lowenkamp, C. T. (2004). *A program level analysis of the relationship between correctional program integrity and treatment effectiveness.* Unpublished doctoral dissertation. University of Cincinnati, OH.

Lowenkamp, C. T., Latessa, E. J., & Smith, P. (2006). Does correctional program quality really matter? The impact of adherence to the principles of effective intervention. *Criminology and Public Policy, 5*(3), 575–594.

Luong, D., & Wormith, J. S. (in press). Applying risk/need assessment in probation practices and its impact on the recidivism of young offenders. *Criminal Justice and Behavior*.

Maruna, S., Lebel, T. P., Mitchell, N., & Naples, M. (2004). Pygmalion in the reintegration process: Desistence from crime through the looking glass. *Psychology, Crime, and Law, 10*, 271–281.

McGuire, J. (2004). *Understanding psychology and crime: Perspectives on theory and action*. Berkshire, England: Open University Press.

Mischel, W., & Ayduk, O. (2004). Willpower in a cognitive-affective processing system: The Dynamics of delay of gratification. In R. F. Baumeister & K. D Vohs (Eds.), *Handbook of self-regulation: Research, theory, and applications* (pp. 99–129). New York: Guilford.

Mischel, W., & Shoda, Y. (1995). A cognitive-affective system theory of personality: Reconceptualizing situations, dispositions, dynamics, and invariance in personality structure. *Psychological Review, 102*, 246–268.

Miller, J. D., & Lynam, D. R. (2001). Structural models of personality and their relation to Antisocial behavior: A meta-analysis. *Criminology, 39*, 765–798.

Ogloff, J. R. P., & Davis, N. R. (2004). Advances in offender assessment and rehabilitation: Contributions of the Risk-Needs-Responsivity approach. *Psychology, Crime and Law, 10*, 229–242.

Patrick, C. J., Curtin, J. J., & Tellegen, A. (2002). Development and validation of a brief form of the Multidimensional Personality Questionnaire. *Psychological Assessment, 14*, 150–163.

Petrosino, A., & Soydan, H. (2005). The impact of program developers as evaluators on criminal recidivism: Results from meta-analyses of experimental and quasi-experimental research. *Journal of Experimental Criminology, 1*, 435–450.

Skeem, J. L., Louden, J. E., Polaschek, D., & Camp, J. (2007). Assessing relationship quality in mandated community treatment: Blending care with control. *Psychological Assessment, 19*, 397–410.

Van Voorhis, P. (1997). An overview offender Classification Systems. In P. Van Voorhis, M. Braswell, & D. Lester (Eds.), *Correctional counseling and rehabilitation* (pp. 81–108). Cincinnati, OH: Anderson.

Vohs, K. D., Baumeister, R. F., & Ciarocco, N. J. (2005). Self-regulation and self-presentation: Regulatory resource depletion impairs impression management and effortful self-presentation depletes regulatory resources. *Journal of Personality and Social Psychology, 88*, 632–657.

7

Assessment and Treatment Strategies for Correctional Institutions

Paul Gendreau and Paula Smith

Since their inception in North America in the early 19th century (see Siegel, 2008), penitentiaries have become a lightning rod for strongly held opinions about their goals (e.g., punishment, rehabilitation, and incapacitation) and the quality of care provided to inmates (Bonta & Gendreau, 1990; Clear, 1995; Haney, 2006; Mitford, 1973; Wright, 1996; Zedlewski, 1987). From our perspective, the issues pertaining to prisons have become particularly troubling since the demise of the rehabilitative ideal in American criminal justice systems that occurred in the 1970s (Cullen & Gilbert, 1982). Due to a variety of factors, the foremost being the politicization of crime as well as Supreme Court and legislative decisions (Haney & Zimbardo, 1998; Tonry, 2004), the United States embarked upon the "mean season" of corrections (Cullen, 1995, p. 340; see also Forer, 1994), a season that has extended to the present time. This disturbing trend has led to concerns being voiced about inhumane prison living conditions (e.g., Aufderheide & Brown, 2005; Gawande, 2009; Haney, 2003; Human Rights Watch, 2003), rising costs due to increased incarceration rates (Chambliss, 1984; Spelman, 2009), and the use of prisons as profit-making enterprises, which has reinforced a management philosophy that has been preoccupied with processing large numbers of inmates through the correctional system as expeditiously as possible (Dyer, 2000; Feeley & Simon, 1992).

In the opinion of some scholars (e.g., Haney & Zimbardo, 1998), it has been disconcerting to discover that those who might be best situated to speak out about these events, namely social scientists (e.g., criminologists, psychologists), have all but abandoned studying the effects of prison life. This has been confirmed from recent reviews of this literature where most of the references dated back 20–40 years ago (Bonta & Gendreau, 1990; Smith & Gendreau, 2010). The reasons for the lack of interest in the social sciences have been varied. They have ranged from the perspective of many criminologists that prisons were, by definition, destructive environments (and thus further research was unnecessary), to the shifting interests of forensic psychologists from prison research to popular diagnostic topics (e.g., psychopathy) and the reality that there were significant disincentives (e.g., poor working conditions, insufficient financial remuneration) to working in prisons (Brodsky, 2000; Cullen, 2007; Gendreau, Goggin, French, & Smith, 2006; Latessa, Cullen, & Gendreau, 2002; Walters, 2003). The consequence of this neglect has been that by failing to speak out against (and evaluate) the negative effects of prison life, social scientists have created an "ethical and intellectual void that undermined both the quality and legitimacy of correctional practices" (Haney & Zimbardo, 1998, p. 721).

In the last decade, however, there have been some tentative signs that the punitive era may have reached its peak. Present-day prison policies are now being questioned by some politicians (see Webb, 2009), the media (e.g., Editorial, 2010)), as well as policy organizations (Gibbons & Katzenbach, 2006). There also have been advances in corrections research in the last decade (Andrews & Bonta, 2010; Gendreau et al., 2006; Davies, Hollin, & Bull, 2008; McGuire, 2004) that counter the pessimistic scenario depicted by Haney and Zimbardo (1998).

While recognizing that the predominant intention of incarceration, especially in the United States, has been punishment, it is our belief that prisons offer the possibility of improving the behavior of offenders, which has beneficial consequences for society as a whole. Thus, the purpose of this chapter is to generate renewed momentum to the sentiment expressed three decades ago by Fowler (1976) and Haney and Zimbardo (1977) that the management of American prisons can profit from the findings of social scientists. We attempt to do this by emphasizing methods of positive change for the management of prisons (for a general review, see Gendreau & Keyes, 2001) by focusing specifically on the recent findings from the offender prediction and treatment research literature (see Chapter 6; Gendreau, Little, & Goggin, 1996).

Evidence on "What Works" to Reduce Recidivism

The findings from these two topics are critical for addressing the two paramount goals in prison work: running prisons in a safe and humane fashion, and protecting the public through effective treatment programming of inmates. The prediction of prison antisocial behavior (e.g., misconducts) is necessary to identify potentially troublesome inmates who then can be enrolled in programs that will reduce their risk of such behavior. The end result will be to reduce the chances of other inmates being victimized and to make the prison a safer place for staff to work. Furthermore, inmates who learn to adjust in prosocial ways to their environment will be placed in better living conditions (e.g., transferred to lower security settings) and have more favorable parole prospects. And, possibly the most important objective of all, the public will receive more protection to the extent that the prosocial skills inmates acquire through programs transfer to the community upon release (i.e., less recidivism).

Before examining the relevant literature, we furnish the reader with a frame of reference to better understand established thinking in corrections on the role and utility of prisons by providing a synopsis of the three major perspectives on the effects of prison life, their predictions as to what happens to offenders while incarcerated, and any long-term effects (e.g., changes in recidivism). This is followed by a brief summary of the evidence for each. Then, we review what is known as the "what works literature" in regard to offender prediction and treatment and consider the evidence that speaks directly to the two goals noted before. We conclude by briefly commenting on three important matters: the measurement of program quality, monitoring program implementation, and what we have called "correctional quackery." The first two are essential for ensuring that programs have therapeutic integrity. The third alerts the reader about a pernicious development in correctional programming.

Three Perspectives on the Effects of Prison Life

Prison as Punishment

This perspective on prisons alleges that individuals who have experienced a more severe sanction, such as incarceration, would be more likely to abstain from crime (Andenaes, 1968; see Gendreau & Ross, 1981; von Hirsch, Bottoms, Burney, & Wikstron, 1999). That is, prisons function as a form of specific deterrence by imposing direct and indirect costs on inmates (e.g., loss of income, psychological costs due to the dehumanizing experience of prison life, social stigmatization) (Nagin, 1998; Pyle, 1995). Arguably, specific deterrence has become the most popular justification for incarceration in the public arena (see DeJong, 1997; Doob, Sprott, Marinos, & Varna, 1998).

There also have been variations on this theme. Orsagh and Chen (1988) suggested that only those offenders who had strong bonds to conventional society (e.g., low risk to reoffend) and the most to lose by being imprisoned would be deterred. They also proposed a drug dosage type of paradigm for deterrence to be most effective. A low dosage, or too little time served, would be insufficient, whereas a high dosage might produce iatrogenic effects. Thus, the goal of specific deterrence was to uncover that precise dosage level (i.e., a moderate level as in a U-shaped function) to achieve optimal results.

There has also been a school of thought that contemporary prisons have become too soft. Deterrence would not work unless the current state of prison life was made more punitive by adopting "no frills" prisons, which would then ensure that prisons become a truly fearful experience. These prisons would have no amenities (e.g., recreation, schooling, TV, visits) and presumably would feature an austere, extreme boot camp–like atmosphere that would resuscitate bygone punishments like the lash (Finn, 1996; Nossiter, 1994; for a justification of corporal punishment for offenders, see Newman, 1983).

The strongest evidence in support of specific deterrence has come from aggregate-level studies where state prison incarceration rates have been found to correlate with decreases in state or national crime rates (e.g., Fabelo, 1996). While these results may support an incapacitation effect, they have been guilty of committing the ecological fallacy because inferences were made about individuals' response to imprisonment based on membership in a group they belong to (see Freedman, Pisani, Purves, & Adhikari, 1991 for descriptions of the fallacy). For specific deterrence to be a viable theory, however, the appropriate level of analysis must attend to the evidence drawing a link between the amount of time served by an individual and his/her recidivism rate, as would be the case for any treatment study. When this type of analysis has been conducted, both standard narrative literature reviews (Bonta & Gendreau, 1992; Gendreau & Ross, 1981; Song & Lieb, 1993) and meta-analyses (Nieuwbeerta, Nagin, & Blockland, 2007; Smith, Goggin, & Gendreau, 2002) have reported no deterrent effect of prisons on recidivism or, in some cases, slight increases.

As a case in point, Smith, Goggin, and Gendreau (2002) examined two large data sets. First, a total of 233 studies encompassing 107,165 inmates were examined. The comparison groups were inmates who spent longer time in prison versus shorter time for four different time periods ranging from 6-month differences in time served to greater than 2 years. The groups in all the comparisons were similar in terms of risk level. On average, the results showed an overall 3% increase in recidivism for those serving more time in prison; moreover, the negative effects increased by 7% for longer incarceration periods (see Table 2 in Smith, Goggin, & Gendreau, 2002). The second set of data looked at periods of incarceration (average of 10 months) versus offenders serving parole conditions. This comparison involved 104 effect sizes ($N = 268,806$). The incarceration group had a 7% higher recidivism rate. In both sets of data, no U-shaped function was discovered favoring deterrence nor were there any effect size interactions with age, gender, quality of research design, or inmate risk level. Unfortunately, the studies in the meta-analyses lacked any information about inmates' quality of life in the prisons or whether they were enrolled in any programs. While proponents of "no frills" might argue that none of the prisons sampled in the meta-analysis met their criteria of "toughness," many of the studies in the Smith, Goggin, and Gendreau (2002) database were conducted 40 years ago when "no frills" prisons were the rule of thumb.

Finally, one would think that supporters of "no frills" prisons would have addressed one of our stated goals; that is, to make prisons safer and more humane. Presumably, if maximum lockup were routinely employed, as in the case of supermax prisons, then inmate-upon-inmate (and staff) violence would necessarily have decreased. As to this point, Briggs, Sundt, and Castellano (2003) conducted an extensive study across four U.S. states and reported that supermax prisons did not reduce inmate-on-inmate violence while there were equivocal results for staff safety. And even if there was such evidence supporting supermax prisons forthcoming in the future, it would have been most unlikely these prison administrative procedures were humane and ethically defensible, especially considering the way in which supermax prisons appear to have been managed (Haney, 2003; Pizarro & Stenius, 2004).

Schools of Crime

The "schools of crime" view has been widely accepted by many criminal justice professionals, and some segments of the public, the media, and political body (Cullen, Fisher, & Applegate, 2001; Lilly, Cullen, & Bal, 1995; Maruna & Toch, 2005; Mason, 1998; Rangel, 1999). In contrast to the deterrence model, proponents of schools of crime declared that prisons produced the opposite results; that is, prisons manufactured criminality. The term used to describe this process, *prisonization*, was " . . . the taking on, in a greater or lesser degree, of the folkways, customs, and general culture of the penitentiary" (Clemmer, 1940, p. 279; see also Sykes, 1958). The learning of antisocial attitudes was predicted to increase in a linear fashion with longer sentences producing the worst effects (Jaman, Dickover, & Bennett, 1972). The strongest statement we have encountered in support of prisonization came from Bukstel and Kilmann's (1980) classic review of the prison literature. Some of the studies they cited (e.g., Buehler, Patterson, & Furniss, 1966) convinced them that there was evidence of "overwhelming positive reinforcement" (Bukstel & Kilmann, 1980, p. 472) by the peer group and staff for a variety of antisocial behaviors.

From this analysis one would assume that all inmates would routinely adopt more criminal values, but subsequent research has pointed to a more complex picture as several other factors have been identified that could possibly moderate or be affected by the prison experience. The most prominent of these have been the inmate's risk level for reoffending, offense history, self-esteem and procriminal attitudes, the stage at which the inmate was in his or her sentence, prison management style, and the availability of programs (for detailed review, see Bonta & Gendreau, 1992; DeLisi & Walters, 2011).

In our opinion, of the aforementioned variables, risk level has offered the best evidence for supporting the prisonization hypothesis, but only in this case of low-risk offenders who would be the most vulnerable to learning more procriminal values through social learning/modeling mechanisms (e.g., Cullen, Wright, Gendreau, & Andrews, 2003; Leschied & Gendreau, 1994). As evidence for this, Walters (2003) found only "novice" inmates ($N = 55$)—and we interpret these as being lower risk—showed increases in criminal identity over time in a penitentiary. Recently, two more studies have reported similar findings. Tanasichuk, Wormith, and Guzzo (2009) compared the recidivism rates of low-risk offenders who were incarcerated versus those remaining in the community under parole. The former group had a 13% higher recidivism rate. Smith and Gendreau (2010) evaluated the prison adjustment and program participation of 5,469 adult male inmates for incarceration periods of 6 months to over 20 years. Prison adjustment was defined by the occurrence of misconducts. Regardless of the type of programming received, low-risk offenders' prison adjustment and postrelease recidivism outcomes worsened as the length of time served increased.

Prisons as a "Behavioral Deep Freeze"

This outlook on prisons evolved from what was known as importation theory (Thomas, 1973). According to Thomas, the characteristics an offender brought to prison (e.g., procriminal attitudes, ongoing community ties, post-prison expectations) largely determined his or her behavior while incarcerated. Initially, importation theory was subsumed under the schools of crime perspective (Bonta & Gendreau, 1992; Irwin & Cressey, 1962), but its recent revivification now distinguishes it as a stand-alone theory. This was due to the research of Zamble and Porporino (1988, 1990) who coined the term *behavioral deep freeze* to describe how inmates coped with imprisonment. Their research found surprisingly little change in prisoners' psychological functioning (i.e., depression, anxiety, etc.) over time, so much so that Zamble (1992, p. 420) stated that "the most striking result was in the total absence of any evidence for general or widespread deteriorative effects" (see Bonta & Gendreau, 1990 for a review of earlier studies that confirmed this observation).

More recently, Camp and Gaes (2005) found little support for the prison environment to have negative effects on inmate misconducts, which are a good index of how well an inmate is adjusting. These authors admitted that their database had little information on inmate culture and prison regime, and this could have affected their results. This problem was overcome to a large extent by Goggin (2008). She analyzed data from all federal prisons in Canada. The sample size was 4,825 for adult male inmates ($N = 4,285$) and 3,595 for prison staff who rated the quality of life in prisons or, in her words, the "personality" of the prison. The items covered 22 domains on how well the prisons functioned (e.g., security and safety, living and working conditions, quality of programs). Her results supported the behavioral deep freeze model. Inmates in prisons that were rated worse on quality of life by both sources had very similar misconduct and recidivism rates to prisons rated higher in quality. It should be noted that the quality of life in Canadian prisons was rated relatively highly by both inmates and staff, which seems to be unlike the case for some American prisons (Haney, 2006).

The behavioral deep freeze theory has left some room for individual differences to occur. Zamble and Porporino (1990) reported some data that offenders ($N = 77$, risk level was not specified) that seemed to cope the worst with prison life over time had the most difficulty adjusting to civilian life (i.e., higher rates of recidivism).

In summary, the three perspectives on the effects of prison life, while intriguing as to how each has conceptualized the effects of prison life, have offered little guidance to correctional managers for running prisons. Two of the theories were silent regarding how to run prisons in a safe and humane fashion unless one (mistakenly) assumes that the deterrence policy of "no frills" prisons meets that goal. As to the matter of treatment, the specific deterrence model is clear about what needs to be done—more punishment—but there is no evidence for its support. The low-risk variation on the schools-of-crime stance would advocate for the sensible policy that low-risk offenders must be diverted from prisons, but there has been little discussion as to what types of treatment programs should be put in place. Within the deep freeze framework, Zamble and Porporino (1990) were more specific to the extent that they subscribed generally to behavioral treatment programs for rehabilitative purposes.

Therefore, we must turn to a different source of evidence, which is otherwise known as the "what works" prediction and treatment literature, to uncover guidelines to meet the two goals we established at the outset.

Effective Treatment in Prisons: Reducing Prison Misconducts and Recidivism

Even though the rehabilitative agenda was pushed aside with the emergence of the "get tough" era in corrections does not mean that it disappeared altogether in the United States. As testimony to this fact, an in-depth survey of the qualitative "management" literature on prisons dating back to the 1970s uncovered 517 published recommendations by correctional experts, most from the United States, on ways to improve the management of prisons (Gendreau & Keyes, 2001). The recommendations fell within the sphere of management principles, inmate services, staff training, and prison housing. Of special interest for our purposes was that the first and third most frequently nominated items within these areas were the provision of effective treatment programs and classification systems (i.e., prediction of criminal behavior).

How accurate were the experts in their clinical wisdom? Considerably so, it seems, based on the evidence that has been generated from correctional meta-analyses. The first set of meta-analyses focused on offender treatment (for a brief history, see Gendreau et al., 2006, pp. 728–733; for recent meta-analyses, see Lipsey, 2009; Smith, Gendreau, & Swartz, 2009). The second set came from the prediction of criminal behavior literature that began to appear in the later 1990s (Bonta, Law, & Hanson, 1998; Gendreau, Little, & Goggin 1996) and continues to this day (Campbell, French, & Gendreau, 2009; Hanson & Morton-Bourgon, 2009). The data from these meta-analyses as well as other source material formed the foundation of the principles of effective treatment programs (see Chapter 6). In order for rehabilitation to produce optimal effects, three principles have been deemed to be absolutely essential. They were as follows: *(1)* employ cognitive-behavioral treatment interventions (e.g., treatments based on behavioral, social learning, and cognitive theories); *(2)* target criminogenic needs (e.g., antisocial attitudes, substance abuse, etc.); and *(3)* deliver more intensive services to higher risk offenders. In studies where these principles were all in effect, reductions in recidivism in the 20%–30% range have been reported (Andrews & Bonta, 2010). Note that for the second and third principles to work in practice, risk prediction instruments that possess adequate predictive validities should be available. Several risk instruments have been identified (e.g., HCR-20, LSI-R, PCL-R, SIR, scale, VRAG) with the LSI-R recommended for measuring change in offenders for treatment and case management purposes (Campbell et al., 2009). Finally, meta-analyses have consistently demonstrated that certain types of programs had minimal or negative effects on recidivism (Andrews & Bonta, 2010; Gendreau, 1996; Lipsey, 2009); these programs were nonbehavioral in nature (e.g., nondirective, psychodynamic, group milieu therapies, programs based on control or coercion). In addition, programs of any type—including cognitive-behavioral interventions—that targeted low-risk offenders and noncriminogenic needs (e.g., self-esteem, anxiety) were not effective in reducing recidivism.

The principles outlined earlier also applied to institutional programs where the reductions in recidivism have been about half those of community-based programs (Andrews et al., 1990). However, the treatment literature for prison programs has been sparse and the prediction literature even more so. This led some correctional psychologists to actively pursue a research agenda to assess how closely the "general" treatment and prediction literature applied to prisons settings.

Here again, meta-analyses, along with one large sample size primary study, have paved the way for understanding what works in the case of prisons. We begin with the prediction literature. With one exception, the Custody Rating Scale, sample sizes have not yet been adequate to make precise conclusions—the confidence intervals are wide—about the magnitude and precision of the utility of risk instruments to predict misconducts. Three instruments (e.g., Custody Rating Scale, HCR-20, LSI-R) that have been identified as useful predictors of recidivism also predict prison misconducts at about the same magnitude (Campbell et al., 2009; Gendreau, Goggin, & Law, 1997; Smith & Gendreau, 2010). Also of significance for correctional managers is that one of the meta-analyses discovered that some situational variables forecast prison infractions (e.g., how staff treats inmates; inmate turnover) while others, like crowding, did not (Bonta & Gendreau, 1990; Gendreau, Goggin, & Law, 1997).

The prison treatment meta-analyses are different from their counterparts in one crucial respect. An important variable is misconducts, not only as a marker for how well a prison is being run safely but because misconducts have been assumed to be a proxy for criminal behavior (Camp & Gaes, 2005; Gendreau, Goggin, & Law, 1997), which, if true, meant that programs that reduced misconducts would decrease recidivism. Fortuitously, for our purposes this has turned out to be the case. The initial meta-analyses in this area, while based on a limited number of effect sizes, indicated that behavioral treatments in prison were associated with reductions in misconducts ($r = 0.17$ to 0.21) (Gendreau & Keyes, 2001; Morgan & Flora, 2002). These results and the ones that follow in this section, expressed in terms of correlation coefficients translate roughly into an equivalent percentage reduction when interpreted using the Binomial Effect Size Display unless base rates are extreme (Gendreau & Smith, 2007; Rosenthal, 1991). In other words, assuming a base rate of 50%, an $r = 0.32$, for example, means that the success rate of the treatment represents a 32% improvement (or 66% vs. 34%) over the control condition (Rosenthal, 1991).

Subsequently, French and Gendreau (2006) analyzed a much expanded database (50 effect sizes, $N = 5,809$). They reported that behavioral treatments reduced misconducts by a magnitude of $r = 0.26$, while the combined effect size for nonbehavioral, educational/vocational and unspecified programs was $r = 0.06$. Consistent with the findings from Andrews and Bonta (2010), the more criminogenic needs targeted, the better the result. French and Gendreau (2006) also rated the programs on a measure of therapeutic integrity—more about that later—and found reductions in misconducts for those rated high, medium, and low to be $r = 0.38, 0.20$, and 0.13, respectively. These results were impressive from a cost savings standpoint. Sampling from a large medium-security prison, Lovell and Jemelka (1996) calculated an average cost of $920 per misconduct.

Now we address the data regarding whether prisons can protect the public by reducing recidivism. French and Gendreau (2006) reported on a subset of programs that attempted to reduce prison misconducts and followed up their clientele after release from prison. They were subdivided as high versus low in their ability to reduce misconducts. Those programs rated high ($N = 12$) reduced recidivism ($r = 0.13$), whereas the ones designated low ($N = 11$) recorded an increase ($r = -0.05$) in recidivism. With so few effect sizes, these results need to be replicated, but if they hold up in future research decreases in recidivism of the magnitude of 10% can be highly cost-effective (see Cohen, 1998; Drake, Aos, & Miller, 2009).

We close this section by commenting on an issue that challenges the foregoing about the usefulness of treatment programs and point to an exemplary prison treatment program that can serve as a model for interested readers. In response to the very favorable meta-analytic results reported by Andrews et al. (1990), Lab and Whitehead (1990) proclaimed that the findings were overly optimistic because they were based on utopian demonstration projects.

These were presumably treatment programs that were generously funded, carefully implemented, and conducted by skilled evaluators and clinicians experienced in delivering effective treatments for offenders (see Andrews & Bonta, 2010; and Lipsey, 2009 for supportive evidence). These characteristics, it would be safe to assume, would not often be found in real-world "routine practice" programs where the treatment outcomes might be expected to be lower (Gendreau, Goggin, & Smith, 1999).

Lipsey (1999) was the first to confirm that "routine practice" programs had attenuated effects on recidivism. He examined 196 such programs for juvenile offenders and reported tremendous heterogeneity in the results. The average reduction in recidivism was 3%, of which eight sites were prison residential programs that produced no (0%) reduction in recidivism. Later on, Lipsey (2009) looked at a subset of juvenile "brand-name model" programs of the type Lab and Whitehead would have labeled as "utopian" and found that they did no better (approximately a 10% reduction across various categories) than routine generic programs. These results have reinforced the importance of the quality of implementation and treatment fidelity associated with cognitive-behavioral programs, rather than the "brand name" of the curriculum per se.

Further confirmation that routine programs have had positive effect came from the largest study yet produced on this topic (Smith & Gendreau, 2010). The sample size of adult male inmates was $N = 5,469$. Of these, 4,207 inmates were moderate to higher risk. The respective reductions in recidivism were 7% and 11% for a class of programs that were defined as appropriate in regard to the Andrews and Bonta principles of effective treatment. Programs that did not fit the principles produced increases of 7% for both risk groups.

The best example of an effective "routine practice" prison program we have come across in the published literature has been the Rideau Correctional Centre program in Ontario, Canada (Bourgon & Armstrong, 2005). It serves as a model that prison policy makers can emulate. First, the programmers established that their program elements met best practices criteria as measured by the CPAI-2000 (described in the next section) to determine the therapeutic integrity of the program and its adherence to the principles of effective intervention. In so doing, programmers ensured that implementing the program would have a greater chance of success. The program concentrated on identifying inmate thought patterns that reinforced antisocial behavior and replacing it by positive prosocial cognitions and skills through modeling, graduated practice, role playing, and relapse prevention. Detailed risk assessments were employed along with other psychological measures to confirm that the criminogenic needs (anger/aggression, criminal attitudes and at-risk lifestyle, substance abuse) of each offender were addressed. Staff matched the level of service (i.e., dosage level as determined by the number of hours of programming) with the risk level of the offender. The evaluators found that dosage was important with the greatest amount (e.g., 300 hours) necessary for high-risk offenders. The reduction in recidivism was 13%, a highly cost effective result (Lipsey, 1999, has suggested that 3% reductions were useful).

This research on "routine practice" programs underscored the need to measure the quality of correctional programs and to attend to the issue of program implementation, which has now become the most important matter in question in the treatment area (Gendreau, Goggin, & Smith, 1999; Lipsey, 2009).

The Importance of Implementation and Assessing Program Quality

Previous studies have demonstrated the importance of attending to program implementation (e.g., Lowenkamp, Latessa, & Smith, 2006; Paparozzi & Gendreau, 2005). Despite the fact that the science of implementation is still in its infancy in the field of corrections, some principles have been put forth (Gendreau, Goggin, & Smith, 1999; 2001; Goggin & Gendreau, 2006). These guidelines fell within four general categories: *(1)* general organizational factors; *(2)* program factors; *(3)* the change agent; and *(4)* staff factors. Please refer to Table 7.1 for a summary of these principles. Gendreau et al. (1999) cautioned that research in this area was in its infancy and as of yet, there was no evidence to clarify the necessary minimum number of factors for successful program implementation. As an aside, both authors, along with colleagues who have been involved in helping programs implement best practices, can attest to the fact that the information is often well received and many programs are genuinely interested in improving their service delivery.

The best way by which to encourage program quality is to engage in program evaluation. A popular measure for this purpose in corrections is the Correctional Program Assessment Inventory-2000 (CPAI-2000), an instrument designed to measure the extent to which programs adhere to the principles of effective intervention (for a brief summary see Gendreau, Smith, & French, 2006). The current version of the measure consists of eight domains: *(1)* organizational culture; *(2)* program implementation/ maintenance; *(3)* management/staff characteristics; *(4)* client risk-need practices; *(5)* program characteristics; *(6)* several dimensions of core correctional practices; *(7)* interagency communication; and *(8)* evaluation (Gendreau, Andrews, & Thériault, 2010). To date, it has been used to evaluate more than 550 offender treatment programs (Gendreau, Goggin, & Smith, 2001; Lowenkamp, 2004), the majority ($\approx$ 70%) of which have failed to achieve a passing grade.

The following two studies provided an example of its use. In the first study, a meta-analysis by Nesovic (2003) analyzed 173 studies from the published offender treatment literature and reported a mean effect of $r = 0.12$ with recidivism across 266 effect sizes. Using program descriptions described in the method sections of the studies, Nesovic (2003) assessed their quality using the CPAI and then correlated scores with the treatment effect reported for each program. Overall, the CPAI program scores correlated well with

Table 7.1 Implementation Guidelines

Organizational Factors

The following guidelines concern the *host agency* where the program will be implemented.

1. The agency has a history of adopting new initiatives.
2. The agency efficiently puts new initiatives into place.
3. The agency resolves issues in a timely fashion.
4. The bureaucratic structure is moderately decentralized, thus allowing for a flexible response to problematic issues.
5. Issues are resolved in a nonconfrontational manner.
6. There is little task/emotional-personal conflict within the organization at the interdepartmental, staff, management, and/or management-staff levels.
7. Staff turnover at all levels has been less than 25% during the previous 2 years.
8. The organization offers a formal program of instruction in the assessment and treatment of offenders on a biannual basis.
9. The agency has formal links with educational institutions or consultants for the purpose of seeking guidelines and training on clinical/service matters.

Program Factors

1. The need for the program has been empirically documented (e.g., surveys, focus groups).
2. The program is based on credible scientific evidence.
3. The program does not overstate the gains to be realized (e.g., recidivism reduction).
4. Stakeholders (i.e., community sources, management, and staff) agree that the program is timely, addresses an important matter, and is congruent with existing institutional and/or community values and practices.
5. Stakeholders agree that the program matches the needs of the clientele to be served.
6. Funding originates from the host agency.
7. The fiscal aspects of the program are cost-effective, do not jeopardize the continued funding of existing agency programs, and are sustainable for the near future.
8. The program is being initiated during a period when the agency is free of other major problems and/or conflicts.
9. The program is designed to maintain current staffing levels, support professional autonomy, enhance professional credentials, and save staff time and/or effort.
10. Program initiation proceeds incrementally, has a pilot/transitional phase, and initially focuses on achieving intermediate goals.

Change Agent

The term *change agent* refers to the person primarily responsible for initiating the program, and it can be either an external consultant or someone within the organization.

1. The change agent has an intimate knowledge of the agency and staff.
2. The change agent has the support of senior agency officials as well as that of line staff.
3. The change agent is compatible with the agency's mandate and goals.
4. The change agent has professional credibility.
5. The change agent has a history of successful program implementation in the agency's program area.

Table 7.1 (Cont'd)

6. In bringing about change, the change agent employs the following techniques: persuasion, motivational interviewing (e.g., empathy, discrepancy, nonconfrontational, self-efficacy support), reciprocity, authority (but does not use threats), reinforcement (e.g., praise), modeling, systematic problem solving, as well as practices advocacy and brokerage.
7. The change agent continues until there are clear performance indications that management and staff are able to maintain the delivery of the program with a reasonable degree of competence.

Staff Factors

In this context, the term *staff* refers to both those who deliver the service as well as the program directors who have direct line authority over treatment staff.

1. The staff members have frequent and immediate access to the change agent.
2. The staff members understand the theoretical basis of the program.
3. The staff members have the technical/professional skill to implement the program.
4. The staff members believe that they can run the program effectively.
5. To run the program efficiently, the staff are given the necessary time, given adequate resources, and provided with feedback mechanisms (e.g., focus groups and workshops).
6. The staff members participate directly in designing the new program.

Sources: From Gendreau, Goggin, and Smith (1999). Reprinted by Permission of SAGE Publications.

reductions in recidivism ($r = 0.46$). The "client assessment" and "program characteristics" domains were among the most robust ($r = 0.41$ and $r = 0.43$, respectively). Nesovic (2003) also examined correlations between individual scale items and effect size. Included among the strongest items (i.e., $r \geq 0.25$) were the following: the program received appropriate clients, offenders' dynamic risk factors are assessed, the program had a written manual, relapse prevention was practiced, staff were trained and hired based on their knowledge of effective relationship and therapeutic skills, and skilled evaluators were involved in the design and maintenance of the program.

In the second study, Lowenkamp, Latessa, and Smith (2006) conducted onsite evaluations of 38 community-based residential programs for adults in Ohio and found that offenders who successfully completed their treatment programs (regardless of program quality) had a 4% lower recidivism rate than their respective comparison groups. Programs categorized as high, medium, and low on the CPAI had respective recidivism reductions of 22%, 10%, and 5% and those categorized as very low actually increased recidivism by 19%. Lowenkamp, Latessa, and Smith (2006) reported robust correlations for the "program implementation," "client assessment," and "program characteristics" domains. With respect to individual items, potent correlations (i.e., $r \geq 0.25$) with outcome were reported on the program dimensions of program designer qualifications (e.g., education/experience, knowledge, and skills related to cognitive-behavioral programming, etc.); staff trained by program director;

program valued by criminal justice stakeholders and "at large" communities; assessment of offenders' risk level and dynamic needs; monitoring of offenders; offender time spent (at least 40% of time) in therapeutic activities; matching of staff to program; external quality controls on program; assessment of in-program progress and community follow-up provided; and ethical guidelines and defined completion criteria for the program.

The Chasm Between Science and Correctional Programming

One of the most vexing problems facing correctional programmers is the fact that a parallel universe to the one science has inhabited has had profound influences on correctional programming. Unlike the hard sciences (e.g., chemistry, neuroscience), applied areas in the social sciences—like corrections—are more likely to be vulnerable to value-based beliefs and ideologies (Gendreau, Goggin, Cullen, & Paparozzi, 2002). These beliefs are not based on the scientific process, which is characterized by repeated attempts at improving measurements, frequent replications of experiments, and analyzed by sophisticated methods like meta-analysis. Instead, when it comes to complex social policy issues such as exist in corrections, what is implemented under the rubric of common sense is often egregiously wrong. This has led to the emergence of programs that had virtually no scientific validity, which Latessa, Cullen, and Gendreau (2002) labeled as correctional quackery (CQ). For examples of CQ, we recommend the interested reader consult the lists compiled by Gendreau et al. (2006) and Gendreau, Smith, and Theriault (2009). It is a sobering, if not alarming experience to see what has occurred under the guise of effective treatments and the potential CQ has for producing harm to inmates (e.g., humiliation programs). The main reason behind the rise of CQ, besides poorly trained treatment staff, has been due to the political system (Gendreau et al. 2002; Gendreau, Smith, & Theriault, 2009; Hunt, 1999). The political tentacles of whoever has been in power have reached further down into government bureaucracies for patronage purposes and control of the bureaucracy and put in place managers that have no content knowledge of the portfolios they manage (Gendreau, Smith, & Theriault, 2009; Hunt, 1999). The end result is that credible programs have been emasculated and CQ allowed to flourish. Gendreau et al. (2009) remained skeptical that CQ will soon disappear, but they did suggest that there were some positive agendas (e.g., program accreditation) that might prove to be at least a partial antidote to the problem.

Another barrier to positive changes has been the conflict between public policy and the interests of powerful labor unions, especially in California (Dr. Joel Dvoskin, personal communication, February 6, 2010). However, when labor unions have advanced their interests of their members beyond the pale as it seems to have happened in some states, we believe that resistance to these changes is based on faulty notions, for example, that less inmate contact is safer than more inmate contact, or that reductions in the use of force endanger staff. Security and treatment are not contradictory roles. In fact, the opposite is true; prisons are safer when treatment programs exist (French & Gendreau, 2006).

One might also ask whether the expanding field of private corrections is poorly suited to implementing these principles. Simply put, this depends upon the nature of the contract under which such prisons exist. If they are paid only to warehouse inmates, then that is what the states are likely to get. On the other hand, if the goal of private prisons is to enhance public safety, then governments should include effective programs and more appropriate outcome measures into the contract's deliverables.

Conclusion

Finally, we leave the reader with this observation. Recalling the results of previous research that an involved evaluator can make a positive difference in treatment outcomes, it is important for social scientists to be involved at the field level to disseminate knowledge and to assist agencies in developing better treatment and training programs. In other words, it is clear that the principles of effective intervention are applicable to institutional programs, and that program integrity can be measured and enhanced. For this to happen, however, it is imperative that correctional agencies proscribe to the three Cs or credentials of correctional management (Gendreau et al., 2002, pp. 371–375). These involve using higher credentialed staff for program administration and delivery, seeing to it that the organization is credentialed itself by adhering to a code of ethics of humane care and evaluating the effectiveness of their programs, and respecting evidence based on rigorous scientific criteria for program development. In this way, we are confident that the principles and guidelines reviewed in this chapter will move our field a step or two closer to better approximating an experimenting society in corrections (Gendreau & Ross, 1987), a society that attends, as much as possible, to the evidence that will help people and agencies in need.

References

Andenaes, J. (1968). Does punishment deter crime? *Criminal Law Quarterly, 11*, 76–93.

Andrews, D., & Bonta, J. (2010). *The psychology of criminal conduct* (5th ed.). Cincinnati, OH: Anderson Publishing Co.

Andrews, D. A., Zinger, I., Hoge, R. D., Bonta, J., Gendreau, P., & Cullen, F. T. (1990). Does correctional treatment work? A clinically relevant and psychologically informed meta-analysis. *Criminology, 28*, 369–404.

Aufderheide, D. H., & Brown, P. H. (2005). Crisis in corrections: The mentally ill in America's prison. *Corrections Today, 37*, 30–33.

Bonta, J., & Gendreau, P. (1990). Reexamining the cruel and unusual punishment of prison life. *Law and Human Behavior, 14*, 347–366.

Bonta, J., & Gendreau, P. (1992). Coping with prison. In P. Suedfeld & P. E. Tetlock (Eds.), *Psychology and social policy* (pp. 343–354). New York: Hemisphere.

Bonta, J., Law, M., & Hanson, K. (1998). The prediction of criminal and violent recidivism among mentally disordered offenders: A meta-analysis. *Psychological Bulletin, 123*, 123–142.

Bourgon, G., & Armstrong, B. (2005). Transferring the principles of effective treatment into a "real world" prison setting. *Criminal Justice and Behavior, 32*, 3–25.

Brodsky, S. (2000). Judging the progress of psychology in corrections: The verdict is not good. *International Journal of Offender Therapy and Comparative Criminology, 44*, 141–145.

Briggs, C. S., Sundt, J. S., & Castellano, T. C. (2003). The effects of super maximum security prisons on aggregate levels of institutional violence. *Criminology, 41*, 1341–1376.

Buehler, R. E., Patterson, G. R., & Furniss, J. M. (1966). The reinforcement of behavior in institutional settings. *Behavioral Research and Therapy, 4*, 157–167.

Bukstel, L. H., & Kilmann, P. R. (1980). Psychological effects of imprisonment on confined individuals. *Psychological Bulletin, 88*, 469–493.

Camp, S. D., & Gaes, G. F. (2005). Criminogenic effects of the prison environment on inmate behavior: Some experimental evidence. *Crime and Delinquency, 51*, 425–442.

Campbell, M. A., French, S., & Gendreau, P. (2009). Predicting violence in adult offenders: A meta-analytic comparison of instruments. *Criminal Justice and Behavior, 36*, 567–590.

Chambliss, W. J. (1984). *Criminal law in action.* New York: Wiley.

Clear, T. R. (1995). *Harm in American penology: Offenders, victims, and their communities.* Albany: State University of New York Press.

Clemmer, D. (1940). *The prison community.* New York: Rinehart.

Cohen, M. A. (1998). The monetary value of saving a high-risk youth. *Journal of Quantitative Criminology, 14*, 5–32.

Cullen, F. T. (1995). Assessing the penal harm movement. *Journal of Research in Crime and Delinquency, 32*, 338–358.

Cullen, F. T. (2007). Make rehabilitation corrections' guiding paradigm. *Criminology and Public Policy, 6*, 717–727.

Cullen, F. T., Fisher, B. S., & Applegate, B. K. (2001). Public opinion about punishment and corrections. In M. Tonry (Ed.), *Crime and justice: A review of research* (Vol. 27, pp. 1–79). Chicago: University of Chicago Press.

Cullen, F. T., & Gilbert, K. E. (1982). *Reaffirming rehabilitation.* Cincinnati, OH: Anderson Publishing Company.

Cullen, F. T., Wright, J. P., Gendreau, P., & Andrews, D. A. (2003). What correctional treatment can tell us about criminological theory: Implications for social learning theory. In R. L. Akers & G. G. Jenson (Eds.), *Social learning and the explanation of crime: Advances in criminological theory* (pp. 339–362). New Brunswick, NJ: Transaction.

Davies, G., Hollin, C., & Bull, R. (2008). *Forensic psychology.* New York: Wiley.

Dejong, C. (1997). Survival analysis and specific deterrence: Integrating theoretical and empirical models of recidivism. *Criminology, 35*, 561–575.

DeLisi, M., & Walters, G. D. (2011). Multiple homicide as a function of prisonization and concurrent instrumental violence: Testing an interactive model–A research note. *Crime and Delinquency, 57*, 147–161.

Doob, A. N., Sprott, J. B., Marinos, V., & Varma, K. N. (1998). *An exploration of Ontario residents' views of crime and the criminal justice system* (C98–931656-4). Toronto, ON: University of Toronto, Centre of Criminology.

Drake, E., Aos, S., & Miller, M. (2009). Evidence-based public policy options to reduce crime and criminal justice costs: Implications in Washington state. *Victims and Offenders, 4*, 170–196.

Dyer, J. (2000). *The perpetual prisoner machine: How America profits from crime.* Boulder, CO: Westview Press.

Editorial. (2010, May 9). They don't often agree. *The New York Times.* Retrieved from http://www.nytimes.com/2010/05/10/opinion/10mon3.html.

Fabelo, T. (1996). *Testing the case for more incarceration in Texas: The record so far.* Austing, TX: Criminal Justice Policy Council, State of Texas.

Feeley, M. M., & Simon, J. (1992). The new penology: Notes on emerging strategy of corrections and its implications. *Criminology, 30*, 449–474.

Finn, P. (1996). No-frills prisons and jails: A movement in flux. *Federal Probation, 60*, 35–44.

Forer, L. (1994). *A rage to punish: The unintended consequences of mandatory sentencing.* New York: Norton.

Fowler, R. (1976). Sweeping reforms ordered in Alabama prisons. *APA Monitor, 7*, 1.

Freedman, D., Pisani, R., Purves, R., & Adhikari, A. (1991). *Statistics* (2nd ed.). New York: W.W. Norton.

French, S. A., & Gendreau, P. (2006). Reducing prison misconducts: What works. *Criminal Justice and Behavior, 33*, 185–218.

Gawande, A. (2009). Hellhole. *The New Yorker.* Retrieved from http://www.newyorker.com/reporting/2009/03/30/090330fa_fact_gawande?currentPage=all

Gendreau, P. (1996). The principles of effective intervention with offenders. In A. T. Harland (Ed.), *Choosing correctional options that work: Defining the demand and evaluating the supply* (pp. 117–130). Thousand Oaks, CA: Sage.

Gendreau, P., Andrews, D. A., & Thériault, Y. (2010). Correctional Program Assessment Inventory – 2010 (CPAI-2010), Beresford, New Brunswick, Canada.

Gendreau, P., Goggin, C., Cullen, F. T., & Paparozzi, M. (2002). The common sense revolution and correctional policy. In J. McGuire (Ed.), *Offender rehabilitation and treatment: Effective programs and policies to reduce re-offending* (pp. 360–386). Chichester, England: Wiley & Sons.

Gendreau, P., Goggin, C., French, S. A., & Smith, P. (2006). Practicing psychology in correctional settings: "What works" in reducing criminal behavior. In I. B. Weiner & A. K. Hess (Eds.), *The handbook of forensic psychology* (3rd ed., pp. 722–750). Hoboken, NJ: John Wiley & Sons.

Gendreau, P., Goggin, C., & Law, M. (1997). Predicting prison misconducts. *Criminal Justice and Behavior, 24*, 414–431.

Gendreau, P., Goggin, C., & Smith, P. (1999). The forgotten issue of effective correctional treatment: Program implementation. *International Journal of Offender Therapy, 43*, 180–187.

Gendreau, P., Goggin, C., & Smith, P. (2001). Implementation guidelines for correctional programs in the "real world." In G. A. Bernfeld, D. P. Farrington, & A. W. Leschied (Eds.), *Offender rehabilitation in practice* (pp. 247–268). Chichester, England: Wiley.

Gendreau, P., & Keyes, D. (2001). Making prisons safer and more humane environments. *Canadian Journal of Criminology, 43*, 123–130.

Gendreau, P., Little, T., & Goggin, C. (1996). A meta-analysis of adult offender recidivism: What works! *Criminology, 34*, 575–607.

Gendreau, P., & Ross, R. R. (1981). Correctional potency: Treatment and deterrence on trial. In R. Roesch & R. R. Corrado (Eds.), *Evaluation and criminal justice policy* (pp. 29–57). Beverly Hills, CA: Sage.

Gendreau, P., & Ross, R. R. (1987). Revivification of rehabilitation: Evidence from the 1980s. *Justice Quarterly, 4*, 349–409.

Gendreau, P., & Smith, P. (2007). Influencing the people who count. *Criminal Justice and Behavior, 34*, 1536–1559.

Gendreau, P., Smith, P., & French, S. A. (2006). The theory of effective correctional intervention: Empirical status and future directions. In F. T. Cullen, J. P. Wright, & K. R. Blevins (Eds.), *Taking stock: The status of criminological theory: Advances in criminological theory* (Vol. 15, pp. 419–446). New Brunswick, NJ: Transaction.

Gendreau, P., Smith, P., & Theriault, Y. L. (2009). Chaos theory and correctional treatment: Common sense, correctional quackery, and the law of fartcatchers. *Journal of Contemporary Criminal Justice, 25*, 384–396.

Gibbons, J., & Katzenbach, N. (2006). *Confronting confinement: A report of the commission on safety and abuse in America's prisons.* New York: Vera Institute of Justice.

Goggin, C. (2008). *Is prison "personality" associated with recidivism?* Unpublished doctoral dissertation, University of New Brunswick, Saint John.

Goggin, C., & Gendreau, P. (2006). The implementation and maintenance of quality services in offender rehabilitation programmes. In C. R. Hollin & E. J. Palmer (Eds.), *Offending behavior programmes: Development, application, and controversies* (pp. 209–246). Chichester, England: John Wiley.

Haney, C. (2003). Mental health issues in long-term solitary and "supermax" confinement. *Crime and Delinquency, 49*, 124–156.

Haney, C. (2006). *Reforming punishment: Psychological limits to the pains of imprisonment.* Washington, DC: American Psychological Association.

Haney, C., & Zimbardo, P. G. (1977). The socialization into criminality: On becoming a prisoner and a guard. In J. L. Tapp & F. J. Levine (Eds.), *Law, justice and the individual in society: Psychological and legal issues* (pp. 198–223). New York: Holt, Rinehard and Winston.

Haney, C., & Zimbardo, P. G. (1998). The past and future of U.S. prison policy: Twenty-five years after the Stanford prison experiment. *American Psychologist, 53*, 709–727.

Hanson, R. K., & Morton-Bourgon, K. E. (2009). The accuracy of recidivism risk assessments for sexual offenders: A meta-analysis. *Psychological Assessment, 21*, 1–21.

Human Rights Watch. (2003) *Ill equipped: U.S. prisons and offenders with mental illness.* New York: Human Rights Watch. Retrieved from http://www.hrw.org/en/reports/2003/10/21/ill-equipped.

Hunt, M. (1999). *The new know-nothings: The political foes of the scientific study of human nature.* New Brunswick, NJ: Transaction Press.

Irwin, J., & Cressey, D. R. (1962). Thieves, convicts, and the inmate culture. *Social Problems, 10,* 142–155.

Jaman, D. R., Dickover, R. M., & Bennett, L. A. (1972). Parole outcome as a function of time served. *British Journal of Criminology, 12,* 5–34.

Lab, S. P., & Whitehead, J. T. (1990). From "nothing works" to "the appropriate works": The latest stop on the search for the secular grail. *Criminology, 28,* 405–417.

Leschied, A. W., & Gendreau, P. (1994). Doing justice in Canada: YOA policies that can promote community safety. *Canadian Journal of Criminology, 36,* 291–303.

Latessa, E. J., Cullen, F. T., & Gendreau, P. (2002). Beyond correctional quackery: Professionalism and the possibility of effective treatment. *Federal Probation, 66,* 43–49.

Lilly, J. R., Cullen, F. T., & Ball, R. A. (1995). *Criminological theory: Context and consequences.* Thousand Oaks, CA: Sage Publications.

Lipsey, M. W. (1999). Can rehabilitative programs reduce the recidivism of juvenile offenders? An inquiry into the effectiveness of practical programs. *Virginia Journal of Social Policy and Law, 6,* 611–641.

Lipsey, M. W. (2009). The primary factors that characterize effective interventions with juvenile offenders: A meta-analytic overview. *Victims and Offenders, 4,* 124–147.

Lovell, D., & Jemelka, R. (1996). When inmates misbehave: The costs of discipline. *The Prison Journal, 76,* 165–179.

Lowenkamp, C. (2004). *Correctional program integrity and treatment effectiveness: A multi-site, program level analysis.* Unpublished doctoral dissertation, University of Cincinnati, Cincinnati, OH.

Lowenkamp, C. T., Latessa, E. J., & Smith, P. (2006). Does correctional program quality really matter? The impact of adhering to the principles of effective intervention. *Criminology and Public Policy, 5,* 201–220.

Maruna, S., & Toch, H. (2005). The impact of incarceration on the desistance process. In J. Travis & C. Visher (Eds.), *Prisoner reentry and public safety in America* (pp. 139–178). New York: Cambridge University Press.

Mason, P. (1998). Systems and process: The prison in cinema. *Images: A Journal of Film and Popular Culture.* Retrieved from http://www.imagesjournal.com/issue06/features/prison.htm

McGuire, J. (2004). *Understanding psychology and crime: Perspectives on theory and action.* Berkshire, England: Open University Press.

Mitford, J. (1973). *Kind and unusual punishment.* New York: Knopf.

Morgan, R. D., & Flora, D. B. (2002). Group psychotherapy with incarcerated offenders: A research synthesis. *Group Dynamics, 6,* 198–213.

Nagin, D. S. (1998). Criminal deterrence research at the outset of the twenty-first century. In M. Tonry (Ed.), *Crime and justice: A review of research* (Vol. 23, pp. 1–42). Chicago: University of Chicago Press.

Nesovic, A. (2003). *Psychometric evaluation of the Correctional Program Assessment Inventory.* Unpublished doctoral thesis, Carleton University, Ottawa, ON.

Newman, G. (1983). *Just and painful: A case for the corporal punishment of criminals.* New York: Macmillan Press.

Nieuwbeerta, P., Nagin, D& Blockland, A. (2007). The effects of imprisonment on the course of criminal careers. *Man and Society, 82,* 272–279.

Nossiter, A. (1994, September 14). Making time harder, states cut jail T.V. and sports. *The New York Times,* pp. A1.

Orsagh, T., & Chen, J-R. (1988). The effect of time served on recidivism: An interdisciplinary theory. *Journal of Quantitative Criminology, 4,* 155–171.

Paparozzi, M. A., & Gendreau, P. (2005). An ISP that worked: Service delivery, professional orientation and organizational supportiveness. *The Prison Journal, 85,* 445–446.

Pizarro, J., & Stenius, V. M. (2004). Supermax prisons: Their rise, current practices, and effects on inmates. *Crime and Delinquency, 84,* 248–264.

Pyle, D. J. (1995). *Cutting the costs of crime: The economics of crime and criminal justice.* London: Institute of Economic Affairs.

Rangel, C. (1999, February 22). America the jailhouse. *Wall Street Journal,* pp. A11.

Rosenthal, R. (1991). *Meta-analytic procedures for social research.* Newbury Park, CA: Sage.

Smith, P., & Gendreau, P. (2010). A longitudinal examination of inmate behaviour and program activities on institutional adjustment and recidivism. *Forum on Corrections Research, 1.* Retrieved from http://www.csc-scc.gc.ca/text/pblct/forum/Vol19No1/v19n1b-eng.shtml.

Smith, P., Gendreau, P., & Swartz, K. (2009). Validating the principles of effective intervention: A systematic review of the contributions of meta-analysis in the field of corrections. *Victims and Offenders, 2,* 148–169.

Smith, P., Goggin, C., & Gendreau, P. (2002). *The effects of prison sentences and intermediate sanctions on recidivism: General effects and individual differences.* Ottawa, ON: Public Works and Government Services Canada.

Siegel, L. J. (2008). *Criminology* (10th ed.). Belmont, CA: Thomson Wadsworth.

Song, L., & Lieb, R. (1993). *Recidivism: The effect of incarceration and length of time served.* Olympia: Washington State Institute for Public Policy.

Spelman, W. (2009). Crime, cash, and limited options: Explaining the prison boom. *Criminology and Public Policy, 8,* 29–77.

Sykes, G. (1958). *The society of captives: A study of a maximum-security prison.* Princeton, NJ: Princeton University Press.

Tanasichuk, C. L., Wormith, S. J., & Guzzo, L. (2009). *The predictive validity of the Level of Service Inventory-Ontario Revision (LSI-OR) with Aboriginal offenders.* University of Saskatchewan, SK, Canada.

Tonry, M. (2004). *Thinking about crime: Sense and sensibility in American penal culture.* Oxford, England: Oxford University Press.

von Hirsch, A., Bottoms, A. E., Burney, E., & Wikstron, P-O. (1999). *Criminal deterrence and sentence severity: An analysis of recent research.* Oxford, England: Hart Publishing.

Walters, G. (2003). Changes in criminal thinking and identity in novice and experienced inmates: Prisonization revisited. *Criminal Justice and Behavior, 30,* 399–421.

Webb, J. (2009, March 29). Why we must fix our prisons. *Parade Magazine*, p.5.

Wright, R. A. (1996). In support of prisons. In B. W. Hancock & P. M. Sharp (Eds.), *Criminal justice in America: Theory, practice and policy* (pp. 252–266). Upper Saddle River, NJ: Prentice Hall.

Zamble, E. (1992). Behavior and adaptation in long-term prison inmates. *Criminal Justice and Behavior, 19*, 409–425.

Zamble, E., & Porporino, F. J. (1988). *Coping behavior and adaptation in prison inmates.* New York: Springer-Verlag.

Zamble, E., & Porporino, F. J. (1990). Coping with imprisonment. *Criminal Justice and Behavior, 17*, 53–70.

Zedlewski, E. W. (1987). *Making confinement decisions: The economics of disincarceration.* NIJ Publication No. NCJ-1054834. Washington, DC: National Criminal Justice Reference Service.

8

Putting Science to Work: How the Principles of Risk, Need, and Responsivity Apply to Reentry

Susan Turner and Joan Petersilia

The explosive, continued growth of America's incarcerated population is now well known. Given the war on drugs, mandatory sentencing, and other "get tough on crime" measures, there are now over 1.5 million prisoners and over 750,000 jail detainees in the United States. America's incarceration rate (737 per 100,000 people) is significantly higher than any other industrialized nation (Pew Charitable Trust, 2008). Despite the fact that the U.S. economy is in recession and states are struggling to fund an increasingly expensive corrections system (now over $60 billion annually), the U.S. prison population continues to grow, up nearly 2% in 2007. By the end of this year (2011), the nation's prison population is projected to reach 1.7 million people (Pew Charitable Trust, 2007).

Virtually all of these inmates will come home. Except for those serving death or life-without-parole sentences (about 7% of all prisoners) and the small number of inmates who die in prison (about 3,000 each year), nearly all prisoners (93%) will be released (Petersilia, 2008). In 2008, nearly 700,000 individuals—1,900 a day—left federal and state prisons to return home. If we add the nation's jails, an additional 12 million people a year will make the difficult transition from incarceration to home (Solomon, Osborne, LoBuglio, Mellow, & Mikamal, 2008).

Prison release rates are expected to accelerate in the next few years, making reentry challenges even more acute. In part, these increases reflect many jurisdictions' reconsideration of harsh drug laws passed in the 1980s and 1990s with their acceleration of prison releases for some drug offenders as a result. For example, Michigan eliminated mandatory minimum sentences and adopted procedures allowing early parole eligibility for certain drug offenders in 2002 (Greene, 2003). The U.S. Supreme Court and the U.S. Sentencing Commission voted in 2007 to allow judges to retroactively reduce crack cocaine sentences for some federal inmates, meaning that thousands of federal inmates—many with serious substance abuse histories—may soon walk out of prison doors (see http://www.ussc.gov/PRESS/rel121107.htm).

"Prisoner reentry" may be defined as the process by which a former inmate returns to the community and hopefully transitions into a law-abiding citizen (Petersilia, 2003). There has been a recent explosion of interest in prisoner reentry, not only because offender populations have increased but also because research shows that inmate work and treatment needs have *increased* at exactly the same time that prison and parole programs designed to meet those needs have *decreased* (Petersilia, 2003, 2006). Today's inmate is likely to have a history of prior convictions, substance abuse problems, unemployment, and/or involvement in gang activities or drug dealing. Each of these factors is known to predict recidivism, yet few are addressed while the inmate is in prison or on parole.

For example, only about one-third of released prisoners receive vocational or educational training while in prison (Lynch & Sabol, 2001). Despite the fact that three-quarters of inmates have alcohol or drug abuse problems, only one-quarter of inmates participate in a substance abuse program prior to release (Beck, 2000). These training and treatment participation figures are lower than rates were a decade ago, according to surveys of state and federal inmates conducted by the Bureau of Justice Statistics (Petersilia, 2003). Even when offenders do participate in substance abuse treatment programs, they consist mostly of inmate self-help groups rather than professionally run programs that studies have found to be most effective (Petersilia, 2003).

This situation—where hundreds of thousands of untreated inmates are released annually—threatens public safety. According to the Bureau of Justice Statistics (BJS), more than two-thirds of released state prisoners are expected to be rearrested for a felony or serious misdemeanor within 3 years after release (Langan & Levin, 2002). These former prisoners account for an estimated 4.7% of *all* arrests for serious crime (murder, rape robbery, aggravated assault, burglary, larceny, and motor vehicle theft; Langan & Levin, 2002). When examined by specific crime type, released prisoners account for an estimated 8.4% of all homicides, 5.4% of all rapes, and 9% of all robberies. Independent estimates also suggest that parolees may be responsible for nearly 10% of all index (serious) arrests occurring in the United States each year (Rosenfeld, Wallman, & Fornango, 2005). This is not inconsequential.

Virtually no one believes that the current prison and parole system is working. The question is, can we do better? Can we provide offenders with educational, literacy, vocational, substance abuse, and/or job placement services that could improve reentry success? The short answer is yes, but this will require investing in reentry programs that incorporate effective principles of correctional treatment (e.g., see Chapter 6), targeting those programs to specific offenders who can most benefit, and continually evaluating and revising program models as the science accumulates.

Alternative Approaches to Reentry and Evidence on What Works to Reduce (Violent) Recidivism

The cry for more correctional services is always met with public skepticism. This is an unfortunate legacy of the Martinson (1974) nothing-works era. But today, there is ample scientific evidence that prison and parole programs *do* work, for *some* people, in *some* settings, and if delivered by appropriately *trained staff.* At the same time, programs that are poorly targeted, poorly designed, and poorly implemented do not work and can actually do harm to those treated. Offenders are not a homogeneous group, and rehabilitation depends on recognizing their diversity in needs, risks, and amenability to treatment.

This chapter considers three different models relevant to reentry: a psychological model (Risk-Need-Responsivity [RNR]; see Chapter 6), an ecological model, and a punitive model that focuses on swift and certain sanctions. We define each model and summarize evidence for or against each one. Much of the evidence on RNR and related correctional principles fails to distinguish between probationers and those reentering the community from prison or jail. Similarly, most research does not distinguish between violent and other forms of recidivism. Where we can, we focus our research review on the reentry population and violent recidivism.

Defining Three Models of Reentry

Risk-Need-Responsivity Model

Because RNR principles are defined by Andrews (see Chapter 6), we simply highlight here that RNR focuses on the psychology of criminal conduct with three principles at the core of effective programming (Andrews & Bonta, 2010; Andrews, Bonta, & Hoge, 1990; California Department of Corrections, 2007). These principles are *(a)* risk—direct intensive services to those at higher risk of recidivism, *(b)* need—target criminogenic needs or strong risk factors for recidivism, and *(c)* responsivity—provide services in a way that is responsive to an offender's learning styles and abilities.

Ecological Model

In his address to the U.S. Congress, Jeremy Travis (2009) stressed the need to move beyond the constraints of a medical model that focuses narrowly on the individual to an "ecological" model that also includes the community context to which offenders return after prison. According to Travis, innovations in reentry should focus on changing the offender's reentry environment. Given such observations, an Expert Panel for the California Department of Corrections and Rehabilitation (2007) developed the California Logic Model, which highlighted community reintegration as a vital part of an eight-step continuous cycle from assessment through release into the community. According to that panel:

> Public safety in our communities is the responsibility of all citizens.
> It is not just the responsibility of the correctional and other justice
> agencies. Research and experience in recent years helped us realize that
> the transition from prison to the community is difficult and filled with
> many obstacles. And, continuity of care is necessary for reducing
> recidivism. In particular, we know that individuals are at higher risk to
> return to prison shortly after their releases. Offenders require the
> assistance of their family members, friends, local support systems, and
> broader communities to sustain the treatment gains they have
> achieved through their participation in correctional programming.
> (California Department of Corrections and Rehabilitation, 2007, p. 38)

The "ecological" approach may be seen as being aligned more closely with historical sociological explanations of crime (e.g., social disorganization, collective efficacy) and rooted in social institutions and structures (see Rose & Clear, 1998; Sampson, Raudenbush, & Earls, 1997) than an individual-based approach, such as RNR. In some ways, the psychological approach of RNR may be viewed as counter to the ecological model.

Swift and Certain Sanctions Model

If one approaches crime control from a perspective in which individuals make the choice about committing crime, depending on the costs and benefits (Wilson, 1975), raising the costs and decreasing the benefits of crime should reduce its commission. Thus, swifter, more certain, and more severe punishments should deter offenders from committing new crimes.

These punishment principles are often difficult to achieve in practice (see Chapter 13). In the United States, only a small fraction of offenses result in arrest, prosecution, and incarceration; justice takes a long time; and the expected level of punishment for a given crime may be low (Nagin, 1998).

Still, U.S. policies heavily feature severe punishment, as is apparent in policies that include the death penalty, three-strikes legislation, and mandatory sentencing. Although drug court models are designed to change behavior by using both "carrot" incentives and "stick" punishments, some heavily emphasize swifter and more certain punishment by incorporating a graduated sanctions approach to noncompliance, where the severity of sanctions is incrementally matched to the seriousness of noncompliance (Marlowe, 2008).

Recently, professional discourse about the severity, certainty, and swiftness of punishment took a somewhat new twist. In his book, *When Brute Force Fails: How to Have Less Crime and Less Punishment*, Mark Kleiman (2009) argued that the certainty and swiftness of punishment, not its severity, will maximize the deterrent effect: "... [T]o the extent that offenders are present-oriented, reckless, and overconfident, swiftness and certainty in punishment will be more important in shaping offense rates" (Kleiman, 2009, p. 93). The focus of this approach is on compliance with the rules, not treatment per se.

Comparing the Three Models

Although there is some overlap among these three models, they broadly differ in their emphasis on the individual (RNR, sanctions) versus his or her community (ecological) as the *target* of change. Moreover, all three emphasize different *mechanisms* of change: positive reinforcement and modeling to shape prosocial behavior (RNR), punishment to extinguish antisocial behavior (sanctions), or educational, social, and community services to address contextual needs (ecological). In this section, we unpack these differences as they are relevant to community supervision.

Ecological Model and Risk-Need-Responsivity

The ecological model envisions the community as a major partner in an offender's reintegration into society. In part, this recognizes that many current policies act as barriers and roadblocks to reentry. Returning offenders may not be permitted to vote, live in publically-funded Section 8 housing, hold certain jobs, or receive public benefits or other services based on their status as felons (Petersilia, 2003; Tarlow, 2011). Sex offenders, in particular, face a host of restrictions (Lussier, Dahabieh, Deslauriers-Varin, & Thomson, 2011). At the same time, evidence shows that having a job and residential stability reduces recidivism (Drake, Aos, & Miller, 2009; Petersilia, 2003). The call, then, for ecological models is to go beyond individual interventions to remove structural barriers for offenders (Travis, 2009). In contrast, the RNR model focuses more on the individual than on changes that should be made in society to assist in recidivism reduction. Still, RNR is not inconsistent with the ecological model. One could argue that RNR would call for barriers to be removed if this directly impacted an offender's criminogenic needs; for example, working to place offenders outside of communities where their criminogenic peers reside.

Sanctions Model and Risk-Need-Responsivity

As Kleiman (2009) notes, the swift and certain sanctions approach is at odds with both RNR and general psychological principles that positive reinforcement generates greater and more lasting behavior change than punishment (see Chapters 6 and 13). As detailed later, however, this model is not completely divorced from RNR. One might argue that the use of swift and certain punishments for offenders who are often impulsive, reckless, and oriented to the present is a more "responsive" approach than the usual delayed, inconsistent, and potentially very harsh sanctions applied for violations under community supervision.

Summarizing Evidence for the Three Models

Risk-Need-Responsivity in Reentry

RISK ASSESSMENT   According to the RNR model, one should assess an offender's risk of recidivism to *(a)* determine the intensity of services to allocate to him or her, and *(b)* target his or her criminogenic needs, that is, dynamic risk factors that could be reduced with particular types of services (e.g., criminal thinking, substance abuse, employment problems).

It is clear that a wide variety of agencies in the United States are systematically assessing offenders' risk of recidivism. As of 2004, 28 states used a prediction instrument for parole decisions, with eight states using the RNR-based Level of Services Inventory-Revised (LSI-R; see Harcourt, 2007). In addition, a national survey of adult prisons, jails, and community corrections agencies revealed than just over one-third uses a standardized risk tool to gauge an offender's risk to public safety (Taxman, Cropsey, Young, & Wexler, 2007)

It is less clear that the field is using risk assessments to allocate treatment resources or to target and reduce criminogenic needs. In fact, there is controversy about whether dynamic risk factors (like criminal thinking) add any utility to static risk factors (like criminal history) in predicting recidivism (compare Andrews, 2009; Baird, 2009). As such, there is debate about whether the pursuits of risk assessment and risk reduction should be separated or integrated. As Skeem and Monahan (2011) note, even if one advocates integration (as in the RNR model), including dynamic risk factors will add no value to simpler approaches unless those factors are translated into an individual supervision and treatment plan (rather than simply filed away), and systematically targeted with appropriate services (rather than ignored in resource allocation).

REENTRY SERVICES   Full tests of RNR in parole have been limited. The field relies heavily upon the results of meta-analyses conducted by two teams led by Andrews and Lipsey (see Chapter 6) to evaluate RNR principles. Most meta-analyses, however, have not been conducted separately for parolees. In a recent analysis of 548 independent study samples, Lipsey (2009) used four categories to classify the type of juvenile justice supervision and control. The probation or parole category represented a third of the studies examined in this meta-analysis. Andrews's meta-analysis (see Chapter 6) compares community corrections (i.e., probation and parole) with prison settings.

Although both teams of investigators find that programs are particularly effective in reducing recidivism when delivered in community settings, they do not separate reentry from other forms of community supervision (e.g., probation).

The Washington State Institute for Public Policy has also conducted relevant meta-analyses. In their review of 291 evaluations of adult corrections programs, Aos, Miller, and Drake (2006) found that programs for the general offender population that applied cognitive-behavioral treatment approaches (which are consistent with RNR; see Chapter 6) significantly reduced recidivism by an average of 8% compared with treatment as usual. That is, without the cognitive-behavioral approach, 49% of offenders will recidivate, and with cognitive-behavioral treatment, 45% of offenders will recidivate. Even with these relatively small effects, cognitive-behavioral treatment programs were cost effective, yielding $2.54 to $11.48 for every program dollar invested. The cost-benefit ratio of programs has been particularly relevant in many program decisions lately—jurisdictions are looking to meta-analyses like these to identify programs that are cost effective.

A handful of recent studies directly test the principles of RNR for the reentry population. Lowenkamp, Latessa, and Holsinger (2006) studied 97 correctional programs and over 13,000 parolees to assess the extent to which programs that followed the risk principle by providing higher risk cases with more intensive services were more successful in reducing return to custody than those that did not. Study findings revealed that, "The correctional programs included in these analyses, whether residential or nonresidential, showed increases in recidivism rates unless offenders who were higher risk were targeted and provided more services for a longer period of time " (Lowenkamp, Latessa, et al., 2006, p. 88).

Lowenkamp and Latessa (2005) tested core principles of RNR with 38 halfway house programs that served parolees and offenders on postrelease control. The authors found that residential programs were effective in reducing recidivism with higher risk offenders and parole violators (but, in keeping with the risk principle, *increased* recidivism for lower risk parolees). Further, they found that the most effective programs were those that targeted the greatest number of criminogenic needs and utilized cognitive-behavioral techniques, as well as role playing and practicing of skills. In addition, programs that were implemented with integrity showed better outcomes.

Although not tested specifically on a reentry population, Taxman and Thanner (2003) tested the effect of the RNR risk principle on recidivism among drug offenders on probation. Half were randomly assigned to receive a "seamless" model in which probation supervision and substance abuse services were integrated, whereas the other half received routine probation and routine referral to treatment. The study stratified offender's risk level, as determined by a validated risk assessment tool. Support for better recidivism outcomes for high-risk offenders were observed in one site, but not in the other. Reconceptualizing the risk variable to include the extent of drug use revealed more consistent support for RNR, leading the authors to argue for more attention in the RNR model to the nature of the criminogenic factors of the target population. Supporters of RNR might counter that the model allows for individualized criminogenic needs (i.e., heavy substance abuse is likely a criminogenic need for many offenders) and for ensuring that services are responsive to the specific problems of an individual.

The Ecological Model in Reentry

According to Travis (2009), several communities have developed promising programs that represent a new frontier in reentry innovation. These programs include comprehensive interagency initiatives (the Boston Reentry Initiative), offender notification forums (Project Safe Neighborhood initiative), reentry courts, and community-based interventions (the Baltimore Reentry Partnership) (Travis, 2009). We next describe the first two, which have been best studied.

The Boston Reentry Initiative (BRI) was established as an interagency collaborative to reduce recidivism among violent offenders released from jail. The program includes mentoring, social service assistance, and vocational development provided by community-based and governmental agencies, as well as the family. At the same time, justice agencies discuss the consequences for misbehaviors and relay to offenders that they are being watched and will be held accountable. Braga, Piehl, and Hureau (2009) conducted a quasi-experimental evaluation of the program's effect on rearrest during a 3-year follow-up period, using a historical control group and propensity score matching to control for differences between the treatment and control groups. Groups were well matched. Results indicated that participants in the BRI group showed longer "time to failure" for any arrest, as well as arrests for violent offenses.

Project Safe Neighborhoods (PSN) was a federally-funded national initiative designed to reduce the level of gun violence in communities. Each jurisdiction was allowed to design its program to fit local legal contexts. Chicago implemented "offender notification forums," in which recently placed parolees were brought to community meetings at which police stressed the consequences of gun use and the choices that parolees had to make to not reoffend. The program included provision of community resources ranging from shelter, education, substance abuse treatment, job training, mentorship, and behavioral counseling. A quasi-experimental design was used in which two adjacent police districts were used as the treatment group and two other districts were used as near equivalent comparison groups. Data were collected over a period of 6 years on homicides, aggravated batteries, and assaults in each area. Using a growth-curve modeling approach and propensity score matching to help control for differences between PSN and comparison districts, researchers found that homicides, but not aggravated batteries and assaults, were lower in the PSN neighborhoods (Papachristos, Meares, & Fagan, 2007).

Although Travis (2009) offers these two initiatives as examples of the ecological approach, one can also see strains of the swift and certain sanctions model in each. Both PSN and the BRI stress the ability of law enforcement to know when misbehavior occurs and to be able to respond to it.

The Swift and Certain Sanctions Model in Reentry

A recently developed program in Hawaii—Hawaii's Opportunity Probation with Enforcement (HOPE)—uses principles of punishment in an effort to improve outcomes for methamphetamine-involved probationers who were not performing well under probation supervision. The logic behind HOPE is to deliver "swift and sure" sanctions that will provide structure to offenders whose lives are often in disarray (Hawken & Kleiman, 2009; National Institute of Justice, 2008). The model focuses on drug use and includes the following key components:

- At the outset of probation, the judge issues a formal warning in open court that any violation will result in an immediate, brief jail stay (which occurs on weekends for employed offenders, to avoid disrupting work schedules).
- Randomized drug tests are conducted weekly to eliminate any "safe window" for undetected drug use.
- Probationers appear before the judge only when a violation is detected.
- There is a short turnaround time between violation and sanction, and bench warrants are served immediately for absconders.
- Fixed sanctions for violations are applied on a fixed schedule, starting at 2 days in jail and increasing in length for subsequent violations.
- Drug treatment is mandated only for probationers who request a treatment referral or repeatedly test positive for drug use; residential treatment may be mandated as an alternative to revocation for repeat offenders. Treatment is provided to a relatively limited proportion of participants.

These components address broken aspects of the application of punishment in current probation supervision, especially for drug offenders in which "drug testing of probationers is too infrequent, because test results come back too slowly, because sanctions are too rare, too delayed, and too severe (months, or occasionally years, in prison)" (Hawken & Kleiman, 2007).

Although early results were positive for the program, they were based on a limited evaluation design (Hawken & Kleiman, 2009). In a much more rigorous evaluation, Hawken and Kleiman (2009) randomly assigned 493 adult probationers in Hawaii with high scores on a risk assessment tool to either HOPE ($n = 330$) or supervision as usual ($n = 163$). Intent-to-treat analyses indicate that, 1 year after random assignment, HOPE probationers had statistically significantly fewer positive drug tests (13% vs. 46%), new arrests (21% vs. 47%), and revocations (7% vs. 15%) than those in the control group.

Although these short-term results are promising, it is unclear whether HOPE actually reduces the risk of recidivism, once probationers are released from formal supervision. One limitation of punishment-based approaches is that behavior change can end once direct monitoring ceases (see Chapter 13).

Moving Science to Practice: Understanding the Knowledge-Practice Gap

Reentry needs and barriers are well documented, and recidivism seems predictable. Scholars have identified approaches to change behavior and provided rigorous evidence that if they are followed, recidivism can be reduced. Yet no one believes the work is finished, because there are many critical knowledge gaps. In this section, we summarize three gaps relevant to the approaches outlined in the first section.

What About Low-Risk Offenders?

The risk principle of RNR suggests that the most intensive resources (treatment and supervision) should be applied to offenders who are at relatively high risk for recidivism. The question remains: What can be done productively with low-risk offenders? Deterrence theory might suggest that if offenders are simply ignored early in their criminal careers, sanctions lose their deterrent value, and criminal careers can escalate.

According to the ecological model, some offenders who may appear "low risk" on risk assessment tools that heavily emphasize individual factors may actually be quite likely to recidivate, given a host of contextual variables and barriers to reentry. These offenders may be assisted by the removal of community barriers and provision of job skills training and other vocational activities that are more skills based and less resource intensive than programs for higher risk offenders. One could envision a field test of this very real possibility and important question in willing and invested communities.

When Is It Best to Intervene?

We also need to explore the timing of service delivery. Research suggests that recidivism often occurs within the first few months of prison release (Petersilia, 2003). Could recidivism outcomes and cost effectiveness be improved if services were "front loaded" and applied to selected parolees immediately after release? The ecological model would suggest so, because community barriers are encountered immediately. The RNR model would suggest so, because those who are at highest risk would be expected to fail most quickly. We can imagine a test of RNR that tests the timing and dosage amount for those at highest risk when they return to the community. The swift and certain model might suggest still another approach. Using that logic, offenders would self-select into high and low risk based on their ability to follow rules; those who could not follow rules would receive intensive services to assist in their treatment.

What Contextual Factors Contribute to Reentry Failure?

Future research must move beyond simple statistical models that attempt to explain parolees' success in the community solely as a function of their individual behavior. In keeping with general premises of the ecological model, the characteristics of the parolee's supervising agent, supervising agency, and community are significant predictors as well. Recent research findings by Lin, Grattet, and Petersilia (2010) examined the impact of these kinds of factors on parolee success using a correlational design. They found that individual offender factors, as well as parole agent and community factors, impacted recidivism for parolees. However, this was not a true test of how *changes* in each of these spheres could improve reentry. This key question needs more definitive answers.

Intersections With Practice

Risk-Need-Responsivity as *Part* of Best Practices Advocated by National Agencies

Several compendiums of reentry program descriptions have been published in recent years, and these descriptions often refer to such RNR principles as using risk/needs assessment instruments, trying to match parolee needs with identified programs, and focusing services on moderate- and high-risk individuals. For example, *The Report of the Reentry Policy Council: Charting the Safe and Successful Return of Prisoners to the Community* (Reentry Policy Council, 2005) offers a 650-page, comprehensive set of bipartisan, consensus-based recommendations for those interested in improving reentry outcomes, along with a variety of program descriptions. Similarly, the American Correctional Association published *Reentry Best Practices* (Wilkinson, 2004), which described eighty reentry programs across the country. Some of those descriptions included vague references to the "what works" literature. Unfortunately, there is no real way to discern the extent to which these principles are influencing daily practices because the program descriptions are not detailed enough.

A report of the American Probation and Parole Association (APPA, 2007) notes that in times of increasing caseloads and major budget cuts, probation and parole agencies must attend to RNR principles in allocating workloads while assuring community safety:

> There is no doubt that evidence-based practices designed to reduce risk of re-offending are infusing the community corrections field

with more scientific approaches. These approaches rely on risk assessments to allow probation and parole agencies to differentiate and typologize offenders based on their relative level of risk to reoffend. This strategy allows for addressing criminogenic needs— anti-social behavior, anti-social personality, anti-social values and attitudes, criminal peer groups, substance abuse, and dysfunctional family relations—through an integrated approach of surveillance, treatment, and enforcement. (APPA, 2007, p.8)

Evidence-based principles have been formally integrated in the National Institute of Corrections (NIC) and the Crime and Justice Institute (CJS)'s model for effective correctional management of offenders in the community (CJI, 2004; APPA, 2007). The integrated model places equal weight in three areas: evidence-based practices, organizational development, and collaboration. RNR principles developed by Andrews and colleagues are at the core of evidence-based practices of the model. Taxman, Shephardson, and Byrne (2005) developed the manual *Tools of the Trade* to help assist practitioners in community corrections translate research findings into practice using RNR concepts. In short, RNR principles are part of recommended best practices, but they seem embedded within other goals and priorities in community corrections.

How Much Does the Current "Brokerage" Approach Overlap with Risk-Need-Responsivity?

In thinking about RNR principles, one often considers a program, its clients, offender assessment, program staff, program model, and outcomes as part of an integrated whole. This model often seems inapplicable to probation and parole supervision, where the agent of supervision often functions as a case manager, perhaps conducting limited risk and needs assessment, but often referring offenders into the community to governmental and private provider agencies that are the actual source of program delivery. Offenders may participate in more than one outside program—drug treatment, anger management, sex offender treatment, and so on. Some refer to this type of arrangement as a "brokerage model." For example in California, the California Department of Corrections and Rehabilitation (CDCR)'s parole division contracts with providers to serve their offenders with outpatient and residential substance abuse services as well as transitional housing. The "brokerage" model becomes quickly complicated with respect to implementation of evidence-based principles. For example, there may be no guarantee that a vendor will follow evidence-based principles for offenders (e.g., targeting criminogenic needs like socialization with antisocial peers, rather than noncriminogenic needs like depression or self-esteem), or that treatment and services received are integrated in a consistent manner. Programs often provide their services as they have done for years, using models that are not necessarily based on evidence, but rather on an accumulation of hands-on experience.

Some corrections agencies, however, are beginning to address the adherence and use of evidence-based principles by using the contracting mechanism itself. Parole agencies may require demonstrated evidence of adherence to evidence-based models in proposal submissions to agencies. CDCR is proposing this as part of their quality assurance for correctional programs. The Correctional Program Assessment Inventory (which encompasses concepts of RNR in review of programs; see Chapter 6) can be used for screening potential programs for funding decisions (Lowenkamp, Pealer, Smith, & Latessa, 2006). Periodic review of programs that have received funding can also be conducted. As part of California Logic Model, CDCR programs are targeted for review using the Correctional Program Checklist (similar to the CPAI) by trained staff from the CDCR research unit. Although the brokerage model may seem to make RNR more complicated to implement and monitor at first blush, the CPAI and related tools make this quite feasible. Indeed, there are no "RNR programs" per se; instead, all programs differ in their adherence to these principles, whether they are provided by corrections agencies or contractors. Brokerage-type contacts can be written to ensure that RNR is implemented.

How Consistent Is the Current Law Enforcement Emphasis with Risk-Need-Responsivity Principles?

Public safety is a major concern in reentry. The prospect of having a parolee commit a horrendous crime may cause agencies to emphasize surveillance and control to the exclusion of RNR principles or long-term behavior change. Although one can view RNR principles as a clear and direct pathway toward improving public safety (see Chapters 6 and 13), some agencies seem to perceive "rehabilitation" and "crime control" as competing goals. This could serve as a barrier to the uptake of RNR.

For example, the National Research Council (NRC) on Parole, Desistance from Crime, and Community Integration reports, "The cost of strict enforcement, whether warranted or not, is borne only by the parolee. The cost of failing to clamp down on a dangerous parolee is borne by an entire agency, or, as in the Willie Horton case, a governor. Consequently agencies have been hard pressed to emphasize rehabilitation or take the process of relapse into account" (NRC, 2007, p. 36). Similarly, APPA (2007) notes that "the community corrections field has changed significantly from its initial focus as a way to help offenders construct pro-social lives by addressing personal and social deficits. The more contemporary view of corrections embraces strategies and services that hold offenders accountable for their criminality, provides cost-effective alternatives to incarceration, and never loses sight of the critical importance of public safety in the near and long term" (p. 9). Recently passed legislation requiring lifelong GPS monitoring of all sex offenders in California (Jessica's law), despite the lack of any sex offender treatment programming in California prisons, is one example of weight still given to enforcement and surveillance.

Conflict remains both at the agent and agency level between evidence-based correctional principles and a law enforcement focus. Parole agents are often required to assume both surveillance and rehabilitation roles. They monitor parolees to assure compliance with the often numerous conditions of parole; yet, as described earlier, they also serve as service brokers to obtain housing, employment, drug treatment, and other services for their clients.

These agents and their agencies face the challenge of how best to integrate RNR into supervision practices that may be more geared toward reducing the short-term "stakes" of supervision failures, rather than the long-term "risks" of reoffending. Similarly, the RNR risk principle suggests that resources be focused on the higher risk; yet the public may demand high levels of supervision for certain "types" offenders (such as sex offenders), regardless of the risk the individual parolee may pose to the community. The "stakes" to the agency for potential crimes committed by certain offender groups often outweigh concerns about effective targeting of resources and money for optimum crime reduction. These potential barriers—and how to address them—are explained by McGuire (see Chapter 12).

Serious and Violent Offender Reentry Initiative

The largest effort to systematically encourage the implementation of evidence-based principles is the federal government's Serious and Violent Offender Reentry Initiative (SVORI). In 2003, 69 agencies representing all 50 states received more than $110 million in federal funds (each receiving $500,000 to $2,000,000 over 3 years) to develop programs to improve the outcomes of serious and violent prisoners coming home (Lattimore, Visher, Winterfield, Lindquist, & Brumbaugh, 2005). SVORI guidelines for these programs were fairly minimal. Grantees were encouraged to do an assessment, but agencies were told to customize their programs to reflect their local needs and resources. SVORI grantees operated nearly 90 distinct reentry programs, many of them expanded during the original funding awards.

SVORI's goals were to improve a variety of outcomes, including family relationships, work, health, community integration, housing, and reduced crime. Researchers from the Research Triangle and Urban Institutes are evaluating SVORI. Thus far, researchers have used project director's self-reports to describe the programs' goals and implementation to explore the extent to which efforts are being made to incorporate evidence-based principles in SVORI program operations. Their reports suggest the following (Lattimore, Brumbaugh, Visher, Lindquist, Winterfield, Salas, & Zweig, 2004; Steffey, Brumbaugh, & Lattimore, 2008):

- Over 90% of SVORI programs report assessing risk and needs using standardized instruments. These instruments are being completed before release (97% of agencies) and also after release (89% completing).

- Unfortunately, SVORI programs do not allocate the most intensive services to only moderate- and high-risk offenders. Certain offenders are eliminated from program participation, but elimination is based upon current conviction crime (usually, sex offenders are excluded) rather than a low recidivism risk score. Moreover, the majority of SVORI programs (75%) do not specifically target populations for program participation based on their type of clinical treatment needs (i.e., substance abuse, mental illness).
- Once accepted into the SVORI program, many programs develop a case management plan in which offenders are provided substance abuse, employment, medical, mental health services, and housing assistance based on an assessment of their needs for those services.
- It is unclear from the available information whether SVORI is using cognitive-behavioral strategies in programming delivered by well-trained staff. It is also unclear whether staff use positive rather than negative reinforcement.
- Most SVORI programs implement a multiphase approach, incorporating at least one prerelease phase and at least one postrelease phase. The programs appear to last at least a year across the two phases. The most common length of combined postrelease phases is 10 to 12 months.
- There is evidence that SVORI projects are engaging ongoing support systems in natural communities, by activating faith-based services, mentors, and family-oriented activities.

Thus, some evidence-based principles are influencing the design and implementation of SVORI, the nation's largest prisoner reentry initiative. Many SVORI sites are doing risk-based assessments, implementing some case management practices, implementing programs that are several months in duration, and collecting process and outcome data. However, SVORI sites are having a more difficult time implementing core risk, need, and responsivity principles, because few programs target resources primarily to moderate- and high-risk offenders, implement cognitive-behavioral programs by trained staff, or create systems that provide positive reinforcement in a consistent and managed way. No SVORI program reported policies specifically to keep low-risk cases out of intensive services. There was also little evidence that programs considered differential treatment with regard to interpersonal maturity, age-, gender- and culturally responsive services.

The SVORI results seem generally consistent with the National Institute of Corrections' Transition from Prison to Home Initiative, where risk and need assessments are routinely completed but delivering intensive cognitive-based programs based on identified needs is more challenging (Byrne, Taxman, & Young, 2004). As best as the authors can tell, there has been limited penetration of evidence-based crime reduction principles to prisoner reentry programs.

The outcome results from SVORI were released in 2010 and appear promising. SVORI program participants were much more likely to receive services and participate in needed programs, and SVORI participants did better across a wide range of domains, including employment and substance abuse (see https://www.svori-evaluation.org/). Rearrest and reincarceration, which may be viewed as the chief outcomes of interest however, were not generally reduced.

These early positive results have encouraged an expansion of federally funded reentry programs. President Bush signed The Second Chance Act of 2007 (H.R. 1593/S. 1934) in April 2008. One hundred fourteen million dollars was appropriated for prisoner reentry programs in FY2010, including $100 million for Second Chance Act programs administered by the U.S. Department of Justice and $14 million for reentry programs administered by the U.S. Department of Labor (http://reentrypolicy.org/government_affairs/second_chance_act, May 12, 2011).

Implications for Practice

Our review of reentry does not offer suggestions surprisingly different from the mainstays of RNR for the supervision of parolees and other former inmates reentering the community. Drawing from the research literature while acknowledging the gaps identified earlier, we recommend the following for facilitating the entry of individual offenders:

1. Assess offenders' risk and needs using validated instruments and use the results to inform supervision plans.
2. Understand the difference between "risks" and "stakes" in parole supervision. An offender may be "high stakes" to the correctional agency, due to his or her index offense, but also low "risk" to the community, given his or her low risk of recidivism.
3. Focus resources on higher risk offenders, recognizing that the definition of higher risk may need to be qualified with need categories.
4. Emphasize rewards and incentives to change behavior, while realizing that for some high-risk offenders, certain and swift sanctions could also be effective.
5. Use cognitive-behavioral treatment (CBT) approaches, while realizing that more work needs to be done to determine how different offender characteristics may affect response. CBT may require modification to be responsive to the needs of some populations (e.g., those with mental illness).
6. Link offenders with community agencies that can help provide services/treatment required, using the brokerage model.

Our review of the evidence on RNR, ecological, and certain and swift sanction models has several more far-reaching implications for reentry agencies and systems. We recommend the following for reentry systems:

1) Explicitly integrate RNR principles with other foci of reentry, including surveillance and control. Because law enforcement goals may seem incompatible with RNR "rehabilitation," explain how behavior change works in the service of increasing public safety.

2) As suggested earlier, recognize the difference between "risk" and "stakes." The stakes may be quite high for some released offenders, should they commit crimes while out, despite the fact that they might be low risk according to validated risk assessment instruments. Systems must find a way to consider both "risk" and "stakes" without completely putting the focus on the risk principle, which is well validated for reducing recidivism.

3) When advocating for the implementation and evaluation of RNR and other evidence-based principles in today's economic climate, emphasize the estimated cost savings using findings from meta-analyses (such as those conducted by the Washington Institute of Public Policy; see earlier). Test those cost savings in evaluation studies.

4) Craft systems that require brokeraged services to demonstrate the implementation of RNR principles. Requests for proposals should require evidence-based programming and services. Those buying the services must be able to distinguish truly evidence-based proposals and programs from other proposals and programs. Providers should be held accountable for the results they achieve.

5) Leverage community support in implementing RNR and other evidence-based principles in reentry. Reentry requires community support; RNR principles need to be integrated into a shared system, in which rehabilitation is one of several goals of the community partners.

6) Work politically toward acceptance of reduced supervision of and services for low-risk offenders. Law enforcement, particularly, may be reluctant to give up search and seizure and other powers that higher levels of (more expensive) formal supervision of parolees allow them.

The current state of reentry programs is marked by enthusiasm and recently focused resources; however, to achieve the desired outcomes, especially reductions in crime, we have provided a series of evidenced-based, sensible recommendations toward aiming resources where they will do the most good. Following these principles of social science will benefit not only the offenders who are released but also the communities in which they will live.

References

American Probation & Parole Association (2007). *Probation and parole's growing caseloads and workload allocation: Strategies for managerial decision*

making, Available at: http://www.appa-net.org/eweb/DynamicPage.
aspx?WebCode=VC_FreePubsReports

Andrews, D.A. (2009). The Level of Service Assessments: A Question, Confusion,
Selectivity and Misrepresentation of Evidence in Baird. Presentation at
International Community Corrections Association Meeting, Orlando, Florida.

Andrews, D. A., & Bonta, J. (2010). Rehabilitating criminal justice policy and
practice. *Psychology, Public Policy, and Law, 16*(1), 39–55.

Andrews, D. A., Bonta, J., & Hoge, R. D. (1990). Classification for effective
rehabilitation: Rediscovering psychology. *Criminal Justice and Behavior, 17*(1),
19–52.

Aos, S., Miller, M., & Drake, E. (2006). *Evidence-based adult corrections programs:
What works and what does not.* Olympia: Washington State Institute for Public
Policy.

Baird, C. (2009). *A question of evidence: A critique of risk assessment models used in
the criminal justice system.* San Francisco, CA: National Council on Crime and
Delinquency.

Beck, A. J. (2000). *State and federal prisoners returning to the community: Findings
from the Bureau of Justice Statistics.* Washington, DC: Bureau of Justice
Statistics.

Braga, A. A., Piehl, A. M., & Hureau, D. (2009). Controlling violent offenders
released to the community: An evaluation of the Boston Reentry Initiative.
Journal of Research in Crime and Delinquency, 46(4), 411–436.

Byrne, J. M., Taxman, F., & Young, D. (2004). Targeting for reentry: Inclusion/
exclusion criteria across eight model programs. *Federal Probation, 68,* 53–61.

California Department of Corrections.and Rehabilitation (2007). *Expert Panel
Report on Adult Offender and Recidivism Reduction Programming.* Sacramento,
CA. Available at www.cdcr.ca.gov/news/docs/Expert_Rpt/ExpertPanel
Rpt_.pdf

Crime & Justice Institute (2004). Implementing evidence-based practice in
community corrections: The principles of effective intervention,
Boston, MA.

Drake, E., Aos, S., & Miller, M. (2009). *Evidence-Based public policy options to
reduce crime and criminal justice costs: Implications in Washington State,*
Washington State Institute for Public Policy.

Greene, J. A. (2003). *Smart on crime: Positive trends in state-level sentencing
and corrections policy.* Washington, DC: Families Against Mandatory
Minimums.

Harcourt, E. H. (2007). *Against prediction: Profiling, policing and punishing in an
acturial age.* Chicago, IL: University of Chicago Press.

Hawken, A., & Kleiman, M. (2007). H.O.P.E. for reform: What a novel probation
program in Hawaii might teach other states. *The American Prospect.* Retrieved
from http://www.prospect.org/cs/articles?article=hope_for_reform

Hawken, A., & Kleiman, M. (2009). *Managing drug involved probationers with swift
and certain sanctions: Evaluating Hawaii's HOPE.* Retrieved from http://www.
ncjrs.gov/pdffiles1/nij/grants/229023.pdf

House of Representatives and Senate, H.R. 1593/S. 1934.

Justice Center, The Council of State Governments (n.d.). Retrieved May 12, 2011,
from http://reentrypolicy.org/government_affairs/second_chance_act

Kleiman, M. (2009). *When brute force fails: How to have less crime and less
punishment.* Princeton, NJ: Princeton University Press.

Langan, P., & Levin, D. (2002). *Recidivism of prisoners released in 1994.* No. NCJ 193427. Washington, DC: Bureau of Justice Statistics.

Lattimore, P. K., Brumbaugh, S., Visher, C. A., Lindquist, C., Winterfield, L., Salas, M., & Zweig, J. M. (2004). *National portrait of SVORI: Serious and Violent Offender Reentry Initiative.* Chapel Hill, NC: RTI International.

Lattimore, P. K., & Visher, C. A. (2009). *The Multi-site Evaluation of SVORI: Summary and Synthesis.* The Multi-site Evaluation of the Serious and Violent Offender Reentry Initiative.

Lattimore, P. K., Visher, C. A., Winterfield, L., Lindquist, C., & Brumbaugh, S. (2005). Implementation of prisoner reentry programs: Findings from the Serious and Violent Offender Reentry Initiative multi-site evaluation. *Justice Research and Policy, 7*(2), 87–109.

Lin, J., Grattet, R., & Petersilia, J., (2010). Back-end sentencing and reimprisonment: Individual, organizational, and community predictors of parole sanctioning decisions, *Criminology, 48*(3), 759–796.

Lipsey, M. W. (2009). The primary factors that characterize effective interventions with juvenile offenders: A meta-analytic overview. *Victims and Offenders, 4*(2), 124–147.

Lowenkamp, C. T., & Latessa, E. (2005). Increasing the effectiveness of correctional programming through the risk principle: Identifying offenders for residential placement. *Criminology and Public Policy, 4*(2), 291–310.

Lowenkamp, C.T., Pealer, J., Smith, P. & Latessa, E. (2006). Adhering to the risk and need principles: Does it matter for supervision-based programs?, *Federal Probation, 70*(3), 3–8.

Lowenkamp, C. T., Latessa, E., & Holsinger, A. (2006). Risk principle in action: What have we learned from 13,676 offenders and 97 correctional programs?. *Crime and Delinquency, 52*(1), 14.

Lussier, P., Dahabieh, M., Deslauriers-Varin, N., & Thomson, C. (2011). Community reintegration of violent and sexual offenders: Issues and challenges for community risk management. In L. Gideon & H-E. Sung (Eds.), *Rethinking corrections: Rehabilitation, reentry, and reintegration.* Los Angeles: Sage.

Lynch, J. P., & Sabol, W. J. (2001). *Prisoner reentry in perspective.* Washington, DC: Urban Institute.

Marlowe, D. (2008). Application of sanctions. In C. Hardin & J. Kushner (Eds.), *Quality improvement for drug courts.* Alexandria, VA: National Drug Court Institute.

Martinson, R. (1974). What Works?: Questions and answers about prison reform. *Public Interest, 35,* 22–35.

Nagin, D. S. (1998). Criminal deterrence research at the outset of the twenty-first century. *Crime and Justice, 23,* 1–42.

National Institute of Justice. (2008). *HOPE in Hawaii: Swift and sure changes in probation.* Retrieved from http://www.ojp.usdoj.gov/nij/pubs-sum/222758.htm

National Research Council. (2007). *Parole, desistance from crime, and community integration.* Committee on Law and Justice, National Academies Press, Washington, D.C.

Papachristos, A. V., Meares, T. L. , & Fagan, J. (2007). Attention Felons: Evaluating Project Safe Neighborhoods in Chicago. *Journal of Empirical Legal Studies, 4*(2), 223–272.

Petersilia, J. (2003). *When prisoners come home: Parole and prisoner reentry.* New York: Oxford University Press.

Petersilia, J. (2006). *Understanding California corrections.* Berkeley: University of California.

Petersilia, J. (2008). California's correctional paradox of excess and deprivation. In M. H. Tonry (Ed.), *Crime and justice: A review of research* (Vol. 37, pp. 207–278). Chicago: University of Chicago Press.

Pew Charitable Trust. (2007). *Public Safety, Public Spending: Forecasting America's Prison Population, 2007-2011.* Retrieved from http://www.pewcenteronthestates.org/uploadedFiles/Public%20Safety%20Public%20Spending.pdf

Pew Charitable Trust. (2008). *One in 100 behind bars in America.* Retrieved from http://www.pewcenteronthestates.org/report_detail.aspx?id=35904

Re-Entry Policy Council. (2005). *Charting the safe and successful return of prisoners to the community.* Council of State Governments, New York, NY.

Rose, D. R., & Clear, T. R. (1998). Incarceration, social capital, and crime: Implications for social disorganizaiton theory: Examining the unintended consequences of incarceration. *Criminology, 36*(3), 441–480.

Rosenfeld, R., Wallman, J., & Fornango, R. (2005). The contribution of ex-prisoners to crime rates. In J. Travis & C. A. Visher (Eds.), *Prisoner reentry and crime in America.* New York: Cambridge University Press.

Sampson, R. J., Raudenbush, S. W., & Earls, F. (1997). Neighborhoods and violent crime: A multilevel study of collective efficacy. *Science, 277*(5328), 918–924.

Skeem, J., & Monahan, J. (2011). Current directions in violence risk assessment. *Current Directions in Psychological Science, 20*, 38–42.

Solomon, A., Osborne, J., LoBuglio, S., Mellow, J., & Mukamal, D. (2008). *Life after lockup: Improving reentry from jail to the community.* Washington, DC: The Urban Institute.

Steffey, D., Brumbaugh, S., & Lattimore, P. K. (2008). *Results from a multi-site evaluation of prisoner reentry programs.* Chapel Hill, NC: Research Triangle Institute.

Tarlow, M. (2011). Employment barriers to reintegration. In L. Gideon & H-E. Sung (Eds.), *Rethinking corrections: Rehabilitation, reentry, and reintegration.* Los Angeles: Sage.

Taxman, F., Cropsey, K., Young, D., & Wexler, H. (2007). Screening, assessment, and referral practices in adult correctional settings. *Criminal Justice and Behavior, 34*(9), 1216–1234.

Taxman, F., & Thanner, M. (2003). Probation from a therapeutic perspective: Results from the field. *Contemporary Issues in Law, 7*(1), 39–63.

Taxman, F., Shepardson, E. & Byrne, J. (2005). *Tools of the trade: A guide to incorporating science into practice.* Report for the National Institute of Corrections, Washington DC. Available at: http://nicic.gov/Library/020095

Travis, J. (2009). *What works for successful prisoner reentry.* Paper presented at the House of Representatives Appropriations Subcommittee on Commerce, Justice, Science and Related Agencies, March 12.

United States Sentencing Commission. (n.d.). Press release. Retrieved July 13, 2009 from http://www.ussc.gov/PRESS/rel121107.htm

Wilkinson, R. (2004). *Reentry best practices: Directors' perspectives.* American Correctional Association, Latham, MD.

Wilson, J. (1975). *Thinking about crime.* New York: Basic Books.

9

Reducing Recidivism and Violence Among Offending Youth

Barbara A. Oudekerk and N. Dickon Reppucci

Violent crime produces staggering costs to juvenile offenders, their victims, and society at large, and these costs multiply if juvenile offenders receive intervention services that are ineffective and/or insufficient in preventing recidivism (Caldwell, Vitacco, & Van Rybroek, 2006). In addition to the more apparent financial burdens involved in criminal justice processing, providing supervision and services, and placing violent offenders in secure confinement (prisons, jails, and mental institutions), violent crime generates numerous human, social, and economic losses that are difficult to quantify. Victims of violent crimes often endure physical, mental, and emotional pain and suffering, which may lead to lasting medical costs and diminished quality of life. Moreover, many young offenders enter the juvenile justice system with histories of severe victimization, neglect, mental health disorders, and unhealthy or weak family attachments (Veysey, 2008), and they demonstrate great risk for poor-quality mental and physical health, interpersonal relationships, and employment and educational outcomes in adulthood (Bullis & Yovanoff, 2006; Laub & Sampson, 1993; Tarolla, Wagner, Rabinowitz, & Tubman, 2002). In turn, society often bears the costs if young offenders, their families, or their victims require medical, welfare, and/or childcare assistance services.

Ideally, contact with the juvenile justice system provides youth with an opportunity to receive intervention services that might encourage their desistance from crime and promote resilience in important adult life functioning domains. Since the inception of the first juvenile court in 1899, juvenile justice has been rooted in the ideology that children and adolescents are developmentally different from adults in ways that increase their amenability to treatment (Feld, 1999). Although the juvenile court penalized juvenile offenders, its fundamental goal was to prevent future crime through the provision of supervision and treatment services (Mears, Hay, Gertz, & Mancini, 2007). Despite recent shifts toward more punitive sentences and adult-like treatment of violent young offenders, recent public opinion surveys suggest that a large majority of community members still endorse the need for preferential treatment of juveniles within a separate justice system (Mears et al., 2007; Scott, Reppucci, Antonishak, & DeGennaro, 2003). A great challenge for juvenile justice professionals, then, is preserving the balance between maintaining community safety and providing these juveniles with opportunities to make positive life changes within their communities.

Notably, many youth naturally desist from violence as they mature into adulthood (Moffitt, 1993; Moffitt, Caspi, Harrington, & Milne, 2002). In an examination of the National Longitudinal Study of Adolescent Health (ADD Health) data, Williams, Tuthill, and Lio (2008) reported that 41.3% of 14,322 seventh through twelfth graders engaged in some form of violence (e.g., serious physical fights, badly hurting someone, using a weapon to get something from someone) in the prior year, but only 12% of these youth reported engaging in a violent offense in adulthood (when the sample ranged from 18–26 years old). Nonetheless, such findings also demonstrate that a small percentage of youth do continue to offend through adolescence and adulthood, and these "chronic" (Loeber, Farrington, & Waschbusch, 1998) or "life course persistent" (Moffitt, 1993) offenders account for a significant portion of violent crimes (Loeber, Farrington, & Waschbusch, 1998). Thus, identifying the most effective interventions for reducing violence among this subset of high-risk juvenile offenders is central to rehabilitating youth, minimizing crime-related financial burdens, and protecting community members.

Fortunately, despite the once popular belief that "nothing works" (Martinson, 1974), today hundreds of intervention studies and dozens of meta-analyses summarizing those studies suggest that intervention services can be effective in promoting desistance among juvenile offenders, if the services are derived and implemented within an empirically validated theoretical framework (Dowden & Andrews, 1999b; Landenberger & Lipsey, 2005; Lipsey & Cullen, 2007; Lipsey & Wilson, 1998). However, many ineffective interventions also exist, some of which have even been associated with *increases* in recidivism, for example, shock incarceration and scared straight programs (Lipsey & Cullen, 2007; Petrosino, Turpin-Petrosino, & Bueler, 2003). In this chapter, we summarize and discuss the literature on what works and what does not work to reduce violent offending among high-risk juvenile offenders. Due to space limitations, our review provides a brief, general overview of the most important issues in implementing treatments with juvenile offenders. It is informed by several excellent resources (see especially, Hoge, Guerra, & Boxer, 2008, on *Treating the Juvenile Offender*, Loeber & Farrington, 1998, on *Serious and Violent Juvenile Offenders,* and Borum, 2003, on *Managing At-Risk Juvenile Offenders in the Community*).

In keeping with the theme of this book, we structure our discussion of "what works" around the principles of Risk, Need, and Responsivity (RNR; Andrews, Bonta, & Hoge, 1990; see Chapter 6). Indeed, crime reduction programs are most successful in reducing recidivism if they *(a)* match the intensity of the intervention to offender's level of risk, *(b)* focus on crimino-genic needs, and *(c)* use empirically validated intervention methods known to increase the offender's responsivity to the treatment. Nevertheless, we recognize and appreciate others' concerns that the theoretical underpinnings of the RNR principles need more attention (Ward, Melser, & Yates, 2007). Furthermore, RNR principles were never designed to promote positive outcomes across multiple settings (e.g., school, work, interpersonal relationships); instead, the RNR principles were solely developed as a framework to reduce crime.

Important Definitions

Given that juvenile justice intervention and treatment programming have been informed by multiple academic and professional disciplines, it is not surprising that inconsistent terminology is normative. Our focus is to identify characteristics of effective programs for reducing *violent* recidivism among high-risk juvenile offenders. Three terms require definitions. First, *risk* refers to offenders' level of risk for recidivism, and therefore *high risk* describes youth who demonstrate significant risk for recidivism. Next, we are most interested in offenders' risk for *violent* recidivism, that is, the probability that offenders will physically injure or attempt to injure another person in the future. Violent recidivism includes (but is not limited to) homicide, attempted homicide, voluntary manslaughter, aggravated assault, child abuse, kidnapping, rape, attempted rape, robbery, armed robbery, and arson of an occupied building. Most of the time researchers do not differentiate between violent and nonviolent recidivism, so we use the term *general recidivism* to represent any new offense, violent or nonviolent. In addition, recidivism can be measured in different ways, varying from self-reported offending, official rearrests, criminal charges, readjudication, to reincarceration (Mulvey, Arthur, & Reppucci, 1993). This review draws heavily upon meta-analyses, which summarize multiple studies and allow researchers to statistically control for different measurements of reoffending.

Finally, the definition of "juvenile offender" varies within the academic and legal realms, in part because the maximum age delimiting whether cases fall within the jurisdiction of the juvenile or adult court is specified within each state. This upper age limit ranges between 15 (e.g., New York), 16 (e.g., Illinois), and 17 years of age (e.g., Virginia), but after penetrating the juvenile justice system, offenders may continue to receive supervision and services even past the maximum age of juvenile court jurisdiction (e.g., until age 25 in California). Nevertheless, federal codes and the majority of the states still define 18 as the "bright line" at which youth become adults. Therefore, unless specifically noted, the terms *youth, juveniles,* and *adolescents* are used to describe samples of youth who are, on average, less than 18 years old.

Distilling Scientific Evidence About What Works for Juvenile Offenders

The Risk Principle: Match the Intensity of the Intervention to the Offenders' Level of Risk

Does Adherence to the Risk Principle Reduce Recidivism?

Although most research has been conducted with predominately or entirely adult samples, initial evidence supports that interventions targeting high-risk versus low-risk juvenile offenders produce the greatest reductions in recidivism. Dowden and Andrews (1999b) conducted a meta-analysis of 229 effect sizes from 134 studies to examine whether adherence to the RNR principles increased effectiveness of interventions with juvenile offenders. Studies were coded as targeting high-risk juveniles if *(a)* the primary authors defined the sample as high risk or *(b)* most of the sample had penetrated the juvenile justice system or had a prior criminal record. The remaining studies were coded as targeting low-risk juveniles. In support of the risk principle, treatment programs implemented with high-risk youth, compared to low-risk youth, were significantly more effective in reducing future general offending. Andrews and Dowden (2006) replicated this finding in a meta-analysis comprising both adults and youth, and found that the risk principle was stronger among adolescents age 19 and younger than among adults age 20 and older.

Importantly, Dowden and Andrews (1999b) and Andrews and Dowden (2006) did not distinguish between violent and nonviolent recidivism, and we know of no research examining whether adherence to the risk principle reduces violent offending specifically for juvenile offenders. Dowden and Andrews (2000) examined intervention effectiveness in reducing *violent* offending and revealed similar findings (although not statistically significant), but their analyses were based on male, predominately adult offenders and did not examine juveniles separate from adults. Nevertheless, allocating more intensive services to high-risk youth is consistent with research showing that only a small percentage of violent juvenile offenders continue to commit offenses, particularly violent offenses, in adulthood (Moffitt, Caspi, Harrington, & Milne, 2002; Williams et al., 2008).

What Is the Best Way to Assess Risk for Violence?

Accurately identifying high-risk juveniles appears to be an integral part of successfully reducing offending, but this is no easy feat, as evidenced by the burgeoning literature discussing the complexity of defining and appraising risk among adolescents (e.g., Hoge, 2008; Mulvey & Iselin, 2008; Olver, Stockdale, & Wormith, 2009). Adolescents who have contact with the juvenile justice system vary greatly in the quantity, type, and gravity of risk factors associated with reoffense, and there is not a single "best practice" assessment of risk. Much research does, however, support structured, standardized assessments of risk producing more reliable, comprehensive, and valid predictors of recidivism than clinical assessments (for reviews see Grove, Zald, Lebow, Snitz, & Nelson, 2000; Hoge, 2008; Mulvey & Iselin, 2008).

The U.S. Office of Juvenile Justice and Delinquency Prevention (OJJDP) has recognized the importance of accurately assessing juvenile offenders' risk, needs, and strengths, and it has published a guidebook, the *Comprehensive Strategy for Serious, Violent, and Chronic Juvenile Offenders*, that advocates for structured decision making through the use of standardized risk assessment tools (Howell, 1995). Although tools were initially designed primarily to predict risk for recidivism, newer tools provide more comprehensive assessments of risks and needs so as to inform intervention and prevent future violence (Olver et al., 2009; Schwalbe, 2008). The most rigorously evaluated tools have been discussed in previous reviews (Edens, Campbell, & Weir, 2007; Hoge, 2008; Odgers, Reppucci, & Moretti, 2005; Onifade et al., 2008; Schmidt, Hoge, & Gomes, 2005; Schwalbe, 2008; Welsh, Schmidt, McKinnon, Chattha, & Meyers, 2008). Three well-known examples assess risk among juvenile offenders and include youth-adapted versions of the Level of Service Inventory (LSI; Andrews & Bonta, 1995) (e.g., Youth Level of Service/Case Management Inventory [YLS/CMI]), Psychopathy Checklist-Youth Version (PCL-YV; Forth, Kosson, & Hare, 2003), and the Structured Assessment of Violent Risk for Youth (SAVRY; Borum, Bartel, & Forth, 2001).

Policy and Practice Relevant Gaps in Knowledge About Risk Assessment

Despite their numerous advantages over nonstructured clinical assessments, caution is warranted when using structured risk assessment tools to inform intervention with and supervision of juveniles. First, even the best structured risk assessment tools are not flawless predictors of future violence. For example, Olver et al.'s (2009) recent meta-analysis of 44 studies compared the predictive accuracy of the PCL-YV, SAVRY, and youth-adapted versions of the LSI (including the YLS/CMI). The combined samples included 8,746 male and female juvenile offenders who were, on average, 15.7 years old. Recidivism data were collected up to an average of 29.1 months post involvement with the juvenile justice system. The average correlations for predicting violent recidivism ranged from 0.25 (PCL-YV) to 0.26 (LSI youth versions) to 0.30 (SAVRY), suggesting that all three tools were reasonable, but not definitive, predictors of recidivism.

Researchers and professionals have also raised concern about whether existing tools can accurately and consistently identify risk for future violent offending across gender, race/ethnicity, and jurisdiction. Most assessment tools have been validated solely or primarily with male offenders, even though girls' and boys' risks and needs may differ (Dornfeld & Kruttschnitt, 1992; Edens et al., 2007; Funk, 1999; Odgers et al., 2005). For example, although prevalent among boys, girl offenders are more likely to experience significant victimization and co-occurring mental health problems (Odgers & Moretti, 2002; Timmons-Mitchell et al., 1997). Odgers et al. (2005) found that victimization experiences significantly predicted general recidivism for girls, even though scores on the PCL-YV did not. Edens et al. (2007) meta-analyzed 21 studies to examine the validity of the PCL-YV to predict violent recidivism among juvenile offenders who were, on average, 16 years old. Although total scores on the PCL-YV significantly predicted violent recidivism, this finding was moderated by gender such that scores only significantly predicted future violence for boys. On the other hand, the meta-analysis by Olver et al. (2009) revealed that the youth-adapted versions of the LSI predicted violent risk comparably for boys and girls, but LSI scores were stronger predictors of general recidivism than violent recidivism. Overall, these findings suggest that more research is needed to investigate gender-specific predictors of violent offending.

Furthermore, given the decades of research on the overrepresentation of minority youth within the juvenile justice system (Feld, 1999), surprisingly few risk assessment tools include cultural-specific risks (e.g., discrimination), needs (e.g., race socialization), and strengths (e.g., strong ties to the religious community or neighborhood). One explanation may be that many of the more popular risk assessment tools have been developed and standardized in Canada, where the racial demographic characteristics are different than in the United States. In fact, a recent comparison of the PCL-YV, LSI youth versions (e.g., YLS/CMI), and SAVRY risk assessment tools provides evidence that these popular instruments might be more robust predictors of risk when administered to Canadian youth than non-Canadian youth (including youth from the United States). Olver et al. (2009) found that the PCL-YV was a significantly better predictor of violent recidivism within Canadian samples ($r = 0.28$) versus non-Canadian samples ($r = 0.18$), and a similar but nonsignificant trend existed for the SAVRY ($r = 0.34$ versus $r = 0.26$). No research has examined the validity of the LSI youth versions to predict *violent* recidivism in non-Canadian samples, but the LSI predicted *general* recidivism significantly better within Canadian samples. Olver et al. (2009) concluded that more research is needed to determine the validity of these instruments within non-Canadian samples.

Finally, caution is warranted because many standardized assessment tools simply generate cumulative risk scores and do not account for the interaction of risk and protective factors or the fact that some risks outweigh others in importance (Carr & Vandiver, 2001; Odgers & Moretti, 2002). For instance, although youth who possess multiple risks are at increased odds for reoffending

(Hawkins et al., 2000), distinct *patterns* of risk might predict recidivism even better than cumulative risk scores. Onifade et al. (2008) found that youth who received a YLS/CMI total risk score in the lower-moderate risk range but scored high on specific subscales (i.e., family, education, leisure, personality, attitudes) recidivated at higher rates compared to youth who received high cumulative risk scores (38% versus 22%, respectively).

To summarize, empirical research reveals that structured risk assessment tools are more comprehensive, valid, and reliable than most clinical assessments, but even the most validated tools should be used with caution. When selecting and employing such tools, evaluators should consider how the various limitations and difficulties associated with assessing risk among juvenile offenders apply within their specific populations (e.g., girls and ethnic minorities). The Professional Override Principle (Andrews et al., 1990) acknowledges that professionals are ultimately responsible for weighing offenders' risks and needs and then choosing the best available treatment. As such, "standardized instruments may be useful in forming opinions about the client, but final decisions must be made by the responsible professional" (Hoge, 2008, p. 57). Professionals who are knowledgeable about cultural and/or gender-specific risk factors will, theoretically, make the most accurate final decisions about an individual offender's risk level.

The Need Principle: Target Criminogenic Needs

The need principle is based on the idea that, although identifying both static and dynamic risk factors is important for determining risk level for reoffending, successfully reducing future violence depends upon alleviating dynamic risk factors (i.e., criminogenic needs) and developing or strengthening factors that might protect against reoffending.

Is There Evidence That Adherence to the Need Principle Reduces Offending Among Youth?

Perhaps the most convincing evidence supporting the validity of the need principle for juvenile offenders stems from Dowden and Andrews' (1999b) examination of treatment effectiveness across 134 studies (described earlier). Although they did not specifically examine *violent* reoffending, they found that interventions which targeted youths' criminogenic needs, compared to noncriminogenic needs, were much more effective in reducing general recidivism. Table 9.1 was adapted from Dowden and Andrews to demonstrate the strength of these findings: the mean effect sizes for interventions targeting criminogenic needs were all positive, indicating a reduction in recidivism; in contrast, the mean effect sizes targeting noncriminogenic needs were all negative, denoting an increase in offending or at least no significant change in offending. In fact, programs that implemented a "fear of official punishment"

Table 9.1 Effect Sizes for Criminogenic Versus Noncriminogenic Treatment Need Targets

Criminogenic Needs	Effect Size (r)	Noncriminogenic Needs	Effect Size (r)
"Other" criminogenic needs	0.36***	Fear of official punishment	−0.18**
Family: Supervision	0.35***	Increase cohesive antisocial peers	−0.12
Family: Affection	0.33***	Family: Other interventions	−0.11
Barriers to treatment	0.30***	Target self-esteem	−0.09
Self-control	0.29***	Vague emotional/personal problems	−0.06
Anger/antisocial feelings	0.28***	Respect antisocial thinking	−0.05
Vocational skills + job	0.26***	Physical activity	−0.03
Academic	0.23***	Increase conventional ambition	−0.00
Prosocial model	0.19**		
Antisocial attitudes	0.13*		
Reduce antisocial peers	0.11		
Vocational skills	0.09		
Relapse prevention	0.07		
Substance abuse treatment	0.04		

*$p < .05$, ** $p < .01$, *** $p < .001$.

Source: Authors' adaptation of Dowden and Andrew's (1999b) Tables 2 and 3, which illustrate evidence in favor of the adhering to the Need Principle (pp. 26–27).

or deterrence approach (e.g., shock incarceration) were related to a significant *increase* in offending.

What Are the Criminogenic Needs (i.e., Dynamic Risk Factors) Related to Violent Offending Among Juveniles?

Relatively little research has focused specifically on identifying the *dynamic* risks associated with *violent* offending. To address this void, OJJDP reviewed, analyzed, and summarized existing literature on risk factors associated with violent offending among youth. As part of this effort, Hawkins et al. (2000) expanded upon Lipsey and Derzon's (1998) chapter on violent and serious offenders and analyzed the degree to which over 25 dynamic risk factors predicted subsequent perpetration of violence. Table 9.2 summarizes their findings. Importantly, the reader must remember that research examining risk factors for violence is correlational, not causational. Many of the risk factors related to violence also predict other negative outcomes and/or problem behaviors, and these interassociations make it difficult to determine which factors *cause* violence.

Table 9.2 Summary of Hawkins et al.'s (2000) Review of Dynamic Risk Factors for Violence

Domain	Risk Factor	Notes
Individual	(1) Hyperactivity, concentration problems, restlessness, and risk taking	
	(2) Aggressiveness	Not consistent for girls
	(3) Involvement in other forms of antisocial behavior	Not consistent for girls
	(4) Beliefs and attitudes favorable to deviant or antisocial behavior	Not consistent for girls
	(5) Substance abuse	Predictor at ages 6–11 but not 12–14; might depend on definition of abuse
Family	(1) Parental criminality	Mixed findings, might depend upon juveniles' age
	(2) Child maltreatment	
	(3) Poor family management practices	Includes inadequate supervision and discipline
	(4) Low levels of parental involvement	Might be weaker among girls
	(5) Family conflict	
	(6) Parental attitude favorable to violence	
	(7) Parent–child separation	Caution: factors related to separation also relate to violence
School	(1) Academic failure	Might be stronger among girls
	(2) Low bonding to school	Mixed findings, might depend upon juveniles' age
	(3) Truancy and dropping out of school	
	(4) Frequent school transitions	Caution: factors related to transitions also relate to violence
	(5) High school delinquency rate	
Peer-related	(1) Delinquent siblings	Might be stronger during adolescence and among girls
	(2) Delinquent peers	Stronger during adolescence
	(3) Gang membership	
Community and neighborhood	(1) Poverty	
	(2) Community disorganization	
	(3) Availability of drugs and firearms	
	(4) Neighborhood crime	
	(5) Exposure to violence and racial prejudice	

Table 9.2 illustrates that several factors across multiple domains are linked to violence. Dysfunctional family contexts are the source of a number of risk factors for violent offending, including deficient family interactions and attachments, inadequate parental supervision and discipline, delinquent siblings, and parental criminality. Enhancing the quality of family relations and cultivating parental competence might decrease the likelihood of recidivism for already offending youth, and it might also protect other children in the family from offending (Alexander, Robbins, & Sexton, 2000). Indeed, results presented in Table 9.1 suggest that targeting family criminogenic needs (e.g., supervision and affection) result in some of the greatest reductions in general recidivism.

Deviant peer groups and dangerous neighborhood contexts also place youth at risk for exposure to and involvement in violence. Moreover, academic failure, including poor school performance, truancy, and negative attitudes about school significantly predict future perpetration of violence. Interestingly, Hawkins et al. (2000) reported that at ages 12–14, school performance is a stronger predictor of future violence than IQ, suggesting that fostering successful academic performance among youth who possess intellectual disabilities might be preventative against violence. Indeed, a significant number of offending youth possess intellectual disabilities and learning deficiencies, compared to nonoffending youth (Grigorenko, 2006).

At the individual level, symptoms of externalizing mental health disorders (e.g., hyperactivity, risk taking, aggressiveness) appear to be predictive of violence, whereas internalizing disorders (e.g., depression) do not appear to increase risk for violence (Vermeiren, Schwab-Stone, Ruchkin, De Clippele, & Deboutte, 2002). It is widely known that the prevalence of mental health and trauma symptoms among boys and girls who engage in criminal behavior is astoundingly high (Teplin, Abram, McClelland, Dulcan, & Mericle, 2002; Veysey, 2008), particularly among incarcerated youth (Lyons, Baerger, Quigley, Erlick, & Griffin, 2001). Although both girls and boys suffer from high rates of mental disorders, research supports that psychiatric symptomology is more frequent and severe among girls (Timmons-Mitchell et al., 1997). Girls experience higher levels of sexual assault, conflict with family members, posttraumatic stress disorder, and co-occurring mental health disorders (Odgers & Moretti, 2002). Notably, high prevalence rates of disorders among offending youth provide evidence that mental health and violence are related, but the complex, multifaceted association between the two is unclear.

Next, Table 9.2 highlights that dynamic risk factors ("criminogenic needs") differ by age and gender. For example, possessing antisocial beliefs and attitudes relates to violence for male juvenile offenders, but for female offenders the findings are mixed. In contrast, encouraging academic achievement appears to be particularly important in reducing violence among girls (Baltodano, Mathur, & Rutherford, 2005). In addition, Lipsey and Derzon (1998) found that involvement in general offenses and substance use were the two strongest predictors of violence for children (ages 6–11), but having few social ties and antisocial peers were strongest in early adolescence (ages 12–14). Interestingly, substance use at ages 12–14 had one of the weakest correlations to future violent offending, possibly because experimentation with drugs and alcohol at this age may be developmentally normative (Shedler & Block, 1990). There is evidence, however, that frequent exposure to substances in early adolescence relates to general offending in adulthood (Odgers et al., 2008).

Policy and Practice Relevant Gaps in Knowledge About Needs Assessment

Overall, these findings demonstrate that validated, reliable needs assessment tools which can be used to inform interventions among diverse populations (e.g., differences in gender, sociocultural characteristics, disability status, and age) are necessary. Although a few assessment tools have been designed to measure criminogenic needs (e.g., YLS/CMI, SAVRY), more empirical work is needed to determine whether these instruments consistently and accurately identify *dynamic* needs, which if modified, relate to decreased violence. Much of existent research on criminogenic needs relies on *assumptions* about which risk factors are dynamic versus static. That is, little research has examined whether risk factors actually change, and whether these *changes* relate to decreased offending. Some basic questions for future research include the following: How do criminogenic needs change as juveniles mature into adults? How can professionals identify changing needs? Which needs, if ameliorated, will produce the greatest reductions in recidivism? How can professionals know when the need has been sufficiently ameliorated?

The Responsivity Principle: Employ Interventions Known to Increase Responsivity and Effectiveness

Implement Highly Structured, Comprehensive, Multilevel Approaches

There are multiple pathways to delinquency and crime, and it is well documented that young offenders possess a wide range of risk factors across multiple domains (Reppucci, Fried, & Schmidt, 2002). Therefore, it is not surprising that the treatments and interventions most likely to reduce recidivism are those that use comprehensive, multilevel (e.g., individual, family, neighborhood) approaches which target multiple criminogenic needs across a number of settings (Mulford & Redding, 2008; Mulvey, Arthur, & Reppucci, 1993). Importantly, broadly disseminating routine services to large groups of juvenile offenders (e.g., offenders in a residential facility) is less effective than interventions, which, through individualized case management, provide offenders with services based on personal needs (Lipsey, 2009; Lipsey & Wilson, 1998).

Implement Cognitive-Behavioral and Social Learning Approaches

Adolescents who engage in aggressive and antisocial behaviors are more likely to possess cognitive distortions or information-processing errors than their nonaggressive peers (Barriga et al., 2000; Dodge, Price, Bachorowski, & Newman, 1990), and these cognitive dysfunctions are thought to interfere with their readiness to participate in and their response to treatments (Chambers, Eccleston, Day, Ward, & Howells, 2008). Chambers et al. (2008) provide a detailed discussion of four categories of cognitive distortions impacting offenders (adapted from Gibbs, Potter, & Goldstein, 1995): (1) self-centered attitudes and beliefs (e.g., "Everyone in society is against me"), (2) placing the blame for offending on others (e.g., "I told him it would be a mistake to hit me"), (3) minimizing and mislabeling violent behavior (e.g., "She was a prostitute; she deserved to be raped"), and (4) using "hostile attributional biases" (Dodge et al., 1990; i.e., assuming the worst of other people). Cognitive-behavioral treatments are designed to correct these dysfunctional thinking patterns and, through the use of various behavioral training techniques (e.g., positive reinforcement, role playing, modeling), teach adolescents to react prosocially in potentially threatening or aggression-provoking situations.

A series of analyses have demonstrated strong support for the effectiveness of cognitive-behavioral approaches with female offenders (Dowden & Andrews, 1999a), violent offenders (Dowden & Andrews, 2000), and juvenile offenders (Dowden & Andrews, 1999b). However, certain components of cognitive-behavioral interventions, or the interaction of certain components, produce greater reductions in recidivism than others. In a meta-analysis of 58 studies, Landenberger and Lipsey (2005) found that cognitive-behavioral treatments emphasizing anger control and interpersonal problem solving were related to significant reductions in general recidivism, whereas programs utilizing victim impact and behavior modification (e.g., behavioral contracts, token economies) did not appear to reduce recidivism. However, caution is warranted in generalizing these findings to juvenile offenders at risk for violent offending because only 29% of the primary studies were conducted with juveniles, and recidivism was not limited to violent offenses. Nevertheless, Lipsey and Wilson (1998) also found that treatments targeting interpersonal skill training consistently reduced general offending among serious and violent juvenile offenders, and this was true for juveniles in both institutional and community-based settings.

Landenberger and Lipsey's (2005) findings highlight the importance of distinguishing between cognitive-behavioral and traditional behavioral programs. Several researchers use the term *behavioral intervention* as inclusive of behavioral, cognitive, and social learning. Indeed, findings are mixed about whether behavioral modification treatments (e.g., token economies) *alone* reduce violent or nonviolent offending (Gottschalk, Davidson, Mayer, & Gensheimer, 1987; Whitehead & Lab, 1989). However, adding a cognitive component (e.g., problem solving, skills training, role playing) to behavioral treatments significantly improves juveniles' responsivity to treatment and reduces general recidivism (Izzo & Ross, 1990; Pearson, Lipton, Cleland, & Yee, 2002), possibly because cognitive-behavioral programs correct youth's dysfunctional thinking patterns in addition to teaching them how to behave prosocially.

Implement Family-Based Approaches

Implementing family-based interventions can potentially ameliorate family risk factors and establish healthy, prosocial attachments and family management practices. Program evaluations, meta-analyses, and extensive literature reviews support the effectiveness of family-based interventions to reduce aggression and/or noncompliance among children (Estrada & Pinsof, 1995; Serketich & Dumas, 1996) and adolescents (Dowden & Andrews, 2003; Eddy, Whaley, & Chamberlain, 2004), but only when implemented within a comprehensive, multilevel treatment plan (Mulford & Redding, 2008). Typically, in family-based interventions a case manager works closely with adolescents and their families to design an individualized, family-based service plan to strengthen family resources and overcome problems which initially placed adolescents at risk for offending. See later descriptions in this chapter of two well-known family-based interventions: multisystemic therapy (MST; Henggeler et al., 1998) and multidimensional treatment foster care (MTFC; Chamberlain & Reid, 1997).

Use Community-Based Approaches

A number of researchers have concluded that implementing highly structured, empirically validated community-based treatment services with high-risk seriously offending youth is more cost-effective than incarceration, and more importantly, yields equal and sometimes greater reductions in violent and nonviolent recidivism (Eddy et al., 2004; Henggeler, Melton, & Smith, 1992). There are multiple reasons why community-based treatments tend to be effective. First, many risk and need factors related to violence stem from within juveniles' homes and communities (Hawkins et al., 2000). Compared to programs implemented in institutions or outside of youths' home communities, community-based interventions are more capable of addressing familial and environmental needs in conjunction with individual needs because professionals will have greater access to offenders' families and friends. Logistical difficulties (e.g., transportation, time) preventing family engagement in treatments are easier to accommodate in community-based programs than remotely implemented programs, which increases the likelihood that families will actively participate in the intervention and that familial risk factors related to violence will be ameliorated. Increased dialogue with family and friends could also provide professionals with valuable information about juveniles' developmental histories, particularly concerning past physical and mental health problems (Perkins-Dock, 2001).

Furthermore, Mulvey et al. (1993) reviewed research on the effectiveness of residential placement treatments and concluded that the improvements in behavior and substance use diminish greatly and/or disappear after youth leave these placements. Providing community-based treatment might promote the generalizability of learned social and behavioral skills across the various settings in which youth function. Importantly, new roles and responsibilities assumed in the transition from adolescence to adulthood offer juvenile offenders "turning points" (Laub & Sampson, 1993) for positive life changes. Providing treatment and services while youth are living in the community and struggling to establish competencies in new developmentally appropriate domains (e.g., employment, marriage) might increase the likelihood that juvenile offenders will mature into self-sufficient, productive adults.

Continually Evaluate the Integrity of Implemented Treatments

Even the best intervention programs will be unlikely to reduce recidivism if they are implemented poorly, that is, without adherence to the validated program model (Henggeler et al., 1997). Yet program implementation has been referred to as "the forgotten issue" (Gendreau, Goggin, & Smith, 1999, p. 180) because programs are rarely evaluated with rigorous control for program implementation characteristics such as treatment duration, total service hours, frequency of contact, staff turnover, staff training, and dropout rates (Lipsey, 2009). Even though few researchers have examined the relationship between program implementation and recidivism, the results have been consistent: Intervention programs are less effective in reducing recidivism if they are not implemented with integrity to the empirically based treatment design (Andrews & Dowden, 2005; Lipsey, 2009).

Gendreau et al. (1999) recognized the scarcity of literature delineating how to initiate and maintain successful intervention programs within various settings. They proposed four categories of guidelines to help professionals weigh the range of potential barriers to successful program implementation so that problems can be contended with before beginning treatment (see also Perkins-Dock, 2001). Specifically, they focus on *(1)* host agency organizational factors (e.g., Is the agency open to adopting new initiatives?), *(2)* specific treatment program factors (e.g., Is the treatment scientifically credible?), *(3)* staff factors (e.g., Do the staff willingly and actively participate in treatments?), and *(4)* change agent factors (e.g., Will the "change agent," or person who is primarily responsible for the program, continue with the program until change is observed?).

Policy and Practice Relevant Gaps in Knowledge About Intervention Responsivity

Research has shed light on the specific components that make certain programs more likely to reduce recidivism, but little of this research has specifically examined *violent* offending. Instead, many researchers measure recidivism as any reoffense, violent or nonviolent. Certain approaches, for example, teaching problem-solving skills, might be more or less effective in reducing violent versus nonviolent recidivism. Similarly, future research is needed to determine whether employing certain combinations of approaches leads to the greatest reduction in violence and other crime for youth with particular risk factors (Guerra, Kim, & Boxer, 2008). For example, for adolescents from risky family backgrounds, individual therapy in conjunction with family group therapy might reduce violence, whereas only receiving one or the other might not. Moreover, including a family therapy component might be particularly important for girl offenders, given that relationships appear to be important to girls' sense of well-being (Odgers & Moretti, 2002). There is a growing body of literature on gender differences in interventions with offending adolescents, but much more research is needed.

Given that addressing family-based criminogenic needs seem to be associated with significant reductions in crime (Dowden & Andrews, 1999b), more research is also needed to determine the best methods for fostering and maintaining family participation (Mulford & Redding, 2008). In practice, there are many obstacles to recruiting and retaining family members' participation in treatment. High dropout rates, noncompliance, time constraints, and other stressors that prevent family participation can jeopardize the potential effectiveness of family interventions (Mulford & Redding, 2008). In addition, family interventions are particularly challenging to implement with institutionalized or out-of-home services youth because families often live far away and are more difficult to access. These circumstances often result in infrequent juvenile–family contact and problems in securing a private and comfortable setting in which to hold family trainings (Mulvey et al., 1993; Perkins-Dock, 2001).

Two Examples of Recognized Crime Reduction Programs: Multisystemic Therapy and Multidimensional Treatment Foster Care

MST and MTFC are two community-based, family-driven, comprehensive programs that have shown long-term reductions in violent and nonviolent crime among high-risk, violently offending youth (Borduin et al., 1995; Eddy et al., 2004). In MST (Henggeler et al., 1998), each adolescent and his/her family is assigned a therapist or case manager who is responsible for coordinating individualized programming based on the family's needs and strengths. MST case managers work collaboratively with a team of service providers to identify and treat individual-, family-, school-, and community-level criminogenic needs. Therapists are trained in empirically based approaches, for example, cognitive-behavioral and functional family therapy. All services are provided at a time and location that is convenient for the family.

Similar to MST, MTFC also provides adolescents and their families with frequent, comprehensive services to overcome criminogenic needs

(Chamberlain & Reid, 1997). However, MTFC is reserved for youth who need to be removed from home, and rather than placing them in a residential facility, families from the youth's community are recruited and trained to act as foster parents. MTFC case managers closely monitor MTFC foster parents through daily phone calls and weekly group meetings. Additionally, MTFC case managers coordinate with other adults (e.g., probation officers, teachers, mentors) to monitor youths' progress within multiple domains. MTFC youth attend weekly individual therapy sessions to learn and practice cognitive-behavioral and social learning skills (e.g., problem solving, perspective taking). Adolescents' biological (or step/adoptive) parents also play an important role in treatment, because the goal is to return adolescents to their homes. Adolescents and their parents complete in-home family therapy sessions and parents are encouraged to monitor their adolescent's progress in the program.

Distilling Scientific Evidence on What *Doesn't* Work

Violent crimes tend to elicit feelings of fear, anger, and retribution, which, in turn, elicit concerns over community safety and often lead to more punitive punishments for violently offending juveniles. Unfortunately, these sanction-based punitive interventions seldom alleviate the risk factors that initially led youth to offend, and therefore are unlikely to reduce future violent and/or nonviolent offending (Dowden & Andrews, 1999a, 1999b, 2000). Indeed, after controlling for methodology, individual offender characteristics (e.g., gender, ethnicity), and the level of juvenile justice supervision, Lipsey (2009) found that all therapeutic interventions (e.g., skills training, counseling) demonstrated relatively equal effectiveness, but justice-oriented programs emphasizing surveillance, deterrence, and discipline showed minimal to no effect on recidivism. In fact, compared to a control recidivism rate of 50%, juveniles enrolled in boot camps and similar discipline-oriented programs showed an 8% *increase* in recidivism rates (Lipsey, 2009).

Strong evidence also exists that transferring youth from juvenile court to adult court increases, rather than decreases, violent and nonviolent offending (Lanza-Kaduce, Frasier, Lane, & Bishop, 2002; McGowan et al., 2007; Reppucci, Michel, & Kostelnik, 2009). In an extensive review, McGowan et al. (2007) analyzed five scientifically credible studies examining the effects of transfer on violent and/or felony recidivism. Importantly, each of these studies statistically controlled for "selection bias," that is, the possibility that the highest risk juveniles were more likely to be selected for transfer to adult court and therefore naturally more likely to recidivate than nontransferred youth. Even after accounting for selection bias, on average, transferred juveniles were 33.7% more likely to recidivate than adolescents retained in the juvenile justice system. McGowan and colleagues (2007) concluded that "transferring juveniles to the adult justice system is counterproductive as a strategy for deterring subsequent violence" (p. 15). In sum, implementing sanction-based treatments without appropriately treating juveniles' risks and needs appears more likely to increase offending than to decrease it (Lipsey & Cullen, 2007).

Recommendations for Structuring Correctional Programs

General Recommendations for Increasing Juvenile Offenders' Responsivity to Treatment

1) Match the intensity of intervention services to offender risk level and target criminogenic needs.
2) Implement highly structured, multilevel, comprehensive treatment programming to address multiple known causes of delinquency.
3) Select treatments with various cognitive-behavioral techniques, for example, programs employing problem solving, cognitive restructuring, role playing, and modeling to address criminogenic needs.
4) Select treatments that emphasize family engagement and promote healthy interpersonal relationships in young offenders' lives.
5) When possible, implement treatment programming in or within close proximity to youths' home communities so as to encourage family involvement and facilitate the development of useful behavioral and social skills within individual communities.

Contextual Recommendations for Increasing Juvenile Offenders' Responsivity to Treatment

1) Form partnerships with researchers to routinely evaluate *(a)* risk and need assessment tools, and *(b)* the integrity of the implementation of empirically supported interventions.
2) Increase the effectiveness of treatment and rehabilitation programs through case management, continuity, and coordination of services for individual offenders.
3) Be aware of how community organizations, settings, and resources might impact the success of treatment programming.

Recommendations for Improving Supervision of and Intervention With Individual Offenders

1) Provide training and/or learning opportunities for juvenile justice professionals to learn about ways individual offender characteristics, including gender, race/ethnicity, and age, might influence the quality and effectiveness of programming.
2) Employ standardized assessments of risks, needs, and strengths, but allow professionals to exercise discretion when they can document circumstances that call for it.

Concluding Remarks

Juvenile justice intervention research has progressed considerably over the past three decades. Initial questions about whether interventions have any effect on recidivism have been replaced by more sophisticated and complex questions about how well certain treatments work for individual offenders under certain circumstances. Two consistent findings have prevailed: *(1)* Interventions based solely on punishment and retribution do not reduce violence among juveniles and may even increase it; *(2)* In contrast, service-based treatment programs, if implemented with integrity, significantly reduce recidivism among high-risk juvenile offenders (Andrews & Dowden, 2005; Lipsey, 2009; Lipsey & Cullen, 2007). Despite these advances in understanding "what works" for treating juvenile offenders, more research examining risks and needs associated with violence in specific populations, particularly female offenders, is warranted. Furthermore, initial evidence suggests that youth who desist from crime do not necessarily experience positive outcomes in other settings, such as school and work (Stouthamer-Loeber, Wei, Loeber, & Masten, 2004). Future research needs to determine how to promote successful outcomes across important adult-functioning domains and increase the likelihood that juvenile offenders will become competent adults. Optimistically, promoting resilience in the transition from adolescence to adulthood might protect against transgenerational patterns of risky and violent behavior.

References

Alexander, J. F., Robbins, M. S., & Sexton, T. L. (2000). Family-based interventions with older, at-risk youth: From promise to proof to practice. *The Journal of Primary Prevention, 21,* 185–205.

Andrews, D. A., & Bonta, J. (1995). *Level of Supervision-Revised (LSI-R): An offender assessment system. User's guide.* Toronto, ON: Multi-Health Systems.

Andrews, D. A., Bonta, J., & Hoge, R. D. (1990). Classification for effective rehabilitation: Rediscovering psychology. *Criminal Justice and Behavior, 17,* 19–52.

Andrews, D. A., & Dowden, C. (2005). Managing correctional treatment for reduced recidivism: A meta-analytic review of programme integrity. *Legal and Criminological Psychology, 10,* 173–187.

Andrews, D. A., & Dowden, C. (2006). Risk principle of case classification in correctional treatment: A meta-analytic investigation. *International Journal of Offender Therapy and Comparative Criminology, 50,* 88–100.

Baltodano, H. M., Mathur, S. R., & Rutherford, R. B. (2005). Transition of incarcerated youth with disabilities across systems and into adulthood. *Exceptionality, 13,* 103–124.

Barriga, A. Q., Landau, J. R., Stinson, B. L., II, Liau, A. K., & Gibbs, J. C. (2000). Cognitive distortion and problem behaviors in adolescents. *Criminal Justice and Behavior, 27,* 36–56.

Borduin, C. M., Mann, B. J., Cone, L. T., Henggeler, S. W., Fucci, B. R., Blaske, D. M., & Williams, R. A. (1995). Multisystemic treatment of serious juvenile offenders: Long-term prevention of criminality and violence. *Journal of Consulting and Clinical Psychology, 63,* 569–578.

Borum, R. (2003). Managing at-risk juvenile offenders in the community: Putting evidence-based principles into practice. *Journal of Contemporary Criminal Justice, 19,* 114–137.

Borum, R., Bartel, P., & Forth, A. (2001). *Manual for the Structured Assessment for Violence Risk in Youth (SAVRY)* (Consultation Ed.). Tampa: University of South Florida.

Bullis, M., & Yovanoff, P. (2006). Idle hands: Community employment experiences of formerly incarcerated youth. *Journal of Emotional and Behavioral Disorders, 14,* 71–85.

Caldwell, M. F., Vitacco, M., & Van Rybroek, G. J. (2006). Are violent delinquents worth treating? A cost-benefit analysis. *Journal of Research in Crime and Delinquency, 43,* 148–168.

Carr, M. B., & Vandiver, T. A. (2001). Risk and protective factors among youth offenders. *Adolescence, 36,* 409–426.

Chamberlain, P., & Reid, J. B. (1997). Comparison of two community alternatives to incarceration for chronic juvenile offenders. *Journal of Consulting and Clinical Psychology, 6,* 624–633.

Chambers, J. C., Eccleston, L., Day, A., Ward, T., & Howells, K. (2008). Treatment readiness in violent offenders: The influence of cognitive factors on engagement in violence programs. *Aggression and Violent Behavior, 13,* 276–284.

Dodge, K. A., Price, J. M., Bachorowski, J-A., & Newman, J. P. (1990). Hostile attributional biases in severely aggressive adolescents. *Journal of Abnormal Psychology, 99,* 385–392.

Dornfeld, M., & Kruttschnitt, C. (1992). Do the stereotypes fit? Mapping gender-specific outcomes and risk factors. *Criminology, 30,* 397–419.

Dowden, C., & Andrews, D. A. (1999a). What works for female offenders: A meta-analytic review. *Crime and Delinquency, 45,* 438–452.

Dowden, C., & Andrews, D. A. (1999b). What works in young offender treatment: A meta-analysis. *Forum on Corrections Research, 11,* 21–24.

Dowden, C., & Andrews, D. A. (2000). Effective correctional treatment and violent recidivism: A meta-analysis. *Canadian Journal of Criminology, 42,* 449–476.

Dowden, C., & Andrews, D. A. (2003). Does family intervention work for delinquents? Results of a meta-analysis. *Canadian Journal of Criminology and Criminal Justice, 45,* 327–342.

Eddy, J. M., Whaley, R. B., & Chamberlain, P. (2004). The prevention of violent behavior by chronic and serious male juvenile offenders: A 2-year follow-up of a randomized clinical trial. *Journal of Emotion and Behavioral Disorders, 12,* 2–8.

Edens, J. F., Campbell, J. S., & Weir, J. M. (2007). Youth psychopathy and criminal recidivism: A meta-analysis of the Psychopathy Checklist measures. *Law and Human Behavior, 31,* 53–75.

Estrada, A. U., & Pinsof, W. M. (1995). The effectiveness of family therapies for selected behavioral-disorders of children. *Journal of Marital and Family Therapy, 21,* 403–440.

Feld, B. C. (1999). *Bad kids: Race and the transformation of the juvenile court.* New York: Oxford University Press.

Forth, A. E., Kosson, D. S., & Hare, R. D. (2003). *Psychopathy Checklist: Youth Version (PCL:YV).* Toronto, ON: Multi-Health Systems.

Funk, S. J. (1999). Risk assessment for juveniles on probation: A focus on gender. *Criminal Justice and Behavior, 26,* 44–68.

Gendreau, P., Goggin, C., & Smith, P. (1999). The forgotten issue in effective correctional treatment: Program implementation. *International Journal of Offender Therapy and Comparative Criminology, 43,* 180–187.

Gibbs, J. C., Potter, G. B., & Goldstein, A. P. (1995). *The EQUIP program: Teaching youth to think and act responsibly through a peer-helping approach.* Champaign, IL: Research Press.

Gottschalk, R., Davidson, W. S., II, Mayer, J. P., & Gensheimer, L. K. (1987). Behavioral approaches with juvenile offenders: A meta-analysis of long-term treatment efficacy. In E. K. Morris & C. J. Braukman (Eds.), *Behavioral approaches to crime and delinquency: A handbook of application, research and concepts* (pp. 399–420). New York: Plenum.

Grigorenko, E. L. (2006). Learning disabilities in juvenile offenders. *Child Adolescence Psychiatric Clinics of North America, 15,* 353–371.

Grove, W. M., Zald, D. H., Lebow, B. S., Snitz, B. E., & Nelson, C. (2000). Clinical versus mechanical prediction: A meta-analysis. *Psychological Assessment, 12,* 19–30.

Guerra, N. G., Kim, T. E., & Boxer, P. (2008). What works: Best practices with juvenile offenders. In R. D. Hoge, N. G. Green, & P. Boxer (Eds.), *Treating the juvenile offender* (pp. 79–102). New York: Guilford Press.

Hawkins, J. D., Herrenkohl, T. I., Farrington, D. P., Brewer, D., Catalano, R. F., Harachi, T. W., & Cothern, L. (2000). Predictors of youth violence. *Juvenile Justice Bulletin.* Washington, DC: U.S. Department of Justice, Office of Justice Programs, Office of Juvenile Justice and Delinquency Prevention.

Henggeler, S. W., Melton, G. B., Brondino, M. J., Scherer, D. G., & Hanley, J. H. (1997). Multisystemic Therapy with violent and chronic juvenile offenders and their families: The role of treatment fidelity in successful dissemination. *Journal of Counseling and Clinical Psychology, 65,* 821–833.

Henggeler, S. W., Melton, G. B., & Smith, L. A. (1992). Family preservation using Multisystemic Therapy: An effective alternative to incarcerating serious juvenile offenders. *Journal of Consulting and Clinical Psychology, 60,* 953–961.

Henggeler, S. W., Schoenwald, S. K., Borduin, C. M., Rowland, M. D., & Cunningham, P. B. (1998). *Multisystemic treatment of antisocial behavior in children and adolescents.* New York: Guilford Press.

Hoge, R. D. (2008). Assessment in the juvenile justice systems. In R. D. Hoge, N. G. Guerra, & P. Boxer (Eds.), *Treating the juvenile offender* (pp. 54–78). New York: Guilford Press.

Hoge, R. D., Guerra, N. G., & Boxer, P. (Eds.). (2008). *Treating the juvenile offender.* New York: Guildford Press.

Howell, J. C. (Ed.). (1995). *Guide for implementing the comprehensive strategy for serious, violent, and chronic juvenile offenders.* Washington, DC: U. S. Department of Justice, Office of Juvenile Justice and Delinquency Prevention.

Izzo, R. L., & Ross, R. R. (1990). Meta-analysis of rehabilitation programs for juvenile delinquents. *Criminal Justice and Behavior, 17,* 134–142.

Landenberger, N. A., & Lipsey, M. W. (2005). The positive effects of cognitive-behavioral programs for offenders: A meta-analysis of factors associated with effective treatment. *Journal of Experimental Criminology, 1,* 451–476.

Lanza-Kaduce, L., Frasier, C. E., Lane, J., & Bishop, D. M. (2002). *Juvenile transfer to criminal court study: Final report.* Report Number 02–02. Tallahassee, FL: Department of Juvenile Justice.

Laub, J. H., & Sampson, R. J. (1993). Turning points in the life course: Why change matters to the study of crime." *Criminology, 31,* 301–325.

Lipsey, M. W. (2009). The primary factors that characterize effective interventions with juvenile offenders: A meta-analytic overview. *Victims and Offenders, 4,* 124–147.

Lipsey, M. W., & Cullen, F. T. (2007). The effectiveness of correctional rehabilitation: A review of systematic reviews. *Annual Review of Law and Social Science, 3,* 297–320.

Lipsey, M. W., & Derzon, J. H. (1998). Predictors of violent or serious delinquency in adolescence and early adulthood: A synthesis of longitudinal research. In R. Loeber & D. P. Farrington (Eds.), *Serious and violent juvenile offenders: Risk factors and successful interventions* (pp. 86–105). Thousand Oaks, CA: Sage.

Lipsey, M. W., & Wilson, D. B. (1998). Effective intervention for serious juvenile offenders: A synthesis of research. In R. Loeber & D. P. Farrington (Eds.), *Serious and violent juvenile offenders: Risk factors and successful interventions* (pp. 313–345). Thousand Oaks, CA: Sage.

Loeber, R., & Farrington, D. P. (Eds.). (1998). *Serious and violent juvenile offenders: Risk factors and successful interventions.* Thousand Oaks, CA: Sage.

Loeber, R., Farrington, D. P., & Waschbusch, D. A. (1998). Serious and violent juvenile offenders. In R. Loeber & D. P. Farrington (Eds.), *Serious and violent juvenile offenders: Risk factors and successful interventions* (pp. 13–29). Thousand Oaks, CA: Sage.

Lyons, J. S., Baerger, D. R., Quigley, P., Erlick, J., & Griffin, E. (2001). Mental health service needs of juvenile offenders: A comparison of detention, incarceration, and treatment settings. *Children's Services: Social Policy, Research, and Practice, 4,* 69–85.

Martinson, R. (1974). What works? Questions and answers about prison reform. *Public Interest, 35,* 22–54.

McGowan, A., Hahn, R., Liberman, A., Crosby, A., Fullilove, M., Johnson, R., Moscicki, E., Price, L., Snyder, S., Tuma, F., Lowy, J., Briss, P., Cory, S., & Stone, G. (2007). Effects on violence of laws and policies facilitating the transfer of juveniles from the juvenile justice system to the adult justice system: A systematic review. *American Journal of Preventative Medicine, 32,* 7–28.

Mears, D. P., Hay, C., Gertz, M., & Mancini, C. (2007). Public opinion and the foundation of the juvenile court. *Criminology, 45,* 223–258.

Moffitt, T. E. (1993). Adolescence-limited and life-course-persistent antisocial behavior: A developmental taxonomy. *Psychological Review, 100,* 674–701.

Moffitt, T. E., Caspi, A., Harrington, H., & Milne, B. J. (2002). Males on the life-course-persistent and adolescence-limited antisocial pathways: Follow-up at age 26 years. *Development and Psychopathology, 14,* 179–207.

Mulford, C. F., & Redding, R. E. (2008). Training the parents of juvenile offenders: State of the art and recommendations for service delivery. *Journal of Child and Family Studies, 17,* 629–648.

Mulvey, E. P., Arthur, M. W., & Reppucci, N. D. (1993). The prevention and treatment of juvenile delinquency: A review of the research. *Clinical Psychology Review, 13,* 133–167.

Mulvey, E. P., & Iselin, A.-M. R. (2008). Improving professional judgments of risk and amenability in juvenile justice. *Future of Children, 18,* 35–57.

Odgers, C. L., Caspi, A., Nagin, D. S., Piquero, A. R., Slutske, W. S., Milne, B. J., Dickenson, N., Poulton, R., & Moffitt, T. E. (2008). Is it important to prevent early exposure to drugs and alcohol among adolescents? *Psychological Science, 19,* 1037–1044.

Odgers, C. L., & Moretti, M. M. (2002). Aggressive and antisocial girls: Research update and challenges. *International Journal of Forensic Mental Health, 1,* 103–119.

Odgers, C. L., Reppucci, N. D., & Moretti, M. M. (2005). Nipping psychopathy in the bud: An examination of the convergent, predictive, and theoretical utility of the PCL-YV among adolescent girls. *Behavioral Sciences and the Law, 23,* 743–763.

Olver, M. E., Stockdale, K. C., & Wormith, J. S. (2009). Risk assessment with young offenders: A meta-analysis of three assessment measures. *Criminal Justice and Behavior, 36,* 329–353.

Onifade, E., Davidson, W., Livsey, S., Turke, G., Horton, C., Malinowski, J., Atkinson, D., & Wimberly, D. (2008). Risk assessment: Indentifying patterns of risk in young offenders with the Youth Level of Service/Case Management Inventory. *Journal of Criminal Justice, 36,* 165–173.

Pearson, F. S., Lipton, D. S., Cleland, C. M., & Yee, D. S. (2002). The effects of behavioral/cognitive-behavioral programs on recidivism. *Crime and Delinquency, 10,* 476–496.

Perkins-Dock, R. E. (2001). Family interventions with incarcerated youth: A review of the literature. *International Journal of Offender Therapy and Comparative Criminology, 45,* 606–625.

Petrosino, A., Turpin-Petrosino, C., & Bueler, J. (2003). Scared straight and other juvenile awareness programs for preventing juvenile delinquency: A systematic review of the randomized experimental evidence. *Annals of the American Academy of Political and Social Science, 589,* 41–62.

Reppucci, N. D., Fried, C. S., & Schmidt, M. G. (2002). Youth violence: Risk and protective factors. In R. R. Corrado, R. Roesch, S. D. Hart, & J. K. Gierowski (Eds.), *Multi-problem violent youth: A foundation for comparative research on needs, interventions and outcomes* (pp. 3–22). Amsterdam, Netherlands: IOS Press.

Reppucci, N. D., Michel, J. L., & Kostelnik, J. O. (2009). Challenging juvenile transfer: Faulty assumptions and misguided policy. In B. L. Bottoms, C. J. Najdowski, & G. S. Goodman (Eds.), *Children as victims, witnesses and offenders: Psychological science and the law* (pp. 295 – 312). New York: Guilford Press.

Schmidt, F., Hoge, R. D., & Gomes, L. (2005). Reliability and validity analyses of the youth level of service/case management inventory. *Criminal Justice and Behavior, 32,* 329–344.

Schwalbe, C. S. (2008). A meta-analysis of juvenile justice risk assessment instruments: Predictive validity by gender. *Criminal Justice and Behavior, 35*, 1367–1381.

Scott, E. S., Reppucci, N. D., Antonishak, J., & DeGennaro, J. T. (2003). Public attitudes about the culpability and punishment of young offenders. *Behavioral Sciences and the Law, 24*, 815–832.

Serketich, W. J., & Dumas, J. E. (1996). The effectiveness of behavioral parent training to modify antisocial behavior in children: A meta-analysis. *Behavioral Therapy, 27*, 171–186.

Shedler, J., & Block, J. (1990). Adolescent drug use and psychological health: A longitudinal inquiry. *American Psychologist, 45*, 612–630.

Stouthamer-Loeber, M., Wei, E., Loeber, R., & Masten, A. S. (2004). Desistance from persistent serious delinquency in the transition to adulthood. *Development and Psychopathology, 16*, 897–918.

Tarolla, S. M., Wagner, E. F., Rabinowitz, J., & Tubman, J. G. (2002). Understanding and treating juvenile offenders: A review of current knowledge and future directions. *Aggression and Violent Behavior, 7*, 125–143.

Teplin, L. A., Abram, K. M., McClelland, G. M., Dulcan, M. K., & Mericle, A. A. (2002). Psychiatric disorders in youth in juvenile detention. *Archives of General Psychiatry, 59*, 1133–1143.

Timmons-Mitchell, J., Brown, C., Schultz, S. C., Webster, S. E., Underwood, L. A., & Semple, W. E. (1997). Comparing the mental health needs of female and male incarcerated juvenile delinquents. *Behavioral Sciences and the Law, 15*, 195–202.

Vermeiren, R., Schwab-Stone, M., Ruchkin, V., De Clippele, A., & Deboutte, D. (2002). Predicting recidivism in delinquent adolescents from psychological and psychiatric assessment. *Comprehensive Psychiatry, 43*, 142–149.

Veysey, B. M. (2008). Mental health, substance abuse, and trauma. In R. D. Hoge, N. G. Guerra, & P. Boxer (Eds.), *Treating the juvenile offender* (pp. 210–238). New York: Guilford Press.

Ward, T., Mesler, J., & Yates, P. M. (2007). Reconstructing the Risk-Need-Responsivity model: A theoretical elaboration and evaluation. *Aggression and Violent Behavior, 12*, 208–228.

Welsh, J. L., Schmidt, F., McKinnon, L., Chattha, H. K., & Meyers, J. R. (2008). A comparative study of adolescent risk assessment instruments: Predictive and incremental validity. *Assessment, 15*, 104–115.

Whitehead, J. T., & Lab, S. P. (1989). A meta-analysis of juvenile correctional treatment. *Journal of Research in Crime and Delinquency, 26*, 276–295.

Williams, K. R., Tuthill, L., & Lio, S. (2008). A portrait of juvenile offending in the United States. In R. D. Hoge, N. G. Guerra, & P. Boxer (Eds.), *Treating the juvenile offender* (pp. 15–32). New York: Guilford Press.

10

Extending Rehabilitative Principles to Violent Sexual Offenders

Judith V. Becker and Jill D. Stinson

Current trends in sex offender legislation and policy are focused on identifying those sexual offenders who present the greatest perceived risk of violent sexual recidivism and finding ways to supervise and contain them apart from the community as a whole. However, this leads to several questions:

1) *Are we only worried about violent sexual recidivism?* Consistent findings in research describing risk indicate that only a small subset of sexual offenders—typically around 10%–15% (e.g., Hanson & Bussière, 1998)—are known to commit future violent sexual acts after their release, but that larger numbers of them commit other violent or criminal acts during the same time period.

2) *Are some offenders riskier than others?* With research suggesting that some groups of sex offenders are more likely to offend and represent a greater proportion of those known to engage in violent sexual recidivism (e.g., Harris et al., 2003), we must evaluate the utility of identifying and responding to these subgroups of sex offenders in accordance with the risk they apparently present to the community.

3) *Do we have reliable ways of differentiating those most at risk from those who are not?* Policy efforts have been affected in a rather indiscriminate manner, suggesting that *all* sex offenders should be subject to the same supervision or notification requirements. Research in this area gives us a mixed presentation of the issue; while risk assessment instruments have shown improvement over time in classifying sexual offenders as high, medium, or low risk (e.g., Hanson & Morton-Bourgon, 2007),

new emerging research suggests that we still have yet to understand the true impact of dynamic variables or treatment influences on future risk (Hanson et al., 2007; Hanson & Morton-Bourgon, 2007).

4) *Is containment really our only option?* Questions have recently arisen regarding the effectiveness of sex offender treatment in reducing sexual recidivism (e.g., Marques et al., 2005). Lack of faith in our ability to treat offenders and prevent future sexual violence has led many to conclude that containment and supervision are the only options. However, other research has suggested strategies allowing for community reintegration for many offenders. Considering the vast differences in cost between an inpatient or residential treatment model and a community supervision model, and also considering the fixed resources available for sex offender treatment and management, intensive supervision in the community may offer a more viable alternative for many offenders as opposed to long-term incarceration or containment for a relative few.

In this chapter, we will address these and other relevant concerns for those directly charged with the responsibility for monitoring and treating sexual offenders in correctional systems. We will consider the empirical literature describing effective strategies and interventions for reducing sexual violence, as well as gaps in our current knowledge. We will also relate the empirical research to pragmatic implications for applied clinical practice and describe a model sex offender program that utilizes the principles outlined here. It is our hope that this information will be relevant for clinicians, researchers, facility administrators, and policy makers in developing effective and empirically driven programs for the sex-offending population in order to reduce violent sexual recidivism.

We offer observations that are informed by and respectful of the existing literature, yet note that there remains a great deal not yet known about this phenomenon. In such a climate, public policy goals should focus on potentially beneficial interventions that are unlikely to cause further harm. Finally, our recommendations are offered with full knowledge that false positives and false negatives in identifying and predicting those at risk can have enormous, even tragic consequences for offenders and victims alike.

Evidence on What Works to Reduce Violent Sexual Recidivism

Advances in our understanding of treatment effectiveness for offender populations are largely attributable to the introduction of the Risk-Need-Responsivity (RNR) model (Andrews, Bonta, & Hoge, 1990; Bonta & Andrews, 2007). In this model, the core principles include the offender's risk to reoffend, the presence of criminogenic needs that should be targeted in treatment, and the offender's responsivity or ability to learn from rehabilitative interventions. These principles are all potentially applicable to sex offender assessment and treatment (Hanson, Bourgon, Helmus, & Hodgson, 2009b; Harkins & Beech, 2007), where paramount are concerns of future violent sexual recidivism and the need to make well-informed decisions regarding offender risk and management.

The use of these principles in sex offender assessment and treatment represents a shift from the traditional views of sex offender management, which rely heavily on a containment and supervision philosophy. Societal expectations have largely supported and maintained this view over time, as people have espoused the belief that all sex offenders are predatory, unchanging individuals who cannot benefit from treatment and deserve extreme punishments for their behaviors. These views, while perhaps understandable from the point of view of victims, do little to solve the problem of continuing sexual violence and the need to work with offenders who are currently in need of treatment. Incorporation of the RNR principles will require a philosophical shift for those responsible for the treatment and management of these offenders.

Assessment: Risk and Future Recidivism

Historically, the assessment of sex offender risk has focused on static risk variables, or those variables that do not substantially change over time. Variables most consistent with increased risk of detected violent sexual recidivism include the number of prior arrests for sexual offenses, number of arrests for nonsexual violent offenses, violence associated with the index sexual offense, degree of psychopathy or other static personality characteristics, certain characteristics of the offender's victims (e.g., victim age, gender, or relatedness to the offender), and offender age (e.g., Hanson & Bussiere, 1996). These static variables have been incorporated into a number of standardized actuarial instruments, including the Static-99 (Hanson & Thornton, 2000), the Static-2002 (Hanson & Thornton, 2003), the Rapid Risk Assessment for Sex Offense Recidivism (RRASOR; Hanson, 1997), the MnSOST-R (Epperson, Kaul, & Hesselton, 2005), and the Sex Offender Risk Appraisal Guide (SORAG; Quinsey, Harris, Rice, & Cormier, 1998). In accordance with the risk principle, these instruments provide estimates of the likelihood of detected recidivism among a comparison sample of sexual offenders over a period of time in the community after release and divide offenders into low, medium, or high risk dependent on their scores on these instruments. While they do not provide individualized estimates of risk, they do describe the likelihood (though not the severity, imminence, or duration) of detected violent sexual recidivism among a group with shared risk characteristics. These risk estimates can then be used to determine appropriate placement, level of supervision, release conditions, or other resource management.

More recent advancements in our understanding of risk have included dynamic risk factors, or those factors that change over time and represent many of the criminogenic needs of offenders. Those criminogenic needs first identified by Andrews, Bonta, and Hoge (1990) include eight variables of interest: antisocial personality pattern, procriminal attitudes, social supports for crime, substance abuse, family/marital relationships, school/work, prosocial recreational activities, and criminal history. Many of these needs also have demonstrated significance as dynamic predictors of detected violent sexual recidivism, including antisocial lifestyle or orientation, attitudes or beliefs supportive of sexual offending, poor social support, and interpersonal conflict with intimate partners (Hanson & Harris, 1998; Hanson & Morton-Bourgon, 2005). Other relevant dynamic factors that have been identified include deviant sexual interests, difficulties with mood regulation and affective control, sexual self-regulation, general self-regulation, control of hostility or anger, and cooperation with supervision (Hanson & Harris, 1998, 2000; Hanson, Harris, Scott, & Helmus, 2007; Hanson & Morton-Bourgon, 2005). A number of new instruments have been designed to incorporate these factors, including the Sexual Violence Risk-20 (SVR-20; Boer, Hart, Kropp, & Webster, 1997), and the Stable-2000/Acute-2000 and Stable 2007/Acute 2007 (Hanson et al., 2007).

Other assessment tools often used to aid decision makers in determining dynamic risk include physiological and self-report measures of sexual interest and behavior, such as the polygraph, the penile plethysmograph, and psychological measures of sexual interest. Some research suggests that individuals who evidence high pretreatment levels of deviant sexual arousal on the penile plethysmograph, for example, are at a higher risk for detected violent sexual recidivism than those who do not (e.g., Malcolm, Andrews, & Quinsey, 1993). Other researchers have examined the utility of the polygraph as a tool for identifying unknown victims, or determining compliance with supervision requirements (Ahlmeyer, Heil, McKee, & English, 2000; Madsen, Parsons, & Grubin, 2004; Wilcox, 2000). However, research also exists suggesting that the use of these tools may provide inaccurate or invalid results for offenders with serious mental illness or intellectual and developmental disabilities, may not be useful over repeated measures, and may not accurately and consistently correspond with actual behavior (e.g., Ahlmeyer et al., 2000; Launay, 1999; Stinson & Becker, 2008).

Whether using actuarial or other assessment tools to evaluate risk, the science underlying the development of these instruments, particularly with regard to dynamic models, is still new, and many factors that appear relevant to risk to the clinician are, in fact, not. Understandably, our ability to assess risk is predicated on our understanding of those variables most related to risk. These limitations will be discussed further later in this chapter.

Treatment: Motivation, Treatment Targets, and Criminogenic Needs

Currently, most sex offender treatment programs in North America are based on a relapse prevention model, which is a cognitive-behavioral intervention focusing on important precursors of sex offender behavior (i.e., risk factors) and preventing sexual relapse or reoffense. Common strategies associated with this approach include an emphasis on cognitive distortions, or problematic beliefs supportive of sexual offending, identification of high-risk situations, and the development of a relapse prevention plan to aid the offender in avoiding potentially risky situations in the community. Relapse prevention models of sex offender treatment have been widely incorporated into correctional, mental health, and community agencies who work with these offenders. Early empirical evidence supported the use of relapse prevention models, indicating that offenders who had successfully completed treatment were in fact less likely to be convicted for a new sexual offense in the community than those who had not (e.g., Hanson et al., 2002). However, criticisms of this research have focused on problematic methodology and questions regarding the stability of the results (Berliner, 2002; Prentky, 2003; Rice & Harris, 2003a), and a large-scale study with a quality research design examining the effectiveness of relapse prevention in reducing rates of violent sexual recidivism failed to replicate these results (Marques et al., 2005).

Despite mixed findings with regard to effective treatment programs, several independent components of treatment, particularly those associated with the RNR model, may have implications for treatment success or the reduction of violent sexual recidivism. Some of these components of treatment have already been introduced as important predictors of risk and are thus potential targets for sex offender treatment.

First, offense-specific fantasies, interests, or arousal are often identified as a crucial component of treatment and have been shown to be related to future risk of detected violent sexual recidivism (Hanson & Morton-Bourgon, 2005). These offense-specific sexual interests or arousal may be addressed in treatment using a variety of methods, including cognitive-behavioral conditioning paradigms (i.e., aversion therapy, masturbatory reconditioning, masturbatory satiation, or covert sensitization) or pharmacological interventions (e.g., anti-androgen therapy), in order to decrease arousal to offense-specific stimuli, such as children or coercive sexual activity, and increase normative and consensual sexual interests in adult partners. Several authors have cautioned that empirical research in this area is mixed with regard to the effectiveness of these methods in reducing violent sexual recidivism (e.g., La Fond, 2005; Prentky, 1997; Rice & Harris, 2003b).

A second treatment target includes identifying precursors to offending behavior, with the goal of determining relevant cues or triggers that can then be incorporated into a behavioral plan, most commonly a relapse prevention plan. This strategy could be similarly employed to not only identify precursors to sex-offending behavior but other criminal behaviors as well, acknowledging that these behaviors may in fact be related. Research regarding the utility of identifying sex offender patterns is mixed, particularly given recent doubts regarding relapse prevention and its impact on future violent sexual recidivism (e.g., Marques et al., 2005).

A third treatment target addresses intimacy, relationships, and social skills. A great deal of research suggests that sexual offenders manifest problematic interpersonal skills and limited experiences with normative and healthy intimate relationships, and that these deficits can contribute to violent sexual behavior in several ways, including failure to form supportive relationships, exacerbation of emotional loneliness, and limitations in the availability of appropriate (i.e., legal) sexual or romantic partners (e.g., Marshall, 1989, 1993; Ward, Hudson, & Marshall, 1995). The development of adaptive interpersonal skills is typically included as a component of many cognitive-behavioral treatments for sexual offending, though findings as to the relatedness of these targets to violent sexual recidivism are inconsistent. For example, empirical research indicates that interpersonal conflicts are predictive of violent sexual recidivism, whereas social skills deficits and loneliness are not (Hanson & Morton-Bourgon, 2005). The success of this component of sex offender treatment thus remains to be determined.

Fourth, offense-supportive attitudes and beliefs, specifically those tolerant of sexual crime, are moderately related to detected violent sexual recidivism (Hanson & Morton-Bourgon, 2004, 2005). Most empirically evaluated treatments for sex-offending behaviors include a strong emphasis on cognitive restructuring of these distorted beliefs. Cognitive-behavioral treatments are typically centered on the idea that these offense-supportive attitudes or beliefs must be identified and challenged during treatment, so that the offender will develop more adaptive or normative beliefs regarding sexual behaviors, victims, and perceptions of self and others in interpersonal interactions. While these beliefs are related to risk, the success of changing them through treatment is inconclusive, as reviews of treatment effectiveness highlight inconsistencies in empirical findings (Hanson & Morton-Bourgon, 2004, 2005; Hanson et al., 2009a).

A fifth factor involves the offender's ability to effectively manage and control emotional states. Emerging research has identified difficulties with self-regulation as a significant etiological component of sex-offending behavior and a relevant treatment target (e.g., Stinson, Becker, & Sales, 2008; Stinson, Sales, & Becker, 2008; Ward, Polaschek, & Beech, 2006). Similarly, risk prediction research has suggested that broad difficulties with self-regulation are in fact correlated with higher levels of risk for future convictions for sexual violence (Hanson & Morton-Bourgon, 2005). Some treatment interventions do include a self-regulatory component but have not yet been empirically validated.

Finally, a sixth broad treatment goal involves management of future risk. Noncompliance with supervision and violation of release conditions have been associated with increased risk of detected violent sexual recidivism (Hanson & Harris, 1998; Hanson & Morton-Bourgon, 2005). The development of a relapse prevention plan outlining conditions to manage potential risk is a primary component in most sex offender treatment programs.

However, methods for incorporating management strategies into treatment need improvement.

In addition to treatment targets or criminogenic needs, responsivity factors are also related to treatment success. While measures of denial, minimization, lack of motivation, and poor treatment progress are viewed by treatment providers as important determinants of future risk, empirical research suggests that these factors are not significantly related to known future sexual offenses (Hanson & Morton-Bourgon, 2005). Other research has identified related responsivity factors that do impact risk, including self-perceptions of risk, disengagement from treatment after release, maintenance of minimization and justification of offenses after release, and lack of insight into potentially high-risk situations when in the community (Hanson & Harris, 1998). This suggests that some responsivity factors have been identified and are useful in determining treatment effectiveness and reduction of risk.

Gaps in Knowledge

While there have been improvements in our understanding of risk and treatment needs of sexual offenders, many questions remain. To treat and manage this population more effectively and thereby reduce rates of continued sexual violence, treatment programming and the assessment of risk should include considerations of these gaps in our empirical knowledge.

What Drives the Behavior, and What Are We Treating?

The struggle to find the most effective treatment for sex-offending behavior is greatly influenced by our understanding of the behavior itself. In other words, to know to how to treat it, we need to know what it is and how it develops. Empirical evidence highlighting the limitations of treatment in reducing the rate of violent sexual recidivism points to our tenuous understanding of etiology. Do thoughts cause behavior? What is the role of opportunity? How do some people develop deviant sexual interests? What roles do psychopathy and other personality characteristics play? These and other etiological questions have been evaluated recently in the literature (e.g., Stinson, Sales, & Becker, 2008; Ward, Polaschek, & Beech, 2006), emphasizing the limitations in our understanding of these behaviors. And while several new theoretical models are emerging that implicate common factors (e.g., self-regulatory processes) in the development of sex-offending behaviors (Stinson, Becker, & Sales, 2008; Stinson, Sales, & Becker, 2008; Ward & Hudson, 2000; Ward, Hudson, & Keenan, 1998; Ward, Polaschek, & Beech, 2006), treatment models based on these self-regulatory processes, including the Good Lives Model (Ward, Yates, & Long, 2006) and Safe Offender Strategies (Stinson & Becker, 2010), need further evaluation to determine their effectiveness in reducing violent sexual recidivism.

The Dynamic Nature of Risk

Risk is not a constant. Evaluating the risk of violent sexual recidivism among people who have a history of violent sexual behavior is complicated by the mutable nature of the risk factors involved. While we may never know with 100% certainty when and how an individual will reoffend, emerging research has identified the importance of dynamic variables, which can inform our understanding of conditions likely to predispose a given individual to reoffend. Considerations of risk *status*, or the long-term static prediction of risk by comparison with other individuals, versus consideration of risk *state*, or the immediate characteristics that would place an individual at risk of some behavior, must be incorporated in order to more fully capture the dynamic nature of risk (Douglas & Skeem, 2005; Skeem & Mulvey, 2002).

As noted by Monahan and Steadman (1996), we should perhaps evaluate violence risk in the context of a weather forecast, where we can predict the seriousness and impact of behavior when we know more about the immediate and changing conditions contributing to it. For example, when the research indicates that poor social support is a critical factor increasing one's risk in the community (e.g., Hanson & Morton-Bourgon, 2005), we have to remember that the availability of a social support network, the person's ability to maintain relationships with those individuals, and the person's willingness to utilize available social supports will change many times over the course of a given follow-up period. Further, the quality and availability of social support depends on other immediate factors, including work or lifestyle stability, antisocial behavior, and the effective regulation of mood or emotion. Simply stating that "good social support" will reduce risk of violent sexual recidivism is insufficient. Our research must move in the direction of explaining how risk changes, how significant risk factors interact with one another to create the right conditions for violent sexual behavior (e.g., Hanson et al., 2009b), and how factors related to risk state may change throughout the course of a treatment intervention.

Role of Motivation, Willingness, and Commitment to Treatment

In the RNR model, responsivity factors are those that refer to the offender's willingness to engage in treatment, commitment to change his or her behavior, and the ability to benefit from the treatment offered. While some of these variables have been linked to risk of violent sexual recidivism, others have not (e.g., Hanson & Harris, 1998; Hanson & Morton-Bourgon, 2005). This illustrates the need for further research into how these factors may subtly differ from one another, in addition to which specific responsivity factors may have a differential impact on treatment completion and risk.

Furthermore, while it is important to say that we need to better understand the role of motivation and responsivity in treatment success and risk reduction, an even more important precursor is having an effective means by which to measure these constructs. How do we truly know if an offender is motivated? We can clearly see treatment behavior, but sex offender treatment is often involuntary (e.g., court-ordered or an institutional requirement), and this would contribute to one's desire to appear motivated in order to achieve secondary gain. We do not know whether motivating factors other than desire to change result in any noticeable difference in terms of crime reduction. However, the point remains that we still do not have sound methods by which to measure motivation, willingness, and commitment to treatment over time.

Most Appropriate Treatment Modalities

How to best address risk of future sexual recidivism in a treatment setting does not just include considerations of what type of treatment to provide or how to most appropriately assign clients to treatment. We must also evaluate the most effective modes of treatment, including group versus individual, outpatient versus residential, adult versus adolescent treatment, treatment frequency and intensity, and inclusion of other relevant treatment targets. While Andrews and Bonta (2006) reported that community treatment was more effective than residential programming for general offenders, other recent treatment reviews suggest otherwise (Hanson et al., 2009a; Lösel & Schmucker, 2005), though only if those at highest risk are targeted (Lovins, Lowenkamp, & Latessa, 2009).

Sexually violent predator (SVP) programs are typically residential treatment programs, though several states, including Arizona and Texas, now include outpatient treatment for some or all of the offenders civilly committed to their programs. Early empirical research regarding one of these programs (i.e., Texas; Bailey, 2002; Meyer et al., 2003) indicates that outpatient SVP treatment may provide a promising alternative to costly residential care for a growing number of sexual offenders. Many more individuals may be targeted for treatment and supervision on an outpatient basis than can be served in a residential setting, given the reality of limited professional and budgetary resources faced by many jurisdictions with civil commitment legislation. This is a promising area for future study.

"Disconnect" Between Policy and Practice

What is done with sex offenders after conviction and what the public thinks should be done with these offenders are often two very different things. SVP laws, lengthy periods of mandatory sentencing, lifetime probation require-ments, and even the possibility of capital punishment in some states suggests little public tolerance for sexual offenders and a desire to see them closely monitored and segregated from the general public. Many of these policies are predicated on the belief that sex offenders are incapable of improving their behaviors, and the consequence of this belief—virtually indiscriminate and indefinite incarceration for all sexual offenders—is extremely costly and perhaps unnecessary. Treatment for sexual offenders, on the other hand, is predicated on the very notion that offenders *can* change their behavior and eventually return to a productive and safer life within the community. While many would acknowledge the importance of treatment, the natural extension of that process—that treated offenders are then sufficiently improved to be released—might cause negative reaction from those in the community.

A significant gap in our knowledge involves the role of the public and their expectations of sex offender treatment. Few prevention or treatment programs have addressed the need for public education. Helping those in the community and those who make decisions regarding sex offender policy understand more about the characteristics of this population, conditions that may increase or decrease risk of violent sexual recidivism, and the role of treatment, would be an important first step in changing the focus from containment and supervision to treatment and building the skills that will allow some sex offenders to live safely in the community. How this would then impact public policy and legislation related to sexual offenders, as well as mandatory sentencing and available funding for treatment and the assessment of risk, still remains to be seen.

Should There Be Special Supervision and Management Efforts for Sexual Offenders?

This is a question seldom addressed in the literature pertaining to sexual offenders. Sexual offenders are segregated from the population of general offenders not only in the literature but also in the minds of the public. For comparison, if the public feared domestic violence to the degree that they fear sexual offenders, then we would have journals, international organizations, entire treatment facilities, special sections of legal code, and generations of specially trained clinicians ready to address domestic assault as we do with sexual offending. It is perhaps because of public sentiment toward sex offenders that we treat them as a separate entity, despite empirical evidence that they are in many ways similar to other criminal groups (Simon, 1997, 2000).

There is also a concern that by targeting sexual offenders in a psychiatric sense, and by using the diagnoses of paraphilias, that a criminal behavior has been transformed into a purported mental illness. This is most evident with rape, which is a legal construct, and the use of persistent coercive sexual behaviors as evidence of a paraphilic interest in rape. This is problematic when a clinician must differentiate sexual interest from repetitive sexual behavior. Whether a behavior represents irresistible urges or simply unresisted ones is likely to remain controversial for many years to come. The current empirical literature has not yet resolved these concerns. This ambiguity is especially salient for those who develop treatment programming and assess risk. Decisions regarding inclusion criteria for sex offender treatment must pay heed to this issue; for example: Do we include only those offenders with paraphilias? Should sex offenders be housed in psychiatric versus correctional versus other residential care facilities? Additionally, decisions about whether the "illness" has been cured or whether the behavior has been managed will depend on the extent to which the clinician or administrator believes sex-offending behavior is a psychological or psychiatric issue, a criminological issue, or both.

Implications for Practice

As noted earlier, research has indicated that the most effective interventions for general offenders are those that follow the risk, need, and responsivity principles (Andrews, Bonta, & Hoge, 1990; Bonta & Andrews, 2007). Integrating findings from the research literature in accordance with the principles of the RNR model can improve current approaches to sex offender treatment and risk management. In fact, recent work by Hanson et al. (2009b) confirms this, because treatment programs adhering to all three of these principles were significantly more effective in reducing known violent sexual recidivism.

With regard to risk, advances have been made both in the development of risk assessment instruments to include static, dynamic, and acute versus stable factors. Empirical evaluation of the accuracy of risk assessment instruments suggests that actuarial instruments are able to identify those offenders most likely to engage in newly detected sexual offenses in the community (Hanson & Morton-Bourgon, 2007, 2009), and instruments designed to specifically assess sexual risk are most accurate in predicting newly detected violent sexual behaviors (Hanson & Morton-Bourgon, 2007, 2009). Thus, a clear assessment protocol should be identified, focusing specifically on these actuarial instruments designed to assess risk of future violent sexual offenses, so that offenders within an institution or treatment program may be classified into groups of low-, medium-, and high-risk offenders. It is recommended that the intensity and level of treatment correspond with identified risk levels. Decisions regarding release and subsequent community monitoring should also follow from these assessments. In addition, risk assessment should be ongoing throughout the course of treatment to identify and account for immediate conditions and treatment interventions that continually impact risk.

With regard to criminogenic needs and treatment targets, research indicates that cognitive-behavioral interventions appear to work best, focusing on both criminogenic and noncriminogenic needs. Treatment programs should focus on those targets specifically and empirically linked to sexual recidivism, including offense-supportive sexual interests, sexual preoccupation, self-regulatory deficits, and the development of supportive relationships (Hanson et al., 2009a). This does not preclude treatment providers from incorporating other components into their treatment, because skills deficits, illicit substance use, and mental illness, including personality disorders and paraphilias, may also be relevant. Sex offenders represent a heterogeneous group, and while some have exclusively engaged in sex-offending behaviors, others have engaged in other forms of criminal behavior that may be crucial treatment targets as well.

With regard to responsivity factors, efforts should be made to determine the most effective treatment modality for the particular individual and to similarly match available resources. Strategies to increase motivation and commitment beyond the immediate treatment environment (i.e., so that it extends to the community after release), such as motivational interviewing (Miller & Rollnick, 2002), would also be crucial in effecting lasting reduction of sexual risk. Assessments of cognitive capacity, educational achievement, or learning style might also aid in increasing engagement and retention of treatment material. As noted earlier, the common use of cognitive-behavioral therapies as part of sex offender treatment is consistent with Andrews and his colleagues, who highly recommend cognitive-behavioral therapy as part of their responsivity principle.

Finally, regarding community management and supervision, the level, type, and intensity of supervision will depend on a number of factors (e.g., whether the offender is at high, moderate, or low risk for known recidivism based on the use of actuarial instruments using static, dynamic, and acute factors; whether the offender's past criminal behavior has been exclusively sexual or if other nonsexual criminal behaviors have occurred). Those offenders who have been in institutional settings and are being reintegrated into the community will additionally need to receive numerous levels of support, including employment, housing, and identifying prosocial individuals within the community who would be willing to serve as a support system for the individual. A comprehensive system for effective monitoring of offenders that complies with local, state, and federal regulatory policies related to sex offenders will need to be established. The effectiveness of some common practices involving specific management techniques, including the use of GPS devices, has not yet been empirically evaluated, though this does not preclude its use if appropriate with certain offender groups. Management techniques should be developed in accordance with risk and supervision need.

A Model Program

Some of the key components outlined in this chapter are those closely related to the RNR model, including accurate assessment of low-, medium-, and high-risk offenders, identification of and treatment addressing the empirically validated criminogenic needs most associated with violent sexual recidivism, and assessing and increasing responsivity (both general and individual) to treatment. Applying these components in practice involves more than just inclusion of empirically validated principles but also considerations of treatment philosophy, method of treatment delivery, other treatment needs beyond those most obviously associated with violent sexual risk, and the role of others involved in the treatment, management, assessment, and supervision of these individuals.

What we need is a treatment program that incorporates new approaches to treatment, utilizes a skills-based approach consistent with the principles of the RNR model, and has been implemented in a large-scale institutional setting where the goal is eventual release into the community. Such an effort has been underway at Fulton State Hospital, in Fulton, Missouri—a forensic state hospital with maximum, intermediate, and minimum security units, which provides treatment to individuals who have been arrested for sexual and other violent crimes (Missouri Revised Statutes 552.020, 552.030). While a forensic mental health rather than correctional setting, client characteristics, environmental security, and release concerns often mirror those of a correctional facility. Programming at Fulton State Hospital involves the use of empirically supported treatments, aided by ongoing research and program evaluation efforts at the facility.

Recent changes in the sex offender treatment programming at Fulton State Hospital have included a change in treatment philosophy, the piloting of a manualized treatment approach authored by Stinson and Becker (2010), extensive staff training, and modifications to the risk assessment process to incorporate more broadly the clients' criminogenic needs and the goals of treatment. These changes were driven by limitations in prior treatment approaches, poor client participation and progress, and concerns related to ongoing risk and supervision needs. This effort began in the fall of 2007 and has resulted in a more comprehensive sex offender program. Further details are provided for those who are interested in how such a program can be implemented in a correctional or forensic residential facility.

Treatment Philosophy

In keeping with the RNR model, client responsiveness is of primary concern in establishing an effective sex offender treatment program. This includes not only client motivation but also the motivation of those who provide treatment, supervision, and daily care for sexual offenders. As in other similar facilities, clients involved in sex offender treatment are typically mandated to do so, whether by the court or the institution. Recognizing this, we must understand that not all offenders want to be in treatment. Similarly, not all treatment providers have sought out the opportunity to provide sex offender treatment; many clinicians have been assigned this role due to facility resource management. This can result in offenders and treatment providers who are not enthusiastic or optimistic about treatment.

With regard to client motivation, it has become a primary focus in the initial stages of treatment. A motivational interviewing approach was incorporated into the treatment manual used at the facility. Clients were allowed to establish their own treatment goals, thus increasing their involvement in the treatment process. At times, goals for unmotivated clients were to simply attend weekly sessions and listen to the concepts discussed. Treatment providers were given a choice regarding their participation, and the voluntariness of participation for both clients and staff has improved commitment to the program (e.g., increase in client participation from 50% group attendance to 85% group attendance over the first 2 years).

Another philosophical shift that occurred involved the perception of the client and the role of the treatment provider. Traditional treatment has emphasized the need for confrontational and directive methods, where the offender is made to describe his or her offense and frequently challenged by peers and treatment providers in a manner intended to elicit more truthful information. The assumption is that offenders are deceptive, regardless of the intentionality of this, and that the role of the treatment provider and fellow group members is to challenge their deception and confront them with their distorted beliefs, biased accounts of the offense, or denial. Unfortunately, this approach has not been shown to increase client motivation, engagement, or treatment success (Beech & Fordham, 1997; Beech & Hamilton-Giachritsis, 2005; Marshall & Serran, 2004; Serran, Fernandez, Marshall, & Mann, 2003). Instead, treatment providers at Fulton State Hospital are viewed as facilitators and use validation strategies to elicit meaningful participation from the clients involved. Client denial or deception is "validated," rather than confronted, because getting a client to "admit" what we typically already know only serves to damage the therapeutic relationship. For example, when a client denies his offense, he may be told, "People make many judgments about sex offending and sex offenders. It can be very frightening to come to treatment and talk about problems like this. A lot of people struggle with understanding their behavior."

Validation, as is used here, comes from a dialectical behavior therapy perspective (Linehan, 1993). Thus, validation is an effort on the part of the therapist to communicate to the client that his or her thoughts, emotions, and behavioral responses are understandable given current situational factors. The emphasis is on acceptance of the client's responses, and his or her efforts in therapy are viewed as serious and meaningful within the current context. Validation is clearly separate from "truth seeking," in which the therapist attempts to determine the veracity of the client's report. Instead, it merely refers to accepting and acknowledging the client's perceptions and emotions related to his or her experiences in that moment. (Further information regarding the use of validation with difficult interpersonal interactions can be found in Linehan, 1993). This strengthens the therapeutic alliance between client and provider, which has been empirically shown to be a crucial factor in treatment success across a variety of psychological interventions (e.g., Horvath & Luborsky, 1993; Horvath & Symonds, 1991).

Staff Training

Because of the large proportion of clients at Fulton State Hospital who are involved in sex offender treatment, it was important for all staff, not just those who provide sex offender treatment, to receive training in working with these individuals. Direct care staff as well as clinicians received basic training in characteristics of sex offenders, sex offender treatment, and monitoring and management of problematic sexual behavior. This was done with all staff at the facility and continues on a monthly basis with new personnel. Those who provide sex offender treatment received more extensive training in the manualized treatment and monthly in vivo adherence monitoring and supervision by the program coordinator. They additionally attend a brief monthly meeting for further training and consultation. These efforts have ensured consistency across treatment groups and treatment providers, provided a preventive education component for direct care staff and case managers, and allowed for feedback from staff members who work with the sexual offenders and observe their behavior on a daily basis. Involving these individuals in the process is critical, because they can continue to motivate and monitor the clients, and especially to reinforce prosocial behaviors at the time they are observed, while they remain in the care of the institution.

Logistics of Treatment Implementation

Treatment at Fulton State Hospital, as it would be at many correctional facilities, is long-term care. Clients are not admitted to the facility for brief periods of time. Understandably, many of these individuals are believed to be at substantial risk for future violent sexual offenses, while others are not. Those at greatest risk will receive longer periods of sex offender treatment; they may be enrolled in groups that meet with greater frequency or may receive supplemental individual therapy. This is consistent with the RNR model's risk principle, as those at the most risk are in need of the greatest intervention.

In keeping with RNR's responsivity principle, treatment groups are kept rather small, ranging from five to eight clients each, so that clients will have the opportunity to engage in group discussions and interact with treatment providers. Clients are selected for groups dependent on a variety of factors, including criminogenic needs, cognitive ability, level of willingness and commitment, severity of psychotic symptoms, or level of treatment need. For example, some groups of highest risk clients are smaller, more focused, and lengthier than those of clients who are at lesser risk. Some groups are designed for those with intellectual or developmental deficits, so that a slower pace and more concrete examples can be presented for these individuals. Each group has two facilitators in order to increase client–facilitator interaction, the use of role plays as examples, and stability of group facilitators over time.

Treatment Targets

Fulton State Hospital utilizes a pilot version of a new treatment manual, Safe Offender Strategies (e.g., Stinson & Becker, 2010), which is a skills-based, self-regulation approach to sex offender treatment. As noted in the literature, some of the critical components of sex offender treatment include addressing offense-specific thoughts and interests, emotion regulation, risk management, social skills and relationships, and precursors to offending behavior. Additionally, the RNR model identifies other targets for treatment, including problematic substance use, antisocial behaviors, and prosocial skills and activities. These needs have been incorporated into treatment, forming a more comprehensive approach to sex offender treatment that references other maladaptive behaviors, including substance use, criminal or aggressive behavior, self-harm behavior, or difficulties with impulse control.

Assessing Risk

Risk of future violent sexual behavior is critical to any transfer or release decision made at Fulton State Hospital. All clients involved in sex offender treatment are assessed before moving to a less restrictive alternative, including movement between security levels within the institution as well as community placement. Risk assessments also determine continued need for sex offender treatment. A combination of actuarial tools and dynamic indicators of criminogenic or psychiatric needs related to their offending behavior are used, along with an emphasis on supports needed to maintain the offender's success in future placements. Recommendations include maintenance of structure, psychiatric medications, supervisory needs, or specific treatment programming which has been effective for the individual. These risk assessment reports are then evaluated by administrative officials at the hospital to determine the most appropriate placement, restrictions, or treatment needs of these offenders.

Summary and Conclusions

Sex offenders in correctional or other forensic residential settings present a number of challenges for those responsible for treating and assessing their risk to the community. The RNR model is applicable to this population, as consideration of their risk to the community, their diverse treatment needs, and factors that affect their willingness and ability to benefit from treatment all effect their likelihood of engaging in future acts of sexual violence. Let us return then to our initial concerns.

Are we only worried about violent sexual recidivism? Research in this area has primarily focused on what we can do to assess and reduce risk of continued sexual offending. However, from an RNR perspective, other criminogenic needs may be relevant and have implications for other problematic behaviors. We should be concerned with the dynamic variables most closely associated with not only sexual risk but also risk of future violence or treatment failure.

Are some offenders riskier than others? Based on what we know from the literature, the answer appears to be yes. The RNR model suggests that these offenders who are at greater risk should be subject to differential supervision, management, and intervention strategies than those whose known risk of violent sexual recidivism is less.

Do we have reliable ways of differentiating those most at risk from those who are not? While we have some consistent information regarding the assessment of risk, the current literature is far from conclusive regarding our ability to accurately predict risk. Future research should focus on the gaps in our knowledge, including the role of dynamic variables, how these variables interact with one another, and how these factors may be impacted by treatment interventions.

Is containment really our only option? Stating that those offenders most "at risk" of violent sexual reoffense should be certainly and indefinitely contained is itself risky, begging several important questions: How certain are we that these offenders are in fact at the highest risk? Does it make sense to manage and treat many fewer offenders in expensive institutions, essentially precluding effective management and treatment of many others? When we are reasonably certain of risk, and when we have a better understanding of dynamic, individualized risk factors for a given individual, we may be more confident in managing an offender with continued treatment, intensive community supervision, and available support services.

References

Ahlmeyer, S., Heil, P., McKee, B., & English, K. (2000). The impact of polygraphy on admissions of victims and offenses in adult sexual offenses. *Sexual Abuse: A Journal of Research and Treatment, 12*, 123–138.

Andrews, D. A., & Bonta, J. (2006). *The psychology of criminal conduct* (4th ed.). Newark, NJ: LexisNexis.

Andrews, D. A., Bonta, J., & Hoge, R. D. (1990). Classification for effective rehabilitation. *Criminal Justice and Behavior, 17*, 19–52.

Bailey, R. K. (2002). The civil commitment of sexually violent predators: A unique Texas approach. *Journal of the American Academy of Psychiatry and the Law, 30*, 525–532.

Beech, A. R., & Fordham, A. S. (1997). Therapeutic climate of sexual offender treatment programs. *Sexual Abuse: A Journal of Research and Treatment, 9*, 219–237.

Beech, A. R., & Hamilton-Giachritsis, C. E. (2005). Relationship between therapeutic climate and treatment outcome in group-based sexual offender treatment programs. *Sexual Abuse: A Journal of Research and Treatment, 17*, 127–140.

Berliner, L. (2002). Commentary. *Sexual Abuse: A Journal of Research and Treatment, 14*, 195–197.

Boer, D. P., Hart, S. D, Kropp, P. R., & Webster, C. D. (1997). *Manual for the Sexual Violence Risk–20: Professional guidelines for assessing risk of sexual violence.* Vancouver, BC: The British Columbia Institute against Family Violence.

Bonta, J., & Andrews, D. A. (2007). *Risk-need-responsivity model for offender assessment and rehabilitation.* User report 2007–06. Ottawa, ON: Public Safety Canada.

Douglas, K. S., & Skeem, J. L. (2005). Violence risk assessment: Getting specific about being dynamic. *Psychology, Public Policy, and Law, 11,* 347–383.

Epperson, D. L., Kaul, J. D., & Hesselton, D. (2005). *Minnesota sex offender screening tool, Revised (MnSOST-R): Development, performance, and recommended risk level cut scores.* St. Paul: Minnesota Department of Corrections.

Hanson, R. K. (1997). *The development of a brief actuarial risk scale for sexual offense recidivism.* User Report 97–04. Ottawa, ON: Department of the Solicitor General of Canada.

Hanson, R. K., Bourgon, G., Helmus, L., & Hodgson, S. (2009a). *A meta-analysis of the effectiveness of treatment for sexual offenders: Risk, need, and responsivity.* User Report 2009–01. Ottawa, ON: Public Safety Canada.

Hanson, R. K., Bourgon, G., Helmus, L., & Hodgson, S. (2009b). The principles of effective correctional treatment also apply to sexual offenders: A meta-analysis. *Criminal Justice and Behavior, 36,* 865–891.

Hanson, R. K., & Bussiere, M. T. (1996). *Predictors of sexual offender recidivism: A meta-analysis.* User Report 96–04. Ottawa, ON: Department of the Solicitor General.

Hanson, R.K. & Bussière M.T. (1998). Predicting relapse: A meta-analysis of sexual offender recidivism studies. *Journal of Consulting and Clinical Psychology, 66*(2), 348–362.

Hanson, R. K., Gordon, A., Harris, A. J. R., Marques, J. K., Murphy, W., Quinsey, V. L., & Seto, M. C. (2002). First report of the Collaborative Outcome Data Project on the effectiveness of treatment for sex offenders. *Sexual Abuse: A Journal of Research and Treatment, 14,* 169–194.

Hanson, R. K., & Harris, A. J. R. (1998). *Dynamic predictors of sexual recidivism.* User report 1998–1. Ottawa, ON: Department of the Solicitor General Canada.

Hanson, R. K., & Harris, A. J. R. (2000). Where should we intervene? Dynamic predictors of sexual offense recidivism. *Criminal Justice and Behavior, 27,* 6–35.

Hanson, R. K., Harris, A. J. R., Scott, T-L., & Helmus, L. (2007). *Assessing the risk of sexual offenders on community supervision: The Dynamic Supervision Project.* User Report 2007–05. Ottawa, ON: Public Safety Canada.

Hanson, R. K., & Morton-Bourgon, K. E. (2004). *Predictors of sexual recidivism: An updated meta-analysis.* User Report 2004–02. Ottawa, ON: Public Safety and Emergency Preparedness Canada.

Hanson, R. K., & Morton-Bourgon, K. E. (2005). The characteristics of persistent sexual offenders: A meta-analysis of recidivism studies. *Journal of Consulting and Clinical Psychology, 73,* 1154–1163.

Hanson, R. K., & Morton-Bourgon, K. E. (2007). *The accuracy of recidivism risk assessments for sexual offenders: A meta-analysis.* User Report 2007–01. Ottawa, ON: Public Safety and Emergency Preparedness Canada.

Hanson, R. K., & Morton-Bourgon, K. E. (2009). The accuracy of recidivism risk assessments for sexual offenders: A meta-analysis of 118 prediction studies. *Psychological Assessment, 21,* 1–21.

Hanson, R. K., & Thornton, D. (2000). Improving risk assessments for sex offenders: A comparison of three actuarial scales. *Law and Human Behavior, 24*, 119–136.

Hanson, R. K., & Thornton, D. (2003). *Notes on the development of Static-2002.* User Report 2003–01. Ottawa, ON: Solicitor General Canada.

Harkins, L. & Beech A.R. (2007). A review of the factors that can influence the effectiveness of sexual offender treatment: Risk, need responsivity, and process issues. *Aggression and Violent Behavior, 12*(6), 615–627.

Harris, G. T., Rice, M. E., Quinsey, V. L., Lalumiere, M. L., Boer, D., & Lang, C. (2003). A multi-site comparison of actuarial risk instruments for sex offenders. *Psychological Assessment, 15*, 413–425.

Horvath, A. O., & Luborsky, L. (1993). The role of the therapeutic alliance in psychotherapy. *Journal of Consulting and Clinical Psychology, 61*, 561–573.

Horvath, A. O., & Symonds, D. B. (1991). Relation between working alliance and outcome in psychotherapy: A meta-analysis. *Journal of Counseling Psychology, 38*, 139–149.

La Fond, J. Q. (2005). *Preventing sexual violence: How society should cope with sex offenders.* Washington, DC: American Psychological Association.

Launay, G. (1999). The phallometric assessment of sex offenders: An update. *Criminal Behaviour and Mental Health, 9*, 254–274.

Linehan, M. M. (1993). *Cognitive-behavioral treatment of borderline personality disorder.* New York: Guilford Press.

Lösel, F., & Schmucker, M. (2005). The effectiveness of treatment for sexual offenders: A comprehensive meta-analysis. *Journal of Experimental Criminology, 1*, 117–146.

Lovins, B., Lowenkamp, C., & Latessa, E. J. (2009). Applying the risk principle to sex offenders: Can treatment make some sex offenders worse? *The Prison Journal, 89*, 344–357.

Madsen, L., Parsons, S., & Grubin, D. (2004). A preliminary study of the contribution of periodic polygraph testing to the treatment and supervision of sex offenders. *Journal of Forensic Psychiatry & Psychology, 15*(4), 682–695.

Malcom, M.B.P., Andrews, D.A., & Quinsey, V.L. (1993). Discriminant and predictive validity of phallometrically measured sexual age and gender preference. *Journal of Interpersonal Violence 26*(5), 486-501.

Marques, J. K., Wiederanders, M., Day, D. M., Nelson, C., & van Ommeren, A. (2005). Effects of a relapse prevention program on sexual recidivism: Final results from California's Sex Offender Treatment and Evaluation Project (SOTEP). *Sexual Abuse: A Journal of Research and Treatment, 17*, 79–107.

Marshall, W. L. (1989). Intimacy, loneliness, and sexual offenders. *Behaviour Research and Therapy, 27*, 491–504.

Marshall, W. L. (1993). The role of attachments, intimacy, and loneliness in the etiology and maintenance of sex offending. *Sexual and Marital Therapy, 8*, 109–121.

Marshall, W. L., & Serran, G. (2004). The role of the therapist in offender treatment. *Psychology, Crime, and Law, 10*, 309–320.

Meyer, W. J., Molett, M., Richards, C. D., Arnold, L., & Latham, J. (2003). Outpatient civil commitment in Texas for management and treatment of sexually violent predators: A preliminary report. *International Journal of Offender Therapy and Comparative Criminology, 47*, 396–406.

Miller, W. R., & Rollnick, S. (2002). *Motivational interviewing: Preparing people for change*. New York: Guilford Press.

Monahan, J., & Steadman, H. J. (1996). Violent storms and violent people: How meteorology can inform risk communication in mental health law. *American Psychologist, 51*, 931–938.

Prentky, R. A. (1997). Arousal reduction in sexual offenders: A review of antiandrogen interventions. *Sexual Abuse: A Journal of Research and Treatment, 9*, 335–347.

Prentky, R. A. (2003). A 15-year retrospective on sexual coercion: Advances and projections. In R. A. Prentky, E. S. Janus, & M. C. Seto (Eds.), *Sexually coercive behavior: Understanding and management* (pp. 13–32). New York: New York Academy of Sciences.

Quinsey, V. L., Harris, G. T., Rice, M. E., & Cormier, C. A. (1998). *Violent offenders: Appraising and managing risk*. Washington, DC: American Psychological Association.

Rice, M. E., & Harris, G. T. (2003a). The size and sign of treatment effects in sex offender therapy. In R. A. Prentky, E. S. Janus, & M. C. Seto (Eds.), *Sexually coercive behavior: Understanding and management* (pp. 428–440). New York: Annals of the New York Academy of Sciences.

Rice, M. E., & Harris, G. T. (2003b). What we know and don't know about treating adult sex offenders. In B. J. Winick & J. Q. La Fond (Eds.), *Protecting society from sexually dangerous offenders: Law, justice, & therapy* (pp. 101–118). Washington, DC: American Psychological Association.

Serran, G., Fernandez, Y., Marshall, W. L, & Mann, R. E. (2003). Process issues in treatment: Application to sexual offender programs. *Professional Psychology, Research, and Practice, 34*, 368–374.

Simon, L. M. J. (1997). The myth of sex offender specialization: An empirical analysis. *New England Journal on Criminal and Civil Commitment, 23*, 387–403.

Simon, L. M. J. (2000). An examination of the assumptions of specialization, mental disorder, and dangerousness in sex offenders. *Behavioral Sciences and the Law, 18*, 275–308.

Skeem, J. L., & Mulvey, E. (2002). Monitoring the violence potential of mentally disordered offenders being treated in the community. In A. Buchanan (Ed.), *Care of the mentally disordered offender in the community* (pp. 111–142). New York: Oxford Press.

Stinson, J. D., & Becker, J. V. (October, 2010). *Safe Offender Strategies*: Pilot data and outcomes from a new manualized treatment approach. Poster presentation. Association for the Treatment of Sexual Abusers. Phoenix, AZ.

Stinson, J. D., & Becker, J. V. (2008). Assessing sexual deviance: A comparison of physiological, historical, and self-report measures. *Journal of Psychiatric Practice, 14*, 379–388.

Stinson, J. D., Becker, J. V., & Sales, B. D. (2008). Self-regulation and the etiology of sexual deviance: Evaluating causal theory. *Violence and Victims, 23*, 35–52.

Stinson, J. D., Sales, B. D., & Becker, J. V. (2008). *Sex offending: Causal theories to inform research, prevention, and treatment*. Washington, DC: American Psychological Association.

Ward, T., & Hudson, S. M. (2000). A self-regulation model of relapse prevention. In D. R. Laws, S. M. Hudson, & T. Ward (Eds.), *Remaking relapse prevention with sex offenders: A sourcebook* (pp. 79–101). Newbury Park, CA: Sage.

Ward, T., Hudson, S. M., & Keenan, T. (1998). A self-regulation model of the sexual offense process. *Sexual Abuse: A Journal of Research and Treatment, 10,* 141–157.

Ward, T., Hudson, S. M., & Marshall, W. L. (1995). Cognitive distortions and affective deficits in sex offenders: A cognitive deconstructionist interpretation. *Sexual Abuse: A Journal of Research and Treatment, 7,* 67–83.

Ward, T., Polaschek, D. L. L., & Beech, A. R. (2006). *Theories of sexual offending.* Chichester, England: Wiley.

Ward, T., Yates, P., & Long, C. (2006). *The Self-Regulation Model of the offense and relapse process: A manual. Volume 2: Treatment.* Victoria, BC: Pacific Psychological Assessment Corporation.

Wilcox, D. T. (2000). Application of the clinical polygraph examination to the assessment, treatment, and monitoring of sex offenders. *Journal of Sexual Aggression, 5,* 134–152.

11

Extending Violence Reduction Principles to Justice-Involved Persons With Mental Illness

John Monahan and Henry J. Steadman

We focus in this chapter on whether—and, if so, how—principles of violence risk reduction can be extended to justice-involved persons who have a serious mental illness. We limit our consideration to interventions that take place with adults, rather than with children or adolescents, and to interventions that occur in the community, rather than in hospitals, jails, or prisons. As with the other chapters in this book, we first address the state of the evidence on reducing violence risk among the population of interest, and we then point out gaps in this evidence base that can only be filled by future research. We conclude by describing what we take to be the implications for current practice of the state of the existing evidence, gaps and all.

Evidence About What Works to Reduce Violent Recidivism Among Justice-Involved Persons With Serious Mental Illness

Context: Serious Mental Disorder and Violence

The vast literature relating serious mental illness and violent behavior can be summarized simply:

- The general public has a grossly exaggerated view of the likelihood that a person with a serious mental illness will be violent to someone else (Pescosolido, Monahan, Link, Stueve, & Kikuzawa, 1999).

- Only a small portion—4% to 5%—of the violence in contemporary American society is committed by people with a serious mental illness (Swanson, 1994).
- That having been said, the likelihood that a person with a serious mental illness will be violent to someone else is in fact modestly higher than the likelihood that a person without a serious mental illness will be violent (Swanson, Holzer, Ganju, & Jono, 1990).
- Most of the violence committed by people with a serious mental illness is associated with their also abusing alcohol or other drugs (Fazel, Gulati, Linsell, Geddes, & Grann, 2009; Steadman et al., 1998).

It is crucial for the purpose of risk reduction to understand *how*, among people who have a serious mental illness and who engage in violence to others, the serious mental illness and the violence relate to one another (Kraemer et al., 1997). There are three possibilities. First, the serious mental illness can be the *cause*—or at least one of the causes—of the violence as, for example, when a person attacks someone whom she delusionally thinks is planning to attack her. Second, the serious mental illness can be a *consequence* of the violence, as would be the case when a person realizes that he has killed his spouse and as a result becomes clinically depressed. Finally, the serious mental illness can be a *concomitant* of the violence, illustrated by a person who has been arrested for a violent crime and is diagnosed in jail with a serious mental illness, analogous to a person who has committed a violent crime and is diagnosed in jail with a serious physical illness, with the illness being independent—neither a cause nor a consequence—of the violence (Douglas, Guy, & Hart, 2009; Silver, Felson, & Vaneseltine, 2008).

For achieving public health goals, serious mental illness should be treated regardless of whether, or how, it relates to violence (Monahan & Appelbaum, 2000). For achieving the goal of increased public safety adopted in this book, however, priority in allocating scarce mental health services should be given to targeting serious mental illness when it is a *cause* of violence, and not when it is a consequence or a concomitant of violence. As Swanson, Van Dorn, Swartz, Smith, Elbogen, and Monahan (2008, p. 240) have written, "we would hypothesize that antipsychotic medication may do little to reduce violence risk in patients whose violence is caused by factors other than psychosis" (see also Lamberti, 2007). Put in terms of Andrew's *needs principle*, which holds that treatment targets "should address dynamic risk factors that have been linked to criminal activity" (Andrews & Dowden, 2005, p. 174; Vieira, Skilling, & Peterson-Badali, 2009; also see Chapter 6), it is only among offenders whose mental illness bears a causal relationship to violence that *specifically mental health treatment* should be expected to reduce violent recidivism.

Among all persons with serious mental illness who also engage in violent behavior, in what proportion of cases does the mental illness bear a causal relationship to the violence? While no definitive answer to this question can be given at this time, findings from three recent studies suggest that the proportion may be surprisingly small.

The MacArthur Violence Risk Assessment Study (Monahan et al., 2001; Steadman et al., 1998) followed 1,136 patients discharged from acute civil psychiatric hospitals. Those patients committed a total of 608 violent acts over the course of their first year after discharge. The patients who had been violent were asked to describe what they were thinking and feeling at the time of the violent incident, and their statements were later rated by clinicians. Only 7% of the patients were rated as having been delusional at the time of the incident, and only 5% were rated as experiencing auditory hallucinations at the time of the incident (with 11% having been *either* delusional *or* hallucinating).

Junginger, Claypoole, Laygo, and Cristiani (2006) interviewed 113 arrestees with serious mental illness and co-occurring substance abuse disorder who were eligible for a jail diversion program. The interviews dealt with the cause of the target offenses. In the view of independent raters, psychiatric symptoms probably to definitely caused only 8% of the crimes for which these offenders had been arrested.

Finally, Peterson, Skeem, Hart, Vidal, and Keith (2010) studied 112 offenders with serious mental illness who had recently been released on parole. Based on an interview and a review of records, independent raters concluded that the criminal behavior of only 5% of these parolees was attributable to delusions, hallucinations, or other symptoms of psychosis.

As Skeem, Manchak, and Peterson (2011) conclude based on their review of these studies, for most offenders with serious mental illness, there is little evidence that untreated illness is a direct or leading cause of criminal behavior.

In this light, it should be clearly recognized that to concentrate the allocation of mental health services on the (evidently small) group of offenders for whom serious mental illness is a cause of their violence is *not* necessarily to concentrate those services on those offenders who are at *the greatest risk* for future violence. In the words of one influential review, "the major predictors of recidivism were the same for mentally disordered offenders as for nondisordered offenders. Criminal history variables were the best predictors, and clinical variables showed the smallest effect sizes" (Bonta, Law, & Hanson, 1998, p. 123). Given this fact, a person with a serious mental illness—*even one that bears a causal relationship to violence*—may have a high (or a low) overall likelihood of violent recidivism for reasons independent of the illness. For example, in the MacArthur Violence Risk Assessment Study (Monahan et al., 2001; Steadman et al., 1998), past violence, substance abuse, a lack of anger control, and violent fantasies all had a stronger relationship to future violence than did serious mental illness. A person for whom serious mental illness is one of the causes of his or her violence may have many (or few) non-mental-illness-related "criminogenic" risk factors for violence, and these criminogenic risk factors may trump the causal effect of mental illness. Put in terms of Andrews' *risk principle*, which holds that "intensive human service is best delivered to higher risk cases, whereas low-risk cases have a low probability of negative outcome even in the absence of service" (Andrews & Dowden, 2006,

p. 89; see Chapter 6), serious mental illness that bears a causal relationship to violence is one of the factors—but only one of the factors—that should go into decisions about allocating scarce services to "higher risk" individuals (see Skeem, Manchak, & Peterson, 2011, for a full account of correctional policy for offenders with mental illness).

How Is It Best to Intervene?

Given the research findings that have just been summarized, it is only for that relatively small group of offenders for whom serious mental illness is causally related to violence that the provision of "traditional" evidence-based mental health services—developed to improve clinical and not justice-related outcomes—can be expected to reduce the risk of future violence. In this regard, it is crucial to appreciate that the vast majority of people with serious mental illness who become involved in the criminal justice system have co-occurring substance abuse disorders (Abrams, Teplin, & McClelland, 2003) and tend to fare poorly in usual systems of care that emphasize *either* mental illness *or* substance use disorder treatments. Since these people do poorly in one or the other type of single-focus treatment program, they often fall out of treatment altogether, ending up in the system of last resort, the criminal justice system. Along the way, they pick up the label of "treatment-resistant" clients. In fact, because of the limited amount of appropriate treatment actually available in most communities for persons with co-occurring mental health and substance use disorders, it is more accurate to characterize the situation as one with "client-resistant services." The available services do not fit the clinical conditions, life histories, or current circumstances of most of the people who need them.

In thinking about appropriate clinical interventions for people with mental illnesses who usually have co-occurring substance use disorders and occasionally have exhibited violent behavior, it is essential to assess the state of the evidence supporting these interventions. Among all mental health treatment practices that have been shown to improve clinical outcomes for people with serious mental illnesses who are justice involved, six interventions have particular relevance to violence reduction (Council of State Governments, 2008; McGuire, 2008; Osher & Steadman, 2007). These include the following:

- Assertive community treatment (ACT), a service delivery model in which a multidisciplinary team of mental health professionals provides individualized treatment (e.g., Lamberti, Weisman, & Fade, 2004)
- Illness self-management and recovery, in which people learn skills to monitor and control their own well-being (e.g., Mueser et al., 2002)
- Integrated mental health and substance abuse services, in which specific treatments are combined to address mental illnesses and substance use disorders (e.g., Drake et al., 2001; Osher, 2006))

- Supported employment, in which people with mental illnesses are employed in competitive, integrated work settings with follow-along supports (e.g., Cook et al., 2005)
- Psychopharmacology, in which medications are used to treat mental illnesses (e.g., Mellman et al., 2001)
- Family psychoeducation, in which people with mental illnesses and their families learn about symptom management techniques and stress reduction (e.g., Substance Abuse and Mental Health Services Administration, 2003)

In addition, two promising mental health treatment practices may improve clinical outcomes for people with mental illnesses, although they are as yet untested for people with mental illnesses in contact with the justice system (Osher & Steadman, 2007):

- Supported housing, such as "Housing First," in which people with mental illnesses gain quick access to housing in addition to case management and other supports (e.g., Robbins, Callahan & Monahan, 2009)
- Trauma interventions, in which people with mental illnesses and extensive histories of trauma (especially among women), including physical and sexual abuse, receive targeted trauma interventions (e.g., Clark, 2002; Manchak, Skeem, Douglas, & Siranosian, 2009)

Finally, interventions based on social learning and cognitive-behavioral principles have long shown considerable success at reducing aggressive behavior among hospitalized civil and forensic inpatients (Bellus et al., 2003; Menditto, Beck, & Stuve, 2000; Paul & Lentz, 1977). Their effectiveness in reducing violence in the community deserves testing.

When Is It Best to Intervene?

As mentioned earlier, there are a number of reasons why justice-involved persons with mental illness should receive treatment. Before and after incarceration, appropriate treatment can improve the quality of life in a community, improve the management of correctional programs, and make more effective use of taxpayer dollars (e.g., prevent costly hospitalization). Here, we focus on providing treatment in order to improve public safety and argue that the justice system should provide multiple opportunities to access services for mentally ill offenders whose illness is causally related to violent offending.

To understand where it may be best to intervene with appropriate treatment for persons who are justice involved, it is instructive to consider the Sequential Intercept Model (SIM) (Munetz & Griffin, 2006) that was developed as a community-based planning tool for developing diversion and reentry programs for justice-involved persons with mental illness. The SIM is presented in Figure 11.1.

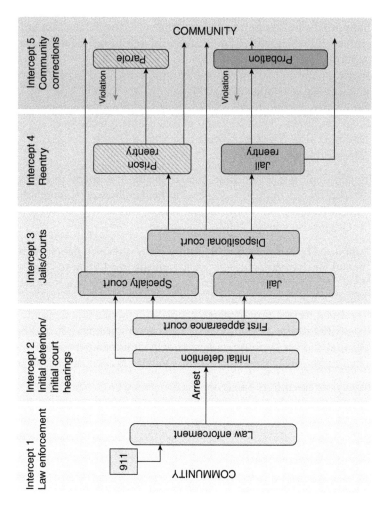

Figure 11.1. The Sequential Intercept Model.

A key underlying premise of this model is that optimum cost-benefit is achieved if a person's penetration into the criminal justice system is minimized. It is to no one's advantage to provide violence-reduction interventions only as the precipitating behaviors get more severe and as the costs of the interventions steadily increase.

A second premise is that interventions should be developed within each intercept in the model for a fully comprehensive system. Ultimately, of course, the question is what are the most effective and cost-effective interventions for each of the five intercepts. Our focus here is on Intercepts 1, 2, 3 and 5, that is, community-based responses before and after incarceration, with the clear understanding that they need to be linked to jails and prisons. Because Intercepts 1, 2, and 3 are focused on diversion and because most diversion programs do not allow violent crimes as target offenses for diversion, and often exclude persons with violent crime histories even if the target offense is nonviolent, most community-based programs that relate to violence reduction will be reentry programs at Intercept 5.

To effectively conceptualize where interventions are and should be offered along the SIM continuum, it is important to recognize that this depiction of the criminal justice system captures its basic linearity. In the criminal justice system a person becomes a "case." The case is processed from booking to arraignment to disposition to penalty, if guilty, and to return to the community. While there can be many twists and turns and glitches along the way, criminal justice case processing is, at its core, linear.

In contrast, the dominant mental health treatment model that has emerged over the past decade is the recovery model (New Freedom Commission, 2003). This model rests on the concept that people can get "better," that treatment is a partnership that should involve client choice, and that the treatment process is nonlinear. There will be advances and declines; perhaps three steps forward and one or two steps backward. Treatment is seen as a long-term process that will involve relapses along with successes.

When the recovery model is overlaid on the criminal justice system as depicted by the SIM, it becomes apparent that interventions for any outcome, including violence, must be available at every intercept in the sequence, since relapse is a possibility even when recovery is well underway. Seen in this light, the concept of criminal justice system linearity and the recovery model of treatment are not at odds, at least when planning for the possibility of relapse is built into the treatment process by the provision of multiple interventions within each intercept in the SIM model.

Must Interventions Be Voluntary?

For offenders whose mental illness is causally related to violent offending, the *leverage* provided by the criminal sanction may provide an important opportunity for maximizing the likelihood of treatment adherence (Kallert, Mezzich, & Monahan, 2011). People with severe mental disorder are sometimes required to adhere with treatment by judges or by other officials acting in the shadow of judicial authority (e.g., probation officers). Making the acceptance of mental health treatment in the community a condition of sentencing a defendant to probation rather than to jail has long been an accepted judicial practice (Skeem & Eno-Louden, 2006), one that has its roots in federal law. Title 18 §3563 of the United States Code provides that "the court may provide, as further conditions of a sentence of probation . . . that the defendant . . . undergo available medical, psychiatric, or psychological treatment." In addition to treatment as a condition of probation, a new specialized type of criminal court—called, appropriately, a "mental health court"—has been developed that makes even more explicit the link between criminal sanctions and adhering to mental health treatment in the community. Adapted from the drug court model, a mental health court offers the defendant intensely supervised treatment in the community as an alternative to jail (Steadman, Redlich, Griffin, Petrila, & Monahan, 2005; Steadman, Redlich, Callahan, Robbins, & Vesselinov, 2011).

A national dialogue is taking place on the legality and morality of making adherence to psychological and psychiatric treatment a condition of probation or of having one's case disposed of in a mental health court. As an illustration, Bonnie and Monahan (2005) have suggested that framing the debate primarily in terms of "coerced" treatment has become counterproductive and that the debate should be reframed in terms of "contract." They believe that language derived from the law of contract often yields a more accurate account of the current state of the law governing community treatment mandated by the justice system, is more likely to be translated into a useful descriptive vocabulary for empirical research, and is more likely to clarify the policy issues at stake than the currently stalemated form of argumentation based on putative rights.

Those who object to the analogy with contract posit that a person's freedom to "choose" to enter an agreement to accept community treatment as a condition of probation or of entry into a mental health court is specious, given stark power imbalances between the individual on whom leverage is imposed and the justice agency doing the imposition. Bonnie and Monahan (2005), on the contrary, argue that using jail as leverage for people who have pled or been found to be guilty of a crime is not properly seen as coercive at all. This is so because the individual's legal "baseline" (Wertheimer, 1987) in treatment as a condition of probation or in a mental health court is "go to jail to serve the sentence for the crime of which you have been convicted." In using the criminal justice system as leverage:

> The key question . . . is whether the prosecutor's proposal is best
> construed as a "threat" to put the defendant in jail if he or she fails
> to adhere to treatment in the community, or as an "offer" of
> treatment in lieu of jail. According to Wertheimer, the prosecutor's
> proposal would be a "threat" if the defendant would be worse off
> than in his or her baseline position if the defendant does not accept
> the proposal, whereas it would be an "offer" (expanding choice) if
> the defendant would be no worse off than in his or her baseline
> position if the proposal is not accepted. [If] incarceration were an
> available sentencing option, as it is in the usual case, probation
> conditioned on [treatment] compliance is properly regarded as an
> "offer," and the agreement is valid. [We] think the agreement is
> valid even if the court would not otherwise have had the authority
> to require treatment because the agreement still represents a choice
> by the defendant between jail and leveraged treatment in the

community—a hard choice, perhaps, but not an unconscionable one. (Bonnie & Monahan, 2005, p. 491)

For some offenders, applying leverage from the justice system may be useful or necessary to achieve adherence to treatment in the community. But that leverage will eventually be terminated—for example, when a probationary sentence or the jurisdiction of a mental health court comes to an end. If postleverage treatment adherence is still needed to prevent violent offending, some way to get the offender to continue adhering to treatment after leverage is lifted must be found.

Motivational interviewing (Miller & Rollnick, 2002) is one promising intervention to get offenders to accept their need for treatment, so that adherence continues after leverage is lifted. Motivational interviewing is "a collaborative, person-centered form of guiding to elicit and strengthen motivation for change" (Miller & Rollnick, 2009, p. 137). Intervention efforts "may be wasted if the individual either does not want to change or has not resolved his or her ambivalence about changing . . . Through motivational interviewing, offenders . . . work to resolve their ambivalence about criminal behavior" (Farbring & Johnson, 2008, p. 307; see also Howells & Day, 2003, on readiness interventions to improve anger management). Motivational interviewing involves a therapist "selectively eliciting and reinforcing the client's own arguments and motivations for change" and promoting "change talk" over "sustain talk" (Miller & Rollnick, 2009, p. 133). "This is true," Miller and Rollnick state, "even in the common situation where MI [motivational interviewing] is provided with clients who have been mandated or otherwise coerced to receive treatment" (2009, p. 131). Put in terms of Andrews' *responsivity principle*, which holds that interventions should be tailored to an offender's motivation for change and other individual characteristics, such as age, gender, and ethnicity (Andrews & Dowden, 2006; see Chapter 6), motivational interviewing could be seen as extending the duration of the positive effect of leverage from the justice system on treatment adherence.

Gaps in Knowledge That Must Be Addressed in Future Research

Much of what we have written is theoretically informed but empirically impoverished. Estimates of the proportion of offenders with serious mental illness for whom the mental illness plays a causal role in their violence, rather than being a consequence of it, or a spurious concomitant, have only recently become available, and there is as yet no convergence in the field around a specific figure. The Risk-Needs-Responsivity model (see Chapter 6) used to organize our conclusions is heuristically useful but scientifically unvalidated in the context of violence reduction among justice-involved persons with serious mental illnesses. Several evidence-based mental health treatment practices have been shown to improve clinical outcomes for people with serious mental illnesses, but the effectiveness of these practices for people with serious mental illnesses in contact with the justice system is still an open question (Council of State Governments, 2008; Osher & Steadman, 2007). The Sequential Intercept Model of providing multiple opportunities for offenders to access services appears to be a useful way to conceptualize the timing of service provision, but whether this framework leads to improved service outcomes is as yet unknown. Motivational interviewing "holds much promise for transferring external motivation for change to internal motivation" among justice-involved persons (Farbring & Johnson, 2008, p. 307). Yet a recent review of 19 studies of motivational interviewing with offenders—including ten randomized controlled trials—concluded that "whether motivational interviewing works to recruit offenders into treatment, to retain offenders in treatment, [and] to reduce offending" remains to be determined (McMurran, 2009, p. 97).

There is another major gap in the research that impedes the development of practical interventions to reduce violence risk among persons with mental illnesses. This gap is the lack of research showing any significant link between improved mental health outcomes and reduced public safety outcomes. As Case, Steadman, Dupuis, and Morris (2009) have demonstrated in a 14-site study of jail diversion programs, the programs were successful at reducing violence, rearrest for new offenses, and jail days, but none of these measures were related to improved mental health outcomes. Likewise, in almost none of the literature on evidence-based practices most relevant to public safety goals reviewed by Osher and Steadman (2007) was violence a dependent measure. Therefore, we must rely most heavily on the general literature on violence and mental disorder (e.g., Fazel et al., 2009; Steadman et al., 1998) showing the link between mental and co-occurring substance use disorders as a prime target for interventions. Unfortunately, we cannot at this time point to specific studies of people with mental illness and co-occurring substance use disorders that report violence reduction as an outcome of a therapeutic intervention.

Implications for Practice

Structuring Correctional Systems

Effective community-based interventions for justice-involved persons who have a serious mental illness may be impossible if basic information about recent contacts with the mental health and the justice systems are not known to all relevant parties. Therefore, we take as the first implication of this review the need for information exchange programs between the mental health and justice systems. Such programs may make a significant contribution to the supervision and monitoring of offenders undergoing community treatment.

We believe that careful information exchange between the mental health and criminal justice systems can be achieved without violating the Health Information Portability and Accountability Act (HIPPA) or similar federal or state laws. This exchange does not mean full disclosure of entire medical records to law enforcement, jails, or probation departments. It does mean conveying basic facts to justice personnel, such as current enrollment in a public mental health program, whether a case manager is currently assigned, any psychotropic medications currently prescribed, and the existence of a psychiatric advance directive (Swartz, Swanson, Van Dorn, Elbogen, & Shumway, 2006). Several successful models of information sharing exist at the state level. Given that recent research reveals that 14.5% of men and 31.0% of women recently admitted to jails have a serious mental illness (Steadman, Osher, Robbins, Case, & Samuels, 2009), many of these programs involve jails.

- In 1999, the Illinois Criminal Justice Authority and the Illinois Department of Human Services/Division of Mental Health implemented a computer database called the Mental Health Jail Data Link that cross-references the daily census of the Illinois correctional facilities with open case records of community mental health centers. The goal of the cross-matching is to establish early identification of individuals who may be eligible for diversion programs. Each identified offender who is receiving services in the facility or has an open case with a community provider is given a case manager. These managers are responsible for making sure that the inmate is linked back to community mental health agencies upon his or her release.
- In 2007, the Texas Legislature passed a bill allowing the Texas Department of State Health Services and the Texas Department of Public Safety (DPS) to share criminal justice/mental health information between departments. This bill permits DPS to access the state mental health database and create a flagging system to notify authorized jail and court personnel whether a person brought before them has had prior contact with the mental health system and whether he or she should undergo further assessment. The bill promotes continuity of care for justice-involved people with mental illness through greater interagency collaboration.
- In Pima County (Tucson), Arizona, the Community Partnership of Southern Arizona (CPSA) Criminal Justice Team (CJT) acts as a link between the justice and treatment systems. To identify clients who have been arrested, a comparison between the jails' booking list and the CPSA member roster is performed twice daily to determine any matches. When matches are identified, the CJT sends notifications to the community provider, informing them a member in their network has been arrested, the charges, the member's classification (type of serious mental illness), the assigned court (jurisdiction), and the next

court date. The CJT also sends notification to the contracted health care provider at the jail, notifying them that an inmate in their custody is enrolled in the community mental health system.

Recently, the CJT has initiated a program that places a team member at the initial court appearance so that a universal consent form can be signed, a quick assessment can be made as to the defendant's ability to safely transport himself or herself home or to treatment, and share information with Pretrial Services and the judge to assist in the decision of whether the defendant with serious mental illness may avoid custody. The community providers are contractually required to submit to the jail health care provider the most recent medications, pertinent case management notes, and any other information relevant to treatment. The health care provider places members with serious mental illness on a specialized caseload and is able to move appropriate individuals to acute or subacute mental health pods within the jail. The most recent pharmacy information is also sent to the health care provider in the jail.

- Other jurisdictions are considering similar information sharing programs. For example, the June 2008 *Report and Recommendations of the New York State/New York City Mental Health-Criminal Justice Panel* stated that "NYS and NYC should pilot an effort to identify individuals with serious mental illnesses who have become involved in the justice system. This information would be shared, with appropriate consent, to facilitate treatment-based alternatives."

Supervising and Treating Individuals Involved in the Justice System

We propose that risk-needs-responsivity principles for violence risk reduction can be extended to justice-involved persons who have a serious mental illness in four ways.

- Given that much and perhaps most of the violence committed by people with serious mental illnesses is associated with co-occurring substance abuse disorders, integrated dual-disorder treatment (IDDT) (Drake et al., 2001), which simultaneously addresses both types of criminogenic disorder, would seem to be an intervention of choice for many justice-involved persons. We note, however, that IDDT has not yet been shown to reduce violence in this population (Chandler & Spicer, 2006; Drake, Morrissey, & Mueser, 2006).
- Given the nonlinear course of many mental illnesses, in which periods of recovery often alternate with periods of relapse, interventions should be developed within each node of the Sequential Intercept Model for a fully comprehensive approach to violence risk reduction.

- For some offenders, the ethical application of leverage deriving from the justice system may be useful or necessary to achieve adherence to treatment in the community.
- If postleverage treatment adherence is still needed to prevent violent offending, motivational interviewing may be one intervention that results in offenders finding added value in continued treatment.

We emphasize the provisional nature of each of these proposals. While theoretically promising, none has yet achieved the status of an evidence-based practice for violence risk reduction among justice-involved persons who have a serious mental illness.

Conclusions

As one recent review concludes, violence-reduction interventions for justice-involved persons with mental illness "tend to construe mental illness as the source of the problem and mental health treatment as the solution" (Skeem et al., 2009). And it is certainly possible—indeed, we believe it is likely—that for a proportion of offenders with mental illness, the illness in a statistically and clinically significant sense *is* one of the causes of their violent offending. The size of this group, however, is likely much smaller than commonly assumed. Successfully treating such offenders, we have argued, entails attending to issues of co-occurring substance abuse, acknowledging the frequently nonlinear course of treatment, applying leverage from the justice system to obtain initial treatment adherence, engaging in motivational interviewing to enhance the duration of treatment adherence, and creating methods for the ethical exchange of information between mental health and criminal justice agencies in the community. Importantly, however, violence-reduction interventions for justice-involved persons with mental illness have much to learn from evidence-based violence-reduction interventions for justice-involved persons *without* mental illness described in other chapters in this book.

References

Abrams, K. A., Teplin, L. A., & McClelland, G. M. (2003). Comorbidity of severe psychiatric disorders and substance use disorders among women in jail. *American Journal of Psychiatry, 160,* 1007–1010.

Andrews, D. A., & Dowden, C. (2005). Managing correctional treatment for reduced recidivism: A meta-analytic review of programme integrity. *Legal and Criminological Psychology, 10,* 173–187.

Andrews, D. A., & Dowden, C. (2006). Risk principle of case classification in correctional treatment. A meta-analytic investigation. *International Journal of Offender Therapy and Comparative Criminology, 50,* 88–100.

Bellus, S. B., Donovan, S. M., Kost, P. P., Vergo, J. G., Gramse, R. A., Bross, A., & Tervet, S. L. (2003). Behavior change and achieving hospital discharge in persons with severe, chronic psychiatric disabilities. *Psychiatric Quarterly, 74,* 31–42.

Bonnie, R. J., & Monahan, J. (2005). From coercion to contract: Reframing the debate on mandated community treatment for people with mental disorders. *Law and Human Behavior, 29,* 487–505.

Bonta, J., Law, M., & Hanson, K. (1998). The prediction of criminal and violent recidivism among mentally disordered offenders: A meta-analysis. *Psychological Bulletin, 123,* 123–142.

Case, B., Steadman, H. J., Dupuis, S. A., & Morris, L. S. (2009). Who succeeds in jail diversion programs for persons with mental illness? A multi-site study. *Behavioral Sciences and the Law, 27,* 661–674.

Chandler, D. W., & Spicer, G. (2006). Integrated treatment for jail recidivists with co-occurring psychiatric and substance use disorders. *Community Mental Health Journal, 42,* 405–425.

Clark, C. (2002). Addressing histories of trauma and victimization in treatment. In S. J. Davidson & H. Hills (Eds.), *Justice-involved women with co-occurring disorders and their children.* Delmar, NY: National GAINS Center. Retrieved from http://gainscenter.samhsa.gov/pdfs/Women/series/Addressing Histories.pdf

Cook, J. A., Lehman, A. F., Drake, R., McFarlane, W. R., Gold, P. B., Leff, S., Blyler, C., Toprac, M. G., Razzano, L. A., Burke-Miller, J. K., Blankertz, L., Shafer, M., Pickett-Schenk, S. A., & Grey, D. D. (2005). Integration of psychiatric and vocational services: a multisite randomized, controlled trial of supported employment. *American Journal of Psychiatry, 162,* 1948–1956.

Council of State Governments. (2008). *Improving responses to people with mental illnesses: The essential elements of a mental health court.* New York: Council of State Governments.

Douglas, K., Guy, L., & Hart, S. (2009). Psychosis as a risk factor for violence to others: A meta-analysis. *Psychological Bulletin, 135,* 679–706.

Drake, R. E., Essock, S. M., Shaner, A., Carey, K. B., Minkoff, K., Kola, L., Lynde, D., Osher, F. C., Clark, R. E., & Rickard, L. (2001). Implementing dual diagnosis services for clients with severe mental illness. *Psychiatric Services, 4,* 469–476.

Drake, R., Morrissey, J. P., & Mueser, K. T. (2006). The challenge of treating forensic dual diagnosis clients: Comment on "Integrated treatment for jail recidivists with co-occurring psychiatric and substance use disorders." *Community Mental Health Journal, 42,* 427–432.

Farbring, C., & Johnson, W. (2008). Motivational interviewing in the correctional system; An attempt to implement motivational interviewing in criminal justice. In H. Arkowitz, H. A. Westra, W. R. Miller, & S. Rollnick (Eds.), *Motivational interviewing in the treatment of psychological problems* (pp. 304–323). New York: Guilford.

Fazel, S., Gulati, G., Linsell, L., Geddes, J. R., & Grann, M. (2009). Schizophrenia and violence: Systematic review and meta-analysis. *PLoS Medicine, 6,* e1000120.

Howells, K., & Day, A. (2003). Readiness for anger management: Clinical and theoretical issues. *Clinical Psychology Review, 23,* 319–337.

Junginger, J., Claypoole, K., Laygo, R., & Cristiani, A. (2006). Effects of serious mental illness and substance abuse on criminal offenses. *Psychiatric Services*, *57*, 879–882.

Kallert, T., Mezzich, J., & Monahan, J. (Eds.). (2011). *Coercive treatment in psychiatry: Clinical, legal, and ethical aspects.* London: Wiley-Blackwell.

Kraemer, H. C., Kazdin, A. E., Offord, D. R., Kessler, R. C., Jensen, P. S., & Kupfer, D. J. (1997). Coming to terms with the terms of risk. *Archives of General Psychiatry*, *54*, 337.

Lamberti, J. S. (2007). Understanding and preventing criminal recidivism among adults with psychotic disorders. *Psychiatric Services*, *58*, 773–781.

Lamberti, J. S., Weisman, R., & Faden, D. I. (2004). Forensic assertive community treatment: Preventing incarceration of adults with severe mental illness. *Psychiatric Services*, *55*, 1285–1293.

Manchak, S., Skeem, J. L., Douglas, K., & Siranosian, M. (2009). Does gender moderate the predictive utility of the Level of Service Inventory—Revised (LSI-R) for serious violent offenders? *Criminal Justice and Behavior*, *36*, 425–442.

McGuire, J. (2008). A review of effective interventions for reducing aggression and violence. *Philosophical Transactions of the Royal Society B*, *363*, 2577–2597.

McMurran, M. (2009). Motivational interviewing with offenders: A systematic review. *Legal and Criminological Psychology*, *14*, 83–100.

Mellman, T. A., Miller, A. L., Weissman, E. M., Crismon, M. L., Essock, S. M., & Marder, S. R. (2001). Evidence-based pharmacological treatment for people with severe mental illness. *Psychiatric Services*, *52*, 619–625.

Menditto, A. A., Beck, N. C., & Stuve, P. (2000). A social-learning approach to reducing aggressive behavior among chronically hospitalized psychiatric patients. In M. Crowner (Eds.), *Understanding and treating violent psychiatric patients* (pp. 87–104). Washington, DC: American Psychiatric Press.

Miller, W. R., & Rollnick, S. (2002). *Motivational Interviewing: Preparing people for change.* New York: Guilford Press

Miller, W. R., & Rollnick, S. (2009). Ten things that Motivational Interviewing is not. *Behavioral and Cognitive Psychotherapy*, *37*, 129–140.

Monahan, J., & Appelbaum, P. (2000). Reducing violence risk: Diagnostically based clues from the MacArthur Violence Risk Assessment Study. In S. Hodgins (Ed.), *Effective prevention of crime and violence among the mentally ill* (pp. 19–34). Dordrecht, Netherlands: Kluwer Academic Publishers.

Monahan, J., Steadman, H. J., Silver, E., Appelbaum, P., Robbins, P. C., Mulvey, E., Roth, L., Grisso, T., & Banks, S. (2001). *Rethinking risk assessment: The MacArthur Study of Mental Disorder and Violence.* New York: Oxford University Press.

Mueser, K. T., Corrigan, P. W., Hilton, D. W., Tanzman, B., Schaub, A., Gingerich, S., Essock, S. M., Tarrier, N., Morey, B., Vogel-Scibilia, S., & Herz, M. I. (2002). Illness management and recovery for severe mental illness: A review of the research. *Psychiatric Services*, *53*, 1272–1284.

Munetz, M. R., & Griffin, P. A. (2006). Use of the sequential intercept model as an approach to decriminalization of people with serious mental illness. *Psychiatric Services*, *57*, 544–549.

New Freedom Commission on Mental Health. (2003). *Achieving the promise: Transforming mental health care in America. Final Report.*

DHHS Pub. No. SMA-03–3832. Rockville, MD: U.S. Department of Health and Human Services.

Osher, F., & Steadman, H. J. (2007). Adapting evidence-based practices for persons with mental illness involved with the criminal justice system. *Psychiatric Services, 58*, 1472–1478.

Paul, G. L., & Lentz, R. J. (1977). *Psychosocial treatment of chronic mental patients.* Cambridge, MA: Harvard University Press.

Pescosolido, B. A., Monahan, J., Link, B. G., Stueve, A., & Kikuzawa, S. (1999). The public's view of the competence, dangerousness and need for legal coercion among persons with mental health problems. *American Journal of Public Health, 89*, 1339–1345.

Peterson, J. K., Skeem, J. L., Hart, E., Vidal, S., & Keith, F. (2010). Analysing offense patterns as a function of mental illness to test the criminalization hypothesis. *Psychiatric Services, 61*, 1217-1222.

Osher, F. C. (2006). *Integrating mental health and substance abuse services for justice-involved persons with co-occurring disorders.* Delmar, NY: CMHS National GAINS Center.

Robbins, P., Callahan, L., & Monahan, J. (2009). Perceived coercion to treatment and housing satisfaction within two housing program models. *Psychiatric Services, 60*, 1251-1253.

Silver, E., Felson, R. B., & Vaneseltine, M. (2008). The relationship between mental health problems and violence among criminal offenders. *Criminal Justice and Behavior, 35*, 405–426.

Skeem, J. L., & Eno-Louden, J. (2006). Toward evidence-based practice for probationers and parolees mandated to mental health treatment. *Psychiatric Services, 57*, 333–342.

Skeem, J. L., Manchak, S., & Peterson, J. K. (2011). Correctional policy for offenders with mental illness: Creating a new paradigm for recidivism reduction. *Law and Human Behavior, 35*, 110–126.

Steadman, H. J., Mulvey, E., Monahan, J., Robbins, P., Appelbaum, P., Grisso, T., Roth, L., & Silver, E. (1998). Violence by people discharged from acute psychiatric inpatient facilities and by others in the same neighborhoods. *Archives of General Psychiatry, 55*, 393–401.

Steadman, H. J., Osher, F. C., Robbins, P., Case, B., & Samuels, S. (2009). Prevalence of serious mental illness among jail inmates. *Psychiatric Services, 60*, 761–765.

Steadman, H. J., Redlich, A., Callahan, L., Robbins, P. C., & Vesselinov, R. (2011). Effect of mental health courts on arrests and jail days: A multisite study. *Archives of General Psychiatry, 68*, 167–172.

Steadman, H. J., Redlich, A. D., Griffin, P., Petrila, J., & Monahan, J. (2005). From referral to disposition: Case processing in seven mental health courts. *Behavioral Sciences and the Law, 23*, 215–226.

Substance Abuse and Mental Health Services Administration. (2003). *Family Psychoeducation: Implementation Resource Kit.* Retrieved from http://www. ct.gov/dmhas/lib/dmhas/cosig/FamilyToolkit.pdf

Swanson, J. W. (1994) Mental disorder, substance abuse, and community violence: An epidemiological approach. In J. Monahan & H. J. Steadman (Eds.), *Violence and mental disorder; Developments in risk assessment* (pp. 101–136). Chicago: University of Chicago Press.

Swanson, J. W., Holzer, C. E., Ganju, V. K., & Jono, R. T. (1990). Violence and psychiatric disorder in the community: Evidence from the Epidemiologic Catchment Area surveys. *Hospital and Community Psychiatry, 41,* 761–770.

Swanson, J. W., Van Dorn, R. A., Swartz, M. S., Smith, A., Elbogen, E. B., & Monahan, J. (2008). Alternative pathways to violence in persons with schizophrenia: The role of childhood antisocial behavior problems. *Law and Human Behavior, 32,* 228–240.

Swartz, M. S., Swanson, J. W., Van Dorn, R. A., Elbogen, E. B., & Shumway, M. (2006). Patient preferences for psychiatric advance directives. *International Journal of Forensic Mental Health, 5,* 67–81.

Vieira, T. A., Skilling, T. A., & Peterson-Badali, M. (2009). Matching court-ordered services with treatment success with young offenders. *Criminal Justice and Behavior, 36,* 385–401.

Wertheimer, A. (1987). *Coercion.* Princeton, NJ: Princeton University Press.

Part IV

A WAY FORWARD

12

Addressing System Inertia to Effect Change

James McGuire

Is it possible to induce criminal justice policy and practice to become more soundly evidence based? Many commentators have recognized the substantial challenge in doing so, given the chasm between science and practice in this field, and the assorted goals of multiple stakeholders pursuing diverse and often conflicting agendas. The scale of the chasm is daunting. Of the numerous factors that appear to drive macro-level policy formulation in criminal justice, and the many others that influence its day-to-day practice, the application of social science evidence appears to be a long way down the priority list. Popular beliefs regarding many aspects of crime and its control are saturated with myths.

Such folk mythology is reinforced daily through the pervasive effects of mass media, political opportunism, and other vested interests. Typically, these purport to present a real-world, no-nonsense, tough-minded analysis of society's ills. Ubiquitously, they do just the opposite, perpetuating simple-minded misconceptions and distortions instead. To cite an example from England and Wales: At a time when all indicators were that the crime rate had been steadily falling (as it currently continues to do), researchers found that many citizens nevertheless believed the opposite; the more so if they read "tabloid" newspapers. Such readers were twice as likely as those who read "broadsheets" (43% versus 21%) to think the national crime rate had increased in the previous 2 years (Lovbakke, 2007).

A new, firmly grounded, wide-ranging, sustained initiative is required to reverse the pernicious trend, apparent in the United States and several other

Western societies, toward ever more futile penal practices and escalating public expense. This book presents an opportunity to embark on such an initiative, by collating key findings of research, presenting them in a coherent and persuasive form, and indicating ways in which they can be applied. The accumulated social science evidence, if marshalled and deployed appropriately, has the potential to transform criminal justice and guide it out of its present self-defeating malaise.

The principal objective of the present chapter is to forward proposals for the reform of criminal justice systems and services and consider how they can be put into effect. Such proposals should first take account of social scientific evidence concerning the reduction of crime and especially violence. A particular aspect of correctional program and service design that can currently be regarded as nonnegotiable is that it should be guided by the *Risk-Need-Responsivity* (RNR) model, as specified in the writings of Andrews (2001, 2006; Andrews and Bonta, 2010) and elsewhere in the present volume. Proposals should also be feasible and realistic, and so offer a genuine and meaningful chance of being adopted and implemented. If as its history suggests, criminal justice policy seems impervious to being evidence led, some means must be found of replacing that scenario and its associated negativist rhetoric, and of creating an impetus to think and act in more constructive and creative directions than before.

The Background

Discouraging though these opening comments might appear, the chronicle of the past four decades suggests that there is *some* connection between basic research on interventions that can reduce criminal recidivism on the one hand, and the expectations and practices of correctional systems on the other. But casting an eye over the recent trajectory of penal policy in the United States, Canada, United Kingdom, and elsewhere, the nature of the research–practice relationship is clearly one that is both intricate and tenuous. The exact parameters of it are quite difficult to define.

Surveys of this history often cite the impact of landmark publications such as those of Martinson (1974) and von Hirsch (1976). According to Gaes (1998, p. 713), for example, the publication of Martinson's article was nothing less than "... a watershed event. In many ways, it ended a 150-year-old era of optimism about the possibilities of reforming the offender." Thus, their views are thought to have steered penal policy, or at least permitted its movement, toward greater harshness; with various other new departures ("intermediate punishment," "three strikes" and so on, now questioned or discredited) as milestones along the way. But paradoxically, although those authors were skeptical about the value of "treatment," broadly defined, they regarded prison as just as much of a failure and urged that it be used only minimally. While decision makers drew on their findings in abandoning what we used to call "rehabilitation," simultaneously many of their more critical observations concerning the futility of imprisonment were deftly overlooked. Whatever the details of policy and practice over the past four decades, the net effect of them in the current circumstances is not far removed from Foucault's (1977) disturbing apparition of a "carceral society," one in which the ethos and techniques of control and discipline have been exported from the penitentiary and permeate "the entire social body."

The Current Context 1: Penal Systems in Crisis

To highlight the urgency of the present situation, it is useful to compare two starkly polarized bodies of information. On the one hand, there is now voluminous evidence that current penal practices are markedly counterproductive. Greatly expanded use of imprisonment and other punitive sanctions has not produced the increase in public safety that many assumed it would. On the contrary, there is evidence that the net effect of increased reliance on prison as the preeminent tool in the criminal justice armoury has been the production of greater harm (Haney, 2006).

Claims that reduced crime rates in the United States and elsewhere are a result of expanded use of incarceration, while superficially plausible, on closer inspection are not supported by the evidence. First, statistical modeling of the incapacitation effect of imprisonment has shown it to be an extremely inefficient route to lowering the crime rate, requiring a 25% increase in the former to yield a 1% decrease in the latter (Tarling, 1993). Second, inconveniently for those who advocate prison as the premier solution to the crime problem, there is no demonstrated connection between incarceration rates and crime rates either historically or cross-nationally. Graphical plots of trends in the two sets of data yield no meaningful relationship (e.g., Zimring & Hawkins, 1994, 1995). Third, the amount of time spent in custody is wholly unrelated to the rate of reconviction on release, as found in a major review by Gendreau, Goggin, and Cullen (1999): Longer sentences have no more of a deterrent effect than shorter ones. Fourth, while we might assume that prisons are reserved for those have committed offenses of personal violence, figures assembled by Haney and Zimbardo (1998) contradict this, with the proportions confined for violent crime in state and federal prisons, respectively, being 47.0% and 13.1% in 1995. The most recent available figures suggest those proportions have changed slightly but remain broadly similar: for state prisons, 53% (December 2005) and for federal prisons 8.7% (September 2007) (West & Sabol, 2008). In 1998, the United States had over 1 million nonviolent offenders behind bars (Irwin, Schiraldi & Ziedenberg, 1999); extrapolating from the available data, that figure is now likely to be in excess of a million and a half.

The much-lauded advent of "three-strikes" policies has been little short of an unmitigated disaster. Its absurdity is exemplified in the case of Curtis Wilkerson, who as described by Kristof (2009) was imprisoned for life after stealing a pair of socks worth $2.50, as he had two previous offenses on record (for abetting robbery when aged 19). Recent findings from California where that policy has been vigorously pursued show that approximately 41,500 offenders have been sentenced under this law since its introduction in 1994. Yet there were large variations in the extent of its use between different counties, some using it up to six times more frequently than others. Analysis of crime data has revealed that the counties where "three strikes" was least used experienced larger reductions in violence and homicide than those that used it most (Center on Juvenile and Criminal Justice, 2008). Judged on this basis, the innovation would appear to have fairly dramatically failed, and possibly backfired.

According to *Confronting Confinement*, a report of the Commission on Safety and Abuse in America's Prisons (Gibbons & Katzenbach, 2006), in 2006 the prisoner population of the United States surpassed 2.2 million, and 13.5 million people spend time in jail or prison in the course of an average year. The position since then has deteriorated further. Expressing things a different way, the Pew Center on the States (2008, 2009) has found that 1 in 100 American adults is in prison or jail; and that when figures for institutions and community supervision are combined, 1 in 31 is under some form of correctional control.

To compound these problems further, this direction of policy is one that results in upwardly spiraling costs. In 2006 the average annual cost of housing a prisoner was $23,000, and annual expenditure on corrections was in excess of $60 billion (Gibbons & Katzenbach, 2006). That is greater than the gross domestic product of two-thirds of the 186 countries on which the World Bank published comparative statistics for 2008. For the fiscal year 2008, the annual *per capita* cost of imprisonment in a Bureau of Prisons facility was $25,894 and in a community correctional center $23,881. By contrast, the annual cost of supervision by a federal probation officer was $3,743 ("Cost of imprisonment. . .," 2009).

The Current Context 2: Outcomes of Intervention

On the other hand, mounting evidence on the effects of constructive efforts toward securing behavior change among frequent offenders has now reached a recognizable "critical mass" (Aos, Miller, & Drake, 2006; McGuire, 2002; Motiuk & Serin, 2001; Sherman, Farrington, Welsh, & MacKenzie, 2002). The volume of work currently available regarding this is such that if parallels were drawn with other areas of public policy (most saliently, health or education), it would be difficult (though regrettably not impossible!) for senior policy officials to ignore it. If we want to find a way forward and escape the present predicament, it is vital to communicate that the latter approaches, however much their critics depict them as "soft," can more effectively achieve the appointed aims of criminal justice. They can yield benefits for individual offenders while maintaining community safety—outcomes that are not only compatible with each other, but reciprocally reinforcing.

There have been numerous short-term endeavors to introduce more constructive initiatives in criminal justice services, both in prisons and the community. The many research investigations that underpin the so-called what works outcome literature are examples. They are not restricted to experimental studies with high investment in researcher-led "demonstration programs" but have often been delivered in routine services as "practical programs" (Lipsey, 1999). Other chapters of the present volume reiterate key messages from that evidence base. In a recent integrative review of methods to reduce violence, McGuire (2008) surveyed findings from 70 meta-analyses of outcome studies, consolidating the now widely established finding that interventions have on average a positive, statistically, and practically significant effect in reducing offender recidivism. Eleven of these meta-analytic reviews focused on the possibility of reducing violent reoffending and demonstrated many successful results.

There is also strong evidence that constructive interventions are more cost-efficient than punitive ones, often remarkably so. It is worth recalling that even if a program evaluation does not produce statistically significant findings in the conventional sense, this does not necessarily mean it has not "worked." Even a small change can be enough for an intervention to have paid for itself (Weisburd, Lum, & Yang, 2003). Large-scale reviews of economic outcomes (e.g., Aos, Phipps, Barnoski, & Lieb, 2001) have concluded that there are financial savings to be made from investment in direct interventions with a range of age groups across both youth and adult corrections. Long-term prevention can generate still higher benefit–cost ratios, but even in the tertiary sector of prisons and parole, where we might consider it is too late to engender change, a worthwhile impact on subsequent criminality and decreased costs can still be secured. Numerous studies have discovered superior benefit–cost quotients for community-based treatment of criminogenic problems as compared with incarceration. Focusing on drug-related offending, for example, several reports vividly illustrate the marked contrast on almost all outcome indicators (recidivism, well-being, cost) between incarceration and community-based treatment. In Maryland, for example, respective yearly costs of the two approaches were $20,000 and $4,000; in California corresponding figures were $27,000 and $4,500 (McVay, Schiraldi, & Ziedenberg, 2004). For Illinois, with a prison population of 64,800 in 2005 and 90,000 persons under probation supervision, it was estimated that providing community-based treatment instead of incarceration for 10,000, plus treatment for 15,000 probationers would yield savings of $223.3 million (Braude, Heaps, Rodriguez, & Whitney, 2007).

Is Departure Long Overdue?

Taking these two compilations of evidence into account there are credible grounds for renewed confidence in the possibility of building genuinely effective links between research and practice. Many authors over the years have called for a "rethink" of priorities in penal policy, though usually with little or no effect. Considerable evidence has now been amassed both on the nature and the extent of the problem, and on the potential best solutions. At present the two sets of information depicted earlier are so sharply polarized that it surely defies sense for things to continue as they are. One might think that simple perusal of these findings would spur criminal justice administrators to immediate and decisive action. What is surely needed now and has been for some time is a concerted effort just to apply what we know (Gendreau, 1996).

Thus, a paramount priority of any sound correctional policy would be to set in motion a major diminution in the size of the prison population. That should entail a moratorium on prison building, adoption of "no entry" policies for a large number of cases, and a comprehensive planning exercise to define what proportion of those in custody could be managed in the community instead. If ever there was a case for what has been called "exnovation," it is in relation to the gross and wasteful overusage of imprisonment as the centrepiece of correctional policy. Exnovation, the converse of innovation, is considered by Frank and Glied (2006, p. 33) to have been an important facet of change in mental healthcare policies, in which ". . . inappropriate, ineffective or inhumane treatments are discontinued as a consequence of new knowledge and new attitudes." Put more colloquially, we might remember the old saying, when you are in a deepening hole, first stop digging!

In addition to its direct benefits, halting and reversing the numbers of lower risk, nonviolent offenders consigned to custody would diminish and could even eliminate overcrowding. The latter factor is one with known noxious effects on all aspects of prison life. The majority of the aforementioned group and even a proportion of those who had committed minor violent offenses could be managed more effectively, beneficially, and economically under community-based supervision. There is already a wide range of options available in community corrections, and many more could be developed. Latessa and Smith (2007) have called for the establishment of a commission to control prison population growth and bring coherence to the range of community sentences. Greatly expanded use of probation and parole is not as "politically seductive" as boot camps, scared straight, and other novelties appeared to be (Paparozzi & Demichelle, 2008, p. 289); but if well resourced and evidence based, it offers a more enticing prospect of actually delivering what the correctional system is supposedly designed to do. Conversely, pursuing such a change would also open opportunities for more effective provision for those for whom prison is genuinely needed for purposes of restraint; who have committed graver offenses or who are assessed as at risk of causing more serious harm.

Thus, the most critical element of a rational, evidence-based correctional policy, and the central proposal of this chapter, would be to initiate a massive transfer of resources from custody to the community. This is not a solitary madcap notion, emanating from liberal sentiments, but one based on illuminating precedents, and bolstered by sound data with reference to both criminal justice and econometric outcomes.

Precedents

Let us first therefore examine three predecessors of the kinds of proposal to be made here. Each is different from the others in crucial respects; each exhibited some problems of its own; yet each has provided lessons that can prospectively guide a larger scale and farther-reaching gamut of policies for ushering in a new phase of correctional policy and practice. While ideally, there would be a perfectly honed "model program" to draw upon, regrettably there is none on hand; no such exemplary case study exists. The first two examples demonstrate the possibility of deinstitutionalization and the relocation of individuals and the resources designed to provide for them to the community. The third drew on similar kinds of research to that reviewed in other chapters of this book and is an illustration of a real-world exercise in evidence-based practice.

Decarceration in Mental Health Services

The transfer of people with severe and enduring mental health problems from long-stay psychiatric hospitals to the community has been carried out on a literally worldwide scale. Though occurring in a different field of service from criminal justice, the history of it is a vivid demonstration both of the possibility that such an apparently cataclysmic transformation can happen at all, and of the different pathways it might take depending on some key features of how it is undertaken.

Based on widespread recognition that long-term hospitalization had numerous damaging (including iatrogenic) effects, countries around the globe progressively closed the asylums of a previous era and enacted policies of community-based provision in their stead. The United Kingdom and the United States were the first countries to instigate this process. In the United States, for example, between 1960 and 1985 the inpatient population of psychiatric hospitals fell from 535,500 to 116,800 (21.8% of the original figure) (Jones, 1988).

Given its global reach, this is possibly the largest planned departure in human services ever to have taken place. Scarcely surprisingly, many aspects of it did not work as expected or planned. The most glaring deficiency was the failure to ensure a minimum standard among the alternative services that were supplied, and the sometimes very poor-quality or even nonexistent support provided in lieu of what had been available in hospital. There were gaps in accommodation, family liaison, employment, education, and other types of provision. After gradual recognition of the inadequacies of the supposed alternative facilities, there has been increased investment in service provision.

In the United States, however, at least during the early stages of this process, considerable thought was given to the impact of deinstitutionalization and what would need to be put in place. Earlier reports had documented the problems of neglect and abuse in long-stay hospitals. A Commission was established and prepared a detailed report and policy proposals, *Action for Mental Health*, presented to Congress in 1961. Subsequently, there was a Presidential Task Force, and legislative changes followed in 1963 specifying the nature and role of the new Community Mental Health Centers that were to be set up (Jones, 1988). Many key elements of a successful policy change were therefore in place. With uneven and sometimes insufficient funding, inconsistencies in quality and level of care, the story of the decades since then has been a more complex one, summed up by Frank and Glied (2006) as a net outcome of "better but not well." Funding changes in the 1980s led to some upheavals and altered the pattern of service provision. Clearly, there is much that can be learnt from the achievements, trials, and errors of this dynamic process both in the United States and elsewhere. From the present standpoint, the fundamental issue is that such a mammoth reconfiguration of services was taken forward against a backdrop of institutional provision that had been in place for a considerable time beforehand and had looked set to stay.

These policy changes gave rise to some concerns over the likelihood of there being a "Penrose effect" (sometimes mistakenly termed a "law"). Based on the work of the British psychiatrist Lionel Penrose in the 1930s, this suggests that there is an inverse relationship between the numbers of people in mental hospitals and the numbers in prison. Closure of the former is likely to lead to an increase in the workload of the latter, in what might be called a process of "transinstitutionalization." That possibility has recently been examined through analysis of statistics for Norway (Hartvig & Kjelsberg, 2009) and such a pattern was indeed observable across a 70-year period. However, these authors did not conclude that the relationship was a causal one, and other tests of the model based on a broader range of countries have provided no support for the supposed "law" nor for the hypothesis that deinstitutionalization is a driver of the rate of violent crime (Large & Nielssen, 2009; Nielssen & Large, 2009). For the period when community mental health was being installed in the United States, Frank and Glied (2006) found no evidence of increased homelessness or incarceration among those discharged from hospitals.

We might of course consider that, notwithstanding the residual stigma that still persists, people with mental health problems are perceived as generally less fortunate and more deserving than persons who have wilfully broken the law. Furthermore, to the extent that serious mental disorders are sometimes associated with crime, it is often through their shared correlation with substance abuse (Fazel, Gulati, Linsell, Geddes, & Grann, 2009). It seems likely too that public fear of mental disorder is probably less than that of crime. Closure of penitentiaries or juvenile correctional centers might therefore cause greater alarm, and only the unwise would be willing even to contemplate it.

Closure of Reform Schools in Massachusetts

The second illustration, however, involved precisely such a departure. Unlike the panoramic changes just outlined, this was localized in a single American state, but it was if anything more dramatic because of the speed with which it was done, the minimal consultation (some would say stealth) involved, and the controversy and vehement opposition it aroused in some quarters. In what is known as the "Massachusetts experiment," all the secure reform schools in that state, which had been in existence for 130 years and housed a total of approximately 1,500 young offenders, were closed within a period of 27 months. All but 49 of the incumbents (3.3% of the original residential population) were diverted to an ad-hoc mixture of alternative, community-based facilities (Guarino-Ghezi, 1988).

Under governmental pressures, attempts at diversion and deinstitutionalization had been made during the 1960s in a number of American states, including, for example, California and Washington. Subsidies were provided to support youth in their local communities rather than transferring them to institutions. However, this failed to lower the numbers in custody, which despite reduced quantities of committals, remained steady as periods of confinement were extended (Macallair, 1993). The seismic changes of 1970–1972 in Massachusetts were attributable to the appointment in late 1969 of Dr. Jerome G. Miller as the state's commissioner for a newly created Department of Youth Services (DYS). Miller (1998) has written a personal account of his work during that period and the repercussions of it over the ensuing years.

An apprehensive public might worry that releasing many hundreds of youthful repeat offenders into the community would result in an increase in delinquency, perhaps even a "crime wave," and Miller (1993) has described some of the myths that surrounded the Massachusetts experiment from its outset. But the upsurge in criminality never came. Independent follow-up studies of the discharged cohorts found no general difference between their subsequent recidivism rates and those of comparable samples (Coates, Miller, & Ohlin, 1978). Where services that were provided in the community included a range of good-quality programs, there was a decrease in recidivism among the DYS samples. A later, 15-year follow-up study found that youth services in Massachusetts relied less on secure units than in comparable states. The state had the lowest recidivism rate in the group with which it was compared, and its services were more cost-effective than those in states that operated with large numbers in secure training schools (Loughran, 1997).

While Massachusetts DYS subsequently restored the usage of some secure institutional beds (though far below the level used prior to 1970), the changes launched in 1970–1972 are not of purely historic interest alone. "These reforms were the most dramatic in the history of corrections in America. Never had an established correctional bureaucracy been so completely altered and recast" (Macallair 1993, p. 114). Such a change ran against the prevailing ethos of the time, but it was nevertheless carried through.

The U.K. Crime Reduction Program

A third and more recent example to draw upon is the British government's *Crime Reduction Programme* (CRP), through which from the late 1990s onward there was extensive transmission of research findings into practice in both prisons and probation. Policy innovations on such a scale do not spring out of nowhere and the CRP was a lengthy time in the making. Taking a retrospective glance at the developments that preceded it, it is possible to identify a number of earlier innovations, each limited in itself, which contributed to a gradual change of direction and an eventual impact on government thinking.

For example, from the 1970s onward there were localized and limited-scale projects in U.K. prisons and probation units, such as day training centers, a concept imported from the United States, which were probation-run alternatives to custody for offenders likely to be given relatively short prison sentences (averaging 18 months). The appearance of the initial meta-analyses from 1985–1990 onward provided further encouragement to practitioners committed to becoming more "evidence based." A series of initiatives in local areas introduced some elements of what is nowadays termed "correctional programming," including, for example, the Mid Glamorgan *Straight Thinking on Probation* experiment (Raynor & Vanstone, 1996). Contemporaneously, there was partial dissemination of interim positive results through what were called the "What Works" conferences and associated publications (McGuire, 1995). In the later 1990s as the governmental drive for greater efficiency found its way into criminal justice, the Home Office embarked on reviews of relevant research, amid an emerging sense that there was scope for trying and testing methods from the expanding treatment–outcome research (e.g., Goldblatt & Lewis, 1998). The resulting major policy initiative (the CRP) was announced in 1998, and implemented in a succession of stages from 2000 onward.

Considerable resources were provided, including investment in dissemination of a portfolio of programs designed in some cases to address general offending behavior, in others with a more concentrated focus on acquisitive, violent, sexual, or substance-related offending. A substantial effort was made to preserve the "treatment integrity" and quality of delivery of interventions. An independent, international expert body, the Correctional Services Accreditation Panel (CSAP), was created to oversee the process of selecting the most appropriate programs and methods to be utilized in both prison and probation settings (Maguire, Grubin, Lösel and Raynor, 2010). This centrally managed process of "program accreditation" has played a pivotal role in the policy as a whole (Hollin & Palmer, 2006). The CSAP developed and has methodically applied a set of 10 criteria for accreditation of programs. They require that to be approved for use in prison or probation settings, a program should achieve satisfactory scores on the following specified elements (CSAP, 2009). It should have *(1)* a clear and explicit model of change; *(2)* clear and appropriate selection criteria; *(3)* materials and methods that target dynamic risk factors; *(4)* use of demonstrably effective methods; *(5)* methods that focus on skill acquisition and development; *(6)* a rationale linking intensity, sequencing, and duration; *(7)* procedures to enhance engagement and participation; *(8)* integration in case management and other services; *(9)* provision of methods for checking and maintaining program integrity; *(10)* ongoing monitoring and regular outcome evaluation.

The results of what has essentially been a correctional experiment on a formidable scale have been evaluated in numerous reports and scientific papers. While not surprisingly the pattern of findings has been uneven, the overall policy can claim a modest measure of success. Hollis (2007) has reported a comparison between predicted and actual reconviction rates for a sizable sample ($n = 25,255$) of offenders who were allocated to accredited probation programs in 2004 and followed up over a period of 2 years. This found significant reductions in actual versus predicted recidivism across programs designed to reduce general, violent, and sexual offending, and substance misuse. Predicted offense rates were based on a well-validated risk assessment measure (the *Offender Group Reconviction Scale*, OGRS-2).

More recently the Ministry of Justice (2008) has reported a study of changes in the national adult reoffending rate, which has been recorded for all those processed by the criminal justice system since the year 2000. Comparing the reoffending results for the 2000 and 2006 adult cohorts reveals some very encouraging trends. The offense frequency rate fell 22.9% from 189.4 to 146.1 offenses per 100 offenders. The number of offenses classified as most serious per 100 offenders fell 11.1% from 0.78 to 0.69 offenses. The proportion of offenders reoffending (expressed as a simple *yes/no* rate) decreased by 10.7% (4.7 percentage points) from 43.7% to 39.0%. The proportion of offenders who reoffended fell by 10.6% when controlling for changes in offender characteristics (Ministry of Justice, 2008). Note that these findings are not derived from controlled experimental trials, but from official criminal statistics. They cannot be exclusively attributed to the impact of the CRP but exhibit uniform trends in the hoped-for direction that grew stronger as that policy was progressively put into effect.

Marsh and Fox (2008) have conducted a review of a number of interventions and compared their effectiveness in terms of both criminal recidivism and benefit–cost ratios relative to that of "standard prison" in the United Kingdom. They found that certain types of community-based services (residential drug treatment, surveillance with or without drug treatment) and prison-based programs (educational/vocational, offending behavior interventions, sex offender treatment) all reduced reoffending relative to standard prison. All of these methods were also more cost-effective than prison sentences alone. These findings add support for the view that the "active ingredient" in securing change in offenders is not the sentence of the court that is imposed on them, but the nature and extent of interventions in which they are able to participate.

As a major policy departure, the CRP and all its accoutrements have also illustrated that there are dangers attendant upon a process of implementation or dissemination of evidence-based policies if it is done too rapidly, on too large a scale, as critics have said was the case. Almost certainly, there was less than uniform commitment on the part of all the "stakeholders" putatively involved, and all of that occurred inside a system that simultaneously had other change expectancies placed upon it. The resultant effects may be diluted and thereby not sufficiently convincing to ensure that subsequent generations of policy makers and program managers will maintain the appropriate service models. Raynor (2004) among others has provided a cogent analysis of the factors at stake in that context.

We should not of course be naïve when it comes to considering the relationship between research findings and public policy. This is evident even from the recent history of the relationship between government, the public, and what are called the "hard sciences." In the United Kingdom there is a widespread perception that as a result of a series of health-related "scares" in the 1990s, public confidence in science and scientists was palpably damaged. Problems over *salmonella* in eggs, *bovine spongiform encephalitis* (BSE), and the triple MMR vaccine, for example, caused substantial public anxiety—out of all proportion, indeed sometimes quite unrelated, to the actual underlying hazard. It was impossible to issue categorical reassurances or plain policy statements denying any risk, and data regarding probabilities are notoriously difficult to communicate. Recently a Parliamentary Group of the House of Commons (2009), the Innovation, Universities, Science and Skills Committee, has alleged that the government is keeping scientists "at arm's length" and marginalizing the considerable contributions they can make to numerous areas of policy. When Professor David Nutt, an eminent research pharmacologist and member of an expert advisory group on drug control policies, expressed dismay at how the panel's advice had been disregarded, he was criticized and denigrated by senior government ministers and subsequently dismissed from his advisory position.

Challenges of Implementation

As some distinguished researchers in this area have previously emphasized (Gendreau, Goggin, & Smith, 1999), despite the positive outcomes found in evaluations, there was inadequate guidance available on the process of implementation. Arguably, however, the accumulated knowledge regarding this phase of projects, with reference to both the pitfalls of "technology transfer" and the means of overcoming them, has now advanced significantly. Palmer (1996) provided an early conceptual analysis; and an edited book by Bernfeld, Farrington, and Leschied (2001) was a landmark in both proposing models of program implementation and documenting examples of successes and failures from which practical lessons can be learned. Recently Andrews (2011) synthesized the messages from research on "nonprogrammatic" factors with the steadily accumulating evidence on correctional effectiveness informed by the RNR model .

There are several widely recognized barriers to change that have impeded previous attempts to increase the adoption and application of evidence-based practice in criminal justice. Obstacles exist at many levels within the complex network of agencies loosely described as the "criminal justice system," and their interactions occur along a number of pathways. Barriers to change and challenges to implementation of evidence-based practice can be classified along various dimensions or in terms of different sets of categories, many of them overlapping. They include, for example, the following: *(a)* lack of knowledge or understanding of the empirical background to offender management and treatment, possibly due to poor communication or dissemination of research; *(b)* limitations with respect to training and availability of staff with appropriate knowledge, skills, or attitudes; *(c)* offenders' difficulties arising from poorly defined objectives in the sentencing and/or corrections process, that is, where practitioners do not sufficiently clarify what is expected of them; *(d)* everyday, practical barriers such as limited physical or monetary resources for provision of rehabilitative programs; *(e)* organizational hurdles arising from rigid procedures and practices (a function of tradition, or of unexamined assumptions); *(f)* internal cultural rifts associated with expectations of staff in different roles, and low cohesiveness between different levels of a hierarchy; *(g)* external cultural barriers due to attributed expectations of court personnel; or of the local community; or the public at large; *(h)* fear of exposure in mass media, of a focus on negative publicity, in the absence of any effort at positive publicity; *(i)* unresolved ethical and ideological dilemmas regarding administration of justice that are generally discussed at only superficial level; and *(j)* politicization of criminal justice and its location on wider agendas regarding perceived electoral advantage.

The foregoing list is by no means exhaustive. It could be longer and more detailed, but it serves to characterize the magnitude of the task. The aforementioned barriers are often interconnected, in some ways that are obvious, in others that are less so. Their cumulative effect can be described as resulting in a form of "system inertia." Very often, key decision makers who may appear authoritative to outside observers feel constrained in the choices available to them. Even more powerful forces maintain the *status quo* and inculcate the bureaucratic imperative of going-by-the-book and limiting change to safe and conservative levels. When this is aggravated by political and media pressures, the position may become intractable.

However, almost all aspects of this situation are subjective or socially constructed, and it is individuals' beliefs that are the key operative factors. As the example of the Crime Reduction Programme indicates, change occurs when several types of factors combine to permit evidence to be applied. Most important, the present contention is that several of those factors exist in many jurisdictions at the present moment. Certainly, pressures for improvement continue to mount, even if (when regarded cynically) they are likely to be impelled primarily by economic rather than justice or humanitarian considerations.

To retain as clear as possible a hold on what could be an extremely confusing picture, it is potentially valuable to adopt a model of barriers and of change derived from a *behavioral systems perspective* (Bernfeld, Blase, & Fixsen, 1990). This entails considering four aspects of innovation, alongside corresponding levels for evaluation of effectiveness, focused, respectively, on the *client, program, organization,* and *society*. It is a crucial aspect of these system components that they are engaged in dynamic interaction over time, and recognition of this will greatly assist any agency planning a new program or policy departure. Too often, programs have failed to flourish because innovators or managers devoted attention to one or two of these levels while ignoring the remainder. Consider, for example, the roles of correctional staff. Attention should be paid to their relational skills and approach to the *client* (offender), because evidence suggests it is perfectly feasible to integrate a caring approach with the exercise of authority (Skeem et al., 2007). They should also of course have knowledge and competence in *program* delivery (Dowden & Andrews, 2004). But their place in the *organization* and factors associated with that should also be understood and addressed (e.g., the need for supervision, accountability, and role enhancement). So also should how they are perceived and valued by *society* (recognition that effective correctional work is demanding and highly skilled). Each of these levels and its multiple linkages with the others should be considered in advance and the framework used as guidance when formulating proposals for change that then encompass ingredients at all four levels of the system.

Dimensions of Change

Notwithstanding the scale of the above challenges, there is an array of possibilities for realistically addressing them, and for moving toward rational, evidence-based correctional policies and systems. Doing so cohesively will amplify the need to construct linkages all the way from abstract concepts of justice and law to the demanding process of everyday supervision of, and intervention with, individual offenders. To make these ideas work in reality, we can consider the central proposition of this chapter as having two interrelated aspects, practical and conceptual.

We should not forget, however, that there is copious evidence that early developmental prevention programs are effective in both clinical and economic terms. Action informed by that evidence should be a key priority in a broad, methodical strategy for crime reduction (Farrington & Welsh, 2007). Other "tertiary prevention" proposals such as those made here can be a direct complement to those initiatives (Keita, 2009).

Practical and Policy Change

The first aspect is *practical* and involves advocating that correctional services embark on a fundamental and far-reaching change, consisting of a significant program of reinvestment of intervention efforts. Given current circumstances and trends, as stated earlier, the most crucial element of this would be a significant reassignment of resources from prison to the community. Given the far higher costs of the former, a detailed organizational planning exercise needs to be undertaken within each jurisdiction, based on auditing the numbers and throughput of individuals likely to require intensive community supervision and correctional programming were they not imprisoned. This would then determine the number of prisons to be closed or the extent of scale-down within each. The process would be allied to a parallel exercise focused on numbers of prisoners who could be candidates for early release and the capacity of reentry provisions required to address their risks and needs. This should also take account of the high rates of mental health problems found in prison surveys worldwide.

In essence, if we apply the RNR principles and evidence base thoroughly, these policy changes and reinvestment options appear irresistible. Reducing prison numbers has a fourfold benefit: It reduces overcrowding; it enables prison staff to work more effectively with those who need to remain; it reduces the criminalizing effect we know prisons have; and it lowers penal costs. The obvious way to achieve it is by removing those who do not need to be there and who can be managed safely in the community. All the evidence suggests that is quite a large number. Such a change is better for them and their families, it does not compromise community safety, and in the process it saves very significant amounts of tax dollars. On any scale we would use to evaluate a policy change—outcome effectiveness, scientific soundness, social justice, and cost-efficiency—it represents an enormous advance on the present status quo.

Econometric methods can be employed to model the relationships between numbers of individuals with different risk-need profiles and the funds released following graduated phases of institutional closure. Usage of prison would be retained on the basis of restraint or incapacitation only, and it would be focused on those individuals assessed as high risk, high need, and most likely to cause harm to others or themselves. Incarceration alone would not of course be expected to have enduring deterrent effects for those who remain subject to it (Tarling, 1993), but the newly available funding that flows from reserving imprisonment for those who need to be there (for incapacitation/public safety purposes) would enable additional offense-focused programming to be introduced.

The Pew Center report (2008) describes two "basic policy levers" that can be pulled to slow the growth of prison numbers. The first is to reduce admissions, either via the "front end," using alternative sentencing and diversion strategies (e.g., drug courts, targeted penalty changes, and revised sentencing guidelines), or the "back end," by facilitating parole and probation while increasing accountability (and using, e.g., intermediate sanctions, short-term residential facilities, and performance incentives). The second lever is to cut the average length of stay in prison, by reducing risk while inside, developing incentive-driven early release schemes, and ensuring there is sufficient reentry program availability. It may be that parts of this task could be undertaken at local level using the methods of *justice mapping*, piloted by the Justice Mapping Center in New York and proposed for use in England and Wales by the House of Commons Justice Committee (2010).

Such broad policy changes need to be accompanied by a series of proposals for direct implementation in everyday routine practice. Incrementally freeing up the resources previously lavished on prison establishments, jurisdictions could thereby afford a commensurate increase in numbers of personnel involved in delivery and supervision of community correctional programming. Preferably, that would be accompanied by a significant elevation of the status and training (and salary) of these groups. This will have a series of practical implications, among other areas, for boosting and consolidating the quality of services in relation to *(a)* offender assessment, case formulation, program allocation, progress monitoring; *(b)* provision of resources for program delivery; *(c)* staff recruitment, qualifications, and training; *(d)* team and organizational management; *(e)* design of correctional facilities and agency sites; *(f)* modes of interagency working; and *(g)* ongoing monitoring and evaluation of all services. These should be guided by the *Risk-Needs-Responsivity* model (Andrews, 2001; Andrews, Bonta, & Wormith, 2006; also see Chapter 6), which remains the best validated approach to design of numerous aspects of correctional interventions. Strategies and methods of service evaluation can be incorporated into the design of delivery systems themselves, and models are available for that purpose (e.g., McGuire, 2001). An invaluable series of proposals for restructuring correctional systems to take account of evidence, and to institute practices of "credentialing" staff, programs, and agencies, has been articulated by Gendreau, Goggin, Cullen, and Paparozzi (2002).

Criminal Justice: Cognitive Restructuring

Anyone proposing changes such as the ones outlined in this chapter might be perceived as having lost touch with reality, and this underpins the need for a second type of change, one that entails a significant reconceptualization of what criminal justice is for and how it is delivered. This necessitates a virtual state transformation rather than a merely incremental shift in thinking and attitudes on the part of key personnel, and communication of this by them to policy makers and the community.

The second category of change is therefore *conceptual* and refers to a range of issues regarding how individuals think of criminal justice and of how it is delivered. Reference was made earlier to the notion of the criminal justice "system," but in most countries the tangled web of national, state, and local services so denoted has developed historically in an uneven and piecemeal fashion. Indeed, to call the end product a system may be, as Ashworth (2005, p. 67) has remarked, ". . . merely a convenience and an aspiration" rather than an accurate description.

The conceptual departure in the present proposal is that the network of criminal justice services genuinely *becomes* a system in a real and meaningful sense. That is, it develops comprehensive coverage and internal coherence in its application of evidence-based practice at all levels of its activity, and the rationale for doing so is enunciated by senior personnel with executive responsibility for its work.

Doing so would require directly engaging in a sustained public relations exercise to redefine the nature and expectations of criminal justice. There is a need to state firmly and repeatedly that criminal justice should be evidence based, following the principles of RNR, and that many of its present procedures are far from optimal. Self-evidently, doing so will arouse considerable cognitive dissonance in many quarters (Tarvis & Aronson, 2007). This would also likely meet with adverse criticism and require careful advance planning and preparation. Many citizens appear to believe that they know a great deal about crime and justice, and remarks to the effect that none of it is "rocket science" are not uncommon. Without wishing to surround this field with some kind of distancing mystique, it is more elaborate than commonsense perspectives imply; there is a scientifically tested evidence base; and the issues and modalities are more complex than often assumed.

Associated with these changes is an affiliated proposal that senior personnel should communicate widespread recognition of the failure of imprisonment as the prime solution to the problem of crime (Haney, 2006). It is, ironically, a failure that was recognized in France within several years of the birth of the modern prison there in the 1820s (Foucault, 1976). More broadly this entails acknowledging the limited power of punishment to act as a deterrent in altering offender behaviour (McGuire, 2004), so calling into question its centrality and preeminence in society's response to crime (Honderich, 2006). There is a need to change the rhetoric and discourse in which discussion of criminal justice issues is conducted. There is an analogous need for more widespread education concerning the factors that influence law-abiding (Tyler, 2006) and law-breaking (Zamble & Quinsey, 1997) patterns of behavior. Such a cognitive shift would resonate with and support the practical and policy change in resource allocations outlined above.

The Implementation Process

Earlier, we noted the importance of adherence to RNR principles as a guiding framework for correctional interventions. Inspection of less successful projects generally uncovers some aspect of implementation that departed from that framework. *Project Greenlight* for example, a promising and apparently soundly based reentry program, produced a higher rate of recidivism than its designated comparison group. But as Rhine, Mawhorr, and Parks (2006) subsequently explained, implementation of this project departed in some important ways from RNR principles; for example, its treatment integrity was diluted, and financial constraints led to discontinuation of the key assessment measure. Reviews of the extent to which programs adhere to RNR principles have emphasized the importance of valid assessment and appropriate allocation along risk-need lines (Andrews & Dowden, 2006; Lowenkamp, Latessa, & Smith, 2006). To the extent that the CRP, described earlier, yielded results that some have considered disappointing, here too the problems appear to reside not in the programs employed but in the process of implementation (Raynor, 2004).

Thus, as noted earlier, attention to program and participant features alone, though indispensable, may be insufficient to ensure positive outcome effects. There is gathering evidence of the importance of a set of "core correctional practices" informing not only the design of programs but their mode of delivery and dissemination (Dowden & Andrews, 2004). The latter facets include the provision of staff training and supervision, an emphasis on the quality of relationships, effective use of reinforcement, effective use of modeling, and management support. Augmenting these findings, there are also strong indications of the impact of some aspects of program quality and overseeing integrity of delivery as imperative factors (Andrews, 2006, 2011; Andrews & Dowden, 2005).

Beyond this, however, there are also numerous organizational variables that must also be taken into account. The starting point of the process of implementation if it is to happen on any meaningful scale is likely to be discussion and reflection among senior staff of an agency contemplating a new direction of policy. If such decision makers (the "people who count") are to be persuaded that a policy change is worth pursuing, it is vital that researchers communicate key findings to them in a comprehensible way. Most important, this resides in how messages are presented and information is conveyed on effectiveness, on the likely sizes of outcome effects, and what they will mean in practice (Gendreau & Smith, 2007).

Leschied, Bernfeld, and Farrington (2001) have identified a series of "critical elements in dissemination" if a policy change is to be effectively pursued. They comprise *(a)* a decision at senior level that sustained effort is needed; *(b)* active fostering, by those with responsibility for managing change, of multilevel ownership of the selected innovation; *(c)* "seeding" the service system with pilot projects; *(d)* ensuring that demonstration sites or centers of excellence have long-term fiscal support; *(e)* maintaining stable leadership, among other things, in order to neutralize "forces of countercontrol"; *(f)* building community investment in the innovation; and *(g)* "top to bottom" training of staff. Leaving out even just one of these stages is likely to lead to a loss of momentum, and it is instructive to learn of programs where there were such gaps and the difficulties that arose as a result. Andrews (2011) analyses a series of examples of disappointing and sometimes damaging outcomes that can be traced to disregard for, or overriding of, some of these crucial elements in the process of trying to propagate effective correctional practices.

Another illustration of this comes from the work of Cissner and Farole (2009), who examined a series of 13 process evaluations of pioneering changes in the field of courtroom procedures and justice administration, such as various types of "problem-solving courts." While this is distinct from direct offender-focused programming to reduce violence or other types of reoffending, the areas are adjacent, their objectives overlap, and there are many informative parallels. Working from the Center for Court Innovation in New York City, these authors sought to identify "common sources of failure" that had arisen in implementing projects and that had partially detracted from otherwise successful performance, and to derive recommendations for improved planning and operation. Their proposals were in four "make-or-break" areas: *(a)* engaging in comprehensive planning, *(b)* identifying key stakeholders, *(c)* responding to emerging challenges, and *(d)* recognizing the need for leadership. For example, some projects despite high-quality indicators in certain aspects of their work, lacked important features of success in others, such as identifying quantifiable objectives and methods of recording relevant data, or issuing a formal program model with accompanying documentation. As Cissner and Farole (2009, p. 5) aptly note, "Given the interdependent nature of the criminal justice system, reform often requires the participation and support of many players, including traditional adversaries, bureaucracies that are not accustomed to change, and disengaged citizens."

These messages are essentially similar to those extracted from other types of projects as exemplified in the volume edited by Bernfeld, Farrington, and Leschied (2001). On the basis of the lessons learned from all these initiatives, it is clear that there is no single prescription or blueprint that guarantees success. However, there are some obvious pitfalls to be avoided, and many more that are less obvious but have emerged from the accumulated, hard-earned experiences of innovators and evaluators.

Conclusion

It is the contention of the present chapter that we can be more confident than ever about two key points: first, regarding the evidence on reducing criminal recidivism, including personal violence; and second, on economic outcomes of more constructive as opposed to more punitive, sanctions-based and predominantly institutional corrections. The spectrum of evidence now available offers a means of escape from the current impasse, and it can be presented as such to policy makers.

There is, sadly, no single model program to emulate and no formulaic process whereby we can arrive at a template of how best to engage in the type and scale of systematic change being envisaged here. It is, however, possible and desirable to learn from previous documented experience and so avoid some of the errors of projects that have done less well than expected or failed to lift off at all. If, for example, we use a kind of "triangulation" and synthesize messages from the three examples cited earlier, it is possible to arrive at a vision of how the type of major reinvestment described here could be feasible. Substantial transfers from hospital to the community of people with mental health problems have been undertaken in many countries throughout the world; and while many services still require improvement, few people nowadays would doubt that this has been a beneficial development. Although prison populations have risen, that is not a consequence of the reform of mental health care systems. As the Massachusetts experiment found, penal institutions can be closed without endangering the public, and the former residents can be managed satisfactorily in a variety of alternative services. As the CRP showed, centralized decisions can be informed by social science evidence and acted upon in a rigorous way. In all three examples, there were things, probably many things, that could have been done better, but each demonstrated something vital about what is possible. Synthesizing the lessons from these innovations, it should not be beyond our ability to address some of the core, long-standing problems of correctional services in a way that makes a real and lasting difference.

Policy departures of the type proposed here would have observable and measurable consequences sooner after they were embarked upon than is the case with many other kinds of organizational change. Preliminary planning exercises would be necessary within each jurisdiction to make decisions regarding numbers of prisoners to be transferred, and reentry resources and services strengthened according to the speed and volume that was feasible in a given area. However, as prison numbers began to reduce with successive phases of policy implementation, as people—offenders, correctional staff, administrators—were reallocated and capital and revenues were reinvested, there would be copious evidence of the extent to which the policy was working. Change would be palpable on many levels, and there would be very little difficulty in monitoring the process and judging the results. Progress reports would not be difficult to write!

If the proposals made here still sound like flights of fancy, consider the August 2009 announcement of a panel of three federal judges who ordered the state of California to reduce its burgeoning prison population by 40,000 within 2 years. That represents 24% of the figure of over 170,000 incarcerated when this judgment was made. Observing that it should be perfectly feasible to achieve this in an orderly manner without endangering the public, the justices required that state officials should bring forward plans as to how they would comply with the order within 45 days (Moore, 2009). In November of that year the state administration forwarded a plan in compliance with the target (Egelko, 2009), whilst also submitting an appeal against the court decision, which was thereby suspended (perhaps an illustration of the forces of countercontrol mentioned earlier). Modest plans were formulated for reducing the number of parole violators returned to prison (McGreevy, 2010). While the dispute remains unresolved, that such a departure should occur at all suggests there is increasing recognition of both the pointlessness and wastefulness of high levels of imprisonment.

Roots of Inertia

The story of human mental evolution is a complex one with many gaps, but findings from the field of cognitive archaeology suggest it was propelled to a significant extent by the gradual development of frontal lobes with which our species could integrate information and plan ahead (Coolidge & Wynn, 2009). Paradoxically when faced with many current predicaments, we all too frequently fall back on "gut reaction" thinking or "caveman logic" that served us well in an earlier evolutionary epoch, but is none too suitably adapted for the world we have now created for ourselves (Davis, 2009; Gardner, 2008). Put bluntly, what we are asking people to do when we point toward evidence concerning "what works" and propose that they act on it is to ignore their automatic fears and listen instead to their forebrains, when many influential interest groups would prefer them to stay just as they are, captives of inertia.

But as the federal judgment mentioned earlier illustrates, in the context of colossal and unsustainable penal expenditures, and contrasted with the positive outcome evidence, we may just be at a tipping point where a coherent statement can significantly shift the balance and overcome "system inertia." Writing on the third anniversary of the publication of the *Confronting Confinement* report, produced by the Commission on Safety and Abuse in America's Prisons, the VERA Institute's Michela Bowman (2009) saw firm reasons to be optimistic. She described the Institute's role, ". . . actively working around the country to strengthen oversight of corrections in line with the Commission's recommendations, and the national conversation around criminal justice reform is increasingly promising." Let us hope the omens, for once, really are good.

References

Andrews, D. A. (2001). Principles of effective correctional programs. In
L. L. Motiuk & R. C. Serin (Eds.), *Compendium 2000 on effective correctional programming* (pp. 9–17). Ottawa, ON: Correctional Service Canada.
Andrews, D. A. (2006). Enhancing adherence to risk-need-responsivity: Making quality a matter of policy. *Criminology and Public Policy, 5,* 595–602.
Andrews, D. A. (2011). The impact of nonprogrammatic factors on criminal-justice interventions. *Legal and Criminological Psychology, 16,* 1–23.
Andrews, D. A. & Bonta, J. (2010). Rehabilitating criminal justice policy and practice. *Psychology, Public Policy, and Law, 16,* 39–55.

Andrews, D. A., Bonta, J., & Wormith, J. S. (2006). The recent past and near future of risk and/or need assessment. *Crime and Delinquency, 52,* 7–27.

Andrews, D. A., & Dowden, C. (2005). Managing correctional treatment for reduced recidivism: A meta-analytic review of programme integrity. *Legal and Criminological Psychology, 10,* 173–187.

Andrews, D. A., & Dowden, C. (2006). Risk principle of case classification in correctional treatment: A meta-analytic investigation. *International Journal of Offender Therapy and Comparative Criminology, 50,* 88–100.

Aos, S., Miller, M., & Drake, E. (2006). *Evidence-based adult corrections programs: What works and what does not.* Olympia: Washington State Institute for Public Policy.

Aos, S., Phipps, P., Barnoski, R., & Lieb, R. (2001). *The comparative costs and benefits of programs to reduce crime.* Olympia: Washington State Institute for Public Policy.

Ashworth, A. (2005). *Sentencing and criminal justice* (4th ed.). Cambridge, England: Cambridge University Press.

Bernfeld, G. A., Blase, K. A., & Fixsen, D. L. (1990). Towards a unified perspective on human service delivery systems: Application of the teaching-family model. In R. J. McMahon & R. D. Peters (Eds.), *Behavioral disorders of adolescence* (pp. 191–205). New York: Plenum Press.

Bernfeld, G. A., Farrington, D. P., & Leschied, A. W. (Eds.). (2001). *Offender rehabilitation in practice: Implementing and evaluating effective programmes.* Chichester, England: John Wiley & Sons.

Bowman, M. (2009). *Commission on Safety and Abuse in America's Prisons: Three years later.* http://www.vera.org/content/three-years-later

Braude, L., Heaps, M. M., Rodriguez, P., & Whitney, T. (2007). *Improving public safety through cost-effective alternatives to incarceration in Illinois.* Chicago: Center for Health and Justice.

Center on Juvenile and Criminal Justice. (2008). *Research update: Does more imprisonment lead to less crime?* http://www.securitytransformation.org/images/documentos/291_Does_more_imprisonment_lead_to_less_crime.pdf.

Cissner, A. B., & Farole, D. J., Jr. (2009). *Avoiding failures of implementation: Lessons from process evaluations.* Washington, DC: Bureau of Justice Assistance, US Department of Justice.

Coates, R. B., Miller, A. D., & Ohlin, L. E. (1978). *Diversity in a youth correctional system.* Cambridge, MA: Ballinger.

Coolidge, F. L., & Wynn, T. (2009). *The rise of homo sapiens: The evolution of modern thinking.* New York: John Wiley & Sons.

Correctional Services Accreditation Panel (2009). *Report 2008-2009.* London: Ministry of Justice, Correctional Services Accreditation Panel Secretariat.

Costs of imprisonment far exceed supervision costs. (2009). *US Courts.gov.* Retrieved from http://www.uscourts.gov/news/NewsView/09-05-12/Costs_of_Imprisonment_Far_Exceed_Supervision_Costs.aspx

Davis, H. (2009). *Caveman Logic: The Persistence of Primitive Thinking in a Modern World.* Amherst, NY: Prometheus Books.

Dowden, C., & Andrews, D. A. (2004). The importance of staff practice in delivering effective correctional treatment: A meta-analytic review of core correctional practice. *International Journal of Offender Therapy and Comparative Criminology, 48,* 203–214.

Egelko, B. (2009). State submits plan to reduce prison population. http://
  articles.sfgate.com/2009-11-13/news/17181317_1_prison-officials-prison-
  construction-prison-law-office
Farrington, D. P., & Welsh, B. C. (2007). *Saving children from a life of crime: Early
  risk factors and effective interventions.* New York: Oxford University Press.
Fazel, S., Gulati, G., Linsell, L., Geddes, J. R., & Grann, M. (2009). Schizophrenia
  and violence: Systematic review and meta-analysis. *PLoS Medicine, 6*(8),
  e100012.
Foucault, M. (1977). *Discipline and punish: The birth of the prison.*
  Harmondsworth, England: Peregrine Books.
Frank, R. G., & Glied, S. A. (2006). *Better but not well: Mental health policy in the
  U.S. since 1950.* Baltimore, MD: Johns Hopkins University Press.
Gaes, G. G. (1998). Correctional treatment. In M. Tonry (Ed.), *The handbook of
  crime and punishment* (pp. 712–738). Oxford, England: Oxford University
  Press.
Gardner, D. (2008). *Risk: The science and politics of fear.* London: Virgin Books Ltd.
Gendreau, P. (1996). Offender rehabilitation: What we know and what needs to be
  done. *Criminal Justice and Behavior, 23,* 144–161.
Gendreau, P., Goggin, C., & Cullen, F. T. (1999). *The effects of prison sentences
  on recidivism.* Report to the Corrections Research and Development and
  Aboriginal Policy Branch. Ottawa, ON: Solicitor General of Canada.
Gendreau, P., Goggin, C., Cullen, F. T., & Paparozzi, M. (2002). The common-
  sense revolution and correctional policy. In J. McGuire (Ed.), *Offender
  rehabilitation and treatment: Effective programmes and policies to reduce
  re-offending* (pp. 359–386). Chichester, England: John Wiley & Sons.
Gendreau, P., Goggin, C., & Smith, P. (1999). The forgotten issue in effective
  correctional treatment: Program implementation. *International Journal of
  Offender Therapy and Comparative Criminology, 43,* 180–187.
Gendreau, P., & Smith, P. (2007). Influencing the "people who count": Some
  perspectives on the reporting of meta-analytic results for prediction of
  treatment outcomes with offenders. *Criminal Justice and Behavior, 34,*
  1536–1559.
Gibbons, J. J., & Katzenbach, N. de B. (2006). *Confronting confinement: A report
  of the commission on safety and abuse in America's prisons.* New York: VERA
  Institute of Justice.
Goldblatt, P., & Lewis, C. (1998). *Reducing offending: An assessment of research
  evidence on ways of dealing with offending behaviour.* Home Office Research
  Study No.187. London: Home Office.
Guarino-Ghezzi, S. (1988). Initiating change in Massachusetts' juvenile
  correctional system: A retrospective analysis. *Criminal Justice Review,
  13,* 1–11.
Haney, C. (2006). *Reforming punishment: Psychological limits to the pains of
  imprisonment.* Washington, DC: American Psychological Association.
Haney, C., & Zimbardo, P. (1998). The past and future of U.S. prison policy:
  Twenty-five years after the Stanford Prison Experiment. *American
  Psychologist, 53,* 709–727.
Hartvig, P., & Kjelsberg, E. (2009). Penrose's Law revisited: The relationship
  between mental institution beds, prison population and crime rate. *Nordic
  Journal of Psychiatry, 63,* 51–56.

Hollin, C. R., & Palmer, E. J. (Eds.). (2006). *Offending behaviour programmes: Development, application, and controversies.* Chichester, England: John Wiley & Sons.

Hollis, V. (2007). *Reconviction analysis of Interim Accredited Programmes Software (IAPS) data.* London: Research Development Statistics, National Offender Management Service.

Honderich, T. (2006). *Punishment: The supposed justifications* (2nd ed.). Harmondsworth, England: Penguin Books.

House of Commons. (2009). *Putting science and engineering at the heart of government policy.* Innovation, Universities, Science and Skills Committee. Eighth Report of Session 2008–2009. (Vol. 1). London: The Stationery Office Limited.

House of Commons Justice Committee. (2010). *Cutting Crime: the case for justice reinvestment.* First Report of Session 2009–10. London: The Stationery Office Limited.

Irwin, J., Schiraldi, V., & Ziedenberg, J. (1999). *America's one million nonviolent prisoners.* Washington, DC and San Francisco: Justice Policy Institute.

Jones, K. (1988). *Experience in mental health: Community care and social policy.* London: Sage Publications.

Keita, G. P. (2009). Improving our prison system begins with prevention. *Monitor on Psychology, 40,* 6–64.

Kristof, N. D. (2009, August 20). Priority test: health care or prisons? *The New York Times,* http://www.nytimes.com/2009/08/20/opinion/20kristof.html?_r=2&th&emc=th.

Large, M. M., & Nielssen, O. (2009). The Penrose hypothesis in 2004: Patient and prisoner numbers are now positively correlated in low and middle income countries but are unrelated in high income countries. *Psychology and Psychotherapy: Theory, Research and Practice, 82,* 113–119.

Latessa, E. J., & Smith, P. (2007). *Corrections in the community* (4th ed.). Cincinnati, OH: Anderson Publishing.

Leschied, A. W., Bernfeld, G. A., & Farrington, D. P. (2001). Implementation issues. In G. A. Bernfeld, D. P. Farrington, & A. W. Leschied (Eds.), *Offender rehabilitation in practice: Implementing and evaluating effective programmes* (pp. 3–19). Chichester, England: John Wiley & Sons.

Lipsey, M. W. (1999). Can rehabilitative programs reduce the recidivism of juvenile offenders? An inquiry into the effectiveness of practical programs. *Virginia Journal of Social Policy and the Law, 6,* 611–641.

Loughran, E. J. (1997). The Massachusetts experience: A historical review of reform in the Department of Youth Services. *Social Justice, 24,* 170–186.

Lovbakke, J. (2007). Public perceptions. In S. Nicholas, C. Kershaw, & A. Walker (Eds.), *Crime in England and Wales 2006/07.* London: Home Office Research, Development and Statistics Directorate. Retrieved from http://www.homeoffice.gov.uk/rds/pdfs07/hosb1107.pdf

Lowenkamp, C. T., Latessa, E. J., & Smith, P. (2006). Does correctional program quality really matter? The impact of adhering to the principles of effective intervention. *Criminology and Public Policy, 5,* 575–594.

Macallair, D. (1993). Reaffirming rehabilitation in juvenile justice. *Youth and Society, 25,* 104–125.

Maguire, M., Grubin, D., Lösel, F. & Raynor, P. (2010). 'What Works' and the Correctional Services Accreditation Panel: Taking stock from an insider perspective. *Criminology and Criminal Justice, 10,* 37–58.

Marsh, K., & Fox, C. (2008). The benefit and cost of prison in the UK: The results of a model of lifetime re-offending. *Journal of Experimental Criminology, 4,* 403–423.

Martinson, R. (1974). What works?–Questions and answers about prison reform. *The Public Interest, 10,* 22–54.

McGreevy, P. (2010). California launches plan to cut prison population. *Los Angeles Times,* January 26. http://articles.latimes.com/2010/jan/26/local/la-me-prisons26-2010jan26

McGuire, J. (Ed.). (1995). *What works: Reducing reoffending: Guidelines from research and practice.* Chichester, England: John Wiley & Sons.

McGuire, J. (2001). Development of a program logic model to assist evaluation. In L. L. Motiuk & R. C. Serin (Eds.), *Compendium 2000 on effective correctional programming* (pp. 208–220). Ottawa, ON: Correctional Service Canada.

McGuire, J. (Ed.). (2002). *Offender rehabilitation and treatment: Effective programmes and policies to reduce reoffending.* Chichester, England: John Wiley & Sons.

McGuire, J. (2004). *Understanding psychology and crime: Perspectives on theory and action.* Buckingham, England: Open University Press/McGraw-Hill Education.

McGuire, J. (2008). A review of effective interventions for reducing aggression and violence. *Philosophical Transactions of the Royal Society B, 363,* 2577–2597.

McVay, D., Schiraldi, V., & Ziedenberg, J. (2004). *Treatment or incarceration? National and state findings on the efficacy and cost savings of drug treatment versus imprisonment.* Washington, DC: Justice Policy Institute.

Miller, J. G. (1998). *Last one over the wall: The Massachusetts experiment in closing reform schools* (2nd ed.). Columbus: Ohio State University Press.

Ministry of Justice. (2008). *Re-offending of adults: Results from the 2006 cohort, England and Wales.* Ministry of Justice Statistics Bulletin. London: Author.

Moore, S. (2009, August 5). California prisons must cut inmate population. *The New York Times,* http://www.nytimes.com/2009/08/05/us/05calif.html

Motiuk, L. L., & Serin, R. C. (Eds.). (2001). *Compendium 2000 on effective correctional programming.* Ottawa, ON: Correctional Service Canada.

Nielssen, O., & Large, M. (2009). Penrose updated: Deinstitutionalization of the mentally ill is not the reason for the increase in violent crime. *Nordic Journal of Psychiatry, 63,* 267.

Palmer, T. (1996). Programmatic and non-programmatic aspects of successful intervention. In A. T. Harland (Ed.), *Choosing correctional options that work: Defining the demand and evaluating the supply* (pp. 131–182). Thousand Oaks, CA: Sage Publications.

Paparozzi, M., & Demichelle, M. (2008). Probation and parole: Overworked, misunderstood, and under-appreciated: But why? *The Howard Journal, 47,* 275–296.

Pew Center on the States. (2008). *One in 100: Behind bars in America 2008.* Washington, DC: The Pew Charitable Trusts.

Pew Center on the States. (2009). *One in 31: The long reach of American corrections.* Washington, DC: The Pew Charitable Trusts.

Raynor, P. (2004). The probation service "pathfinders": Finding the path and losing the way? *Criminal Justice, 4,* 309–325.

Raynor, P., & Vanstone, M. (1996). Reasoning and rehabilitation in Britain: The results of the Straight Thinking on Probation (STOP) programme. *International Journal of Offender Therapy and Comparative Criminology, 40,* 272–284.

Rhine, E. E., Mawhorr, T. L., & Parks, E. C. (2006). Implementation: The bane of effective correctional programs. *Criminology and Public Policy, 5,* 347–358.

Sherman, L. W., Farrington, D. P., Welsh, B. C., & MacKenzie, D. L. (Eds.). (2002). *Evidence-based crime prevention.* London and New York: Routledge.

Skeem, J. L., Louden, J. E., Polaschek, D., & Camp, J. (2007). Assessing relationship quality in mandated community treatment: Blending care with control. *Psychological Assessment, 19,* 397–410.

Tarling, R. (1993). *Analysing crime: Data, models and interpretations.* London: Home Office.

Tarvis, C., & Aronson, E. (2007). *Mistakes were made (but not by me).* London: Pinter and Martin.

Tyler, T. R. (2006). *Why people obey the law.* Princeton, NJ: Princeton University Press.

Von Hirsch, A. (1976). *Doing justice: The choice of punishments.* Report of the Committee for the Study of Incarceration. New York: Hill and Wang.

Weisburd, D., Lum, C. M., & Yang, S-M. (2003). When can we conclude that treatments or programs "don't work"? *Annals of the American Academy of Political and Social Science, 587,* 31–48.

West, H. C., & Sabol, W. J. (2008). *Prisoners in 2007.* Washington, DC: Bureau of Justice Statistics.

Zamble, E., & Quinsey, V. L. (1997). *The criminal recidivism process.* Cambridge, England: Cambridge University Press.

Zimring, F. E., & Hawkins, G. (1994). The growth of imprisonment in California. *British Journal of Criminology, 34,* 83–96.

Zimring, F. E., & Hawkins, G. (1995). *Incapacitation: Penal confinement and the restraint of crime.* New York: Oxford University Press.

13

What If Psychology Redesigned the Criminal Justice System?

Joel A. Dvoskin, Jennifer L. Skeem,
Raymond W. Novaco, and Kevin S. Douglas

When we embarked upon this project, it arose from a simple question: How can expert psychological knowledge about shaping prosocial behavior be applied to design a criminal justice system? Our point of departure was the widely shared recognition that the criminal justice system was falling far short of its elementary objective of protecting public safety. The focus of our project and book is on violent offending, and we have portrayed what behavioral science has established about its causes and its remedies.

Violent offending has serious implications for public health and public spending. Violence imposes a major burden on the well-being of populations, both worldwide (Krug, Dahlberg, Mercy, Zwi, & Lozano, 2002) and in the United States (Centers for Disease Control and Prevention [CDC], 2006). In the United States, the costs of gunshot and stab wounds in 1992 were $53 billion (Miller & Cohen, 1997), and the costs associated with nonfatal injuries and deaths due to violence in 2000 were more than $70 billion (Corso, Mercy, Simon, Finkelstein, & Miller, 2007). When one adds the value of lost life and the value of injuries to simple monetary costs, the true costs of violent crime in the United States have been estimated to exceed $574 billion annually (Anderson, 1999). Soares (2006) estimated the social cost of violence across 73 countries and put the yearly cost of violence in the United States at 2.9% of gross domestic product. While such cost estimates and criteria vary, it is unmistakable that violence imposes a substantial burden for society

Violent offending also threatens public safety, evokes fear, and can serve as a political lightning rod. In this book, we have attempted to leave behind divisive political rhetoric that can stand in the way of effective criminal justice policy. Simply put, we do not believe in ideologies as a way of preventing crime; we believe in results. Good ideas are not the exclusive province of either wing of the political continuum, and all too frequently, claims of being tough on crime have been euphemisms for being tough on criminals. When one considers strong risk factors for violent crime, such as deficits in life skills, association with criminal peers, and anger dysregulation, the weaknesses of mass incarceration as a crime reduction strategy become all too clear.

Who lives in U.S. prisons? According to the entertainment and "news" media, prisons are filled with superpredators and criminal geniuses. The truth is quite different. Put simply, prisons are filled with people who are bad at life and are not much better at crime. Typically, they are undereducated, unskilled, and often traumatized, with little realistic hope for a better life. Our current policy is to imprison these individuals for relatively long periods of time, with little or no correctional programming. Incarceration has many intended purposes (see Blumstein, Chapter 1, and Hollin, Chapter 2), including punishment, deterrence, incapacitation, and risk reduction. However, if we take various measures of recidivism rates as evidence for the effectiveness of imprisonment, the recurrent verdict is that the current policy is not working from the standpoint of either harm reduction or economic wisdom, as James McGuire (Chapter 12) has so aptly articulated.

For our purposes, we assert that protecting public safety is the overarching goal of imprisonment and, indeed, the entire criminal justice system. Although reasonable experts will disagree about the optimal pathway (e.g., deterrence, treatment, or retribution), there can be little argument that the ultimate goal is to make our communities safer. Using this simple yardstick, we conclude that the current response to crime is failing, in large part because it ignores what the social sciences have learned about why people behave as they do and how to change behavior for the better. The criminal justice system would look quite different, if it were guided by psychological knowledge about behavior change. In this chapter, we outline key principles of behavior change, many of which overlap with the content covered throughout this book. Next, we summarize how these principles could be applied to make key changes to our criminal justice system. We conclude by arguing that we cannot afford *not* to implement these principles as soon as possible.

Principles of Behavior Change for Correctional Intervention

Donald Meichenbaum is one of the leading contemporary thinkers on behavior change. We asked Professor Meichenbaum to summarize core principles that he had learned in his lifetime that were relevant to changing antisocial behavior via the correctional system. Because his reflections are consistent with the research and principles presented throughout this book, we distill his reflections (in italics) and elaborate on them below.

1. *Tailor behavior change programs to the individual. Given the heterogeneity of the offender population, there is a need to recognize that "one size does not fit all."* This principle runs counter to rigid policies applied in the U.S. criminal justice system, which tend to treat low-risk offenders with the same sorts of programs that were designed for high-risk, persistent, and/or violent offenders.

2. *Use risk factors and protective factors to inform supervision and treatment. Interventions should be strength based and build upon existing resilience and prosocial skills that the offender possesses, along with social and community resources.* To live a crime-free life after prison, offenders must possess prosocial skills that can translate to a successful work, family, and social life in the "free world." Treatment programs should prioritize offenders with high-risk profiles.

3. *Clearly identify both wanted and unwanted behaviors and establish a positive reinforcement protocol that systematically reinforces the wanted behaviors. Consider the "functional value" of unwanted behavior, including how it helps obtain perceived desirable consequences (e.g., resources, freedom, or personal safety) or avoid perceived undesirable consequences (e.g., behavioral restrictions, loss of resources, or personal harm).* Our basic philosophy is that the best way to influence offenders' behavior is to "catch them doing something right" and reward them for it. However, we must first understand what each offender finds rewarding, given his or her beliefs, expectations, and value system. In other words, people do what rewards them, but before we can change their ways of getting rewards, we have to understand what motivates them.

4. *Limit use of punishment as a tool for behavioral change. Intervention programs that are "punitive" and confrontational in nature have poor long-term outcomes.* First, although punitive programs may lead to some short-term behavioral changes when applied under direct scrutiny, they rarely lead to long-term behavior change (Bandura, 1973, 1977; Matson & Kasdin, 1981). Application of punitive contingencies will not shape internalized values and self-regulatory skills that are necessary for lasting behavior change. True desistance from crime requires development of internalized controls that punishment cannot instill. Second, in the U.S. criminal justice system, punishment is rarely used in an effective manner, although there are exceptions (Marlowe & Kirby, 1999). Punishment can promote short-term behavior change when the following occur:
   • Punishment is predictable. That is, offenders can reasonably expect to be caught every time they commit crime and to be assigned a particular penalty for that crime. This is not the case in the U.S.

system. The clearance rate by arrest for violent crime (Federal Bureau of Investigation, 2008) is 45.1%, ranging from 26.8% for robbery to 63.6% for murder and nonnegligent manslaughter. Even when offenders are caught and convicted, the plea bargaining process by which virtually all cases are resolved means that the sentence assigned is unrelated to that advertised in the criminal law.

• There is temporal contiguity (i.e., timeliness) between the undesirable behavior and punishment, such that punishment is clearly associated with the unwanted behavior. In the U.S. system, consequences do not occur soon after the crime. To take an extreme example, many executions take place literally decades after the crime. When the crime is a distant memory, punitive consequences have diminished effects.

• There is a period of scrutiny (i.e., close supervision after the punishment is inflicted). This is not the case in the U.S. system, where burgeoning probation and parole caseloads preclude meaningful scrutiny after incarceration.

• The offender has the skills necessary to accomplish the desired changes. It is useless to punish repeatedly violent people for failing to control their anger, if they have not been helped to develop the capacity for such control, and they are recurrently exposed to anger activators.

• Punishment is perceived as adverse. For inmates whose long sentences have left them utterly unprepared for modern life in the free world, the prospect of returning to prison may seem less frightening than release.

In short, when held up to the principles of effective punishment, our criminal justice system falls breathtakingly short. Nevertheless, its ineffective punishment framework remains refractory. Prison segregation (colloquially, being placed in "the hole") was previously used only for the most dangerous inmates, but it has now blossomed into the fastest growing segment of U.S. corrections. Many inmates are now released directly from segregation to the streets of our communities. In a carefully controlled study, Lovell, Johnson, and Kane (2007) found that direct release from segregation dramatically increases former inmates' likelihood of reoffending. Nevertheless, we are aware of only one state (Michigan) that has begun making systematic attempts to incrementally resocialize these long-time segregated inmates prior to their release to the streets. As currently applied in our criminal justice system, punishment is not working. Programs using positive reinforcement procedures that encourage prosocial skills would seem to have a greater chance of success.

5. *Attend to issues of motivation and incorporate methods of facilitating treatment engagement, such as Motivational Interviewing* (MI; Miller & Rollnick, 2002). There is considerable merit to the

perspective that many offenders are less "treatment resistant" than lacking in "readiness for change" (Howells & Day, 2003) or challenged by "offender-resistant services" (see Monahan & Steadman, Chapter 11). To ameliorate this problem and to foster reinforcing offender–provider interactions, programs could incorporate MI components, such as building the participatory involvement of offenders in considering the pros and cons of behavioral change and in setting behavioral change goals.

6. *Establish high-quality relationships with offenders. In group-based interventions, establish cohesive groups with mutual prosocial goal setting.* In correctional settings, staff are sometimes cautioned *against* establishing any relationship with offenders, based partially on fear that the relationship will be used for "manipulation" purposes. Similarly, the idea of a cohesive group is discouraged in most U.S. prisons, because it seems closely related to gang activity. This is inconsistent with research knowledge. Psychologists have known for decades about the importance of the therapeutic relationship for optimizing clinical outcomes (Norcross, 2002; see also Ackerman & Hilsenroth, 2003; Lambert & Barley, 2001). A growing body of work suggests that firm, fair, and caring relationships between offenders and community supervision officers is a powerful predictor of criminal justice outcomes (Skeem, Eno Louden, Polaschek, & Camp, 2007). For such reasons, Burnet and McNeill (2005) have argued for reinstating the officer–offender relationship as a core condition for changing offender behavior and the social circumstances associated with recidivism. Similarly, Andrews (see Chapter 6) advocates respectful, caring, and collaborative relationships with offenders.

7. *Use and establish real evidence-based programs. Evaluation measures and procedures should be built in to programs so that progress can be monitored and ongoing feedback provided to both staff and offenders.* For every program, the same questions should be asked: "How do you know it works?" "How strong is the evidence?" Those who choose interventions and implement them must be critical consumers, mindful of fads and questionably grounded procedures that are actively sold to various criminal justice agencies. For some interventions, the phrase "evidence based" is not much more than a marketing slogan. Rigorous and meaningful controlled evaluations of programs (not pre/post tests) are essential for establishing an evidence base.

8. *Implement a training approach that nurtures prosocial skills, encourages prosocial affiliations, and promotes a positive lifestyle* (see also Andrews, Chapter 6, and Oudekerk & Reppucci, Chapter 9). What skills are likely to be used in a variety of life situations to prevent general antisocial behavior? Skills in solving problems, communicating and negotiating effectively with others, resolving conflicts, and

planning for the future. What skills are likely to prevent violent behavior, specifically? Because most violence is impulsive or reactive, self-regulation skills are central. Programs should boost internal control capability, as opposed to reliance on external controls. Offenders must learn to monitor themselves and control anger and other emotions of distress that lead to violent behavior. Although this self-regulatory orientation may seem axiomatic, it flies in the face of most correctional practice, where obedience to authority is rewarded and disobedience punished. If an offender only learns how to obey, there will be no positive effect on offending after release. Individually and personally, the offender must make prosocial choices without the benefit of an authority figure's explicit instructions. Instead of learning how to obey, offenders must learn how to make better decisions.

9. *Incorporate procedures to increase the likelihood of generalization and maintenance of intervention effects.* This requires behavioral rehearsal and skills practice (e.g., role plays) that approximate real-life situations. This principle is vital. Intervention should not be limited to didactic instruction, because offenders' active participation is critical. Beyond experientially teaching reentry skills, Meichenbaum recommends involving significant others in the intervention and providing community-based social supports with prosocial peers. The goal is to establish a prosocial lifestyle and a new "possible self" by engaging offenders in supportive, meaningful relationships, helping them find good jobs, and helping them avoid "high-risk" people, places, and things. To maintain prosocial behavior, booster sessions that reinforce learning and help offenders identify and establish community resources can be helpful.

10. *Incorporate a relapse prevention component that actively involves the offender in considering possible obstacles to behavior change efforts and in formulating "game plans" and "backup plans" to confront each obstacle.* Relapse prevention strategies are relevant to preventing repetition of internally rewarding and exciting behavior, such as substance abuse (Marlatt & Gordon, 1985) and criminal offending (Hodge, McMurran & Hollin, 1997). The goal is for offenders to foresee situations that might elicit violence and to develop self-management skills tailored to those situations, thereby reducing the risk of reoffending. Risk is elevated by negative emotional states (e.g., anger, disappointment, depression, shame), interpersonal conflicts, and social pressures. Avoidance and/or escape from high-risk situations, self-regulation of emotional distress, and enhanced communication and problem-solving skills are marshaled to prevent relapse. In their analysis of 24 studies of relapse prevention programs with offenders, Dowden, Antonowicz, and Andrews (2003) found that the most effective elements of such

programs were training of significant others, role playing the situations, and focusing on precursors in the offense chain. Programs with multiple elements produced significantly higher gains.

Toward a Justice System of the Future

The chapters of this volume have probed the strengths and weaknesses of today's justice systems, especially in the United States. The results of the inquiries have led to a surprisingly simple but important array of changes that can improve our justice systems.

1. *Stop incarcerating low-risk offenders and provide more intensive services to high-risk offenders.* As our late colleague Professor Don Andrews so eloquently argued, correctional programming for low-risk offenders is worse than wasteful; it actually *increases* crime! Yet we continue to waste tens of thousands of dollars per offender on incarceration of relatively low-risk offenders. Incarcerating fewer inmates will allow more resources to be aimed at effective programs for high-risk offenders.

2. *Conduct risk and needs assessments of every offender.* Assessing risk and criminogenic needs of each offender is essential to meet the demands of a scientifically informed justice system. The results of these assessments must then be used to guide the system's response to each offender and crime. Our authors' guidance is clear and incontrovertible: To be effective, programs must be aimed at criminogenic needs. If one does not address the reasons that crimes are committed, one stands little chance of preventing them in the future.

3. *Staff correctional institutions and community corrections programs adequately.* With adequate staffing, the criminal justice system can be both safe *and* effective. Budgetary constraints induce correctional administrators to choose the former at the expense of the latter. However, the system must get back into the business of correcting behavior, with programs that have been shown to improve motivation, enhance acquisition of prosocial life skills, enhance protective factors, and maximize the offender's chances of successful desistance from crime. Adequate staffing is not just a matter of workforce numbers—it also means having personnel with the appropriate skill set. Since resources are at a premium, if it is not feasible to increase correctional staffing, an equally effective measure would be to reduce the number of low risk inmates. Because incarceration is neither necessary nor effective for low risk inmates, reducing their incarceration would reduce staff-to-inmate ratios at no cost.

4. *Teach staff to use the most powerful behavior change agent at our disposal: positive reinforcement of prosocial behaviors.* Despite the

power of positive reinforcement (see earlier), to our knowledge, no large correctional agency has ever systematically trained its line staff to use this weapon with accuracy and consistency. Each offender should be instructed in the specific areas of skill deficit that have led him or her to crime. Staff should be oriented toward identifying prosocial and violence-antithetical behaviors when they occur, and to reinforce them. This reinforcement can be material (e.g., tokens that can be exchanged for desired goods), social (e.g., verbal praise), or enhanced privileges, and must only be given contingent upon the prosocial behavior. Fundamentally, for rewards to be meaningful, we must shift the person's valuations in a prosocial direction.

5. *Create and implement individualized release and reentry plans.* Fortunately, one area of recent improvement is in the form of release planning. Community corrections agencies increasingly are using risk-needs assessment tools to inform supervision. Nevertheless, parole and probation officers remain overwhelmed by caseloads that typically exceed 100 offenders. Agencies that match caseloads to risk level, with minimal or no supervision of the lowest risk offenders and intensive supervision of the highest risk offenders, represent one advance. Until intensive supervision is matched with intensive services for high-risk offenders, however, there will be few returns in recidivism reduction (see Turner & Petersilia, Chapter 8).

6. *Stop sending low-risk and juvenile offenders to "crime school."* As is the case with adult offenders (see Andrews, Chapter 6), correctional programs that include high-quality services reduce recidivism for youth, whereas programs based solely on punishment do not (see Oudekerk & Reppucci, Chapter 9). To reduce the staggering number of graduates of juvenile institutions who go on to adult prisons, juvenile justice systems must match the intensity of intervention services to offender risk level and target criminogenic needs. Equally important is the implementation of multi-level, comprehensive treatment programs to address multiple known causes of delinquency, with special attention to the effects of trauma. Finally, whenever possible, programs must emphasize family and community engagement in close proximity to the youth's home.

7. *Leverage new tools for prevention and intervention.* As one example, the power of the media is undeniable. As Saleem and Anderson (see Chapter 4) show, entertainment and news media could be applied in a manner that reduces, rather than exacerbates, the violence potential of at-risk youth and adults. There are many possibilities for intervention. Witness the incredible efficacy of television advertizing to change the behavior of consumers throughout the world. Why hasn't television been used creatively, as a reinforcer, as a teacher, and as a means of changing values and attitudes toward crime? In the prison of the future, television should be used not as an unearned

babysitter, but as a powerful tool for reinforcing behavior, teaching skills, and changing attitudes.

There are many uses for media productions in treatment programs that target self-control. For example, Walker, Novaco, O'Hanlon and Ramm (2009) incorporated film and television video segments into an anger treatment program at a high security forensic hospital. The video segments are integrated within a group-based treatment protocol to engage patients in the therapeutic material of each session, including considering the costs of anger dysregulation, taking other people's perspectives, and preventing relapse. The video materials serve many purposes. For example, viewing film segments in the initial stages of treatment can provide violent offenders with a safe opportunity to talk about themselves and their life circumstances indirectly through the characters in the film. As they discover that it is safe to talk about anger, they progressively open to treatment with group leader guidance. Film segments can also be used to demonstrate the multifaceted aspects of an anger episode, which can be replayed and discussed to facilitate learning of self-monitoring. Moreover, film segments can demonstrate alternative ways of responding to provocation, providing visual-motor imagery for effective coping. As participants grow accustomed to viewing film segments as part of treatment, they become more amenable to having themselves filmed in doing role plays. That then can provide material for treatment staff to coach participants and to support their efforts at behavior change.

The Costs of the Status Quo

An objective look at today's criminal and juvenile justice programs reveals the sad truth: If this were a boxing match, there would be an investigation, because it looks like we are trying to lose. In the United States, billions of dollars are spent annually on a punitive system that consistently fails to increase public safety. Given our policy of mass incarceration, generations of minority children are growing up without a father in their home. Money that could be spent on community development and the creation of jobs is being poured into the construction and operation of prisons. The tremendous cost of this strategy to our nation's communities certainly is not offset by the jobs that prisons create in small towns, regardless of how fiercely local residents protest against sensible downsizing.

Arguably, opportunistic politicians from all sides of the political kaleidoscope have helped to create this system of ineffective and counterproductive punishment. Mindless punishment makes people more likely to commit crimes, by eroding existing prosocial skills, increasing anger, and destroying ties to family and prosocial friends. We need to ask ourselves, "Making people worse—how is it working out so far?"

Can we afford the changes suggested in this book? All it takes to answer this question is to compare the dramatic increases in correctional budgets to those of higher education, or the average cost of a prison bed to a year of community college or university. Sociological research tells us that as high-risk teenagers develop into adults, they are likely to desist from crime, *if* they get a job or go to college (Elliott, 1994). Simply put, prison costs more than college, both literally and figuratively. Can we afford to make these changes? Yes. In fact, we cannot afford not to change.

It is hard to find a politician who does not claim to be "tough on crime," but our justice systems are not tough on crime; they are merely tough on criminals. As a result, America's approach to changing criminal behavior (with other developed nations close behind) has devolved into one simple and ineffective answer: mass imprisonment. Worse, the conditions of imprisonment fly in the face of social science, leaving offenders more angry, less skilled (except perhaps at crime), and less capable of a crime-free life when they leave prison than they were when they entered. In this book, we have proposed that the unabashed goal of justice systems should be to enhance the safety of the men, women, and children who live in our communities. We have argued for a more scientifically informed justice policy—one where offenders can be helped and expected to learn the skills they will need to succeed in avoiding crime upon release. We have long known the limitations of punishment as a behavioral change agent, as well as the immense power of targeted reinforcement of prosocial behavior.

We recognize that there are impediments to change that make for system inertia, but we are fortified in our optimism by existing prototypes that have produced both violence reduction and economic efficiencies (see McGuire, Chapter 12). We do not oppose the use of incarceration; to the contrary, in many cases, it is an obvious necessity. However, if we are going to spend enormous amounts of public funds on locking people up, this most costly intervention should be reserved for the most dangerous offenders, and we owe it to our communities to make sure that the prison experience is likely to make people better, not worse.

We have dedicated this book to our friend and colleague Don Andrews, who devoted his life to the optimistic notion that "nothing works" is an angry lie. Simply put, psychologists know a great deal about changing human behavior for the better, and it was Don's dream, and ours, that these lessons might be put to use in America's courts, jails, juvenile halls, and prisons. Mohatma Ghandi wrote, "An eye for an eye makes the whole world blind." It is our hope that justice systems in America and throughout the world will turn away from a self-defeating and seductive investment in revenge and stop turning a blind eye to the lessons of psychology and social science about how to reduce violent behavior. It would be far better to embrace rational, evidence-based approaches to crime and punishment. As Nelson Mandela famously said, "It always seems impossible until it is done."

References

Ackerman, S. J., & Hilsenroth, M. J. (2003). A review of therapist characteristics and techniques positively impacting the therapeutic alliance. *Clinical Psychology Review, 23*, 1–33.

Anderson, D. A. (1999). The aggregate burden of crime. *Journal of Law and Economics, 42*, 611–642.

Bandura, A. (1973). *Aggression: A social learning analysis.* Englewood Cliffs, NJ: Prentice-Hall.

Bandura, A. (1977). *Social learning theory.* Englewood Cliffs, NJ: Prentice Hall.

Burnett, R., & McNeill, F. (2005). The place of the officer-offender relationship in assisting offenders to desist from crime. *Probation Journal, 52*, 221–242.

Centers for Disease Control and Prevention (CDC). (2006). Homicides and suicides - National violent death reporting system, United States, 2003–2004. *Journal of the American Medical Association, 296*, 506–510.

Corso, P. S., Mercy, J. A., Simon, T. R., Finkelstein, E. A., & Miller, T. R. (2007). Medical costs and productivity losses due to interpersonal and self-directed violence in the United States. *American Journal of Preventive Medicine, 32*, 474–482.

Dowden, C., Antonowitz, D., & Andrews, D. A. (2003). The effectiveness of relapse prevention with offenders: A meta-analysis. *International Journal of Offender Therapy and Comparative Criminology, 47*, 516–528.

Elliot, D. S. (1994) Serious violent offenders: Onset, developmental course, and termination—The American Society of Criminology 1993 Presidential Address. *Criminology, 32*(1), 1–21.

Hodge, J. E., McMurran, M., & Hollin, C. R. (1997). *Addicted to crime?* Chicester, England: John Wiley & Sons.

Howells, K., & Day, A. (2003). Readiness for anger management: Clinical and theoretical issues. *Clinical Psychology Review, 23*, 319–337.

Krug, E. G., Dalhberg, L. L., Mercy, J. A., Zwi, A. B., & Lozano, R. (2002). *World report on violence and health.* Geneva, Switzerland: World Health Organization.

Lambert, M. J., & Barley, D. E. (2001). Research summary on the therapeutic relationship and psychotherapy outcome. *Psychotherapy, 38*, 357–361.

Lovell, D. L., Johnson, L. C., & Kane, K. C. (2007). Recidivism of supermax prisoners in Washington state. *Crime and Delinquency, 53*, 633–656.

Marlatt, G. A., & Gordon, J. R. (1985). *Relapse prevention: Maintenance strategies in the treatment of additive behavior.* New York: Guilford.

Marlowe, D. B., & Kirby, K. C. (1999). Effective use of sanctions in drug courts: Lessons from behavioral research. *National Drug Court Institute Review, 2*(1), 1–32.

Matson, J. L., & Kazdin, A. E. (1981). Punishment in behavior modification: Pragmatic, ethical, and legal issues. *Clinical Psychology Review, 1*, 197–210.

Miller, T. R., & Cohen, M. A. (1997). Costs of gunshot and cut/stab wounds in the United States, with some Canadian comparisons. *Accident Analysis and Prevention, 29*, 329–341.

Miller, W. R., & Rollnick, S. (2002). *Motivational interviewing: Preparing people for change.* (2nd ed.). New York: Guilford.

Norcross, J. C. (2002). *Psychotherapy relationships that work: Therapists contributions to the responsiveness of patients*. New York: Oxford University Press.

Skeem, J. L. Eno Louden, J., Polaschek, D., & Camp, J. (2007). Assessing relationship quality in mandated community treatment: Blending care with control. *Psychological Assessment, 19*, 397–410.

Soares, R. R. (2006). The welfare costs of violence across countries. *Journal of Health Economics, 25*, 821–846.

Walker, C., Novaco, R. W., O'Hanlon, M., & Ramm, M. (2009). Anger treatment protocol. The State Hospital, Scotland.

Index

Ingram Content Group UK Ltd.
Milton Keynes UK
UKHW020642080523
421358UK00008B/32